T0295892

Entrepreneurship and Development for a Green Resilient Economy

LAB FOR ENTREPRENEURSHIP AND DEVELOPMENT

Series Editors: Bruno S. Sergi and Cole C. Scanlon

Lab for Entrepreneurship and Development is Emerald's innovative book series on the study of entrepreneurship and development, striving to set the agenda for advancing research on entrepreneurship in the context of finance, economic development, innovation, and the society at large.

The Lab for Entrepreneurship and Development, a now-independent research lab that first started at the Institute of Quantitative Social Sciences at Harvard University, with the overarching and ambitious aim of using the book series to synthesize interdisciplinary research by academics and students to advance our understanding of modern entrepreneurship and development across cultural and disciplinary boundaries.

Previous volumes:

Entrepreneurship and Development for a Green Resilient Economy

EDITED BY

ADRIANA GRIGORESCU

National University of Political Studies and Public Administration, Romania; National Institute for Economic Research "Costin C. Kiritescu" (INCE), Romanian Academy, Romania

AND

JEAN VASILE ANDREI

Petroleum-Gas University of Ploiesti, Romania; National Institute for Economic Research "Costin C. Kiritescu" (INCE), Romanian Academy, Romania

United Kingdom – North America – Japan – India – Malaysia – China

Emerald Publishing Limited
Emerald Publishing, Floor 5, Northspring, 21-23 Wellington Street, Leeds LS1 4DL.

First edition 2024

British Library Cataloguing in Publication Data
A catalogue record for this book is available from the British Library

ISBN: 978-1-83797-089-6 (Print)
ISBN: 978-1-83797-088-9 (Online)
ISBN: 978-1-83797-090-2 (Epub)

Printed and bound by CPI Group (UK) Ltd, Croydon, CR0 4YY

INVESTOR IN PEOPLE

Contents

About the Editors

Adriana Grigorescu is a Full Professor and PhD Supervisor in Management at the National University of Political Studies and Public Administration, a Senior Researcher at the National Institute for Economic Research Costin C. Kirițescu – Romanian Academy, and a full member of the Academy of Romanian Scientists. Her research areas are management and marketing in business and public administration, innovation and knowledge transfer, circular economy, labor economics, education management, and especially integrated, interdisciplinary studies of global economy and governance. Her last published studies explored the digital transformation side effects of various aspects of business models, education, and the world of work. Sustainable development and environmental protection also represent a significant part of her work from the perspective of their impact on education and skills or business models. Moreover, she is preoccupied with finding models to measure people's readiness for the nowadays challenges and spatial analysis.

Jean Vasile Andrei is Full Professor at Petroleum-Gas University of Ploiesti, Department of Business Administration; Managing Director of Center for Renewable Energies and Energy Efficiency within National Institute for Economic Research "Costin C. Kirițescu," Romanian Academy; and PhD Mentor in Economics at Bucharest University of Economic Studies, Romania. He is Co-founder and Scientific Coordinator of the Research Network on Resources Economics and Bioeconomy. He holds a PhD in Economics from the National Institute for Economic Research – Romanian Academy of Sciences. He has earned a BA degree in Administrative Sciences (2005) and in Banks and Finances (2007) from the Petroleum-Gas University of Ploiesti. He has an MA degree in Economics, Administrative and Business Management (2007) earned at the same university. He is also Associate Editor of *Economics of Agriculture* (Serbia), scientific reviewer, and committee member for numerous international conferences. He is member of scientific organizations: The Balkan Scientific Association of Agrarian Economists, Serbia (2008), DAAAM Vienna, and Information Resources Management Association (2011). Issues like agricultural economics and rural development, energy and resource economics, and business economics are among his research and scientific interests.

About the Contributors

Dorel Berceanu is an Associate Professor at the Faculty of Economics and Business Administration and Vice Rector of the University of Craiova, with a PhD in Economics since 2001. He has over 27 years of experience in didactic and scientific research. His main areas of interest are research financial management, financial policy, evaluation and financing of investments, and financial decisions, and he has published numerous scientific papers in journals or volumes of national and international conferences.

Claudiu George Bocean is a Professor and PhD Supervisor at the Faculty of Economics and Business Administration at the University of Craiova. In 2007, he obtained a PhD in Economics from the Faculty of Economics, University of Craiova, Romania, and in 2015 Habilitation title in Management from the Academy of Economic Sciences in Bucharest, Romania. Since 2002, he has been teaching at the Faculty of Economics and Business Administration, the University of Craiova, taking courses on human resource management, business management, labor economics, organization theory, project management, business negotiation techniques, business ethics, and co-operating within research projects of national and international universities and organizations. His main areas of interest are CSR, business ethics, human resource management, and digital transformation.

Karoly Bodnar is a Professor at the Hungarian University of Agriculture and Life Sciences Szent Istvan Campus in Szarvas (Hungary). Previously, he taught and researched at the Faculty of Agriculture of the University of Szeged. The author's main research interests are animal husbandry and its economic aspects, as well as the study of factors affecting the consumption of animal products, with particular attention to domestic rabbits and game meats. He is a member of the World Rabbit Science Association. In 2011, the University of Agriculture and Veterinary Medicine of the Banat in Timisoara (Romania) awarded him the title of doctor honoris causa.

Alina Gabriela Brezoi currently holds the position of University Lecturer at Faculty of Economic Sciences, Petroleum-Gas University of Ploiesti (Romania). Starting with 2022, she is also the Vice Rector of the Petroleum-Gas University of Ploiesti (Romania). Her work experience derives from and includes teaching courses and seminaries, research activities, and organizing and participating in scientific conferences. Regarding research results, these are represented by publishing 3 books and over 20 scientific papers in the following field of interest: sustainable development, corporate social responsibility, ethics, and financial market. She has published articles in leading international journals, including *Sustainability and Economic Insights: Trends and Challenges.*

Marian Cazacu is a PhD student in Management at the Faculty of Economics and Business Administration at the University of Craiova, Romania. In 2006, he graduated with a bachelor's degree in Management at the University of Craiova. In 2008, he graduated with a master's program in diagnostic analysis and business assessment at the Faculty of Economics and Business Administration, University of Craiova. His areas of interest are social responsibility, ethics, and human resource management.

Luminița Chivu is Senior Researcher in Economics (since 1992) and currently the General Director and President of the Scientific Council of the National Institute for Economic Research "Costin C. Kirițescu" – Romanian Academy (since 2011). She is the author of 18 books in foreign and national publishing houses and more than 200 articles in economics. She is the member of the Consultative Council for Research, Development and Innovation of the Ministry of Research, Innovation and Digitization in Romania. She holds expertise in agricultural models and agricultural policies and competitiveness, sustainable rural development, labor market, industrial relations, working conditions, economic growth and restructuring, and European integration. She has experience in managing and coordinating more than 15 international and 20 national projects working with multidisciplinary teams of research experts. She is the Co-chair of the Scientific Council of the international conference "Economic Scientific Research-Theoretical, Empirical and Practical Approaches" – ESPERA, editions 2013–2022.

Drago Cvijanovic is a Scientific Advisor and Full Professor at the Faculty of Hotel Management and Tourism in Vrnjačka Banja, University of Kragujevac, Republic of Serbia. He has been a member or President of the Commission for Defense of Degree Essays, MA Theses, and PhD Theses for more than 130 times and more than 105 times member or President of the Commission for Selection of Research or Scientific Topics – Research Vocation. He led or was a member of the research team of more than 69 projects. He published as author or co-authored more than 590 papers delivered at national and international conferences and published in national and international journals. He published as author or co-authored over 58 monographs. He is the Chief Editor of the journal *Economics of Agriculture* (Belgrade, Serbia), and *HiT Management* (Vrnjačka Banja, Serbia), He is member of the Balkan Environmental Association and member of the Presidency of the Balkan Scientific Association of Agrarian Economists. He is a president and regular member of Developmental Academy of Agriculture of Serbia. He is an Honorary Professor at Stavropol State Agricultural Universities in Stavropol, Russia. Now, he is the Dean of the Faculty of Hotel Management and Tourism in Vrnjacka Banja, Serbia.

Gheorghe Dan Isbășoiu is a University Lecturer at the Petroleum-Gas University in Ploiesti, specializing in economic and social statistics, as well as the study of probabilistic models applied in industrial processes. His doctoral thesis, "Reliability of the Human Factor Integrated into Industrial Technological Processing Systems," defended at the Petroleum-Gas University in Ploiesti, Romania, laid the groundwork for a methodology to determine the probability of human error and the connection between the human factor and the reliability level of systems. His subsequent research has focused on applied statistical analyses in the field of sustainable development. In multidisciplinary teams, he has delved into aspects related to sustainable tourism, equal opportunities in education, sustainable development of rural areas, and the social responsibility of enterprises.

George Georgescu is Senior Researcher and Deputy General Director of the National Institute of Economic Research "Costin C. Kirițescu" – Romanian Academy. He has over 30 years of experience in scientific research and has published, as author and co-author, over 23 books (including chapters in books) and over 70 articles. He has participated in the implementation of over 40 projects/research programs, including financed from European funds. He has contributed to the elaboration of the Development Strategy of Romania in the next 20 years in the vision of the Romanian Academy. His professional career is completed by activities carried out within government institutions in the field of macroeconomic forecasts, foreign trade and economic diplomacy, as well as the banking system. He is a member of the Fiscal Council of Romania, of the National Statistical Council, and a Lecturer within the SCOSAAR Doctoral School. He is a National Expert for IFO World Economic Survey.

Boris Kuzman has a PhD in Agricultural Economics. He works as Senior Research Associate at the Institute of Agricultural Economics, Belgrade, Serbia. He participated in 4 international projects and 20 domestic projects. His fields of interest are agricultural markets and agricultural marketing, bioengineering, agricultural futures markets, and risk hedging in agribusiness. He is an author/co-author of 17 papers published in international journals with impact factors. He held several public functions in the institutions of the Republic of Serbia.

Mădălina Giorgiana Mangra is an Associate Professor at the Faculty of Economics and Business Administration, University of Craiova, with a PhD in Economics since 2005. She has over 26 years of experience in didactic and scientific research. Her main areas of interest are insurance and reinsurance, insurance and social protection, financial management, finance and credit, firms' evaluation, international finance, investments, financial systems, and reporting, and she has published numerous scientific papers in journals or volumes of national and international conferences.

Augustin Mitu, PhD, is a member of the Business Administration Department from the Petroleum-Gas University of Ploiesti, Faculty of Economic Sciences, and Professor since 2015. He is the author of 2 books on marketing and co-author of 4 books and 31 scientific articles. He participated in implementation of four research projects as Project Manager and was a member in implementing two European Social Fund (ESF) projects at the Petroleum-Gas University level. His relevant research activities are four articles presenting original scientific contributions, in extenso, published in an ISI-rated journal; author or co-author of six books; and one chapter published in *Organizational Culture and Behavioral Shifts in the Green Economy*, IGI Global, 2018.

Gordana Nikolić, PhD, is a Founder of Business Academy Rijeka which promotes lifelong learning from 2007 through different projects and cooperation modalities with international scientific institutions, and in partnership with BA Nordhessen, she has started the first international professional study in Rijeka. As a Vice President of Croatian Council of University of Applied Science and University College, she oversees international cooperation and standards for quality assurance in the European Higher Education Area. For her work, she received several awards, out of which the most important one is for the women entrepreneur of the year in Croatia in 2014. In 2015, she was honoured for her exceptional international contributions to advancing science, educational development, and fostering female entrepreneurship in regional countries. Additionally, in 2016, she received a special award for her extraordinary efforts in higher education and entrepreneurship within her city, notably for establishing and launching the first private higher education institution. She is still the only woman in Croatia who is an Owner and a Dean of a higher education institution. Apart from the managerial position, she also leads a successful science career. She is an author and co-author of several books and more than 50 scientific and professional papers and has worked on different programs and projects for the Croatian Ministry of Science, Education and Sports and EU Commission. She was a Guest Professor at the Iacocca Institute, Lehigh University at the Global Village Program for future leaders of business and industry. She is also the President of the Program and Organizational Committee of the PAR International Leadership Conference and member of many professional and scientific associations, regional summer schools, and the board of directors.

Bianca-Florentina Nistoroiu embarked on her academic journey at the Bucharest University of Economic Studies, where she is currently pursuing her doctoral studies. Her educational background, combined with a remarkable enthusiasm for research, has propelled her into the world of sustainable development, agriculture, and gender equality. Her research is characterized by a multifaceted approach, encompassing the exploration of sustainable agricultural practices and the pivotal role of gender equality in fostering resilient economies. Her work resonates with the global need for sustainable practices in agriculture while promoting inclusivity and gender equity as fundamental components of this process. Among the publications, we can note the following articles "Sustainable Development Through Gender Equality," "Rural Development Through Smart Village Initiatives," "Gender Trends in Modern Agriculture: The Case of Female Farmers in

Europe," and "Role of Digitalization in Sustainable Agriculture: Benefits, Challenges and Use Cases."

Gabriela Oprea is an Associate Professor at the Oil and Gas University from Ploiesti, Department of Business Administration. She is passionate and dedicated to the education system, with extensive experience in the academic and research fields. She shares her rich knowledge and experience with students, significantly contributing to the development of higher education and research in entrepreneurship, managerial simulations, and other areas. With rigorous work and deep involvement in impactful research projects, she has become a trusted mentor for young students, inspiring them to realize their potential in the complex world of business, making her an exemplar in the academic community.

Nataša Papić-Blagojević is a Professor of Applied Studies in undergraduate and master's study programs at the Department for Quantitative Analysis and Business Informatics in the Novi Sad School of Business, Republic of Serbia, since 2005. She has significant experience as a coordinator and researcher at national and international projects, and her research experience is presented by writing over 80 scientific papers in journals, monographs, and national and international conferences. She is the author or co-author of the books *Quantitative Methods, Financial and Actuarial Mathematics, Financial Mathematics,* and *Tariff Calculation in Life Insurance,* and publications *EU Handbook, How Well Do We Know Each Other?* and *EU for Youth – Challenges and Opportunities.*

Catalin Popescu is Professor of Management at the Petroleum-Gas University of Ploiesti, Romania. His research and consulting interests includes project management, quantitative methods for business and management, operations management, statistical analysis, energy management, and sustainable development. He has 32 years of experience in higher education. Starting with 2016, he is PhD advisor in the engineering and management domain. He has published over 230 articles, 9 books, and 12 book chapters; he participated in 45 international conferences (in more than 27 different countries); he was involved in more than 30 scientific research grants and international projects. He was also a member of scientific committees within more than 50 international conferences, and he was plenary speaker for six times. He is Editor-in-Chief of two scientific journals: *Journal of Innovation and Business Best Practices* (JIBBP), Stamford Publishing, USA, and *Economic Insights: Trends and Challenges Journal*, Romania.

Lukman Raimi holds the position of Assistant Professor and Program Coordinator in the Entrepreneurship Major at Universiti Brunei Darussalam, Brunei. He obtained his PhD in Entrepreneurship and CSR from De Montfort University, UK. Formerly, he served as the Graduate Program Coordinator at the School of Business and Entrepreneurship and as the Director of the Center for Entrepreneurship at the American University of Nigeria. His diverse research interests encompass various areas, including business-oriented entrepreneurship, social entrepreneurship, halal entrepreneurship, and innovation management. Notably, he currently serves as the Associate Editor of the *Journal of Business and Economic Analysis* at Universiti Brunei Darussalam, Brunei, as well as the Associate Editor of the *GUSAU Journal of Entrepreneurship Development* at Federal University Gusau, Nigeria. Furthermore, he is a valued member of the Editorial Board for several esteemed journals, including the *Indonesian Journal of Sustainability Accounting & Management* in Indonesia, *Emerald Emerging Markets Case Studies* in the United Kingdom, the *Journal of Developmental Entrepreneurship* in the United States, *African Journal of Innovation and Entrepreneurship* in the United Kingdom, and *International Journal of Circular Economy and Waste Management* published by IGI Global in the United States.

Felizia Arni Rudiawarni is an Associate Professor at Faculty of Business and Economic at University of Surabaya and Project Director of Social Science & Business Research Network (SSBRN). She holds Certified Financial Planner and Certified Data Analytics. She is active as financial consultant and trainer. Her research interests are in the field of financial accounting and capital market.

Dalia Simion is Associate Professor and Vice Dean at the Faculty of Economics and Business Administration, University of Craiova, with a PhD in Cybernetics and Economic Statistics since 2001. She has over 26 years of experience in didactic and scientific research. Her main areas of interest are financial management, firms' investments, firms' evaluation, financial and economic analysis, financial systems and reporting, corporate finance, and financial markets, and she has published numerous scientific papers in journals or volumes of national and international conferences.

Biljana Stankov is a Professor of Applied Studies at the Department for Trade and International Business of Novi Sad School of Business, Republic of Serbia. She has 16 years of experience educating on undergraduate and master's study programs which deal with EU economy, trade, and international economies. She participated as a coordinator and researcher in several international and national scientific projects. She held webinars on EU topics and, as an author, published the book *European Union: Trade, Investments and Competitiveness* and as co-author publications *EU Handbook, How Well Do We Know Each Other?* and *EU for Youth – Challenges and Opportunities*. She participated in numerous national and international conferences and published scientific papers in journals, monographs, and thematic proceedings. She is the coordinator for the publishing activities, the assistant editor-in-chief of the international scientific journal, and the organizer of the national and international scientific conferences in Novi Sad School of Business.

Daniela Steluța Uță is a PhD Lecturer at the Petroleum-Gas University of Ploiesti, Faculty of Economics, Business Administration Department; author of a book on consumer attitude research; and co-author of 4 books, 2 published in international volumes, and 31 scientific paperworks. She published in 2018, under IGI Global, the chapter entitled 'Advertising and Organization's Green

Behavior', as part of the book with the title *Organizational Culture and Behavioral Shifts in the Green Economy*. Her expertise and consulting interests are marketing research, monitoring and evaluation of socio-economic projects, simulated enterprise expert, communication and publicity expert, and students' guidance in order to facilitate insertion on the labor market.

Anca Antoaneta Vărzaru is a Lecturer at the University of Craiova (Romania), Faculty of Economics and Business Administration, with a PhD in Accounting since 2010. She obtained a Habilitation title in Management in 2022 and a Habilitation title in Accountancy in 2023. Since 2006, she has taught at the same faculty basic accounting, public accounting, financial accounting, management accounting, financial management, financial economics, and management of banking risks, and she also co-operated in national research projects. Her main areas of interest are CSR, business ethics, sustainability accounting and reporting, and digital transformation.

Sergej Vasic was born in 2001. In June 2023, he obtained his bachelor's degree in Business and Management at the MCI Innsbruck, Austria. He is currently attending master's studies at the MCI Innsbruck, alongside working as a Transport Manager at the LKW Walter in Kufstein. He is a member of American Marketing Association and a Vice President of the Youth Forum of the European Marketing and Management Association. His research interest is mostly in human resource management. His chapter was created for the purpose of completion of his bachelor studies (bachelor thesis) and is his second published work.

Dana Volosevici is a University Lecturer at the Petroleum-Gas University in Ploiesti and a Lawyer specialized in labor law and business law. Her research focuses on reshaping the relationship between enterprises and society, considering the increasing importance that enterprises have in communities and the growth of their financial and strategic power. Her doctoral thesis, defended at the Université de Bretagne Sud in France, titled "Multifaceted Analysis of Employee Integration in Commercial Companies in France and Romania," serves as an example of such analysis. It addresses the reshaping of the relationship between the enterprise and its employees. Through a series of other studies, she has analyzed the impact of labor and business legislation on industrial processes and transformations. Additionally, she explores how enterprises can, voluntarily and by adopting sustainable practices, establish a framework of action that ensures increased protection for vulnerable groups affected by these processes or transformations.

Predrag Vuković is Senior Research Associate and graduated in 2003 from the Faculty of Economics, University of Belgrade. He finished his postgraduate specialist studies in 2006 and master's degree in 2008. He earned his doctoral degree in 2016 from the Faculty of Economics, University of Kragujevac. He has been working at the Institute of Agricultural Economics, Belgrade, since 2004. He has been actively engaging as a member of the research team on projects of the Ministry of Education, Science and Technological Development of the Republic of

Serbia. He has also been engaged in numerous projects of the Institute of Agricultural Economics, as well as the development of numerous development strategies for cities, municipalities, and local communities as a member of research teams and manager of project teams. In his doctoral thesis, master's thesis, specialist thesis, and numerous scientific articles published in national and international professional journals, presented at scientific conferences of national and international importance, he dealt with the issues of tourism marketing, management of tourist destinations, rural tourism, rural development, and agriculture issues of economics. He is a member of scientific organizations: Balkan Scientific Association of Agricultural Economists, Serbian Association of Agricultural Economist, European Rural Development Network,and Research Network on Resources Economics and Bio-economy Association.

Lidija Weis, PhD, serves as the Dean of the Ljubljana School of Business. Her research expertise encompasses marketing and management, and she is the author of numerous scholarly and professional articles. She has actively participated in various domestic and international projects. Additionally, she holds the position of President of the Program and Organizational Committee of the Eastern European Conference of Management and Economics and is a member of several professional and scientific associations. Furthermore, she holds the role of Vice President in the honorary board of the international organization European Marketing and Management Association and is the President of the Women's Forum. She holds the distinguished title of Professorship at Woxsen University. As Slovenia Country Chair, she is a member of G100: GROUP OF 100 GLOBAL WOMEN LEADERS. On a national level, she is a member of the Inter-ministerial Working Group for Sustainable Development in Education until 2030 at the Ministry of Education. Her contributions extend to being actively involved in shaping educational policies. In addition, she serves as an assessor for quality in higher education, both domestically and internationally. She plays a pivotal role in evaluating and ensuring the standards of excellence in higher education institutions, contributing to the enhancement of academic quality on a global scale. Her expertise as an assessor further solidifies her commitment to maintaining and elevating the standards of educational institutions, both at home and abroad. Her commitment and leadership roles underscore her dedication to advancing the fields of marketing and management, both at the national and international levels, while also contributing to the broader goals of sustainable development in education.

Cliff Oliver Winoto graduated from the Faculty of Business and Economics, Universitas Surabaya, Indonesia. He holds a Master of Accounting degree and a Bachelor of Accounting degree from Universitas Surabaya. He is a practicing accountant and tax consultant for a diverse range of clients. His area of interest includes taxation, financial accounting, and banking.

Alina Zaharia Lecturer at the Bucharest University of Economic Studies (ASE) from Romania within the Department of Agrifood and Environmental Economics, where she teaches economics of environmental and agrifood organisations, environmental economics, and consumer protection in the agrifood sector. Also, she is an Associate Researcher of Center for Renewable Energies and Energy Efficiency within National Institute for Economic Research "Costin C. Kirițescu," Romanian Academy. She has a PhD in Economics from the same university, graduated in 2017, focusing on energy policies and sustainable development, and a MA in Environmental economics. Dr. Zaharia is a Fulbright-RAF Scholar Award Alumni after taking part in a USA stage on agricultural extension services of approximately 4.5 months in Athens, Georgia, between August and December 2023. Also, she has benefited from an Erasmus exchange for a semester in Verona, Italy, during 2012-2013. Further, she was involved in several international and national research projects on developing sustainable food systems, waste recovery, improving agro-food chains, while she also was scientific reviewer, and committee member for various scientific events.

Dejan Živkov has a PhD in Economics. He works as a Professor at Novi Sad Business School, University of Novi Sad, Serbia. He participated in one international project and two domestic projects. His fields of interest are international financial and commodity markets, risk hedging and portfolio management, and financial econometrics. He is an author/co-author of 59 papers in international journals with impact factors.

Foreword

In transitioning from traditional economic frameworks to models prioritizing efficiency, environmental sustainability, and inclusivity, green entrepreneurship has emerged as a key component in forging and defining this new economic approach. The transition toward a more balanced and equitable model recognizes green entrepreneurship as both a valuable and effective tool. It plays a pivotal role in realizing the potential and addressing the challenges inherent in achieving a fair and balanced transition that adheres to resilient economies' principles and anticipates future technological advancements.

Achieving a green and resilient economy based on an entrepreneurship paradigm and developing sustainable business call for a holistic approach. It requires redefining how resources are allocated and used, advocating for policies that support sustainable business models, and encouraging a culture that values long-term ecological health alongside immediate economic gains. In essence, green entrepreneurship is becoming synonymous with a progressive, forward-thinking approach to business and economic development that promises to reshape our economic landscape into one that is more equitable, sustainable, and inclusive. In this context, it is no longer just about maintaining profitability; it's about integrating sustainability into the core of business practices. Therefore, green entrepreneurs are not just business creators but integral in driving a new economic paradigm that values ecological stewardship and economic growth.

Green entrepreneurship represents a vital component in redefining economic paradigms and plays a crucial role in addressing the opportunities and challenges associated with achieving a fair and balanced economic transformation. The new paradigm transition is underpinned by the criteria of resilient economies, prospective technological advancements, and the cultivation of green entrepreneurship, which is a pressing need for innovative approaches in harnessing and allocating economic resources and promoting entrepreneurship.

Green entrepreneurs are employing the new and green factors as their competitive advantage in highly competitive and often unstable markets, value the inherent opportunities and challenges in achieving a balanced economic development and transition to a more competitive entrepreneurial economy, and diversify the instruments of valuing the economic and business potentials. The new entrepreneurial paradigm considers not only resilient economies, technological development, or the lack or limited access to financial and human resources, raw materials, capital, or the optimal combination between traditional factors or instruments in assuring the production process and promoting sustainable consumption, but also provide innovative and cutting-edge entrepreneurial solutions in achieving a green economic model for business communities. Green entrepreneurship creates a tight link between technological development, green entrepreneurship philosophy, and the New Normal requirements. Resilient economies, technological development, and green entrepreneurship provide a highly impacted environment for implementing a balanced, just transition.

Entrepreneurship and development for a green, resilient economy cover extensive ground in contemporary green entrepreneurship, from fundamental theories such as business investments and venturing capital to emerging and new concepts that reflect the critical challenges of the current times, including technological development slowdowns, economic resilience, economic systems downfalls, digitalization, green business footprints, and many more actual topics.

Promoting green entrepreneurship in contact with the New Normal could be a necessary and not mandatory step to limit the negative effects of classical economic and business policies based on a linear production process and stimulus consumption and attracting green and new resources to the economic process by valuing the opportunities and challenges for achieving a balanced, just transition. In this context, the analysis of promoting technological development and green entrepreneurship in the New Normal in terms of opportunities and challenges in achieving a balanced, just transition may represent a further step in understanding the role and importance of diversifying the economic resources and potentials in contemporary economies and designing new business paradigms.

The actual research on entrepreneurship and development for a green, resilient economy has been upon entrepreneurial ventures and venturing capital, and using the traditional business philosophy usually neglects wider economic and social contexts within which they operate and the changes imposed by the transitional patterns, as in the New Normal or assuring balanced economic transformation. Designing an extensive context that deals with technological development and green entrepreneurship in contemporary economies fulfills a need to better understand the inner core of the New Normal paradigm.

This book offers insights into promoting green entrepreneurship, a vital component in steering economies toward a green, resilient economy. In addressing business traditions, this book acknowledges the challenges of integrating new, sustainable practices within established business models. It provides a comprehensive analysis of navigating highly competitive and transformative markets, emphasizing the need for businesses to adapt and innovate continually. Also, the content examines the potential of entrepreneurs in this dynamic landscape, highlighting how their ingenuity and adaptability can drive economic growth and sustainability. Furthermore, this book provides a comprehensive overview of the current state of green business, including case studies and practical examples. These real-world insights offer valuable lessons on how businesses, from start-ups to established corporations, can adapt and thrive in an eco-conscious market.

The editors
Adriana Grigorescu,
Faculty of Public Administration, National University of Political Studies
and Public Administration, Bucharest, Romania
National Institute for Economic Research "Costin C. Kirițescu,"
Romanian Academy, Romania
Academy of Romanian Scientists, Romania

Jean Vasile Andrei,
Faculty of Economic Sciences, Petroleum-Gas University of Ploiesti, Romania
National Institute for Economic Research "Costin C. Kirițescu,"
Romanian Academy, Romania

Acknowledgments

The editors would like to express their gratitude and special acknowledgments to the book series *Lab for Entrepreneurship and Development* coordinator Professor Bruno S. Sergi for giving us this opportunity and to all the contributors to this book. Your expertise, insights, and commitment have been determinant in designing this comprehensive book on entrepreneurship and development for a green, resilient economy.

In addition, we extend our profound gratitude to the National Institute for Economic Research "Costin C. Kirițescu" – Romanian Academy and Research Network on Resources Economics and Bioeconomy Association. The development and advent of this book would hardly have been possible without their diligent support.

As editors, we express our profound gratitude to everyone who has been directly involved in supporting this book throughout its development process. The dissemination of ideas, help, insightful reviews, and guidance received during this book writing and collecting process has been integral to its success.

Finally, we are grateful to the Emerald Editorial team for providing us with the opportunity to publish this edit and for all the support provided. We would like to extend a special thanks to Ms Sashikala Balasubramanian for her direct implication in making possible this book.

Chapter 1

Discussing the Role of Innovation in Green Entrepreneurship and Development

Lidija Weis[a] and Gordana Nikolić[b]

[a]*Ljubljana School of Business, Slovenia*
[b]*PAR University of Applied Science, Croatia*

Abstract

This chapter elucidates the significance of innovation in fostering green entrepreneurship and cultivating a resilient, eco-friendly economy. It underscores the three categories of innovation available to green entrepreneurs: product innovation, process innovation, and business model innovation. These avenues empower green entrepreneurs to craft sustainable products and services, enhance operational efficiency, and establish novel markets for eco-friendly goods and services. This chapter also explores green entrepreneurs' challenges, including lack of funding, limited market demand, and regulatory barriers, provides strategies to overcome these challenges, and discusses the role of public–private partnerships (PPPs) and cross-sector collaboration in promoting green entrepreneurship and sustainable development. It also highlights the benefits of these collaborations, such as access to funding and resources, technical expertise, market development, networks, collaboration, and shared knowledge and expertise. Finally, this chapter emphasizes that green entrepreneurship can be supported through partnerships that combine the strengths and resources of multiple sectors, such as the government, private industry, non-profits, and academia. Ultimately, this chapter provides a roadmap for green entrepreneurs to overcome challenges and leverage collaborations to create sustainable products and services, improve efficiency, and develop new markets for sustainable goods and services.

Keywords: Innovation; sustainability; green entrepreneurship; environmental responsibility; resilience

Entrepreneurship and Development for a Green Resilient Economy, 1–21
Copyright © 2024 by Lidija Weis and Gordana Nikolić
Published under exclusive licence by Emerald Publishing Limited
doi:10.1108/978-1-83797-088-920241001

Introduction

Green entrepreneurship is a fundamental driver of the green economy. A green economy refers to a low carbon and resource-efficient economy where growth is driven by investments that aim at decreasing carbon emissions and pollution, improve energy, and resource efficiency, and prevent the loss of biodiversity (UNEP, 2011). Green economy cannot be driven solely from top-down by the policymakers; instead, it needs to be implemented by green entrepreneurs that also benefit from policy incentives through green innovation and green technology. However, governments should enable better circumstances for green innovation that are large scale and aid in the global transformation of business to become more eco-friendly and not just subsidize green niche markets (Saari & Joensuu-Salo, 2020).

Entrepreneurs play a crucial role in introducing novel concepts to the market and instigating transformative shifts in economies. This holds particularly true in the realm of green entrepreneurship, where emerging startups possess the potential to disrupt entrenched practices (Phan et al., 2005). Green entrepreneurs capitalize on opportunities stemming from environmental market failures. However, the paradox within green entrepreneurship arises from the fact that the environmental benefits derived from these ventures constitute a public good, rendering them non-excludable. This non-excludable nature may push green entrepreneurs, along with their innovative breakthroughs, into transitional spaces where additional costs create a competitive disadvantage, thereby limiting their economic impact compared to non-green counterparts (Demirel et al., 2019).

Green entrepreneurship, as a distinct subset, is dedicated to formulating and implementing solutions to environmental challenges while advocating for social change to prevent harm to the environment. There's a perspective suggesting that green entrepreneurship could represent a novel business paradigm rather than merely a subset of entrepreneurship, given the broader motivations of green entrepreneurs beyond launching eco-friendly products for a niche market. The realm of environmental or green entrepreneurship can be elucidated through the lens of entrepreneurship theories and ecological and welfare economics, positioning it as a subset of sustainable entrepreneurship. The environmental economics discourse posits that environmental degradation arises from market failures, while entrepreneurship literature contends that business opportunities emerge from such failures (Dean & McMullen, 2007). The target of green entrepreneurship is to improve the business ecosystems where businesses operate and, at the same time, promote changes in business practices that have an impact on the natural environment and society (Gast et al., 2017), which can be on the level of business and production processes or products themselves. Green entrepreneurship is responding to the growing demands for the termination of environmentally degrading businesses and consumers' growing willingness to pay for reducing activities that harm the environment. Green entrepreneurs are seizing business opportunities that can improve ecological sustainability (Dean & McMullen, 2007), and sustainability has become one of the key factors for long-term business success.

Innovation is a crucial economic growth and development driver and plays a critical role in green entrepreneurship (Acs & Audretsch, 2010). In green entrepreneurship, innovation refers to creating new products, services, technologies, and business models that promote sustainability and environmental responsibility. Green entrepreneurship is essential in building a resilient, green economy, and innovation is a critical component of that effort. This chapter will examine the role of innovation in green entrepreneurship and development and how it can contribute to creating a resilient, green economy.

Creating a resilient, green economy requires a comprehensive approach encompassing various strategies and initiatives. Some key strategies that can help to create a resilient, green economy include (Schiederig et al., 2012):

- *Investing in renewable energy*: Shifting from fossil fuels to renewable energy sources such as wind, solar, and hydroelectric power can help to reduce greenhouse gas emissions and promote a more sustainable energy system. Governments, businesses, and investors can play a crucial role in supporting renewable energy development by providing funding, incentives, and regulatory support.
- *Promoting sustainable transportation*: Encouraging the use of public transportation, biking, and walking, as well as supporting the development of electric and hybrid vehicles, can help to reduce transportation-related emissions and promote a more sustainable transportation system through congestion charges, parking policies, and incentives for electric vehicle adoption.
- *Adopting circular economy principles*: A circular economy is one in which resources are used more efficiently, and waste is minimized through reuse, recycling, and repurposing. We can achieve this through product redesign, waste reduction, and recycling programs.
- *Supporting green entrepreneurship*: Green entrepreneurship can help to drive innovation in sustainable technologies, products, and services. Governments and investors can support green entrepreneurship by providing funding, training, and regulatory support and creating markets for sustainable products and services.
- *Building resilient infrastructure*: Investing in resilient infrastructure can help to reduce the impact of climate change and natural disasters and promote a more sustainable and resilient economy, which can include initiatives such as building sea walls to protect against rising sea levels, improving water management systems, and developing green infrastructure such as parks and roofs.
- *Encouraging sustainable agriculture*: Sustainable agriculture practices such as organic farming, agroforestry, and regenerative agriculture can help to reduce greenhouse gas emissions, improve soil health, and promote biodiversity. Waste is one of the examples of how much the green entrepreneurship that solves it is much needed and the green entrepreneurs that find the most sustainable solutions can make profits from it or eliminate it as much as possible. Governments and businesses can support sustainable agriculture by providing funding, incentives, and regulatory support.

- *Fostering sustainable tourism*: Sustainable tourism can help promote economic development while minimizing negative environmental impacts, which can be achieved through initiatives such as ecotourism, responsible tourism practices, and sustainable tourism certification programs.
- *Investing in green education and research*: Investing in green education and research can help to promote knowledge sharing, drive innovation, and build capacity for sustainable development, which can include initiatives such as green education programs, research centers, and partnerships between academia and industry.

The Importance of Innovation in Green Entrepreneurship

In today's dynamic and tumultuous global environment, we are witnessing a wave of megatrends, including the rapid pace of change in globalization and technological advancements, giving rise to new market forces. For any organization to survive and thrive in such an environment, innovation is essential. This entails generating brilliant entrepreneurial ideas that offer sustainable solutions with global applications, contributing even more significantly to environmental conservation. However, innovation is no longer confined to creating value solely for individuals, organizations, or societies. The goal of innovation should extend much further, aiming to help shape a smart future where people can experience the highest possible quality of life.

In this context, innovation must actively seek intelligent solutions to address major social challenges, adopt more proactive approaches to anticipate an uncertain future, and pursue strategies to overcome barriers to this smart future (Canton, 2015; Drucker, 1985). The benefits of innovation can accrue to individuals, groups, communities, industries, societies, nations, regions, and the world. What unites all these entities is their shared pursuit of innovation for better future preparedness. However, innovation shouldn't passively prepare for a smart future by being predictive, adaptive, and agile; rather, it should be aggressively proactive in creating a smart future that offers more opportunities for an improved quality of life (Lee et al., 2016).

Green entrepreneurship, a distinct subset of entrepreneurship, addresses the creation and implementation of solutions to environmental challenges, with the aim of promoting social change to safeguard the environment. Some argue that green entrepreneurship could represent a new business paradigm rather than just a subset of entrepreneurship because green entrepreneurs harbor broader motivations beyond launching eco-friendly products and services for niche markets (Kirkwood & Walton, 2010). Green entrepreneurship can be conceptualized based on entrepreneurship theories, environmental economics, and welfare economics, positioned as a subset of sustainable entrepreneurship (Dean & McMullen, 2007).

The objective of green entrepreneurship is to enhance the business ecosystems in which businesses operate while simultaneously advocating for changes in business practices that impact the natural environment and society (Gast et al., 2017). This impact can manifest at the level of business and production processes and/or the products themselves. Green entrepreneurship responds to the increasing demands for the cessation of environmentally degrading business activities and the growing willingness of consumers to pay for reducing activities that negatively impact the environment. Green entrepreneurs are seizing business opportunities that can lead to improvements in ecological sustainability (Dean & McMullen, 2007).

Innovation is essential in green entrepreneurship for several reasons (Hockerts & Wüstenhagen, 2010):

(1) Innovation enables entrepreneurs to develop new products and services that are environmentally sustainable. These products and services can address various environmental challenges, from reducing greenhouse gas emissions to improving resource efficiency.
(2) Innovation can lead to the development of new technologies that can enable businesses to operate more sustainably. For example, developing renewable energy technologies has enabled businesses to reduce their reliance on fossil fuels and transition to cleaner energy sources.
(3) Innovation can lead to the development of new business models that are more environmentally sustainable.

These models can help businesses reduce waste, improve resource efficiency, and operate sustainably. Innovation is crucial in green entrepreneurship because it drives the development of sustainable technologies, products, and services. Green entrepreneurs must constantly innovate to meet the growing demand for sustainable solutions and to stay ahead of competitors. Innovation can lead to more efficient and effective resource use, reducing waste and emissions and promoting a more sustainable economy.

One of the critical ways that innovation is driving green entrepreneurship is by developing clean energy technologies. Innovations in solar, wind, and other renewable energy technologies have helped to make them more efficient and cost-effective, driving down the cost of renewable energy and making it more competitive with fossil fuels, which has led to a significant increase in the adoption of renewable energy globally, which has helped to reduce greenhouse gas emissions and promote a more sustainable energy system.

Innovation is also driving the development of sustainable products and services. Green entrepreneurs are developing new and innovative ways to reduce waste and promote the circular economy, such as by developing products made from recycled materials or introducing innovative business models that promote reuse and recycling. These innovations help reduce waste and emissions and create new market opportunities for green entrepreneurs.

Moreover, innovation is driving the development of sustainable agriculture practices. Innovations in agriculture, such as regenerative agriculture and vertical farming, are helping to reduce the environmental impact of agriculture while also increasing efficiency and productivity. These practices are also helping to promote food security and support rural livelihoods.

Finally, innovation is driving the development of sustainable transportation solutions. Innovations in electric and hybrid vehicles, public transportation, and bike-sharing systems are helping to reduce emissions and promote more sustainable transportation systems. These innovations are not only helping to reduce the environmental impact of transportation, but they are also creating new market opportunities for green entrepreneurs.

In the green management literature, the focus has been lately shifting more to sustainability and innovation, the important role of small- and medium-sized enterprises (SMEs), and the increasing demands from the consumer markets for more green products (Schaper, 2016). The role of businesses in future sustainable development is crucial. Green economies and green entrepreneurs are change agents that can introduce the environmental, social, and ethical transformation of society (Affolderbach & Krueger, 2017).

Types of Innovation in Green Entrepreneurship

Innovation can take many different forms in green entrepreneurship. Some of the most common types of innovation include product innovation, process innovation, and business model innovation.

Product Innovation

In recent years, an increased debate and interest in green product innovation was clearly observed. Pujari (2006) points out that green product innovation is increasingly being portrayed as an opportunity. Nowadays, product innovation has become a significant means of firms' survival and a weapon to sustain market competitive advantage (Gronhaug & Kaufmann, 1988). A good product innovation performance can help firms to improve market position, affirm brand name, leapfrog competition, create a breakthrough, and attract new customers (Lin et al., 2013). Commission of the European Communities (2001) defines green product innovation as products that reduce the negative impacts and risks to the environment, utilize less resources, and prevent waste generation in the product's disposal phase. In other words, green product innovation not only protects the natural environment but also provides environmental benefits higher than conventional products. Green product innovation can serve as a means for firms to gain sustainable development and achieve their business targets (Lin et al., 2013).

Product innovation refers to creating new products or improving existing products that are more environmentally sustainable. Green product innovation aims to change or modify product designs by using nontoxic compounds or biodegradable materials during the production process to reduce the disposal impact on the environment and to improve energy efficiency (Lin et al., 2013). For example, a green entrepreneur might develop a new type of biodegradable packaging material to replace plastic or a new energy-efficient lighting system to reduce energy consumption. Product innovation can also involve using new materials or applying new technologies to improve the environmental performance of existing products.

Product innovation is a critical aspect of green entrepreneurship because it drives the development of sustainable products and services. Product innovation involves the creation of new or improved products that are more sustainable, environmentally friendly, and socially responsible. By developing innovative products, green entrepreneurs can meet the growing demand for sustainable solutions and gain a competitive advantage in the market.

One way that green entrepreneurs innovate in product development is by using sustainable materials. Sustainable materials, such as recycled or biodegradable materials, are environmentally friendly. Green entrepreneurs use these materials to create new and innovative products, such as clothing made from recycled plastic bottles or furniture made from reclaimed wood. Green entrepreneurs use sustainable materials to reduce waste, conserve resources, and promote a circular economy.

Another way that green entrepreneurs innovate in product development is by using renewable energy. Renewable energy can power the production of products, reducing reliance on fossil fuels and helping to reduce greenhouse gas emissions. For example, solar panels can power manufacturing facilities, or wind turbines can power shipping fleets. Green entrepreneurs use renewable energy to promote sustainable production practices and reduce their products' environmental impact.

Green entrepreneurs are also developing innovative business models promoting sustainable consumption. For example, Rent the Runway and ThredUp promote clothing rental and resale, reduce the need for new clothing production, and reduce textile waste. Similarly, companies such as Loop promote reusable packaging for consumer products, reduce the need for single-use packaging, and promote the circular economy. These innovative business models are not only reducing waste and promoting sustainability, but they are also creating new market opportunities for green entrepreneurs (Hockerts & Wüstenhagen, 2010).

These innovations are geared toward mitigating environmental repercussions by judiciously utilizing natural resources, implementing effective waste management, and embracing renewable energy sources. They also prioritize the upholding of human rights and ethical treatment of animals, whether destined for production or experimentation, signifying a substantial departure from conventional processes within the agri-food sector (El Bilali, 2018). Moreover, these innovations necessitate significant short-term investments, with their outcomes typically manifesting in the long term (Bartoloni, 2013; Berrone et al., 2013). This underscores the imperative to assess the economic and financial viability of such investments, considering that resources allocated to innovative projects in sustainable products could potentially be diverted to endeavors with lower costs and risks for the company.

In summary, product innovation stands as a pivotal facet of green entrepreneurship, steering the creation of sustainable products and services. Green entrepreneurs leverage sustainable materials, renewable energy, and inventive business models to address the escalating demand for solutions, fostering a more sustainable and resilient economy. With consumers increasingly cognizant of the environmental impact associated with their consumption choices, the clamor for sustainable products and services is set to intensify, underscoring the indispensability of product innovation for the triumph of green entrepreneurs.

Process Innovation

Process innovation refers to developing or improving new production processes to reduce waste, improve resource efficiency, and reduce environmental impact. Green process innovation is defined as "the application or exploitation of production processes that is novel to firms and which results in the reduction of environmental pollution compared to relevant alternatives" (Ma et al., 2017, p. 1). Green process innovation includes measures to minimize the waste from within the production process (Mendes, 2012; Severo et al., 2017). It also concerns the end-of-pipe technology using pollution-control equipment to ensure compliance with environmental regulations. Using such technology and processes, a significant amount of waste is reduced or recycled, and energy is utilized more efficiently. Thus, companies often implement green process innovations to improve production efficiency, gain cost advantages, and help their organizations develop new market opportunities to promote their competitive advantage. Overall, green process innovation is often considered a vital factor for firms and industries, as well as for business and innovation scholars.

For example, a green entrepreneur might develop a new manufacturing process that uses less water or energy or a new recycling process that recovers more materials from waste streams. Process innovation can also involve using new technologies or adopting new practices to improve the environmental performance of existing processes.

Process innovation is a critical aspect of green entrepreneurship, as it drives the development of sustainable production processes that reduce waste and promote environmental sustainability. Process innovation involves the creation of new or improved production methods, technologies, and systems that are more efficient, environmentally friendly, and socially responsible. By innovating in production processes, green entrepreneurs can reduce costs, increase efficiency, and gain a competitive advantage in the market, especially because customers are becoming more sensitive to environmental issues, they are demanding an end to polluting technologies while calling for products made using green technologies. Therefore, firms must adopt green production technologies and related equipment in their production process to retain their customer base, whose interest in such technologies has been increasing exponentially (Khan et al., 2021).

One way that green entrepreneurs are innovating in process development is through the adoption of circular production practices. Circular production is a system that aims to eliminate waste and promote the reuse and recycling of materials. Green entrepreneurs are adopting circular production practices by designing products with recyclable or reusable components, implementing closed-loop manufacturing systems that minimize waste, and creating supply chains that prioritize sustainable materials and production methods.

Another way green entrepreneurs innovate in process development is by using automation and digital technologies. By automating production processes, green entrepreneurs can reduce waste, increase efficiency, and reduce the environmental impact of production. In addition, digital technologies such as artificial intelligence and machine learning can also be used to optimize production processes, reduce waste, and improve efficiency.

Green entrepreneurs also innovate in process development by adopting sustainable energy and water management practices. Sustainable energy practices involve using renewable energy sources such as solar, wind, and geothermal energy and implementing energy-efficient technologies and systems. In addition, sustainable water management practices involve using water-efficient technologies, such as low-flow toilets and faucets, as well as the implementation of water recycling and rainwater harvesting systems.

There is no doubt that process innovation is a critical aspect of green entrepreneurship because it drives the development of sustainable production processes that promote environmental sustainability. By adopting circular production practices, automating production processes, and implementing sustainable energy and water management practices, green entrepreneurs can reduce waste, increase efficiency, and gain a competitive advantage in the market. As consumers become increasingly aware of the environmental impact of production processes, the demand for sustainable production practices will only continue to grow, making process innovation essential for the success of green entrepreneurs.

Business Model Innovation

Business model innovation assumes a dual role within the realm of innovation. First, it serves as a conduit for innovation, empowering managers to introduce inventive products and technologies to the market. Second, it functions as a wellspring of innovation, transcending conventional dimensions such as product, process, and organizational innovation by reshaping the established approaches to conducting business. The innovation of business models involves a reconfiguration of elements within the business model, encompassing innovation in the content (introduction of new activities), structure (relationships and sequencing of activities), or governance (control/responsibility over an activity) of the activity system between the company and its network. Through business model innovation, an organization can redefine its connections to external stakeholders and reshape its economic exchanges with them to generate value for all partners. Consequently, it becomes instrumental in coordinating technological and organizational innovations that involve a broader spectrum of stakeholders within a value network (Nußholz, 2017).

Furthermore, business model innovation extends to the development of new business methods that prioritize environmental sustainability. The cultivation of green and sustainable business models is indispensable for establishing environmentally conscious and sustainable businesses. This encompasses both the dismantling of existing business models and the creation of novel approaches to generating and capturing value (Roome & Louche, 2016). With the sustainability requirements, businesses need to develop innovative ideas and business models and not just add superficial fixes to current non-sustainable solutions (Bocken et al., 2014). If companies improve their energy efficiency, but simultaneously their production and sales grow because of enhanced affordability, the companies are generating a rebound effect. This means that even though companies develop their eco-design and eco-efficiency, it is not necessarily decreasing their resource usage, and there is a negative impact of the products on the environment due to the increasing sales and demand on the markets (Bocken et al., 2014). The focus on green companies should be on creating more durable and repairable products, and thus, the revenue would be collected from other sources than just sales of products. Sustainable and green business model creation is multidisciplinary, and different kinds of stakeholders need to be involved from the very early phases. A business model usually has three main components: the value proposition, the value creation and delivery, and the value capture (Osterwalder & Pigneur, 2010). In a green and sustainable business model, the economic, environmental, and social levels of the business need to be included, and different kinds of stakeholders need to be involved from the three levels of the business environment (Bocken et al., 2014).

Business model innovation refers to a new integrated logic of how the firm creates value for its customers or users and how it captures value and is the implementation of a business model that is new to the firm (Björkdahl & Holmén, 2013). Contrasted with product or service innovation, business model innovation does not necessarily discover a new product or service; instead, it uses new ways to create and deliver the existing product or service and new ways to capture value from it. Business model innovation is changing how to do business, rather than what to do, and that it goes further than purely innovations in technology, product, and process (Amit & Zott, 2012).

As an illustration, a green entrepreneur may devise a novel business model that advocates for resource sharing or relies on renewable energy sources. The innovation of business models can extend to the formulation of fresh supply chain frameworks or the adoption of innovative marketing strategies geared toward promoting environmental responsibility.

The pivotal role of business model innovation in green entrepreneurship cannot be overstated, as it propels the formulation of inventive approaches to conceive and deliver sustainable products and services. Business model innovation entails the creation or enhancement of business models that prioritize environmental sustainability, social responsibility, and economic viability. Through this innovative approach to business models, green entrepreneurs can unearth new market prospects, curtail costs, and distinguish themselves from competitors. Green entrepreneurs innovate in business model development by adopting circular business models. Circular business models emphasize the prioritization of material reuse and recycling, the advocacy for the sharing economy, and the minimization of waste. In the pursuit of these principles, green entrepreneurs are embracing circular business models by designing products and services with reusability or recyclability in mind, instituting initiatives for product take-back, and collaborating with other enterprises to establish sharing platforms.

Another avenue through which green entrepreneurs' manifest innovation in business model development is the establishment of sustainable supply chains. These supply chains place a premium on the utilization of sustainable materials and production methods, uphold fair labor practices, and mitigate the environmental impact associated with transportation and logistics. Green entrepreneurs actively shape sustainable supply chains by sourcing materials responsibly, implementing sustainable production methods, and forming partnerships with suppliers and logistics providers who share a commitment to sustainability (Schaltegger et al., 2016). The creation of a sustainable supply chain is paramount in green entrepreneurship, serving to minimize the environmental, social, and economic footprint of a company's supply chain operations. This involves prioritizing the use of sustainable materials, advocating for equitable labor practices, and reducing the environmental consequences of transportation and logistics.

In particular, green entrepreneurs can champion sustainability by prioritizing the use of responsibly sourced materials, including those harvested, recycled, or biodegradable. This not only diminishes the environmental impact of production processes but also contributes to environmental sustainability. Moreover, the conscientious selection of materials supports fair labor practices and benefits local communities.

Furthermore, green entrepreneurs can contribute to sustainable supply chains by adopting production methods that minimize waste, decrease energy consumption, and foster environmental sustainability. This encompasses the incorporation of circular production practices, automation of production processes, and reliance on renewable energy sources. Through the adoption of such sustainable production methods, green entrepreneurs not only mitigate their environmental impact but also gain a competitive edge in the market.

The establishment of sustainable supply chains is further facilitated by collaborations with suppliers and logistics providers who share a commitment to sustainability. This involves working with partners who prioritize environmental sustainability, fair labor practices, and social responsibility. Through such collaborations, green entrepreneurs ensure that their entire supply chain aligns with their sustainability objectives.

It is imperative to acknowledge that a sustainable supply chain stands as a pivotal component of green entrepreneurship, serving to mitigate the environmental, social, and economic repercussions of a company's supply chain operations. By placing an emphasis on sustainable materials, adopting eco-friendly production methods, and partnering with sustainable suppliers and logistics providers, green entrepreneurs can forge sustainable supply chains that not only promote environmental sustainability but also champion fair labor practices. As consumer awareness of the environmental and social impact of business practices grows, the demand for sustainable supply chains is poised to escalate, underscoring the necessity for green entrepreneurs to steadfastly prioritize sustainability in their supply chain endeavors. Green entrepreneurs further showcase their commitment to sustainability by innovating in business model development through the adoption of new financing and revenue models. For example, crowdfunding platforms and impact investing funds can give green entrepreneurs access to capital, while revenue models such as subscription services and performance-based contracts can provide stable and predictable revenue streams.

Overcoming Barriers to Innovation in
Green Entrepreneurship

Despite the importance of innovation in green entrepreneurship, several barriers can hinder the development and adoption of new technologies, products, and business models. The existing literature indicates that impediments to green entrepreneurship encompass various business-related challenges, including constraints on capital availability (Mrkajic et al., 2019) and limitations in securing funding (Demirel et al., 2019). Additionally, these barriers extend to factors such as perceptions of political and technological risks, challenges in scalability, and the protracted payback periods associated with green entrepreneurship (Migendt et al., 2017). Other hindrances can be linked to competencies (Santini, 2017), considerations related to environmental issues and health consciousness (Kirkwood & Walton, 2010), as well as consumer awareness from the perspective of products and services (Walley & Taylor, 2002). Abdullah et al. (2016) note that the barriers to green products, processes, and system innovations are different. Environmental resources, attitude and perception, business practices, government support, and customer demand were found to be barriers to green product innovation, while attitude and perception, business practices, poor external partnerships, insufficient information, lack of customer demand, and environmental commercial benefits have been identified as factors that negatively affect green process innovation. In terms of green system innovation, environmental resources, attitudes and perceptions, business practices, technical barriers, government support, and environmental and commercial benefits were presented as internal and external barriers to be addressed. Given that governments are less willing to adopt alternative technologies if they compromise their economic and industrial growth, green technologies are particularly promising as they help in energy efficiency and emission reduction at the same time (Khan et al., 2021).

One of the most significant barriers to innovation in green entrepreneurship is a lack of funding. Many green entrepreneurs struggle to secure the capital they need to develop and commercialize new technologies, products, and business models, which is particularly true for early-stage startups, which often have limited financial resources and struggle to attract investors. To overcome this barrier, green entrepreneurs may need to explore alternative funding sources, such as crowdfunding, impact investing, or government grants. They may also need to develop a strong business plan demonstrating their innovation's potential financial and environmental benefits.

The lack of funding can be a significant obstacle for green entrepreneurs developing innovative products and services promoting environmental sustainability. However, there are several strategies that green entrepreneurs can use to overcome this challenge and secure the funding they need to drive innovation in their businesses.

Seek government funding and grants: Local, state, and federal government entities frequently provide funding opportunities and grants aimed at supporting sustainable businesses and fostering innovation. Green entrepreneurs can conduct thorough research to identify and apply for such funding opportunities that align with their business goals and sustainability objectives.

Collaborating with impact investors presents another avenue for green entrepreneurs to secure financial support. Impact investors prioritize funding businesses that not only yield financial returns but also create positive social and environmental impacts. By actively seeking out impact investors who share similar values and sustainability objectives, green entrepreneurs can present their businesses and innovative concepts, making a compelling case to secure funding for their endeavors.

Crowdfunding: Utilizing crowdfunding platforms like Kickstarter and Indiegogo presents a direct avenue for green entrepreneurs to secure funding from individuals with an interest in supporting sustainable businesses and innovative initiatives. Beyond financial support, crowdfunding can serve as a means for green entrepreneurs to validate their businesses and innovative concepts by garnering feedback and support directly from their target market.

Engaging in collaborations with strategic partners is another viable approach for green entrepreneurs to explore. These strategic partners may include suppliers, customers, and fellow businesses. By forming partnerships, green entrepreneurs can leverage shared resources and expertise to drive innovation. Additionally, such collaborations can open up funding opportunities and provide access to resources that may otherwise be unavailable to green entrepreneurs working independently.

Leverage sustainable financing options: Certain financial institutions provide financing solutions tailored for sustainable businesses and innovation. Green entrepreneurs can explore these financial options, conducting thorough research to identify those that align with their business goals and sustainability objectives. In summary, the challenge of securing funding for green entrepreneurs driving innovation in their businesses can be addressed by exploring government funding and grants, partnering with impact investors, utilizing crowdfunding, engaging in collaborations with strategic partners, and leveraging sustainable financing options. Through these avenues, green entrepreneurs can overcome funding challenges and secure the resources needed to drive innovation and establish sustainable businesses.

Another prevalent hurdle to innovation in green entrepreneurship is the limited demand within the market. Many consumers remain unaware of the environmental advantages associated with sustainable products and services, and this lack of awareness may hinder their willingness to pay a premium. Consequently, green entrepreneurs may encounter difficulties in generating revenue and scaling their businesses. Nevertheless, various strategies can be employed to surmount this challenge and cultivate demand for innovative products and services.

Educate the market: Green entrepreneurs can enlighten their target audience about the benefits inherent in their sustainable offerings. These benefits may include reducing environmental impact, promoting social responsibility, and enhancing health and wellness. Through awareness campaigns and educational initiatives, green entrepreneurs can create demand among environmentally conscious consumers.

Target niche markets: Focusing on niche markets with a heightened interest in sustainability and a willingness to pay a premium for eco-friendly products and services can be a strategic approach. Niche markets may encompass eco-tourists, green commuters, and health and wellness enthusiasts.

Collaborate with other businesses: Collaboration with other businesses presents an opportunity for green entrepreneurs to collectively generate demand for sustainable products and services. For instance, a sustainable clothing company could collaborate with a sustainable fashion retailer to jointly promote sustainable fashion and drive demand for eco-friendly clothing.

Competitive pricing: Green entrepreneurs can strategically price their sustainable offerings to be competitive with non-sustainable alternatives. This approach makes sustainable products and services more accessible and appealing to consumers, fostering demand among those who are price sensitive.

Utilize social media and digital marketing: Leveraging social media and digital marketing channels allows green entrepreneurs to raise awareness and generate demand for sustainable products and services. Through engaging and informative content that highlights the benefits of sustainability, entrepreneurs can attract environmentally conscious consumers and cultivate demand for their offerings.

To address the challenge of limited market demand, green entrepreneurs may need to educate consumers about the environmental advantages of their products and services. Additionally, incentivizing sustainable choices through discounts, rewards, or partnerships with other businesses can be explored as creative strategies.

The Role of Collaboration in Green Entrepreneurship

The term "Green Entrepreneurship" is very broad and includes both "Startups" and "Existing Businesses" working toward the betterment of the environment. It includes any such activity which provides for environmental upgradation and reduction or slowdown of environmental degradation (Navarathinam & Amutha, 2022). Collaboration is another critical component of green entrepreneurship. Collaboration can help to overcome barriers to innovation, promote knowledge sharing, and create new opportunities for sustainable growth (Makki et al., 2020). Collaboration can take many forms, from partnerships between businesses and governments to collaborations between different sectors and stakeholders.

Public–Private Partnerships

Contemporary theoretical perspectives on PPPs and effective approaches to implementing large-scale investment projects globally go beyond the conventional role of the private sector in delivering public services. The concept of PPPs, as elucidated by Vassileva (2022), extends to long-term collaborations between government entities and private entities on national and international levels. These collaborations aim to address socio-economic challenges, provide public assets or services, and foster sustainable development in economies and civil societies.

The scope of PPPs, in a broader context, encompasses a comprehensive spectrum of interactions between the public and private sectors. Any association involving a blend of private, non-governmental, or public sector activities falls under the umbrella of a "partnership." Lindner (1999), an American author, defines PPP as a "form of cooperation between the state and private business" (p. 35). In the United States, PPPs extend beyond constructing transport facilities and toll roads to include private involvement in areas such as education policy, social work, health and medical services, and numerous other public initiatives, ranging from education to urban renewal and environmental policy.

This expansive framework encompasses partnerships at both the "policy level" and the "project level," particularly in endeavors related to environmental conservation and the pursuit of economic growth through sustainable development aligned with green economy objectives. Policy-level partnerships entail joint efforts from the public and private sectors in decision-making and policy formulation for various projects. In the energy sector, for instance, policy-level partnerships evaluate the merits of different energy sources, including renewables, establish operational guidelines, devise investment strategies, and outline dispute resolution mechanisms. In contrast, project-level partnerships concentrate on specific initiatives, such as the construction of new power stations, to attract private investment and ensure effective project management. While some countries seamlessly integrate partnerships at the policy, program, and project levels, others may not consistently adopt this comprehensive approach (UN, 2016, pp. 3–8). PPPs are a common form of collaboration in green entrepreneurship and an instrument to contribute to sustainable development (Vassileva, 2022). These partnerships bring together businesses, governments, and other stakeholders to work together on environmental challenges. For example, a PPP might bring together a renewable energy company, a local government, and a community organization to develop a new solar energy project. These partnerships can provide various benefits, including access to funding, technical expertise, and regulatory support.

PPPs are a form of collaboration between the public and private sectors to address shared challenges, including environmental sustainability. PPPs can be a powerful tool for green entrepreneurs looking to drive innovation and create sustainable businesses. Here are some ways that PPPs can support green entrepreneurship:

- *Access to resources*: PPPs can provide green entrepreneurs access to resources that may not be available through the private sector alone, such as government funding, technical expertise, and research and development facilities.
- *Shared expertise*: PPPs allow green entrepreneurs to access the expertise of both public and private sector partners. Public sector partners can provide expertise on environmental regulations and sustainability policies, while private sector partners can offer expertise on business development and commercialization.
- *Risk-sharing*: PPPs can help green entrepreneurs to share the risks associated with developing and commercializing sustainable products and services. Green entrepreneurs can leverage their resources and expertise by partnering with public sector entities to reduce the risks of developing and bringing sustainable products and services to market.

- *Scale and impact*: PPPs can help green entrepreneurs scale up their businesses and have a more significant environmental impact. Public sector partners can provide access to markets, distribution networks, and infrastructure, allowing green entrepreneurs to reach a wider audience and significantly impact sustainability.
- *Policy and regulatory support*: PPPs can provide green entrepreneurs with policy and regulatory support, helping them to navigate complex environmental regulations and policies. Public sector partners can also advocate for policies and regulations that support green entrepreneurship and sustainability.

In conclusion, PPPs can be a valuable form of collaboration for green entrepreneurs looking to drive innovation and create sustainable businesses. By providing access to resources, shared expertise, risk-sharing, scale and impact, and policy and regulatory support, PPPs can help green entrepreneurs overcome the challenges of developing and commercializing sustainable products and services and promote sustainability and innovation in their businesses.

Cross-sector Collaboration

The importance of cross-sector collaboration and partnership as a vehicle for sustainability transformations are widely acknowledged in practice and academia (Doh et al., 2019). Addressing sustainability challenges often transcends sectoral boundaries, necessitating the active involvement of the state, market, and civil society. While there is a shared acknowledgment of the advantages associated with collaborative efforts across sectors, our comprehension of the extent to which such collaboration can generate value for diverse stakeholders involved remains incomplete. Despite this, it is recognized that collaborative business models, in many instances, have the capacity to instigate, oversee, and yield outcomes that prove advantageous for both business entities and society at large (Pedersen et al., 2021). Cross-sector collaboration is an important form of collaboration in green entrepreneurship, which involves collaboration between sectors such as business, government, academia, and civil society. Cross-sector collaborations, among firms, governmental and civil society actors, seem essential to address the systemic nature of sustainability which can help to bring together different perspectives and expertise and create new opportunities for innovation and growth (Stål et al., 2022). Cross-sector collaborations have the potential of providing voice to new stakeholder groups whose needs and wants are often underrepresented in conventional business-led sustainability interventions (Pedersen et al., 2021).

For example, the cross-sector collaboration between a university research team, a technology startup, and a community organization might lead to the development of a new technology to monitor air quality in urban areas.

Cross-sector collaboration can help green entrepreneurs address complex environmental and social challenges and promote sustainability and innovation. Here are some ways in which cross-sector collaboration can support green entrepreneurship:

- *Access to resources*: Cross-sector collaboration can provide green entrepreneurs access to a wide range of resources, including funding, expertise, and networks. For example, the cross-sector collaboration between a non-profit organization and a private sector firm can fund research and development of sustainable products and services.
- *Shared expertise and knowledge*: Cross-sector collaboration can bring together the expertise and knowledge of different sectors to address complex environmental and social challenges. For example, a collaboration between a government agency and a non-profit organization can leverage the expertise of the government agency in policy and regulation and the knowledge of the non-profit organization in community engagement and sustainability.
- *More significant impact*: Cross-sector collaboration can help green entrepreneurs to achieve a more significant impact in promoting sustainability and innovation. By working with multiple sectors, green entrepreneurs can leverage the strengths and resources of each sector to address environmental and social challenges at scale.
- *Access to diverse perspectives*: Cross-sector collaboration can provide green entrepreneurs with access to diverse perspectives, which can help to identify new opportunities and solutions. By working with stakeholders from different sectors, green entrepreneurs can better understand the needs and interests of different stakeholders and develop solutions that meet their needs.
- *Collaboration on policy development*: Cross-sector collaboration can help to develop policies and regulations that support sustainable development and promote innovation. By collaborating with government agencies and other stakeholders, green entrepreneurs can provide input on policy development and advocate for policies that support sustainability and innovation.

In conclusion, cross-sector collaboration is a necessary form of collaboration in green entrepreneurship that can provide green entrepreneurs with access to resources, expertise, and networks and help them to achieve a more significant impact in promoting sustainability and innovation. By working with stakeholders from different sectors, green entrepreneurs can identify new opportunities and solutions and collaborate on policy development to support sustainable development.

Conclusion

Green entrepreneurship assumes a pivotal role, particularly in the face of the increasingly evident impact of climate change, reshaping our environment and available resources. It propels a shift in mindset, fostering contemplation on sustainable development. The significance of green entrepreneurship in the realm of sustainable development is underscored by its emphasis on the environment, an uncontrollable factor, while concurrently managing other factors, be they economic or social.

In the context of green entrepreneurship and sustainable development, innovation emerges as a crucial element. Innovation serves as the catalyst for the creation of novel products, services, technologies, and business models that champion sustainability and environmental responsibility.

Nevertheless, the journey of green entrepreneurship is not without obstacles. Barriers to innovation in this domain include challenges such as insufficient funding, restricted market demand, and regulatory impediments. Overcoming these barriers necessitates the exploration of alternative funding sources, the dissemination of environmental benefits to consumers, and active engagement with policymakers and regulators to advocate for supportive policies that foster sustainable innovation. Collaboration stands out as a pivotal facet of green entrepreneurship, fostering knowledge sharing, surmounting innovation hurdles, and opening avenues for sustainable growth.

The promotion of green entrepreneurship and the establishment of a resilient, green economy emerge as imperative for sustainable development. This chapter accentuates the significance of innovation in attaining this objective, emphasizing the continual need for green entrepreneurs to pioneer new products, services, and business models aligned with environmental sustainability. The arsenal of tools available to green entrepreneurs includes product innovation, process innovation, and business model innovation. These tools serve to not only create sustainable offerings but also enhance efficiency and cultivate new markets for sustainable goods and services.

Nonetheless, the path of green entrepreneurship is laden with challenges, encompassing insufficient funding, limited market demand, and regulatory obstacles. Overcoming these challenges demands a multifaceted approach, with strategies ranging from PPPs to cross-sector collaborations. Such collaborative endeavors offer access to funding, technical expertise, networks, shared knowledge, and expertise, empowering green entrepreneurs to identify fresh opportunities, develop sustainable offerings, and advocate for policies conducive to sustainable development. In addition, PPPs and cross-sector collaborations can foster a supportive ecosystem for green entrepreneurship, where stakeholders from different sectors work together toward a common goal of sustainable development. This ecosystem can promote innovation, knowledge sharing, and collaboration, leading to a more robust and resilient, green economy.

In summary, promoting green entrepreneurship and building a resilient, green economy requires multiple stakeholders' joint efforts. By leveraging innovation and collaboration, green entrepreneurs can overcome challenges, develop sustainable products and services, and promote policies that support sustainable development. Ultimately, a resilient, green economy benefits the environment and society, leading to a more sustainable future.

Based on the discussion above, the following are recommendations for the future:

- *Foster an innovation culture*: Governments and organizations should promote a culture of innovation that supports green entrepreneurship, which can be achieved through funding for research and development, training, and education, supporting startup incubators and accelerators and solutions like green product/service and green design, green production. The green idea and innovation means to have unique solution to the green challenges.

- *Increase funding for green entrepreneurship*: Governments and organizations should increase funding for green entrepreneurship, specifically for product innovation, process innovation, and business model innovation, which can include PPPs, venture capital, and grants.
- *Support sustainable supply chains*: Organizations should support sustainable supply chains by partnering with suppliers who prioritize sustainability, implementing sustainable procurement practices, and engaging with suppliers on environmental and social issues.
- *Encourage cross-sector collaboration*: Governments, businesses, academia, and non-profits should work together to promote cross-sector collaboration, which can provide access to funding, technical expertise, networks, and shared knowledge and expertise.
- *Championing supportive policy measures*: Green entrepreneurs ought to actively champion policies conducive to sustainable development, including initiatives such as setting renewable energy targets, implementing carbon pricing mechanisms, and adopting sustainable procurement policies.
- *Fostering sustainable consumption*: Organizations are encouraged to foster sustainable consumption patterns by crafting eco-friendly products and services, coupled with educational efforts to enlighten consumers about the environmental and social implications of their choices.

Through the implementation of these recommendations, we can establish a more robust and environmentally conscious economy that places a premium on sustainability and social responsibility.

References

Abdullah, M., Zailani, S., Iranmanesh, M., Jayaraman, K. (2016). Barriers to green innovation initiatives among manufacturers: the Malaysian case. *Review of Managerial Science, 10*(4), 683–709.

Acs, Z. J., & Audretsch, D. B. (2010). *Entrepreneurship and innovation.* MIT Press.

Affolderbach, J., & Krueger, R. (2017). "Just" ecopreneurs: Re-conceptualising green transitions and entrepreneurship. *Local Environment, 22*(4), 410–423.

Amit, R., & Zott, C. (2012). Creating value through business model innovation. *MIT Sloan Management Review, 53*, 41–49.

Bartoloni, E. (2013). Capital structure and innovation: Causality and determinants. *Empirica, 40*(1), 111–151. https://doi.org/10.1007/s10663-011-9179-y

Berrone, P., Fosfuri, A., Gelabert, L., & Gómez-Mejia L. R. (2013). Necessity as the mother of 'green' inventions: Institutional pressures and environmental innovations. *Strategic Management Journal, 34*(8), 891–909. https://doi.org/10.1002/smj.2041

Björkdahl, J., & Holmén, M. (2013). Editorial: Business model innovation – The challenges ahead. *International Journal of Product Development, 18*(3), 213–225.

Bocken, N. M. P., Short, S. W., Rana, P., & Evans, S. (2014). A literature and practice review to develop sustainable business model archetypes. *Journal of Cleaner Production, 65*, 42–56.

Canton, J. (2015). *Future smart: Managing the game-changing trendsthat will transform your world.* Da Capo Press.

Commission of the European Communities. (2001). *Green paper on integrated product policy*. http://eur-lex.europa.eu/LexUriServ/site/en/com/2001/com2001_0068en01.pdf

Dean, T. J., & McMullen, J. S. (2007). Toward a theory of sustainable entrepreneurship: Reducing environmental degradation through entrepreneurial action. *Journal of Business Venturing, 22*(1), 50–76.

Demirel, P., Qian, C. L., Rentocchini, F., & Tamvada, J. P. (2017). Born to be green: New insights into the economics and management of green entrepreneurship. *Small Business Economics, 52*, 759–771. https://doi.org/10.1007/s11187-017-9933-z

Doh, J., Tashman, P., & Benischke, M. H. (2019). Adapting to grand environmental challenges through collective entrepreneurship. *Academy of Management Perspectives, 33*(4), 450–468.

Drucker, P. (1985). The discipline of innovation. *Harvard Business Review, 63*(3), 67–72.

El Bilali, H. (2018). Relation between innovation and sustainability in the agro-food system. *Italian Journal of Food Science, 30*(2), 200–225. https://doi.org/10.14674/IJFS-1096

Gast, J., Gundolf, K., & Cesinger, B. (2017). Doing business in a green way: A systematic review of the ecological sustainability entrepreneurship literature and future research directions. *Journal of Cleaner Production, 147*, 44–56.

Gronhaug, K., & Kaufmann, G., (1988). *Innovation: A cross disciplinary perspective.* Norwegian University Press.

Hockerts, K., & Wüstenhagen, R. (2010). Greening Goliaths versus emerging Davids—Theorizing about the role of incumbents and new entrants in sustainable entrepreneurship. *Journal of Business Venturing, 25*(5), 481–492.

Khan, S. J., Kaur, P., Jabeen, F., & Dhir, A. (2021). Green process innovation: Where we are and where we are going. *Business Strategy and the Environment, 30*(7), 3273–3296.

Kirkwood, J., & Walton, S. (2010). What motivates ecopreneurs to start businesses? *International Journal of Entrepreneurial Behavior & Research, 16*(3), 204–228.

Lee, S. M., Trimi, S., & Kim, C. (2016). Innovation for creating a smart future. *Journal of Innovation & Knowledge, 3*(1), 1–8.

Lin, R. J., Tan, K. H., & Geng, Y. (2013). Market demand, green product innovation, and firm performance: Evidence from Vietnam motorcycle industry. *Journal of Cleaner Production, 40*, 101–107.

Lindner, S. H. (1999). Coming to terms with the PPP. *American Behavioral Scientists, USA, 43*, 35–51.

Ma, Y., Hou, G., & Xin, B. (2017). Green process innovation and innovation benefit: The mediating effect of firm image. *Sustainability, 9*(10), 1778.

Makki, A. A., Alidrisi, H., Iqbal, A., & Al-Sasi, B. O. (2020). Barriers to green entrepreneurship: An ISM-based investigation. *Journal of Risk and Financial Management, 13*, 249.

Mendes, L. (2012). Clean technologies and environmental management: A study on a small dairy industry in Brazil. *Resources and Environment, 2*(3), 100–106.

Migendt, M., Polzin, F., Schock, F., Täube, F. A., & von Flotow, P. (2017). Beyond venture capital: An exploratory study of the finance-innovation-policy nexus in cleantech. *Industrial and Corporate Change, 26*, 973–996.

Mrkajic, B., Murtinu S., & Scalera. V. G. (2019). Is green the new gold? Venture capital and green entrepreneurship. *Small Business Economics, 52*, 929–950.

Navarathinam, K., & Amutha, V. (2022). Green entrepreneurship: a sustainable development initiative with special reference to selected districts. *Journal of Positive School Psychology, 6*(3), 7517–7526.

Nußholz, J. L. K. (2017). Circular business models: Defining a concept and framing an emerging research field. *Sustainability, 9*(10), 1810.

Osterwalder, A., & Pigneur, Y. (2010). *Business model generation: A handbook for visionaries, game changers, and challengers.* John Wiley and Sons.

Pedersen, E. R. G., Lüdeke-Freund, F., Henriques, I., & Seitanidi, M. M. (2021). Toward collaborative crosssector business models for sustainability. *Business & Society, 60*(5), 1039–1058.

Phan, P., Siegel, D., & Wright, M. (2005). Science parks and incubators: Observations, synthesis and future research. *Journal of Business Venturing, 20*(2), 165–182. https://doi.org/10.1016/j.jbusvent.2003.12.001

Pujari, D. (2006). Eco-innovation and new product development: Understanding the influences on market performance. *Technovation, 26*(1), 76–85.

Roome, N., & Louche, C. (2016). Journeying toward business models for sustainability: A conceptual model found inside the black box of organisational transformation. *Organization & Environment, 29*(1), 11–35.

Saari, U. A., & Joensuu-Salo, S. (2020). In W. L. Filho, A. Azul, L. Brandli, P. Özuyar & T. Wall (Eds.), *Responsible Consumption and Production* (Encyclopedia of the UN Sustainable Development Goals, pp. 302–312). Springer.

Santini, C. (2017). Ecopreneurship and ecopreneurs: Limits, trends, and characteristics. *Sustainability, 9*, 492.

Schaltegger, S., Hörisch, J., Freeman, R. E. (2019), Business Cases for Sustainability: A Stakeholder Theory Perspective. *Organization and Environment, 32*, 191–212.

Schaper, M. (2016). Understanding the green entrepreneur. M. Schaper, (Ed.), *Making Ecopreneurs: Developing Sustainable Entrepreneurship* (2nd. ed., pp. 27–40). Routledge.

Schiederig, T., Tietze, F., & Herstatt, C. (2012). Green innovation in technology and innovation management–an exploratory literature review. *R&D Management, 42*(2), 180–192.

Severo, E. A., Guimarães, J. C. F. d, & Dorion, E. C. H. (2017). Cleaner production and environmental management as sustainable product innovation antecedents: A survey in Brazilian industries. *Journal of Cleaner Production, 142*, 87–97.

Stål, H. I., Bengtsson, M., & Manzhynski, S. (2022). Cross-sectoral collaboration in business model innovation for sustainable development: Tensions and compromises. *Business Strategy and the Environment, 31*(1), 445–463.

UN. (2016). *PPPs for sustainable development in Asia and the Pacific, country guidance, UN ESCAP.* https://ppp.worldbank.org/public-private-partnership/sites/ppp.worldbank.org/files/2022-02/PPP_and_SDGs_Draft_20_December.pdf

UNEP. (2011). *Towards a green economy: Pathways to sustainable development and poverty eradication – A synthesis for policy makers.* United Nations Environment Programme. http://www.unep.org/greeneconomy

Vassileva, A. G. (2022). Green public-private partnerships (PPPs) as an instrument for sustainable development. *Journal of World Economy: Transformations & Transitions (JOWETT), 2*(5), 22.

Walley, E. E., & Taylor, D. W. (2002). Opportunists, champions, mavericks …? *Greener Management International, 38*, 31–43.

Chapter 2

The Role of Entrepreneurship as Catalysts for Sustainability and a Green, Resilient Economy: Critical Discourse Analysis

Lukman Raimi

University Brunei Darussalam, Brunei Darussalam

Abstract

Entrepreneurship, sustainability, and the creation of a resilient, green economy are intricately linked, particularly as conventional economic models grapple with existential challenges. However, empirical research addressing the connection between entrepreneurship and sustainability for a more balanced and resilient future is notably scarce. This chapter aims to bridge this gap by investigating the role of entrepreneurship in advancing sustainability and establishing a resilient, green economy. Through comprehensive research utilizing critical discourse analysis (CDA), three research questions were explored to draw insightful managerial and practical implications. In the intersection of entrepreneurship, sustainability, and a green, resilient economy, opportunities are seized by entrepreneurship amid limitations, while sustainability presupposes responsible management of resources for current needs without compromising the future. A green economy ensures adaptability, growth, and ecological stability even in resource-scarce conditions. The CDA affirms the influential role of entrepreneurship in pursuing sustainability and a green, resilient economy, drawing from 18 cases across public, private, and social sectors to highlight environmental, social, and economic impacts. Furthermore, the CDA uncovers power dynamics, ideologies, and social structures affecting entrepreneurship's role in fostering sustainable and resilient, green economies. Collaborations between governments, corporations, and social ventures in diverse countries promote sustainability within existing social structures, fostering comprehensive development. However, imbalanced power dynamics pose challenges, risking potential social exclusion. This chapter concludes by addressing practical

Entrepreneurship and Development for a Green Resilient Economy, 23–46
Copyright © 2024 by Lukman Raimi
Published under exclusive licence by Emerald Publishing Limited
doi:10.1108/978-1-83797-088-920241002

implications and limitations, aiming to contribute to an ecologically balanced and socially equitable future by understanding entrepreneurship's role in promoting sustainability and green resilience within the context of power dynamics, ideologies, and social structures.

Keywords: Entrepreneurship; green economy; environmental impact; social impact; economic impact; resilience

1. Introduction

The link between entrepreneurship, sustainability, and the green economy has received significant attention in the literature on sustainable development and green entrepreneurship in recent years. As the world faces pressing, unprecedented environmental challenges such as climate change, famine, desertification, deforestation, scarcity-driven conflict, and depletion of natural resources, there is a growing realization that traditional entrepreneurship and economic models that ignore social and environmental externalities are no longer sustainable and acceptable. In response, entrepreneurship as a transformative process is increasingly being reinvented as a tool to promote sustainability and build a green, resilient economy. Sustainability, on the other hand, has become a critical issue in today's world as entrepreneurship, particularly human, agricultural, commercial, and industrial activities, increasingly brings with it negative externalities and poses an existential threat to social, environmental, and economic well-being (Heim et al., 2023; Lindell et al., 2022). Entrepreneurship across human, agricultural, commercial, and industrial activities can directly strengthen the achievement of sustainable development goal (SDG) 1, SDG 2, SDG 3, SDG 8, SDG 9, SDG 10, SDG 11, SDG 12, SDG 14, SDG 15, and SDG 17 and indirectly affect other SDGs (Dhahri & Omri, 2020; Raimi et al., 2021; Raimi & Lukman, 2023).

The contemporary sustainability agenda toward a green, resilient economy provides a framework for directly addressing the challenges arising from destructive entrepreneurship (otherwise described as the irresponsible use of resources and unsustainable production), the environment (the planet), society (the people), the economy (profit), etc. The alignment of entrepreneurship and sustainability is further understood as a solution to resource scarcity and emphasizes the need for people and businesses to adopt a new development paradigm that meets current needs without compromising the ability of future generations to meet their own needs (Raimi, 2022). Several studies in both developed and developing countries have stated that sustainability, which encompasses responsible resource use, ecosystem protection, flora and fauna conservation, and reforestation, is laudable, yet complex and controversial. Its realization is entangled in a web of social, economic, and political considerations driven by multiple stakeholders with differing interests, powers, and priorities (Hirons, 2020; Macharis et al., 2012; Tønnesen et al., 2023; Wearing et al., 2010). Sustainability probably consists of several pillars. It was originally embodied by the people, planet, and profit (3Ps) model. Later, as the concept of sustainability became more widespread, partnerships and peace were added, expanding it into the 5P model. Broadly speaking, the 5Ps of sustainability still revolve around the age-old environmental, social, and economic dimensions of sustainable development. The term sustainable development, used interchangeably with sustainability, is legendary as it transcends multidisciplinary boundaries, including religion.

The concept of sustainable development emerged in the 1980s due to increasing economic and population pressures, environmental degradation, and resource scarcity. It was first recognized at the United Nations Conference on Environment and Development in June 1992 in Rio de Janeiro, Brazil. Subsequently, the Brundtland Report defined sustainable development as a development process that meets the needs of the present without jeopardizing the capacity of future generations to meet their own needs (Bartiromo & Ivaldi, 2023; Gialeli et al., 2023). More recently, another term, SDGs, was established in New York by the United Nations in 2015 to address humanity's greatest sustainability challenges, namely: poverty, inequality, hunger, climate change, pandemics and disease, and loss in ecosystems and biodiversity (Raimi, 2022). At the height of industrialization in the international business landscape, developed and developing countries enjoying economic prosperity were oblivious to sustainability issues and less concerned about existential threats posed by irresponsible and unsustainable production and use of our planet's resources. However, in recent years, there has been a rethinking and reconsideration of the need to address the interconnected issues of environmental degradation, social inequality, and economic instability, making the green, resilient economy a priority in academic and political circles. Additionally, today's socially and environmentally conscious consumers, businesses, and communities prefer green products and solutions over traditional products that harm people, the planet, and profits. As a result, multiple manufacturing sites, trading companies, and entrepreneurs are proactively innovating, reinventing, and redesigning their products, services, processes, and solutions to become green and environmentally sustainable – a phenomenon known as green entrepreneurship, green innovation, or a sustainable business model (Haldar, 2019; Todeschini et al., 2017; Xie et al., 2023).

The green, resilient economy as a new paradigm shift in the development process has fully developed as humanity finds a connection with nature and ecology as reciprocity. Green policies and environmentally friendly practices are being vigorously promoted in academic and political circles to conserve natural resources and comply with climate change mitigation strategies. Therefore, the use of colors, especially green, has helped raise concerns about pollution, deforestation, and environmental degradation. It is gaining increasing importance and is frequently used in the political discourse of the international community, governments, and environmentalists. Similarly, a distinct field of green economics has fully emerged, emphasizing sustainability, resource efficiency, and environmental stewardship to achieve economic growth while minimizing negative environmental impacts. It is a widely held concept that emphasizes the need to integrate environmental concerns into human activities to ensure a sustainable and balanced relationship with the natural world.

Across multidisciplinary boundaries, the theoretical and ideological stance of sustainability and a green, resilient economy represents a conscious shift toward more responsible, responsive, and sustainable practices to protect people, the planet, profit, prosperity, and peace (5Ps). These dimensions serve as a comprehensive approach to addressing the complex and interrelated challenges of sustainable development. By considering these five dimensions, individuals, businesses, and governments can work toward a more sustainable and resilient future. To achieve sustainability, it is important to consider three interrelated pillars: the environmental, social, and economic aspects of sustainability, which underlie all 17 SDGs. The environmental pillar focuses on minimizing negative impacts on natural resources, biodiversity, and ecosystems. The social pillar aims to ensure social equity, equity, and inclusivity for all individuals and communities. The economic pillar aims to promote economic growth, innovation, and prosperity while ensuring the efficient use of resources (Raimi, 2022; Raimi et al., 2023).

Many studies in developed and developing countries have examined the link between entrepreneurship and economic sustainability, neglecting social and environmental sustainability. There is a growing body of studies looking at the link between entrepreneurship and social and environmental sustainability, with the goal of leading to a green, resilient economy. The insufficient empirical research on the relationship between entrepreneurship and sustainability justifies this qualitative study. With the background outlined above, the purpose of this chapter is to use CDA to qualitatively examine the role of entrepreneurship in promoting sustainability and building a green, resilient economy. In particular, this chapter aims to answer three research questions: (a) What are the interrelated definitions of entrepreneurship, sustainability, and a green, resilient economy? (b) What is the role of entrepreneurship in promoting sustainability and a green, resilient economy? (c) How do power dynamics, ideologies, and social structures significantly shape the role of entrepreneurship in promoting sustainability and building green resilience?

The contributions to theory and practice are threefold. First, we logically provide a theoretical explanation for the link between entrepreneurship and sustainability leading to a green, resilient economy through CDA. Second, we significantly expand the body of knowledge by providing interconnected definitions of entrepreneurship, sustainability, and a green, resilient economy. This chapter qualitatively contributes to theoretical advances in both areas. Third, by explaining how power dynamics, ideologies, and social structures influence entrepreneurship in promoting sustainability and building green resilience, this study provides a useful framework for researchers and policymakers to explore the relationship between entrepreneurship and sustainability in the global business landscape. According to the introduction (Section 1), this chapter is divided into five sections. Section 2 explains the methodological approach of the CDA. Section 3 provides a conceptual, theoretical, and empirical literature review on the relationship between entrepreneurship and sustainability leading to a green, resilient economy. Section 4 presents the results of the qualitative study. Section 5 concludes with a summary of the study, its implications, and limitations, including further research directions.

2. Methodology

In writing this chapter, the methodology of qualitative research is followed. To obtain answers to the research questions, we reviewed academic papers using

CDA to understand the language and communication of how entrepreneurship advances three pillars of sustainability, with a particular focus on building a green and resilient economy. CDA is an interdisciplinary approach that focuses on the analysis of language in academic discourses with the aim of recognizing, assessing, and combating perceived power imbalances, injustices, and social inequalities (Briant Carant, 2017; Mullet, 2018). In the current context of this chapter, CDA is used to understand how power dynamics, ideologies and social structures significantly influence the role of entrepreneurship in promoting sustainability and building green resilience. Our selected articles focus on three thematic research questions. The application of CDA not only addresses conceptual aspects and the roles of various entrepreneurial actors – entrepreneurs, policymakers, and environmentalists – in promoting sustainability but also highlights the crucial influence of power dynamics, ideologies, and social structures that underlie entrepreneurship's role in significantly shaping the development of green resilience.

For reasons of methodological robustness, CDA was preferred to critical literature review (CLR) because it involves an in-depth study of language and social dynamics. The CDA places great emphasis on a differentiated understanding of linguistic structures, cultural contexts, and power dynamics within the concept of the phenomenon being studied and studied (Catalano & Waugh, 2020; Fairclough, 2023). CDA selected 57 articles and texts from the Google Scholar and Web of Science databases using a targeted sampling technique and pre-developed selection/inclusion criteria (relevance, language, and timeliness). The selected papers were analyzed systematically with the CDA. This approach makes it easy to see the strengths and limitations of the link between entrepreneurship and sustainability in creating a green, resilient economy – an achievement that qualitatively contributes to theoretical advances in both fields. Regarding the steps to carry out the CDA, the current study followed a 12-step approach as explained and illustrated in Fig. 2.1.

1. No Poverty
2. Zero Hunger
3. Good Health and Well-being
4. Quality Education
5. Gender Equality
6. Clean Water and Sanitation
7. Affordable and Clean Energy
8. Decent Work and Economic Growth
9. Industry Innovation and Infrastructure
10. Reduced Inequities
11. Sustainable Cities and Communities
12. Responsible Consumption and Production
13. Climate Action
14. Life Below Water
15. Life on Land
16. Peace, Justice and Strong Institutions
17. Partnerships for the Goals

Fig. 2.1.   List of the 17 SDGs. *Source*: Author's creation (2023).

(i)   *Selection of texts*: In this phase, articles and texts are selected from the Google Scholar database and Consensus website using a targeted sampling technique and selection/inclusion criteria (relevance, language, and recency).

(ii) *Familiarization*: In this phase, the author reads and familiarizes himself with the selected articles to understand their context, content, and possible discursive features that fit our CDA.

(iii) *Transcription*: Various information from different contexts and content in the selected articles were integrated, harmonized, and synthesized at this stage to form a unique multi-source transcribed text. This step ensures the accuracy of your analysis.

(iv) *Segmentation*: In this step, the transcribed text from multiple sources is divided into meaningful sections and subsections according to the CDA.

(v)   *Identification of discursive features*: In this step, we identify linguistic and rhetorical elements within the segments, such as sustainable development and SDGs; discourse on pillars of sustainability; entrepreneurship as a driver of sustainability and a green, resilient economy, environmental impacts of entrepreneurship (ENIE), social impacts of entrepreneurship (SIE), economic impacts of entrepreneurship (ECIE) and how entrepreneurship fosters an entrepreneurial ecosystem that promotes sustainability. We have paid attention to how these elements of critical discourse contribute to the construction of meaning and ideology.

(vi) *Contextualization*: Building on the unique insights from Step (v) we analyze insightful data based on the environmental, social, and economic contexts in which selected articles describe the link between entrepreneurship and sustainability as promoting a green, resilient economy. The contexts in which entrepreneurship acts as a driver for sustainability in creation have a major impact on the meaning and interpretation of its discursive features.

(vii) *Interpretation*: In the fifth step, we interpret the discursive features of the relationship between entrepreneurship and sustainability in terms of three a priori research questions: (a) What are the interrelated definitions of entrepreneurship, sustainability, and a green, resilient economy? (b) What is the role of entrepreneurship in promoting sustainability and a green, resilient economy? (c) How do power dynamics, ideologies, and social structures significantly shape the role of entrepreneurship in promoting sustainability and building green resilience?

(viii) *Identification of ideologies*: This step is about identifying the underlying ideologies and assumptions anchored in the selected articles that discuss the relationship between entrepreneurship and sustainability. The process of identifying the underlying ideologies and assumptions involves uncovering hidden meanings, biases, and narratives that dominate entrepreneurship and sustainability discourse and how both worldviews foster a green, resilient economy.

(ix) *Critical reflection*: In this step, we engage in a critical reflection on the impact of the three identified research findings on discursive features and ideologies, including detailed explanations of how these aspects contribute to perpetuating or challenging power imbalances and social norms in the global economy.

(x)   *Comparison*: In this phase, the author compares the final reflections with previous insights to identify areas of convergence and divergence, patterns, and contrasts to highlight systemic issues and recurring themes for the development of tables and other visual representations.

(xi) *Writing the analysis*: In this step, the author presents the qualitative results in a well-structured analysis. In doing so, the discursive features of the relationship between entrepreneurship and sustainability are presented to reflect how both worldviews promote a green, resilient economy in broader social, environmental, and economic contexts.

(xii) *Discussion and conclusion*: In the final phase, the author documents the intellectual reflection on the meaning of the CDA's insightful findings and discusses their implications for theory and practice, particularly how the discourse on entrepreneurship and sustainability and its role in promoting a green, resilient economy shapes the understanding of its social issues, discourse practices, and power dynamics.

3. Critical Discourse Analysis

Three concepts underlying this CDA are entrepreneurship, sustainability, and a green, resilient economy. The disruptive capacity of entrepreneurship is evident across all industries and sectors, driving national innovation and organizational competitiveness (Acs, 2010; Idrees & Sarwar, 2021; Raimi & Hazwan, 2024). Entrepreneurship also has the potential to improve the performance of a green economy and sustainable development, while promoting environmentally friendly practices such as green entrepreneurship and resilient agro-tourism, among others (Ahmad et al., 2015; Chaaben et al., 2022; Drăgoi et al., 2017).

3.1. Defining Entrepreneurship

Entrepreneurship is a tricky concept with varying definitions. Stevenson et al. (2021) defines it as the pursuit of opportunity beyond the resources available to individuals (entrepreneurs) and firms (business entrepreneurs) at any given time or context. The essence of entrepreneurship is opportunity. Therefore, the term "opportunity" upon which entrepreneurship depends refers to a favorable and often unique set of circumstances that enable an individual or corporate entrepreneur to create value or achieve a specific goal. Opportunities include contextual situations where potential gains can be realized through innovative ideas, actions, or solutions. Such opportunities typically arise from the identification of unmet needs, market gaps, information asymmetry, friction, emerging trends, technological advances, or evolving customer preferences (Amit & Han, 2017; Arend, 2023). This creates opportunities in four ways: (a) pioneering work with innovative products, (b) development of new business models, (c) further economic development of existing products, and (d) development of untapped customer segments (Eisenmann, 2013). The assessment of entrepreneurship includes national indicators such as self-employment rates, business ownership, creation of new businesses, and comparison of new and defunct businesses (Audretsch & Fritsch, 2002; Bjørnskov & Foss, 2016). Empirical studies consider indicators such as self-employment (Desai, 2017), availability of startup funding, human capital support, access to business services, and investment in innovative knowledge (Ahmad & Hoffmann, 2008; Avanzini, 2011; Hilmi, 2023). Entrepreneurship is recognized worldwide as a catalyst for economic growth (Vazquez-Rozas et al., 2010). It is also a self-help tool to help the disadvantaged and marginalized become self-employed (Álvarez & Barney, 2014) and a powerful policy tool to financially empower women amid socio-cultural challenges (Alsaad et al., 2023; Ginting-Carlström & Chliova, 2023).

In theory and practice, entrepreneurship matters in politics, technology development, and sciences, as it is seen as a dynamic force that drives the economy, addresses social inequalities, and empowers women in challenging contexts. Entrepreneurship is instrumental in shaping various aspects of today's society. In summary, entrepreneurship drives innovation, economic growth, resource efficiency and social justice, all of which are essential components of sustainability and a green, resilient economy. It serves as a force for positive change, paving the way for a greener and more economically resilient future (Ellis, 2010; Mensah, 2019).

3.2. Defining Sustainability

Sustainability refers to the practice of meeting current needs without compromising the ability of future generations to meet their own needs. This includes using resources responsibly, maintaining ecological balance, and considering social, economic, and environmental factors to ensure lasting well-being and continuity. Sustainable practices aim to minimize negative environmental impacts, promote social justice, and maintain economic viability for the benefit of current and future generations. Notable variants of sustainability that have recently gained prominence are sustainable development and SDGs (Zamora-Polo & Sánchez-Martín, 2019). Sustainable development describes a development approach that addresses the needs of the current generation without compromising the needs of the next generation (Kirkby et al., 2023; Raimi & Lukman, 2023). SDGs, on the other hand, comprise a comprehensive set of 17 interconnected global goals designed to serve as a common blueprint for current and future peace and prosperity for both people and the planet (Bantekas & Akestoridi, 2023). These 17 goals span a wide range of social, economic, and environmental concerns and aim to address key existential challenges, including poverty, inequality, climate change, environmental degradation, peace, and justice (Raimi et al., 2021). The Islamic point of view enriches ongoing discussions by regarding sustainability as the harmonious and simultaneous realization of consumer welfare, economic efficiency, the achievement of social justice and ecological balance within the framework of Islam's evolutionary, knowledge-based, and socially interactive principles of reasoning (Abumoghli, 2022). Consequently, the use of the earth and its abundant resources is considered a trust of God, requiring their use because of equality and justice between individuals (Abumoghli, 2022; Moneim, 2023). Furthermore, the SDGs address a range of global social, economic, and environmental challenges (Hales & Birdthistle, 2023). In contrast, sustainability is the practice of meeting immediate needs without compromising the ability of future generations to meet their own needs. It includes the responsible use of resources, the maintenance of ecological balance, and the consideration of social, economic, and ecological aspects to ensure lasting well-being and continuity. Sustainable practices aim to reduce negative environmental impacts, promote social equity, and maintain economic viability for both current and future generations (Raimi et al., 2021).

In numerous scholarly discussions, the definitions of sustainability, sustainable development, and SDGs have converged again and again (Boar et al., 2020). By intertwining these definitions, sustainability presupposes the need to protect future generations from the harm caused by irresponsible actions by humans and businesses. This is achieved by striking a harmonious balance between economic, social, and environmental dimensions while promoting peace, prosperity, and the well-being of the planet. This approach is proving crucial for tackling a wide range of global challenges in the social, economic, and environmental fields.

3.3. Defining a Green, Resilient Economy

A green, resilient economy refers to an economic system that is both environmentally sustainable and resilient to shocks and socioeconomic and environmental disruptions while supporting practices that reduce negative environmental impacts while promoting long-term economic growth and stability (Almalki et al., 2021). Functionally, a green, resilient economy focuses on renewable energy sources, efficient use of resources, reduced waste generation, and green technologies that leave neither a carbon footprint nor polluting impacts (Ali et al., 2021; Ragapriya & Rudrappan, 2018). The inclusion of resilience in the context of a green economy means the ability to withstand and recover from various challenges such as climate change, natural disasters, economic downturns, and other disruptions while maintaining ecological balance and sustainable development (Ali et al., 2021). The 10 commonly cited classic examples of green, resilient economic models include the shift to renewable energy, sustainable agriculture, the circular economy, green infrastructure, climate-resilient buildings, nature-based solutions, ecotourism, green technologies and sustainable finance, and disaster preparedness and response (El-Hermisy, 2021; Lubchenco & Haugan, 2023).

At the operational level, the renewable energy transition is about switching from fossil fuels to renewable energy sources. Sustainable agriculture means adopting regenerative agricultural practices to ensure food security (Schattman et al., 2023). The circular economy minimizes resource consumption by recycling and upcycling waste. Green infrastructure includes urban planning that incorporates green spaces, urban forests, and sustainable transport systems, thereby increasing the resilience of cities (Janiszek & Krzysztofik, 2023). Scientists explain that climate-resilient buildings focus on building energy-efficient and climate-resilient structures, reducing energy use and climate change impacts, and that nature-based solutions leverage natural ecosystems for flood defense, water treatment, and carbon sequestration. While ecotourism promotes sustainable tourism practices that respect local culture, support conservation, and provide economic opportunities without environmental harm (Meetei et al., 2023; Rebar et al., 2023). Green technologies include the adoption of smart grids, energy-efficient appliances, electric vehicles, and sustainable technologies to reduce resource consumption and environmental impact. Sustainable finance aligns investment practices with environmental and social goals and sustainable development. Disaster preparedness and response involves establishing robust disaster management systems to mitigate the impact of natural disasters and emergencies (El-Hermisy, 2021; Orr et al., 2022; Seidu, 2020).

Many countries are actively promoting green and resilient economies by incorporating sustainable practices into their economic policies and entrepreneurship development strategies to avert the looming climate catastrophe. For clarity, here are some classic examples. Denmark has become a frontrunner in the field of renewable energy by aiming to reduce greenhouse gas emissions and increase the use of renewable energy, particularly through its wind energy sector (Calero et al., 2023). Germany is thereby another reference model of a green energy system, a resilient economy, its energy transition policies aimed at switching the country from fossil fuels to renewable energies such as wind, solar, and hydropower, as well as investments in energy efficiency, electric vehicles, smart grids, smart homes, smart neighborhoods, and green buildings (Quitzow, 2023). The third example is Sweden, which as the most sustainable country is passionately aiming for carbon neutrality by 2045, in addition to advances in renewable energy adoption, waste management, sustainable urban planning, efficient transport, and circular economy practices (Mansson, 2016). Next is Norway, a pioneer in electric vehicles that, alongside government commitments to cut greenhouse gas emissions by 55% by 2030 and 90%–95% by 2050, uses abundant hydropower for clean energy and significant deployment of electric vehicles (Malka et al., 2023).

In the development context, Costa Rica is known for making steady and enviable strides in renewable energy and environmental commitment, promoting the replacement of fossil fuels with renewable energy sources. A goal is being developed to produce almost 100% renewable electricity from hydroelectric, geothermal, wind, and solar energy by 2030 (Elliott, 2023). Similarly, Finland also focuses on sustainable forestry and bioeconomy, combining circular economy principles with a culture of waste minimization and optimizing resource efficiency. South Korea is also investing heavily in green technology and renewable energy while pursuing its 2050 carbon neutrality goals by focusing on solar, wind, electric vehicles, and green industries (Calero et al., 2023). China is known for its pollution and carbon footprint, yet it is a leader in green practices, producing the most solar panels and wind turbines in the world and investing heavily in infrastructure for its industrial fabric geared toward reducing carbon emissions and renewable energy (Zhao et al., 2023). The Hainan Island region of China plans to ban ground vehicles with internal combustion engines from 2030 as part of its green resilience (Snchez et al., 2023). Like other developed countries in its geographic zone, New Zealand is targeting 100% renewable electricity generation by 2030. Therefore, policy-makers are prioritizing sustainable agriculture, conservation, and circular economy initiatives. In this context, the Netherlands combats sea-level rise and sustainable urban planning through innovative flood management and environmentally friendly transport solutions (David, 2023). The explanation for the disruptive impact of entrepreneurship on sustainability, leading to the transition to a green and resilient economy that meets all 17 SDGs, is shown in Fig. 2.1.

3.4. Entrepreneurship, Sustainability and Green, Resilient Economy Nexus

This section examines cases of conscious efforts by governments, business-minded corporations, and social enterprises that have taken the lead in advancing the three dimensions of sustainability and have contributed to the advancement of green, resilient economies through responsible entrepreneurship. In particular, nations and companies are actively promoting green and resilient economies by incorporating sustainable practices into their economic policies and entrepreneurship development strategies, respectively, with the aim of averting the looming climate crisis. For clarity, several illustrative examples are given below. In both theory and practice, entrepreneurship has the potential to build a green and resilient economy that underpins sustainability in three areas: (a) the EIE, (b) the SIE, and (c) the economic impact of entrepreneurship (EIE).

First, the EIE relates to the responsible use and conservation of natural resources and the protection of ecosystems and biodiversity. This includes minimizing pollution, reducing waste, and promoting efficient use of resources while conducting business. Therefore, corporate entrepreneurs, social entrepreneurs, and sole proprietors in business have the potential to make a positive impact on the environment through innovative ideas, strategies, technologies, products, services, business solutions, and practices. In countries such as Norway, Denmark, the United States, Germany, Sweden, South Korea, and China, among others, governments, entrepreneurs, and entrepreneurs have seized the opportunities created by climate change and other externalities to develop and implement environmentally sustainable solutions. This has led to the creation of a resilient, green economy in areas such as renewable energy, waste management, sustainable agriculture, and green transport.

Second, the SIE refers to entrepreneurial initiatives and endeavors that directly address social issues such as social inequality, poverty, and the low quality of life of large segments of the population. Social entrepreneurship, sharing economy, circular economy, and social inclusion models have the potential to address societal challenges and bring about positive social change through innovative social enterprise models and sustainable business practices. Through their various social actions, social entrepreneurs, change makers, and sustainability advocates have made a significant positive impact on society. This class of entrepreneurs identifies and leverage opportunities to address social issues and contribute to social sustainability in critical sectors and industries where entrepreneurs can have a significant social impact, such as B. in health care, education, poverty alleviation and community development.

Third, the economic impact of entrepreneurship (EIE) relates to the promotion of economic growth, prosperity, and stability in the economy while ensuring ethical, responsive, and responsible use of resources. Entrepreneurship plays a crucial role in promoting economic sustainability and sustainable development through its ability to create jobs, foster innovation, and generate economic value. Entrepreneurs and entrepreneurs in small, medium, and large companies are known to identify and capitalize on new opportunities to drive economic sustainability across diverse sectors and industries. These sectors and industries include fintech, AI, robotics, green technology, sustainable tourism, circular economy, and social enterprise. Tables 2.1 and 2.2 each explain the cooperative and collaborative roles of the public, private, and social sectors in mainstreaming entrepreneurship and sustainability to promote green, resilient economies in different contexts.

Based on the public, private, and social sector cases (government, corporate, and social enterprise, respectively) discussed above, it is important to note that entrepreneurship, especially green entrepreneurship, plays a crucial role in promoting sustainability and green, resilient economies in different parts of the world. Entrepreneurial governments, corporate entrepreneurs, and social entrepreneurs have chosen to be innovative and imaginative in identifying and capitalizing on socio-environmental opportunities to create sustainable businesses, products, processes, and solutions for projects and programs that address environmental, social, and social issues. Economic problems in the world deal with the corporate landscape.

4. Findings from the CDA

At the end of the CDA, the following three major findings emerged as answers to the three thematic research questions.

Research Question 1: What are the interconnected definitions of entrepreneurship, sustainability, and a green, resilient economy?

Finding 1: The CDA established that definitions of entrepreneurship, sustainability, and a green, resilient economy intricately intersect. Entrepreneurship, pursued by individuals and corporate entities, entails seizing opportunities beyond available resources. Sustainability revolves around responsibly managing resources, maintaining ecological balance, and considering social, economic, and environmental aspects to meet present needs without compromising future generations. A green, resilient economy merges environmental sustainability and adaptability, aiming to minimize adverse impacts while promoting enduring growth and stability amid shocks and disruptions. Insights drawn from CDA underscore that entrepreneurship spurs innovative sustainable solutions. Simultaneously, a green, resilient economy encompasses a sustainable practice and an entrepreneurial mindset, ensuring a harmonious equilibrium among economic, social, and environmental facets – ultimately cultivating long-term green resilience.

Table 2.1. Role of Public and Private Sectors Driving a Green, Resilient Economy.

Case	National and Cultural Contexts	Language, Social, and Power Dynamics
1.	Denmark has become a frontrunner in renewable energy, thanks to its commitment to curbing greenhouse gas emissions and significantly increasing the use of renewable energy sources. Denmark has carved a significant niche in the wind energy sector, positioning itself at the forefront of global advances in sustainable energy solutions (Calero et al., 2023)	Government and the private sector jointly shape policy, using language and communication to promote greener solutions and sustainability awareness
2.	Germany's green, resilient economy, exemplified by the "Energiewende policy," shifts from fossil fuels to renewables like wind, solar, and hydroelectric power. Accompanying strategies include energy efficiency, electric vehicles, smart grids, and eco-friendly buildings (Quitzow, 2023)	Government and the private sector jointly shape policy, using language and communication to promote greener solutions and sustainability awareness
3.	Sweden's global recognition of green technology and sustainability is evident in its commitment to carbon neutrality by 2045. Progress includes renewable energy adoption, waste management, sustainable urban planning, efficient transportation, and circular economy practices (Mansson, 2016)	Sector jointly shapes policy, using language and communication to promote greener solutions and sustainability awareness
4.	Norway is a pioneer in electric vehicles and uses its rich hydroelectric resources to generate clean energy. The country has also made significant progress in EV adoption, further supported by the government's determined commitment to reduce greenhouse gas emissions by 55% by 2030 and the ambitious target of a 90%–95% reduction by 2050 (Malka et al., 2023)	Government and the private sector jointly shape policy, using language and communication to promote greener solutions and sustainability awareness

(Continued)

Table 2.1. *(Continued)*

Case	National and Cultural Contexts	Language, Social, and Power Dynamics
5.	Costa Rica's remarkable progress in renewable energy and environmental dedication is evident in its goal of nearly 100% renewable electricity, including hydropower, geothermal, wind, and solar by 2030 (Elliott, 2023)	Government and the private sector jointly shape policy, using language and communication to promote greener solutions and sustainability awareness
6.	Finland prioritizes sustainable forestry, a thriving bioeconomy, and carbon neutrality through circular economy principles, technology adoption, and waste reduction (Alola & Adebayo, 2023; Smith et al., 2022)	Government and the private sector jointly shape policy, using language and communication to promote greener solutions and sustainability awareness
7.	In Nigeria, while political discourse focuses on the relationship between entrepreneurship, sustainability, and the emerging green economy, practical strides involve energy efficiency, sustainable finance, climate-conscious agriculture, solar innovations, and renewable energy to tackle deforestation, gas flaring, and carbon emissions (Ewim, 2023; Raimi et al., 2023)	Government and the private sector jointly shape policy, using language and communication to promote greener solutions and sustainability awareness
8.	South Korea's commitment to green initiatives includes investments in advanced technology, renewable energy, achieving carbon neutrality by 2050, and prioritizing solar, wind energy, electric vehicles, and eco-friendly industries for environmental preservation and technological advancement (Calero et al., 2023)	Government and the private sector jointly shape policy, using language and communication to promote greener solutions and sustainability awareness

| 9. | Despite its environmental challenges, China excels in green practices, manufacturing solar panels and wind turbines, and investing in renewable energy infrastructure to reduce carbon emissions (Zhao et al., 2023). Hainan, China, plans to ban ground combustion vehicles by 2030 for increased green resilience (Sánchez et al., 2023) | Government and the private sector jointly shape policy, using language and communication to promote greener solutions and sustainability awareness |
| 10. | New Zealand and similar developed nations target 100% renewable electricity by 2030, emphasizing sustainable agriculture, nature preservation, and circular economy. The Netherlands addresses sea-level rise and urban planning via inventive flood management and green transportation (David, 2023) | Government and the private sector jointly shape policy, using language and communication to promote greener solutions and sustainability awareness |

Source: Authors' compilation from Calero et al. (2023), Quitzow (2023), Mansson (2016), Malka et al. (2023), Elliott (2023), Alola and Adebayo (2023), Smith et al. (2022), Raimi et al. (2023), Ewim (2023), Sánchez et al. (2023), and David (2023).

Table 2.2. Role of Private and Social Sectors Driving a Green, Resilient Economy.

Case	National and Cultural Contexts	Language, Social, and Power Dynamics
1.	Elon Musk's Tesla has shown how entrepreneurship drives sustainable cars, pioneering high-performance electric cars with longer range and fast-charging capabilities. Tesla's innovative technology and model lowers emissions and inspires competitors to invest in electric vehicles to advance sustainable transportation (Zhang et al., 2023)	Tesla aligns its policies and actions with government regulations for a green, resilient economy
2.	Patagonia, an outdoor clothing, and gear company is a sustainable business pioneer. It adopts a holistic approach, incorporating environmental and social aspects. Initiatives include using recycled materials, repairing, and reselling garments, and advocating for environmental causes. This strategic integration not only reduces environmental impact but also enhances brand reputation and customer loyalty (Schatz & Pfoertsch, 2023)	Patagonia aligns its policies and actions with government regulations for a green, resilient economy
3.	Grameen Bank, a Bangladeshi microfinance institution, empowers low-income individuals through small loans, fostering financial inclusion and poverty reduction. Beyond microfinance, it promotes sustainable enterprises via social business initiatives, addressing societal issues with financial returns. By empowering marginalized communities, Grameen Bank drives grassroots sustainable development (Datta & Sahu, 2023)	Grameen Bank aligns its policies and actions with government regulations for a green, resilient economy
4.	EcoPost contributes to green resilience by collecting commercial waste, improving local conditions, and reducing plastic pollution, especially where official waste systems are absent. Addressing broader environmental concerns like sewer blockages and urban flooding, EcoPost promotes healthier living conditions and community well-being, exemplifying their commitment to sustainability (Ineza, 2021)	EcoPost aligns its policies and actions with government regulations for a green, resilient economy

5.	Angaza Design Inc., a US social enterprise, addresses energy poverty with its "Pay-As-You-Go" tech. This innovation enables base-of-the-pyramid customers to access affordable solar lights, water pumps, and cookstoves via a convenient payment model, combating energy scarcity sustainably (Raimi et al., 2022)	Angaza EcoPost aligns its policies and actions with government regulations for a green, resilient economy
6.	TOMS Shoes, a Los Angeles-based for-profit company, innovates in shoe production, addressing issues like Poverty, Health, and Education. Its CSR model donates shoes for every pair sold, funding wellness projects for water, sight, birth, and anti-bullying initiatives (Raimi et al., 2022)	TOMS Shoes aligns its policies and actions with government regulations for a green, resilient economy
7.	Solar Sister, a Tanzanian non-profit social enterprise, empowers women in off-grid communities to establish affordable energy businesses, tackling poverty and Lack of access to electricity and clean fuels sustainably (Raimi et al., 2022)	Solar Sister aligns its policies and actions with government regulations for a green, resilient economy
8.	Mekong Quilts empowers underprivileged women in Vietnam and Cambodia through sustainable employment, addressing poverty, financial exclusion, and gender imbalance. They produce and sell eco-friendly products, reinvesting earnings to support local communities, children's scholarships, and micro-financing programs (Raimi et al., 2022)	Mekong Quilts aligns with government regulations for a green, resilient economy
9.	Malô in Ségou, Mali, builds and operates modern rice processing facilities, milling, fortifying, and marketing rice grown by West African smallholder farmers. Their vitamin-fortified rice, cheaper than non-fortified options, combats rice insecurity, hidden hunger, and childhood malnutrition. This innovative approach transforms Africa's rice value chain, providing affordable, nutritious, and high-quality rice (Raimi et al., 2022)	Malô aligns with government regulations for a green, resilient economy

Source: Authors' compilation from Zhang et al. (2023), Schatz and Pfoertsch (2023), Datta and Sahu (2023), Ineza (2021), and Raimi et al. (2022).

Research Question 2: What is the role of entrepreneurship in driving sustainability and building green resilience?

Finding 2: The 18 classic cases in Tables 2.1 and 2.2, from the public, private, and social sectors of different countries, underscore how entrepreneurship contributes to building a green and resilient economy, with impacts in (a) environmental, (b) social, and (c) economic domains as shown in Fig. 2.2. Countries such as Norway, Denmark, the United States, Germany, Sweden, South Korea, and China, among others, show examples where entrepreneurs and companies use climate change and externalities to develop environmentally friendly solutions. This initiative promotes a robust green economy in areas such as renewable energy, waste management, sustainable agriculture, and green transport. Social entrepreneurs and sustainability advocates drive meaningful positive change by addressing social issues in critical areas such as health care, education, poverty alleviation, and community development. In addition, governments and companies are promoting economic sustainability in sectors such as fintech, AI, robotics, green technology, sustainable tourism, circular economy, and social enterprise.

Research Question 3: In what way do power dynamics, ideologies, and social structures significantly shape the role of entrepreneurship in driving sustainability and building green resilience?

Finding 3: The 18 cases presented in Tables 2.1 and 2.2 reveal a strong link between power dynamics, ideologies, and social structures, which significantly shape the role of entrepreneurship in promoting sustainability and building green resilience. Four key findings emerge. First, governments, businesses, and social enterprises globally play pivotal roles in advancing sustainability and green, resilient economies. Entrepreneurial governments, corporate entrepreneurs, and social entrepreneurs demonstrate innovation in identifying and capitalizing on socio-environmental opportunities, addressing environmental, social, and economic issues. Second, within social structures, corporate activities' impact on sustainability is influenced by existing setups in the public and private sectors. The synergy between sectors promotes inclusive development and empowerment of marginalized groups, while ineffective collaboration exacerbates social inequalities. Looking at the national perspective of entrepreneurship, sustainability,

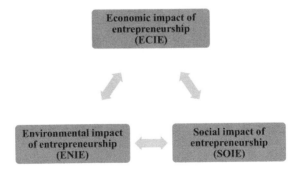

Fig. 2.2.   Three-dimensional Impacts of Entrepreneurship.

and the green economy nexus, governments and the private sector collaborate to drive policies, communication, and strategic actions. For corporate strategies, businesses align their actions with government regulations. Third, power dynamics reveal that corporate entities, governments, and social entrepreneurs engage with stakeholders to advance sustainable and green economic policies. Strong stakeholders influence sustainability entrepreneurship, while balanced power distribution enables collective efforts. Conversely, imbalances can lead to resource exploitation. Fourth, ideological shifts, driven by green ideologies and theoretical perspectives, influence corporate aspirations and sustainability awareness. Ideological alignment fosters innovation in line with sustainable practices. Ventures founded on conservation, circular economy, and social responsibility ideologies contribute to greener solutions. Conflicting ideologies hinder progress.

5. Conclusion, Implications, Limitation, and Further Research Direction

This chapter qualitatively discusses the role of entrepreneurship in promoting sustainability and building a green, resilient economy. The aim is to answer three research questions using CDA. The results of the 12-step CDA approach are as follows: First, the intersection of the three concepts shows that entrepreneurship seizes opportunities amid constraints, while sustainability uses resources responsibly for present needs without compromising the future. A green economy ensures adaptability, growth, and ecological stability even when resources are scarce. Second, the CDA strongly affirms its influence, drawing on 18 cases in the public, private, and social sectors to shed light on the environmental, social, and economic implications. Third, the CDA uncovers power dynamics, ideologies, and social structures that impact entrepreneurship's role in fostering sustainable and resilient, green economies. In different countries and companies, governments, companies, and social enterprises promote sustainability within existing social structures in the public, private, and social sectors. While these collaborations foster inclusive development, imbalanced power dynamics pose challenges and risk potential social exclusion. In addition, the CDA identifies how dominant green ideologies among stakeholders significantly shape entrepreneurship and sustainability awareness, enabling greener solutions, while conflicting ideologies impede progress.

The CDA results have four implications. First, the alignment of entrepreneurship, sustainability, and a green economy underscores entrepreneurship's ability to seize opportunities, the resource management of sustainability, and the adaptability of a green economy amid scarcity. Second, the CDA underscores its impact with 18 cases from different sectors showing environmental, social, and economic impacts. Finally, the influence of power dynamics, ideologies, and social structures on the role of entrepreneurship in promoting sustainability and green resilience is revealed. Government, business, and social enterprise working together within established social frameworks promote inclusive development, although power imbalances pose a risk of exclusion. Dominant green ideologies are driving greener solutions, but conflicting ideologies are impeding progress. Ultimately, conscious sectoral efforts to redefine the role of entrepreneurship within power dynamics, ideologies, and social structures contribute to ecological balance and social justice. Despite the practical implications outlined, this study, like other desk-based qualitative studies, has limitations. First, it does not purport to solve all the mysteries surrounding entrepreneurship's role in sustainability and green resilience. Future empirical studies using quantitative data and interviews could provide a deeper understanding of how entrepreneurship paves the way for a green, resilient economy that supports sustainable development.

References

Abumoghli, I. (2022) *The Islamic principles on sustainable development*. https://www.ecomena.org/islam-sustainable-development/

Acs, Z. J., & Audretsch, D. B. (Eds.). (2010). Introduction to the 2nd Edition of the Handbook of Entrepreneurship Research. In *Handbook of entrepreneurship research: an interdisciplinary survey and introduction* (pp. 1–19). Springer.

Ahmad, N. H., Halim, H. A., Ramayah, T., & Rahman, S. A. (2015). Green entrepreneurship inclination among Generation Y: The road towards a green economy. *Problems and Perspectives in Management, 13*(2), 211–218.

Ahmad, N., & Hoffmann, A. (2008). *A framework for addressing and measuring entrepreneurship*. OECD.

Ali, E. B., Anufriev, V. P., & Bismark Amfo, B. (2021). Green economy implementation in Ghana as a road map for a sustainable development drive: A review. *Scientific African, 12*, e00756. https://doi.org/10.1016/j.sciaf.2021.e00756.

Almalki, F. A., Alsamhi, S. H., Sahal, R., Hassan, J., Hawbani, A., Rajput, N. S., Saif, A., Morgan, J. & Breslin, J. (2021). Green IoT for eco-friendly and sustainable smart cities: Future directions and opportunities. *Mobile Networks and Applications, 28*, 1–25.

Alola, A. A., & Adebayo, T. S. (2023). Are green resource productivity and environmental technologies the face of environmental sustainability in the Nordic region? *Sustainable Development, 31*(2), 760–772.

Alsaad, R. I., Hamdan, A., Binsaddig, R., & Kanan, M. A. (2023). Empowerment sustainability perspectives for Bahraini women as entrepreneurs. *International Journal of Innovation Studies, 7*(4), 245–262.

Álvarez, S. A., & Barney, J. B. (2014). Entrepreneurial opportunities and poverty alleviation. *Entrepreneurship Theory and Practice, 38*(1), 159–184.

Amit, R., & Han, X. (2017). Value creation through novel resource configurations in a digitally enabled world. *Strategic Entrepreneurship Journal, 11*(3), 228–242.

Arend, R. J. (2023). Opportunity on Mars? Roving for theory in the re(a)d dust rather than beyond. *Journal of Business Venturing Insights, 19*, e00397.

Audretsch, D. B., & Fritsch, M. (2002). Growth regimes over time and space. *Regional Studies, 36*, 113–124.

Avanzini, D. B. (2011). Designing composite entrepreneurship indicators. In W. Naudé (Ed.), *Entrepreneurship and economic development.* (pp. 37–93). Palgrave Macmillan/ United Nations University.

Bantekas, I., & Akestoridi, K. (2023). Sustainable development goals, between politics and soft law: The emergence of "political normativity" in international law. *Emory International Law Review, 37*(4), 499–560.

Bartiromo, M., & Ivaldi, E. (2023). A gender sustainable development index for Italian regions. In C. Chakraborty & D. Pal (Eds.), *Gender inequality and its implications on education and health: A global perspective* (pp. 247–258). Emerald Publishing Limited.

Bjørnskov, C., & Foss, N. J. (2016). Institutions, entrepreneurship, and economic growth: What do we know and what do we still need to know? *Academy of Management Perspectives, 30*(3), 292–315.

Boar, A., Bastida, R., & Marimon, F. (2020). A systematic literature review. Relationships between the sharing economy, sustainability and sustainable development goals. *Sustainability, 12*(17), 6744.

Briant Carant, J. (2017). Unheard voices: A critical discourse analysis of the millennium development goals' evolution into the sustainable development goals. *Third World Quarterly, 38*(1), 16–41. https://doi.org/10.1080/01436597.2016.1166944

Calero, M., Godoy, V., Heras, C. G., Lozano, E., Arjandas, S., & Martín-Lara, M. A. (2023). Current state of biogas and biomethane production and its implications for Spain. *Sustainable Energy & Fuels, 7*(15), 3584–3602.

Catalano, T., & Waugh, L. R. (2020). *Critical discourse analysis, critical discourse studies and beyond.* Springer International Publishing

Chaaben, N., Elleuch, Z., Hamdi, B., & Kahouli, B. (2022). Green economy performance and sustainable development achievement: Empirical evidence from Saudi Arabia. *Environment, Development and Sustainability, 26*, 1–16.

Datta, S., & Sahu, T. N. (2023). Financial inclusion, microfinance institutions and women empowerment. In S. Datta & T. N. Sahu (Eds.), *Financial inclusion and livelihood transformation: Perspective from microfinance institutions in rural India* (pp. 15–85). Springer Nature.

David, L. S. Y. (2023). Should policymakers encourage the development of specific green energy technologies? Advantages and risks. In R. Leal-Arcas (Ed.), *Climate and energy governance for a sustainable future* (pp. 83–94). Springer Nature https://doi. org/10.1007/978-981-19-8346-7_7.

Desai, S. (2017). Measuring entrepreneurship: Type, motivation, and growth. *IZA World of Labor.* Article 327. DOI: 10.15185/izawol.327

Dhahri, S., & Omri, A. (2020). Foreign capital towards SDGs 1 & 2 – Ending poverty and hunger: The role of agricultural production. *Structural Change and Economic Dynamics, 53*, 208–221.

Drăgoi, M. C., Iamandi, I. E., Munteanu, S. M., Ciobanu, R., Țarțavulea, R. I., & Lădaru, R. G. (2017). Incentives for developing resilient agritourism entrepreneurship in rural communities in Romania in a European context. *Sustainability, 9*(12), 2205.

Eisenmann, T. R. (2013). Entrepreneurship: A working definition. *Harvard Business Review, 10*(5), 1–3.

El-Hermisy, H. (2021). The economic effects of environmental and climatic changes on the economic sector. *International Journal of Modern Agriculture and Environment, 1*(1), 51–78.

Elliott, E. (2023). Leadership & ambition: Comparative insights from France and Costa Rica's fossil fuel moratoria. *On Politics, 16*, 38–59.

Ellis, T. (2010). *The new pioneers: Sustainable business success through social innovation and social entrepreneurship.* John Wiley & Sons.

Ewim, D. R. E. (2023). Integrating business principles in STEM education: Fostering entrepreneurship in students and educators in the US and Nigeria. *IJEBD (International Journal of Entrepreneurship and Business Development), 6*(4), 590–605.

Fairclough, N. (2023). Critical discourse analysis. In M. Handford & J. P. Gee (Eds.), *The Routledge handbook of discourse analysis* (pp. 11–22). Routledge.

Gialeli, M., Troumbis, A. Y., Giaginis, C., Papadopoulou, S. K., Antoniadis, I., & Vasios, G. K. (2023). The global growth of 'sustainable diet' during recent decades, a bibliometric analysis. *Sustainability, 15*(15), 11957.

Ginting-Carlström, C. E., & Chliova, M. (2023). A discourse of virtue: How poor women entrepreneurs justify their activities in the context of moderate Islam. *Entrepreneurship & Regional Development, 35*(1–2), 78–102.

Haldar, S. (2019). Green entrepreneurship in theory and practice: Insights from India. *International Journal of Green Economics, 13*(2), 99–119.

Hales, R., & Birdthistle, N. (2023). The sustainable development goals – SDG# 11 sustainable cities and communities. In N. Birdthistle & R. Hales (Eds.), *Attaining the 2030 sustainable development goal of sustainable cities and communities* (pp. 1–9). Emerald Publishing Limited.

Heim, I., Vigneau, A. C., & Kalyuzhnova, Y. (2023). Environmental and socio-economic policies in oil and gas regions: Triple bottom line approach. *Regional Studies, 57*(1), 181–195.

Hilmi, M. (2023). Entrepreneur, entrepreneurship and enterprise in agricultural mechanization hire service enterprises in developing economies. *Middle East Journal of Agriculture Research, 12*(3), 434–461.

Hirons, M. (2020). How the sustainable development goals risk undermining efforts to address environmental and social issues in the small-scale mining sector. *Environmental Science & Policy, 114*, 321–328.

Idrees, A. S., & Sarwar, S. (2021). State effectiveness, property rights and entrepreneurial behaviour as determinants of National Innovation. *Australian Economic Papers, 60*(3), 392–423.

Ineza, A. (2021). Review of case of social entrepreneurship: EcoPost for a green and prosperous society. *Academia Letters, 2*, 1–7. https://kompozit.org.tr/wp-content/uploads/2021/07/Review_of_case_of_social_entrepreneurshi.pdf

Janiszek, M., & Krzysztofik, R. (2023). Green infrastructure as an effective tool for urban adaptation – Solutions from a big city in a postindustrial region. *Sustainability, 15*(11), 8928.

Kirkby, J., O'Keefe, P., & Timberlake, L. (2023). Sustainable development: An introduction. In J. Kirkby, P. O'Keefe, & L. Timberlake (Eds.), *The Earthscan reader in sustainable development* (pp. 1–14). Routledge.

Li, Y., Liao, T., & Li, J. (2023). Optimizing higher education for sustainable development through the design and implementation of the global engagement program. *Sustainability, 15*(13), 10098.

Lindell, L., Sattari, S., & Höckert, E. (2022). Introducing a conceptual model for wellbeing tourism – Going beyond the triple bottom line of sustainability. *International Journal of Spa and Wellness, 5*(1), 16–32.

Lubchenco, J., & Haugan, P. M. (2023). Coastal development: Resilience, restoration and infrastructure requirements. In J. Lubchenco, & P.M. Haugan (Eds.), *The blue compendium: From knowledge to action for a sustainable ocean economy* (pp. 213–277). Springer International Publishing. https://doi.org/10.1007/978-3-031-16277-0_7

Macharis, C., Turcksin, L., & Lebeau, K. (2012). Multi actor multi criteria analysis (MAMCA) as a tool to support sustainable decisions: State of use. *Decision Support Systems, 54*(1), 610–620.

Malka, L., Bidaj, F., Kuriqi, A., Jaku, A., Roçi, R., & Gebremedhin, A. (2023). Energy system analysis with a focus on future energy demand projections: The case of Norway. *Energy, 272*, 127107.

Mansson, M. (2016). Sweden – The world's most sustainable country: Political statements and goals for a sustainable society. *Earth Common Journal, 6*(1), 16–22.

Meetei, K. B., Tsopoe, M., Giri, K., Mishra, G., Verma, P. K., & Rohatgi, D. (2023). Climate-resilient pathways and nature-based solutions to reduce vulnerabilities to climate change in the Indian Himalayan Region. In A. Kumar, W. D. Jong, M. Kumar, & R. Pandey (Eds.), *Climate change in the Himalayas* (pp. 89–119). Academic Press.

Mensah, J. (2019). Sustainable development: Meaning, history, principles, pillars, and implications for human action: Literature review. *Cogent Social Sciences, 5*(1), 1653531.

Moneim, Y. A. (2023). The green Islamic approach on environmental sustainability: A contemporary perspective. *Manchester Journal of Transnational Islamic Law & Practice, 19*(2), 43–68.

Mullet, D. R. (2018) A general critical discourse analysis framework for educational research. *Journal of Advanced Academics, 29*(2), 116–142.

Orr, A., Ahmad, B., Alam, U., Appadurai, A., Bharucha, Z. P., Biemans, H., … & Wescoat, J. L. Jr. (2022). Knowledge priorities on climate change and water in the Upper Indus Basin: A horizon scanning exercise to identify the top 100 research questions in social and natural sciences. *Earth's Future, 10*(4), e2021EF002619.

Quitzow, L. (2023). Smart grids, smart households, smart neighborhoods–contested narratives of prosumage and decentralization in Berlin's urban Energiewende. *Innovation: The European Journal of Social Science Research, 36*(1), 107–122.

Ragapriya, R., & Rudrappan, D. (2018). Climate resilient green economy: Prospects. *International Review of Business and Economics, 1*(3), 1–6. https://digitalcommons.du.edu/cgi/viewcontent.cgi?article=1287&context=irbe

Raimi, L. (2022, September 25). *Mastery of sustainable development skills and sustainability plans* [Paper presentation]. Presentation at HAVEK Leadership Fellowship Programme. Lagos, Nigeria. https://doi.org/10.13140/RG.2.2.20603.08485

Raimi, L., & Lukman, F. M. (2023). Rethinking sustainable development under climate change in Nigeria: A strategic analysis. In S. Seifi & D. Crowther (Eds.), *Corporate resilience: Risk, sustainability and future crises* (pp. 73–91). Emerald Publishing Limited.

Raimi, L., Che, F. N., & Mutiu, R. M. (2021). Agricultural information systems (AGRIS) as a catalyst for sustainable development goals (SDGs) in Africa: A critical literature review. In F. Che, K. Strang, & N. Vajjhala (Eds.), *Opportunities and strategic use of agribusiness information systems* (pp. 109–133). IGI Global. https://doi.org/10.4018/978-1-7998-4849-3.ch007

Raimi, L., Dodo, F., & Sule, R. (2022). Comparative discourse of social enterprises in the developed and developing countries using theory of change framework: A qualitative analysis. In D. Crowther & F. Quoquab (Eds.), *Social entrepreneurs* (Vol. 18, pp. 29–54). Emerald Publishing Limited.

Raimi, L., Ridwan, L. I., & Olowo, R. (2023). Determining the nexus of energy efficiency and sustainable development in Nigeria: Time series analysis. In D. Crowther & S. Seifi (Eds.), *Achieving net zero: Challenges and opportunities* (pp. 153–176). Emerald Publishing Limited.

Raimi, L., & Haini, H. (2024). Impact of entrepreneurial governance and ease of doing business on economic growth: Evidence from ECOWAS economies (2000–2019). *Journal of Public Affairs, 24*(1), e2887.

Rebar, R. A., Palma-Oliveira, J. M., Pescaroli, G., Kiker, G. A., Stennett-Brown, R. K., Saunders, C., Gregory, E., & Lambert, J. H. (2023). Principles of systemic resilience to climate change in Caribbean small island developing states. In C. D. Metcalfe & E. R. Bennett (Eds.), *Building resilience to climate change in small island developing states (SIDS) in the Caribbean* (pp. 13–33). Springer Nature.

Sánchez, F. G., & Govindarajulu, D. (2023). Integrating blue-green infrastructure in urban planning for climate adaptation: Lessons from Chennai and Kochi, India. *Land use policy, 124*, 106455.

Sánchez, A. S., Junior, E. P., Gontijo, B. M., de Jong, P., & dos Reis Nogueira, I. B. (2023). Replacing fossil fuels with renewable energy in islands of high ecological value: The cases of Galápagos, Fernando de Noronha, and Príncipe. *Renewable and Sustainable Energy Reviews, 183*, 113527.

Schattman, R. E., Rowland, D. L., & Kelemen, S. C. (2023). Sustainable and regenerative agriculture: Tools to address food insecurity and climate change. *Journal of Soil and Water Conservation, 78*(2), 33A–38A.

Schatz, C., & Pfoertsch, W. (2023). Case study: Patagonia – A human-centered approach to marketing. In P. Kotler, W. Pfoertsch, U. Sponholz, M. Haas (Eds.), *H2H marketing: Case studies on human-to-human marketing* (pp. 195–213). Springer International Publishing. https://doi.org/10.1007/978-3-031-22393-8_12

Seidu, D. (2020). *Green recovery and green jobs in Africa: The case of Ghana* [Policy Briefing 227], South African Institute of International Affairs, pp. 1–17. https://saiia.org.za/wp-content/uploads/2020/12/Policy-Briefing-227-seidu.pdf

Smith, T., Ehrnström-Fuentes, M., Hagolani-Albov, S. E., Klepp, I. G., & Tobiasson, T. S. (2022). Rethinking the (wool) economy. In I. G. Klepp & T. S. Tobiasson (Eds.), *Local, slow and sustainable fashion: Wool as a fabric for change* (pp. 133–170). Springer International Publishing.

Stevenson, K., Hoeber, L., & Heffernan, C. (2021). Critical discourse analysis as theory, methodology, and analyses in sport management studies. *Journal of Sport Management, 35*(5), 465–475.

Todeschini, B. V., Cortimiglia, M. N., Callegaro-de-Menezes, D., & Ghezzi, A. (2017). Innovative and sustainable business models in the fashion industry: Entrepreneurial drivers, opportunities, and challenges. *Business Horizons, 60*(6), 759–770.

Tønnesen, A., Guillen-Royo, M., & Hoff, S. C. (2023). The integration of nature conservation in land-use management practices in rural municipalities: A case study of four rural municipalities in Norway. *Journal of Rural Studies, 101*, 103066.

Vazquez-Rozas, E., Gomes, S., & Vieira, E. (2010). Entrepreneurship and economic growth in Spanish and Portuguese regions. *Regional and Sectoral Economic Studies, Euro-American Association of Economic Development, 10*(2), 110–126.

Wearing, S. L., Wearing, M., & McDonald, M. (2010). Understanding local power and interactional processes in sustainable tourism: Exploring village–tour operator relations on the Kokoda Track, Papua New Guinea. *Journal of Sustainable Tourism, 18*(1), 61–76.

Xie, X., Khan, S., Rehman, S., Naz, S., Haider, S. A., & Kayani, U. N. (2023). Ameliorating sustainable business performance through green constructs: A case of manufacturing industry. *Environment, Development and Sustainability, 26*(1), 1–33.

Zamora-Polo, F., & Sánchez-Martín, J. (2019). Teaching for a better world. Sustainability and sustainable development goals in the construction of a change-maker university. *Sustainability, 11*(15), 4224.

Zhang, W., Fang, X., & Sun, C. (2023). The alternative path for fossil oil: Electric vehicles or hydrogen fuel cell vehicles? *Journal of Environmental Management, 341*, 118019.

Zhao, B., Wang, K. L., & Xu, R. Y. (2023). Fiscal decentralization, industrial structure upgrading, and carbon emissions: Evidence from China. *Environmental Science and Pollution Research, 30*(13), 39210–39222.

Chapter 3

Green Transition, Labor Shortages and Employment Policies

Luminiţa Chivu[a], George Georgescu[a] and Drago Cvijanovic[b]

[a]*National Institute for Economic Research "Costin C. Kiriţescu" – Romanian Academy, Romania*
[b]*Faculty of Hotel Management and Tourism in Vrnjacka Banja, University of Kragujevac, Serbia*

Abstract

Under the circumstances of the accelerated technological advance and the overlapping of various global crises in the recent years, one of the main strategic priorities of the European Union in medium and long terms consists of building resilient regional and local communities which implies the aim to protect citizens against the impact of climate changes. Considering the essential role of the human capital in this endeavor, this chapter aims to investigate the relationship between human resources and economic development focusing a SWOT analysis in the case of Romania taking into account recent developments and trends of the European and global labor market related to various aspects induced by the green transition. The analysis of the structural demo-economic characteristics of Romania's population revealed a decline of the total population, against the background of negative demographic and net migration, the increase in the average and median age of the total population, the rise in demographic and economic dependency ratios representing serious challenges for the development strategy on short, medium and long terms. To these, increasing quantitative and qualitative shortages in the labor market are added, which complicate the advancement of the green transition in Romania. In the conclusions of this chapter, strategic milestones on policies and measures in the short, medium and long terms at macroeconomic and labor market levels are proposed.

Keywords: Green transition; demo-economic structures; labor market; labor shortages; employment policies

Entrepreneurship and Development for a Green Resilient Economy, 47–83
Copyright © 2024 by Luminiţa Chivu, George Georgescu and Drago Cvijanovic
Published under exclusive licence by Emerald Publishing Limited
doi:10.1108/978-1-83797-088-920241003

1. Introduction

Indispensable and essential driver for the progress of any economic activity, human resources leave their decisive mark on the quality of the development policies of each nation, through which solutions are proposed to capitalize on the mix of natural resources, human resources and capital, with the aim of achieving the targeted economic and social objectives.

The starting point of any development strategy, including for Romania, should be represented by the size of the total population and its demo-economic structures as well as the forecasts regarding their evolution in the short, medium and long terms.

As concerns the labor market and employment policies, the extremely fragile balance, permanently under the pressure of divergent influences, at the confluence between the determining factors of labor demand and supply, needs complex approaches. Technological progress, the internationalization of the economy and the green and digital transition require a rethinking of strategies and policies in the field of employment, in close connection with the other components of the macroeconomic framework as well as with social issues.

In what follows, the relationship between human resources and economic development will be investigated as shown by the international literature reviewing, conducting a SWOT analysis of this relationship in the case of Romania and an overview of recent developments and trends of the European and global labor market under the circumstances of the accelerated global technological advance and the overlapping of various global crises, focusing on the structural demo-economic characteristics of Romania's population and its dynamics, revealing the quantitative and qualitative shortage in the labor market, existing and foreseeable to deeper on medium and long terms, making necessary adequate policies and measures to alleviate them, all the more in the conditions of the green and digital transitions.

2. Literature Review

The relationship between human resources and economic development has attracted the interest of many generations of researchers, the studies developed highlighting the complexity of interdependencies and, at the same time, providing important reference points regarding the multiple aspects that must be taken into account in the context of the integration of the human resources component in a strategy targeting the long-term development.

Resorting to the approach from the perspective of the components of national wealth, the ratio between the natural capital and the produced capital of a nation depends essentially on how human resources are capitalized, the central role being the size of human capital and investments in it.

In contrast to the situation of a relatively closed economy (with a minor dimension of the international trade exchanges), in which the population–economy relationship was primarily treated from the perspective of the ratio between human and land resources, more precisely the optimal dimension of the agricultural land to meet the needs of consumption, for feeding the population (an important role being, in this context, of the population employed in agricultural activities) (Malthus, 1798) in the contemporary period, the unprecedented increase in the international trade (stimulated by the significant progress in the field of transport) and the setting up of regional free trade areas requires rethinking on other bases of this relationship.

Successive industrial revolutions, technological progress, including the mechanization and automation of agricultural works, the results obtained by scientific research, of phyto-sanitary protection, innovations in technological processing in the food industry (highlighting the role more and more important of neo-factors, intangible assets), have conducted to major changes in the population–economy equation (Garcia-Lazaro & Pearce, 2023).

The population–agricultural land balance has undergone new connotations in the context of paradigm changes in the theory and practice of economic strategies, being marked, in recent decades, by the sustainable development requirements, the measures imposed to protect the natural areas from the intensive exploitation and the restrictions for carrying out economic activities in these areas. The progress recorded in the field of definition, quantification and integration the ecosystem services in the equation of the economic growth (Prato, 2012), simultaneously with the pressures felt regarding the changes of the destinations of important agricultural land areas (many of them located in the immediate neighborhood of inhabited urban and rural areas), to productive activities (industrial parks, commercial areas, residential ensembles or solar and wind parks), under the conditions of the green transition and, respectively, to a new mix of energy production, lowering the impact on the environment, preventing and mitigating climatic changes (CEDEFOP, 2022; Jie et al., 2023).

Recent studies conclude that the green transition involves massive processes of industrial transformation, with a profound impact on the labor market from multiple perspectives: the need for graduates to acquire transversal knowledge allowing them for a rapid adaptation to innovations; strengthening environmental knowledge among citizens, workers and businesses becomes a priority; the investments of individuals, but also of companies, in education, training and acquiring new skills become essential for facilitating the green transition; inclusive social protection systems are required, providing support for workers who will lose their jobs and supporting services for professional reconversion and labor market reintegration (Vandeplas et al., 2022).

As underlined by Roubini and Bundy (2023), for overcoming the rising climate-driven costs and the general belief according to which investments on a long term related to the green transition are associated with a predominantly social impact but a low profitability, the policymakers urgently should rethink how to channel the capital so as to secure reliable returns to investors, including assets that provide a hedge against geoeconomic risks and avoid "greenflation" caused by decarbonization impact on prices.

The lessons of previous transitions have highlighted a need to adapt to the specific assets of each territory, respectively, the importance of the role played by strategies to strengthen local investments (including public investments and public–private partnerships), the attractiveness of the territory (by providing access to healthcare, education, culture, etc.), optimizing complementarities, by effective systems of multi-level governance (with a strong presence at the national level) and with the involvement of all interested parties (including a relevant social dialogue).

The size of the population and its demographic and demo-economic characteristics are essential benchmarks for shaping the consolidated budget of each state and the main aggregated macroeconomic indicators. The age group structure of the population, the demographic dependency ratio, provides essential information on the ratio between the population with the potential to contribute to the creation of added value (working-age population, 15–64 years) and the young population (under 15 years) which requires financial efforts from the family and the state for education and health, etc. up to the age of employment as well as the elderly population (over 65 years old) whose contribution to the society development has to be rewarded by ensuring the income necessary for a decent living, through unrestricted access to health and social assistance services.

The structure of the total population according to professional status provides additional information, by grouping it into two important categories: active population (employed and unemployed population) and inactive population (pupils and students, pensioners, householders, dependents of the state aids, other persons supported by other sources). The information provided by these structures is an essential input for the sizing of the education system, employment and professional training services for adults, services for people looking for a job, the state social insurance system and pensions, social assistance and its corresponding budgets (Temsumrit, 2023).

Many studies in the specific literature associate economic growth with an increase in population size, a decreasing average and median age, reduced demographic and economic dependency ratios. The trends recorded in recent decades, in Romania, showing a decline of the total population, against the background of negative demographic and net migration, the increase in the average and median age of the total population and the rise in demographic and economic dependency ratios, represent huge challenges for any development strategy on short, medium and long terms (Fig. 3.1).

Recent studies draw attention to the fact that the dynamics of Romania's economy will be severely affected by the demographic crisis (Albu, 2023). Under the circumstances of the population decline, the long-term support of economic growth is fundamentally dependent on shifting the emphasis from the quantitative component of human resources to the qualitative one (Fanti & Gori, 2009; Peterson, 2017); increasing investment in human capital, which supposes combined efforts, from the part of the state, by allocating additional resources for initial education and professional training of adults, and from the part of companies as well as from the part of individuals, depending on the increase in their income level (Bucci, 2023; Tanzila et al., 2022); increasing companies' appetite for innovative investments, with consequences on the increase of total factor productivity (TFP; Burkhard & Irmen, 2014); and increasing investments in

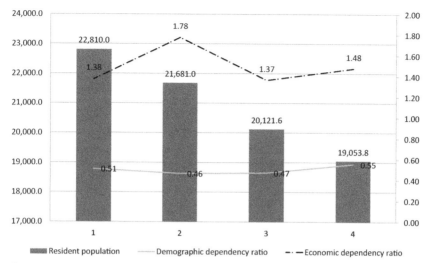

Fig. 3.1. Total Population (Thousand Persons) in Romania, Demographic and Economic Dependency, in 1992–2021. *Source*: Author's own calculations based on population and housing census in 1992–2021.

research–development–innovation, with a preponderance of those with a high potential for transposing the results in the economy and societal impact, generating technical progress and stimulating economic agents to invest in human capital (Bucci, 2008).

Other authors cite the need to improve the performance of the pension system (Burkhard & Irmen, 2014) and capitalize on the opportunities offered by active aging, increasing the median age of the working-age population (Cylus & Lynn, 2021). The coexistence in the workplace of several generations (15 successive generations co-existing at present) (Fougère & Mérette, 1999) offers important opportunities, in the context of a suitable work climate, for the transfer of experience and knowledge acquired at the workplace (Choi & Shin, 2015).

Among the solutions identified are also: the increase in the participation rate of women in the circumstances of the decrease in fertility rates (Peterson, 2017; Polyzos et al., 2022); the modification of the human resources strategies of institutions and companies to ensure the balance between the needs and aspirations of exponents of different coexisting successive generations, both among own employees and customers (Harnphattananusorn & Puttitanun, 2021); increasing the quality of institutions (Polyzos et al., 2022); the transition to a model based on processes and technologies with low labor intensity (Choi & Shin, 2015).

Last but not least, some authors believe that the negative impact of demographic decline on economic growth can be mitigated by the transition from investments in capital-oriented technologies, which require the continuous training of new young workers, to human capital-oriented technologies, which ensure support for the employed elderly population (Elgin & Tumen, 2012); and strategies that combine maintaining (reducing losses through migration) and increasing the stock of human capital (attracting highly qualified labor from abroad) in parallel with new investments in human capital (Škare & Lacmanović, 2015) and/or investments in education and strengthening of strong university centers, able of inducing significant changes in the areas where they operate, including by stabilizing the population, in general, and the working-age population, in particular (Andrei, 2023).

3. SWOT Analyses

In the Appendix, the main indicators for SWOT analyses of human resources and green transition during the period of 2007–2022 are presented.

3.1. Strengths

- *Important and quality human resources.* According to Eurostat data, Romania ranks seventh among the 27 European Union (EU 27) Member States in terms of active (8.2 million people, 2022) and employed (8.1 million people, 2022) population. In recent years, the unemployment rate has been at a low level: 5.6% in 2022 (15th place among EU 27 Member States). The high qualification of human resources enjoys international recognition in numerous fields: health, IT, etc. Romanians who have worked abroad and return to the country contribute to the development of new skills and specializations.
- *Material import dependency* (calculated as the ratio of imports over direct material inputs, for example, the sum of internal extraction and physical imports), represents an indicator which is part of the Circular Economy indicator set. This ratio is very low in the case of Romania, which ranked first in the hierarchy of EU Member States from this point of view, both in 2007, with a share of imports over direct material inputs in the economy of 11.1%, and in 2021, with a ratio of 10.0%. These percentages are half compared with the average recorded at the EU 27 level, being much lower compared to Luxembourg (91.4%), the Netherlands (82.6%), Belgium (74.3%), Italy (45.5%), Germany (40.6%) or France (34.8%). Romania's favorable situation from the perspective of the internal availability of material flows entering production or internal consumption, which can also be explained by a relatively lower level of industrial development, should be corroborated, especially in a volatile international context regarding raw materials prices, with national efforts to expand value-added chains and increase the degree of domestic processing, supported by appropriate investment and fiscal policies.
- *Low rate of energy dependency* (calculated as net energy imports divided by gross inland energy consumption). Romania is endowed with important energy resources, both fossil (crude oil, coal, natural gas, to which nuclear energy is added) and renewable (hydropower, solar-photovoltaic, wind, geothermal, biomass and hydrogen). The energy security risk score is higher than the EU average and better than its neighbors, which, in an international context marked by volatility, represents an asset for the development of the energy sector so that, through the implementation of the strategic investment program, it will

strengthen Romania's position of regional supplier of energy security (Romanian Government, 2020). Romania's energy dependency rate is at a low level compared to most other EU Member States, which represents a significant comparative and competitive advantage in the perspective of sustainable economic development and green transition. In 2007, the energy dependency rate was 31.5%, Romania being in the fourth position in the EU from this point of view, and in 2020, an improvement of the indicator was recorded at the level of 28.2%, which led to the country's advancement to the second place in the ranking of EU Member States.

- *The relatively low greenhouse gas (GHG) emissions*, namely 5.9 tons per inhabitant recorded in 2021 (against 7.1 tons in 2007), placed Romania in the second place in the EU 27 ranking in terms of this indicator, compared to an European average of 7.4 tons, which represents another strength when it comes to the green transition.
- *The energy productivity* measures the amount of economic output that is produced per unit of gross available energy. This indicator is part of the set of sustainable development goals (SDGs) of the EU, monitoring the progress toward SDG 7 on affordable and clean energy. The European Green Deal includes energy efficiency as a key measure for reducing cross-sectoral GHG emissions establishing climate targets by 2030 in a fair, cost-effective and competitive way (European Commission, 2019). Reducing primary energy consumption and CO_2 emissions mainly requires the optimization of the energy mix, the promotion of infrastructure investments energy and the orientation toward clean and high-yield technologies. In the case of Romania, the energy productivity recorded a favorable evolution, from 3.2 euro/kg of oil equivalent in 2007 to 5.3 euro/kg of oil equivalent in 2021, which led the advancement of the country from the 25th position to the 18th in the EU ranking from this point of view, as well as reducing the gap with the EU average (6.7 euro/kg oil equivalent and, respectively, 8.5 euro/kg oil equivalent in 2021) from 54% in 2007 to 38% in 2021, respectively, by 16 percentage points.
- *The forests wood timber* (without bark), an indicator recently introduced by Eurostat, which is still undergoing methodological adjustments to ensure comparability at the level of EU Member States (Pilli & Grassi, 2021), reflects the availability of using this important resource in the economy, respecting the requirements of protecting forests, respectively, the environment, and reducing the carbon footprint as well as mitigating the impact of climate change, which have become priority objectives of the EU in the medium and long terms. Romania, with over 2,100 million cubic meters in 2007 and over 2,350 million cubic meters in 2020, is one of the best endowed countries from this point of view, ranking sixth in the EU hierarchy in the two reference years.
- *The existence of a strategic framework appropriate to the new realities.* Approving the National Strategy for Employment and the Action Plan for the period 2021–2027, monitoring and evaluating the implementation of the strategy through annual progress reports for adaptation to developments in the real economy (Romanian Government, 2021).

- *The increase in the fiscal stimulus* granted in recent years for certain categories of employees and companies to boost activities, combined with other measures of social assistance that need to be taken, which can lead to a reduction in emigration and an increase in repatriations.
- *The important value of human capital and its weight in intangible assets.* Romania ranks 15th among the EU27 Member States in terms of National Wealth – the human capital component and 10th in terms of the share of human capital in intangible assets.
- *Increasing the monthly minimum wage in purchasing power standard (PPS).* Mentioning that a number of six EU Member States (Denmark, Italy, Cyprus, Austria, Finland and Sweden) have not established by legislation a certain minimum monthly salary, there are some issues regarding the comparability of this indicator calculated by Eurostat on a monthly basis for the other EU countries, due to the differences regarding the number of hours in the working week, the amount of salary taxation, the conversion of national currencies into euros, respectively, in terms of PPS, etc. To these, particularities of each state, among these the proportion of employees remunerated at the minimum salary level are added. According to Eurostat data, Romania registered the fastest dynamics among all EU Member States of the monthly minimum wage at PPS, which increased from 184 euros in 2007 to 943 euros in 2022, allowing the country to advance from the 27th position to 18th place in the EU ranking from this point of view (respectively, from 20th position to 13th place if Member States that have not established a minimum wage are excluded).
- *The accumulated experience in attracting European funds* used for the development of human resources in the financial exercises for the periods 2007–2013 and 2014–2020; the absorption rate of these nonreturnable funds was close to 90%, benefiting of the $n + 3$ rule.
- *The physical productivity of work is competitive at the international level*, in the case of certain fields and specializations, as automotive and information and communication technology (ICT).
- *The high value of personal transfers* (between non-resident and resident households in Romania). The level of 3.4 billion euros recorded in 2020 ranks Romania the first place in the EU.

3.2. Weaknesses

- *Unfavorable demographic trends and demo-economic indicators.* From the perspective of human capital, Romania is in the 33rd year of negative demographic growth. In the period 1990–2020, the natural decline of the population exceeded 1 million inhabitants. The net balance of migration in the same period is estimated by official statistics at over 2.6 million people. In the case of Romania, according to the projections of the European Commission, the demographic and employment indicators will register a severe deterioration in the coming decades, with a negative impact on the labor market. Despite the lower impact of net migration on a long term, the employed population is expected to decrease from 8.2 million people in 2020, to 7.3 million people in the year 2030 and, respectively, to 5.3 million people in the year 2070.

According to the EU projections, the dependency rate of the public pension system, expressed as a percentage ratio between the number of pensioners and the number of employed people, is on an unfavorable trajectory, difficult to sustained, expected to increase from 63% in 2020, to around 71% in 2030 and, respectively, to almost 100% in 2060.

- *The labor market is a tense one*, in which the quantitative and qualitative labor force shortages (estimated at over 500,000 people in 2020) caused mainly by discrepancies between the offer provided by the education system and the needs of the labor market coexist with significant contingents of unused human resources (Chivu et al., 2019). These estimates, based on Eurostat data, led to the conclusion that, in Romania, for the training of approximately 1 million NEETs, the state spent approximately 11.1 billion euros and families approximately 13.6 billion euros, resulting in a total of 24.7 billion euros of the value of expenditures on unutilized human capital.

- *The socio-professional structure of the employed population in Romania differs substantially from that of the other EU Member States*. The relatively low share of employees and the high share of workers in subsistence agriculture induce a risk of a different response to labor market-specific adjustment policies in the other Member States, characterized by a high share of employees. According to Eurostat data, in 2022, of the total number of employed persons in Romania, approximately 85.8% were salaried persons, 11.5% were self-employed and 2.7% were unpaid family workers. Among the self-employed, approximately 87.6% had no employees.

- *High risk of poverty and social exclusion*. Although there is a general downward trend, the number of people at risk of poverty and social exclusion remains at a high level. In 2020, according to Eurostat data, in Romania, 5.9 million people were in this situation (compared to 9.9 million people in 2009), representing 32.5% of the total population (compared to 43.0% in 2007). From this perspective, it is worth mentioning the high and increasing territorial disparities.

- *Having a job is not always a guarantee for a decent living*. According to Eurostat data, in 2020, the in-work poverty rate in Romania was 14.9%, compared to the 9.4% average at the EU 27 level. If in the case of employees, the in-work poverty rate was only 4.2%, in the case of the other categories (respectively, self-employed and unpaid family workers), the in-work poverty rate was 53.8% (compared to 21.0% EU 27 average).

- *The waste recycling* rate represents the share of material resources coming from waste recycling in the total material resources used in the economy. This indicator is part of the EU framework for monitoring the Circular Economy, having a particular economic and environmental importance. Moreover, according to a December 2020 EU Council Decision on own resources (Member States' contributions to the EU Budget), a tax of 0.8 euro/kg paid by Member States is imposed on plastic packaging waste that is not recycled. In the case of Romania, the amount related to this tax amounts to several hundred million euros per year. If in 2008, the first year for which Eurostat calculated the waste recycling rate, Romania recorded a percentage of 3.5% and occupied the 20th place in the European ranking from this point of view, and in 2021, the recycling rate had dropped to 1.4%, descending the country to the last position. This difference must be judged considering the gap with the EU average for this indicator (7.3% in 2008 and 10.3% in 2021), which increased by 3 percentage points in the reference period.

- *Lack of a real institutionalized dialogue.* The legislative reform carried out by the law on social dialogue (Law No. 62/2011) had a negative impact on social partnership at all levels, collective negotiations and the quality of employment and working conditions. The cumulative effect of abolishing the collective labor agreement at the national level, supplementing the representativeness conditions at the sectoral level and introducing the absolute majority criterion for obtaining representativeness for collective bargaining at the company level was that over 1.2 million workers, in particular those employed in enterprises with less than 20 employees, were excluded from collective bargaining, a fact that induces a negative impact on the salary level and the quality of working conditions in general. The legislative changes promoted during 2023 partially solved these problems.

3.3. Opportunities

- *The opportunity to attract additional sources of financing from non-reimbursable funds and the improvement, in recent years, of their absorption capacity.* According to the data provided by the Ministry of Finance (2023), in the period January 1, 2007–December 30, 2022, Romania received 81.3 billion euros from the EU and contributed to the EU budget with 26.7 billion euros (a positive balance for Romania of 54.6 billion euros). In the following period, Romania benefits from the European Union allocations of 51.5 billion euros related to the financial exercise 2021–2027 (31.5 billion euros from the cohesion policy and about 20 billion euros from the Common Agricultural Policy), adding to these – 12.2 billion euros in grants and 15 billion euros in the form of loans, related to the implementation of the National Recovery and Resilience Plan financed from the EU Recovery and Resilience Facility.
- *Significant potential in the field of renewable energies.* Approximately 40% of the electricity mix is composed of energy from renewable sources, respectively, 58% energy without GHG emissions and 72% with relatively low CO_2 emissions.
- *The Human Capital Operational Program, the Sustainable Development Operational Program and the Just Transition Operational Program* provide important funds dedicated to the adaptation of the workforce to the profound changes included in the strategic documents related to the 2021–2027 period, mainly as regards the green and digital transition.
- *Growing stock of foreign direct investment (FDI).* According to the UNCTAD (2022) data, at the end of 2021, in Romania, the stock of FDIs was 108.7 billion euros (over 40.0% of which were located in industry), compared to 60.9 billion euros in the year 2007. In many cases, they brought new generations of technologies, contributed to the development of leading industries and increased exports. Romania has an important industrial tradition, benefiting from a skilled workforce and an attractive labor cost for foreign investors. This has contributed to the development of some dynamic industrial sectors, particularly in the field

of motor vehicle production but also some activities in the field of IT (information technology) and transport services. One of the competitive advantages that stimulated FDI inflows was represented by the reduced average hourly wage cost recorded in Romania, respectively, of 9.5 euros in 2022 (second place from the point of view of this indicator in the hierarchy of the EU 27 Member States), compared to an average on the entire EU 27 of 30.5 euros.

- *Broadband Internet download speed* measured in megabits per second (Mbps) represents an extremely important indicator in the context of the green and digital transition, as it facilitates and accelerates online interactions, both in the case of home users and the business environment. From this point of view, both in 2007 and in 2023, Romania ranks first in the EU, but also in the Top 10 worldwide, which is explained, paradoxically, by the delay in the introduction and expansion of Internet networks, developed progressively and extensively in our country only after the 2000s, when the fixed connection infrastructure was based on more advanced technologies, mainly on optic fiber networks as a support for fastest data transmission. The high speed of broadband Internet connections, in conditions of low costs, is a special comparative and competitive advantage for Romania, as it can capitalize at a much higher level than the current one in terms of added value and contribution to gross domestic product (GDP) growth, by promoting of state-of-the-art business software solutions (customer relationship management (CRM) and/or enterprise resource planning (ERP)), including for small- and medium-sized enterprises (SMEs), the creation of cloud development tools, the development of online markets and e-commerce, with implications for increasing the productivity of employees' work, as well as the improvement of the education process, continuous professional training and the reduction of labor force deficits.

3.4. Threats

- *Government effectiveness* is an indicator that captures the perception of the quality of public services and their degree of independence from political pressures, the coherence of policy formulation and implementation and the credibility of the government's commitment to these policies. The World Bank ranking indicates the country's position in relation to all states covered by the aggregate indicator of government effectiveness, with 0 corresponding to the lowest rank and 100 to the highest rank. Romania, both in 2007 and in 2021, ranks last among the Member States of the EU, which reflects the persistence of some structural weaknesses of government institutions and administrative capacity, the inconsistency and incoherence of public policies reflected by the poor results of their implementation as well as the low degree of adoption and completion of deep structural reforms, both in the economic and social fields.
- *The fragility of the economic growth model of recent years*, based on consumption, also reflected by the measures promoted, in the period 2018–2022, as concerns the significant increase in the income of the population (increasing salaries in the public sector and pensions).

- *Current redistribution mechanisms* do not ensure the transposition of economic growth into well-being for all categories of inhabitants.
- *Slow social progress compared to the other Member States.* In the "2022 Social Progress Index" (Social Progress Imperative, 2023), an indicator that measures the quality of life and social well-being of the inhabitants of 146 countries, based on three dimensions, namely basic human needs, the foundations of well-being and the opportunities offered, Romania was in the penultimate position among EU 27 Member States.
- *Fiscal burden* is an indicator that measures the degree to which labor taxation discourages (or encourages) employment. In Romania, from this point of view, the labor taxation was at a high level in 2007 (39.9%) and, even if in a slight decrease, also in 2021 (37.2%). The country occupied the 22nd position in the EU ranking for this indicator. This situation, despite relatively low wage costs, does not represent an incentive for employment, including for attracting FDI.
- *The high rate of early leaving the education system* (15.6% in Romania, in 2022, compared to 9.6% EU 27 average), especially in rural areas.
- *The low integration rate of graduates on the labor market* (69.6% in Romania in 2022, for ISCED (International Standard Classification of Education) Levels 3–8, aged 20–34 and who graduated from the education system 1–3 years before the reference year, compared to 81.5% the EU 27 average) represents important factors of exposure to the risk of poverty and social exclusion.
- *The physical and social infrastructure* (education, research–development–innovation, health, social assistance, etc.) *poorly developed and unevenly distributed in the territorial profile* constitutes a serious obstacle for the sustainable development. A decisive role was played by the extremely low-budget allocations for these sectors, in terms of their share in GDP, Romania retaining the last positions among the EU Member States. The smallness funds allocated for of education, for example, the GDP share of education expenditure representing 3.2% in 2021, compared to 4.8% EU 27 average. Chronic underfunding of research–development–innovation (last place among Member States (MS) in 2021, in terms of average RDI expenditure per inhabitant) has a negative impact, including by substantially reducing the number of researchers, as well as showing a weak relationship between research–industry–market. The extremely low level of absorption of European funds allocated for research–development–innovation is added.

4. Recent Developments and Trends of the European and Global Labor Market

In recent years, the international and domestic context has undergone major changes, with significant effects on the configuration of labor markets determined, on the one hand, by the accelerated global technological advance (including Industry 4.0, Big Data, IoT & IoE, 6G Network, Machine Learning, AI (artificial intelligence) and Quantum Computing) and, on the other hand, by the overlap of crises on a global scale (sanitary, economic, financial, energy and raw materials, geopolitical and armed conflicts), whose combined effects have amplified the intensity and scope of these changes, often in directions that are difficult to anticipate, putting to the test the ability of policymakers to manage their adverse impact with the most appropriate policies and instruments.

Among the few certainties highlighted by these evolutionary spasms and fragmentations is *the importance of human capital and its capacity to adapt and innovate*, as well as the development of metacognitive, creative and integrative skills in relation to the new realities of the labor market and an increasingly complex global economy.

The configuration of employment in any type of economy is determined by its sectoral structure and the availability of human capital skills to support it. From here, it results that developments toward a new balance of the labor market, in the conditions of structural changes determined by the emergence of new activities and sectors to the detriment of traditional ones, depend decisively on investments in human capital (along with infrastructural ones and appropriate regulations) that can endow it with the skills and competences corresponding to these changes. Otherwise, the development of an emerging sector with strong growth potential is dimmed by the lack of ability to provide it with labor resources with the necessary qualifications (Oxford Economics, 2023).

Macroeconomic trends and determinants of foreseeable changes in labor markets globally, in terms of job creation/transformation and/or destruction, point to a complex picture in the sectoral structure and the related skills. A recent report by the World Economic Forum (2023), based on the results of a survey of the most important companies in all regions of the world, shows that, on the 2027 horizon, major changes in the structure of employment are expected as a result of new job creation and the elimination of some existing ones.

It was estimated that in the next five years, 69 million jobs will be created, while 83 million jobs will be lost. By dividing their sum i.e. 152 million jobs to the 673 million employees, is resulting a percentage of 23%, which reflects a significant measure of distortions in labor markets due to the compounding effects induced, mainly, by economic and technological factors. Sectoral, the fastest dynamics are seen for telecommunications, financial services and capital markets, and from the point of view of qualifications, the fastest growth is predicted for specializations related to new technologies, especially in AI and machine learning, environment and energy and business intelligence. It should be noted that among the macrotrends indicated by companies as having the strongest impact on net job creation are investments that facilitate the green transition, the widespread application of ESG (environmental social governance) standards and the concentration of supply chains.

At the level of the EU, various surveys among employers and employees in representative sectors, including in Central and Eastern European countries (European Commission, 2021), the results of which are in line with observed trends on a global level, highlight the tactical approaches and long-term strategies that must be adopted in the transition to a labor market in a digitized world, emphasizing the qualifications and skills of the workforce that need to be adjusted and adapted (including concrete ways to develop them), which, without being limited to these and with the mention that they must be constantly updated in line with technological progress at a galloping pace, include (potentially cumulative) social/interpersonal skills, critical thinking skills (ability to observe, analyze, conclude, communicate and problem-solving), cognitive flexibility and adapt to changes/unforeseen events, capacity for innovation and creativity, intercultural, interdisciplinary, transversal, resource management, technical, digital and self-confidence.

In terms of the concept of hybrid work (Eurofound, 2023a), recently entered the analytical language of the labor market, at least in the European space under the impact of the COVID-19 pandemic, it is defined as the form, practiced on an increasingly wide scale (European Commission, 2023d), of organization of work through the interference of four main components, namely physical, temporal, virtual and social, each of which has sub-components that interact with each other, which can be combined in various forms. One of the conclusions resulting from the implementation of hybrid schedule work is that telework and office work, for example, although seen as performing differently, have complementary functions. Thus, as the case may be, depending on the object of activity, the employer's preferences and the nature of the workplace, telework is more appropriate for the situation where social interaction is not important, while office work involves and stimulates the exchange of ideas and innovation.

Consistent with the fundamental objective of the EU aimed at the functionality of the European model of the social economy, the reference framework for monitoring employment, the labor market and social performance is represented by the European Pillar of Social Rights (EPSR) launched in 2017, structured on three categories of principles: equal opportunities and access to the labor market, fair working conditions and social protection and social inclusion.

The EPSR was completed in 2021 by an Action Plan for its implementation which contains a series of main targets to be achieved by 2030 regarding employment (the employment rate of people aged 20–64 to be at least 78%), qualifications (at least 60% of adults participate annually in training courses, including for the development of digital skills) and poverty reduction (the number of people at risk of poverty or social exclusion should be reduced by 15 million).

In the context of the profound changes in the configuration of the labor market at the level of the EU, one of the most difficult challenges to the policies in this field and the guidelines recommended to the Member States is the quantitative and qualitative shortages of labor force, already felt in many countries, although differentiated in scope and intensity, which complicates the development and implementation of coherent and viable long-term European strategies, able to adequately respond to current and anticipated changes in global trends under the impact of macrotrends and new technologies, previously highlighted.

Thus, at the EU level, in order to support economic and social progress, as well as green and digital transitions, strengthen the industrial base of the Union and ensure competitive and resilient labor markets, it is recommended that Member States pay priority attention to solving the problem of the quantitative shortage and workforce structure, promoting quality education, training courses, future-oriented vocational education, lifelong professional development and retraining programs, as well as promoting active policies on the labor market, improving career opportunities by strengthening ties between the educational system and the requirements recognized by the labor market, including through knowledge or skills acquired during non-formal and informal educational processes (European Commission, 2023b).

The main influence on the evolution of the labor market, including as regards the labor shortages, comes from the introduction of new technologies, whose impact produces changes on the demand side in the proportion of production factors (labor vs capital) but also in the sectoral structure of the economy, implicitly of qualifications required on the labor market. Thus, within the EU, between 2002 and 2020, the trend of increasing the share of highly qualified personnel in total employment from 35% to 42% was highlighted, exclusively due to the decrease, in the same proportion, of those with an average degree of qualification, while the share of personnel with a low level of qualification remained constant, around the figure of 10% (European Commission, 2022).

A particular aspect of labor shortages within the EU in the post-pandemic period is the finding that they are not only caused by the qualification discrepancies, which are the focus of debates and public policies, especially regarding the need to develop digital skills and those related to the green transition, but they are also acutely felt in occupations with low salary and qualification levels, characterized by poor working conditions and/or a specific work regime (fixed- or part-time contracts, in shifts, in the evening/at night, on weekends, under pressure, etc.) likely to lead to the deepening of wage and social inequalities (Zwysen, 2023). To mitigate them, revisions of the Charter of Fundamental Rights and the regulations on working conditions, the minimum wage, and collective labor contracts are being considered at the EU level.

A recent report on employment and social developments in Europe warns that, despite limited data, the available metrics show growing labor shortages in sectors and occupations crucial to the green transition, mainly in construction (bricklayers, carpenters, jointers, plumbers and pipe fitters) and manufacturing (metal working machine tool setters and operators) also facing obstacles to investment in climate change, among these, due to the lack of environmental and climate assessment skills, together with digital skills, engineering and other technical skills and regulatory understanding (European Commission, 2023a).

5. Quantitative and Qualitative Deficits of the Labor Market in Romania

According to a Eurofound report (Eurofound, 2023b), the quantitative shortage of labor in Romania was about 500,000 people in 2022 (about 10% of the number of employees), determined mainly by demographic causes but also by the massive emigration of the population aged work, including qualified personnel, mostly in the Western states of the EU, motivated by significant salary differences.

The issue of quantitative and qualitative labor force deficits in Romania was the subject of a study published by Chivu et al. (2019), in which, based on the analysis of labor supply and demand, from a structural perspective, as well as the main factors of influence, projections and scenarios on long-term evolution were made, highlighting deficits on a national scale and in a sectoral profile, proposing a series of solutions and measures to mitigate them, aiming at improving the macroeconomic correlations between the supply and demand of the workforce, attracting different categories of the inactive population to the labor market, increasing the performance of the education and professional training system, etc.

It has been estimated that the losses of companies in Romania as a result of the labor shortage amount to about 7 billion euros, representing about 3% of GDP. From a structural point of view, this deficit is of two types, one caused by the lack of highly qualified labor in sectors such as IT and some occupations in industrial branches, and the other due to the shortage of personnel with a low level of qualification, in sectors such as HORECA and constructions. To mitigate the latter deficit, Romania had to import foreign workers from outside the EU in 2022, increasing the quota to 100,000 workers (four times higher than the previous year) and in 2023 to 140,000 workers. It should be noted that in 2022, a number of over 11,000 Romanian companies hired foreign workers, compared to about 5,000 companies in 2021.

In addition to the employment difficulties and the staff shortage experienced by companies (estimated at similar dimensions to those assessed by Eurofound), the report on the financial stability of Romania (National Bank of Romania, 2022) indicates important gaps between the level of training and job requirements. Thus, in 2019, more than 25% of the workforce worked in other fields compared to those for which they had trained (horizontal gap), and about 16% of the workforce was overqualified compared to the requirements of the job occupied (vertical gap). The analysis of differences at the sectoral level showed that the largest horizontal gaps were registered in the service sector (60%) and in sectors that require knowledge in science, mathematics or programming, and the largest vertical gaps were registered in the transport sector (41%) and trade (28%).

In the context of the first European Semester of 2023, based on the analysis of the National Reform Program and the Convergence Program sent to Brussels by the Romanian authorities, the European Commission made a series of economic policy recommendations, mainly of a fiscal-budgetary nature, which compliance is important, including through the implementation of the National Recovery and Resilience Plan (European Commission, 2023c).

At the same time, attention is drawn to the fact that in 2022, serious labor shortages have been reported for several occupations that require specific qualifications or in-depth specialized knowledge to achieve the green transition and the implementation of zero-emission technologies, including plumbers, construction engineers and site managers, which creates significant blockages and obstructs the acceleration of this transition, a priority objective of the EU.

In order to reduce the structural deficits of the labor force, the importance of the quality of education and training systems is emphasized, so that they can respond to the needs of the labor market and the requirements of upgrading the qualification and professional reconversion, benefiting from the support of active policies on the labor market, in the case of Romania, especially in the sectors and regions most affected by the green transition.

The country diagnosis updated by the World Bank for Romania (World Bank, 2023) reveals a series of particularities regarding the labor shortage, felt in key occupations (the case of doctors, for example), the skills gap and distorted salary claims, against the background of the decrease in real labor productivity, anticipating that deficits and inconsistencies between labor demand and supply will become more acute as the digital and green transition advances.

It is also pointed out that the low level of skills development and activation, as well as the shortcomings of the current skills provision system in Romania, represent a major obstacle to the country's adaptation to changes in the world context. Starting from the fact that the education and training system hardly manages to provide the skills that Romania needs (World Bank, 2020) and that there is no functional connection between employers, workers and education and training providers, it is estimated that only 20% of the current needs of the labor market are covered (World Bank, 2023).

On the one hand, Romanian companies invest little in skills training, and on the other hand, the low and relatively ineffective public expenditures for active policies in the labor force field make the total of these expenditures represent less than 0.1% of GDP, respectively, below 10% of the amount spent on average at the EU 27 level.

Conclusions

The reconsideration of the role of the labor force as a factor of economic growth requires the understanding of the severity of the unfavorable trajectory that Romania is on. From this point of view, the major risks are induced by the chronicling of these trends making vital need for an integrated approach to demo-economic imbalances, the relationship between demographic developments, human capital and GDP, the impact of labor force shortages on the country's green transition and sustainable development prospects. On the other hand, the relationship between labor productivity, labor costs and competitiveness, as well as the labor/capital substitution ratio in Romania's concrete conditions (Chivu & Georgescu, 2021).

At the macroeconomic level, it is necessary to change the perspective of Romania's development model and related public policies, including employment, through the lens of the main factors of production, labor and capital and, respectively, their combination (TFP).

Thus, in order to achieve these objectives, at the macroeconomic level, the following strategic milestones need to be taken into account:

I. *Development of an integrated demographic strategy and a related action plan* to stop the demographic decline and the emigration exodus. Combining measures aimed at maintaining the stock of human capital (reducing losses through migration) and increasing it (by attracting skilled labor from abroad) with investments aimed at accumulating new human capital, support mechanisms for reconciling professional life with family life, support services affordable for raising children, etc.

II. *The foundation of the analytical framework of the decision-making process and public policies specific to the labor market* by setting up a statistical and informational system that ensures the collection of adequate data and information for monitoring their application, updating, revising and permanently adapting to the rapidly changing realities of the economy and society.

III. *Reducing the population employed in the agricultural sector*, especially the subsistence sector, and facilitating relocation to non-agricultural sectors, especially in the activities targeted by the green and digital transition, those in rapid development and/or having labor shortages.

IV. *Stimulating the growth of investment in human capital*, which involves combined efforts from the state by allocating additional resources for initial education and vocational training of adults, from companies as well as from individuals.

V. *Stimulating the growth of the companies' appetite for innovative investments* with consequences on the increase of the total factor productivity.

VI. *Identifying and measuring the quantitative and qualitative shortages* of sectoral, regional and occupation categories as support for the promotion of public policies aimed at mitigating them.

VII. *Elaboration of forecasts regarding the evolution of labor force shortages*, which allow the provision of relevant information to decision-makers and social partners, for the foundation and implementation of specific policies, adapted to future skills needs, which also form the basis of the educational and professional training system of adults.

VIII. *Elaboration of strategies, policies and operational measures for regional and local development* that could lead to counteracting the manifested trends and reducing territorial disparities, increasing the mobility of the workforce and companies at the regional and local levels.

IX. *Extending the active life duration of the population* by implementing the objectives of reaching the target of 78% in 2030 of the employment rate of the population aged between 20 and 64 through policies that stimulate the maintenance of the Romanian population within the labor resources.

X. *Reconsidering the role and importance of the educational and professional training system* through a strategic, sectoral and territorial approach to the educational process and the labor market, which allows the correlation of the skills acquired during the educational process with the realities of the Romanian economy, in relation to the evolution of labor market requirements and employers' needs.

XI. *Stimulating the growth of investments in R&D* (research and development), with a preponderance of those with high potential for transposing the results in the economy and societal impact, generators of technical progress, which stimulate economic actors to invest in human capital.

XII. *Investments in education and in the consolidation of strong university centers* that demonstrate the ability to induce significant changes in the regions in which they operate through the effect of stabilizing the population and, in particular, the working-age population.

XIII.   *Modernizing professional and technical education,* increasing the degree of student participation in this form of education by promoting the future benefits generated and revising study programs to ensure relevance for the needs identified on the labor market and increasing the employment rate of young people aged between 20 and 34 years, not included in education and training.

XIV.   *Support and development of dual* education that makes investments in human capital more efficient by adapting professional training to the real, present needs of companies.

XV.   *The creation of a county-level web portal* that brings together the county's education and vocational training offer (high school, vocational, post-high school and foreman technical, university, adult vocational training), increasing the degree of accessibility and ensuring the transparency of related information.

XVI.   *Increasing the attractiveness of STEM studies* (science, technology, engineering and mathematics) in order to reduce the gap between demand and supply for highly qualified professionals in technical and IT fields considering the role of technological progress in increasing productivity and competitiveness, as well as in accelerating economic and social development.

At the level of the labor market, the active and passive measures only prove their effectiveness in the short term, becoming more and more obvious that employment is not a simple result of the economic mechanisms functioning, but a consequence of economic strategies and policies at national, regional and sectoral levels, of financial and monetary policies in accordance with the European ones. The measures to maintain the balance of the labor market should be the result of the *ex ante* analysis of the impact of such strategies and policies, as well as their essential components, updated and adjusted *ex post,* depending on the practical results and their efficiency, related to macro- and microeconomic developments and the changing coordinates of the international context.

Following, mainly, the correlation of the demand with the labor supply, *as strategic benchmarks for policies and measures in the short, medium and long terms to mitigate the quantitative and qualitative deficits of the labor force balance,* can be considered:

I.   *Stimulating the increase in the employment rate at the level of the population* regarding the extension of active life, both through measures at the level of public systems and policies as well as at the level of practices in companies.

II.   *Reducing the tax burden on labor income* in general and on labor in particular.

III.   *Stimulating the increase of the internal mobility of workers* by activating the unemployed and inactive people from regions with a lower labor supply and encouraging the transfer to unoccupied jobs in other regions of the country.

IV.   *Capitalizing on the opportunities offered by the Education and Employment Operational Program 2021–2027* for financing studies on addressing labor shortages for certain occupations, in certain sectors or certain areas.

V.   *Improving the administrative-institutional framework of the labor market* by expanding the role and responsibilities of the National Agency for Employment (ANOFM), digitizing its activity in order to provide the services offered in an integrated manner, strengthening its administrative capacity in managing the real problems of the labor market and increasing the level of employment, as well as for correlating the labor demand with the labor supply.

VI.   *The application of integrated measures packages* in order to reduce the number of young people who do not have a job, do not follow a form of education and do not participate in vocational training activities (NEETs).

VII.   *Firmly combating undeclared work* by intensifying control actions, information campaigns on the rights and obligations of employers and employees, as well as the risks to which people who accept undeclared jobs are exposed.

VIII.   *Management of the labor shortage by companies* through a set of measures aimed at attracting and retaining talented employees, measures to increase labor productivity through the technological advances of operational activities (automation, robotization and digitalization), strengthening the workforce strategic planning process, the creation of partnerships with educational institutions in order to initiate connections with potential candidates from the time of school, the introduction of a scholarship program for students with potential, outsourcing processes that do not represent key activities for the business.

IX.   *Establishing appropriate methods of attracting social aid beneficiaries* (that ensure the minimum guaranteed income) to the labor market (estimated at over 500,000 people), respectively, increasing the chances of integration on the labor market the members able to work in the social aid beneficiary families.

X.   *Increasing the degree of female participation in the labor market* in the context of the reduction in fertility rates.

XI.   *Increasing the degree of participation in the labor market of people with disabilities* (estimated at around 850,000 persons, adults and children), a resource insufficiently capitalized on the labor market in Romania.

XII.   *Increasing the degree of participation on the labor market of people of Roma ethnicity* (estimated at around one million persons).

XIII.   *Rethinking the human resources strategies of institutions and companies* to capitalize on the opportunities offered by active aging (increasing the median age of the working-age population) and the coexistence of several generations, which offer important opportunities, in the context of an appropriate work climate, for the intergenerational transfer of experience and knowledge at work.

XIV. *Incentivizing companies to combine capital-oriented investments,* which require the continuous training of new young workers, with those in human capital-oriented technologies, which provide support for the aged employed population.

XV. *Managing the phenomenon of emigration,* in particular, reducing the "brain drain" through specific measures to prevent and mitigate this phenomenon, to manage its negative effects and to determine the retention of talents, thus supporting the development of a knowledge based economy.

XVI. *Supporting the phenomenon of repatriation of emigrant Romanians* aimed at both attracting emigrants and reintegrating them and their families, influencing the decision to return to the country, especially of highly qualified Romanians, from areas declared priority and having labor shortages.

XVII. *Recourse to the controlled import of labor force from abroad,* especially those from the extra-EU space, by making the entry and access conditions on the labor market more flexible for foreign workers, as well as the attraction and retention of international researchers and students.

References

Albu, L. L. (2023). *Criza demografică va afecta major dinamica economiei în România.* Institutul de Studii Financiare.

Andrei, T. (2023). *Îmbătrânirea populației rezidente, fenomen greu de oprit.* Retrieved May 14, 2023, from www.stiripesurse.ro

Bucci, A. (2008). Population growth in a model of economic growth with human capital accumulation and horizontal R&D. *Journal of Macroeconomics, 30*(3), 1124–1147.

Bucci, A. (2023). Can a negative population growth rate sustain a positive economic growth rate in the long run? *Mathematical Social Sciences, 122,* 17–28.

Burkhard, H., & Irmen, A. (2014). Population, pensions, and endogenous economic growth. *Journal of Economic Dynamics and Control, 46,* 50–72.

CEDEFOP. (2022). *An ally in the green transition* [Briefing Note 9166]. CEDEFOP, Thermi, https://www.cedefop.europa.eu/ro/publications/9166.

Chivu, L., & Georgescu, G. (2021). *Employment and labour market vulnerabilities during COVID-19. The case of Romania* [Working paper]. NIER, pp. 1–26 https://www.econstor.eu/bitstream/10419/233969/1/wpince210325.pdf.

Chivu, L., Racovițeanu, M., Georgescu, G., & Băncescu, I. (2019). *Piața muncii în România. Repere cantitative și calitative privind deficitele de forță de muncă.* CIDE.

Choi, K. H., & Shin, S. (2015). Population aging, economic growth, and the social transmission of human capital: An analysis with an overlapping generations model. *Economic Modelling, 50,* 138–147.

Cylus, J., & Lynn, A. T. (2021). Health, an ageing labour force, and the economy: Does health moderate the relationship between population age-structure and economic growth? *Social Science & Medicine, 287,* 114353.

Elgin, C., & Tumen, S. (2012). Can sustained economic growth and declining population coexist? *Economic Modelling, 29*(5), 1899–1908.

Eurofound. (2023a). *Hybrid work in Europe: Concept and practice.* Publications Office of the European Union, https://www.eurofound.europa.eu/en/publications/2023/hybrid-work-europe-concept-and-practice.

Eurofound. (2023b). Industrial relations and social dialogue. Romania: Developments in working life 2022. Publication Office of the European Union https://www.eurofound.europa.eu/en/topic/industrial-relations-and-social-dialogue?sort_by=title_asc&page=%2C31%2C169%2C1%2C0%2C0.

European Commission. (2019). *The European green deal [COM(2019) 640 final].* European Commission, https://eur-lex.europa.eu/legal-content/EN/TXT/?uri=COM%3A2019%3A640%3AFIN.

European Commission. (2021). *Guidebook for employees and employers* [Work Transition CEE, VS/2021/0094]. European Commission https://worktransition.eu/wp-content/uploads/2023/02/20230223_slide-deck-Ghid-de-bune-practici-pt-angajati-si-angajatori.pdf.

European Commission. (2022). *Science, research and innovation performance of the EU 2022 – Building a sustainable future in uncertain times.* DGRI, Publications Office of the European Union https://op.europa.eu/en/publication-detail/-/publication/52f8a759-1c42-11ed-8fa0-01aa75ed71a1/.

European Commission. (2023a, July). *Employment and social developments in Europe. Addressing labour shortages and skills gaps in the EU (Annual review).* European Union. https://ec.europa.eu/social/main.jsp?catId=738&langId=en&pubId=8553&furtherPubs=yes

European Commission. (2023b, May 24). *Proposal for a council decision on guidelines for the employment policies of the member states* [COM(2023) 599 final 2023/0173 (NLE)]. European Commission, https://eur-lex.europa.eu/procedure/EN/2023_173.

European Commission. (2023c, May 24). *Recommendation for a council recommendation on the 2023 National Reform Programme of Romania and delivering a council opinion on the 2023 Convergence Programme of Romania* [COM(2023) 623 final]. European Commission, https://commission.europa.eu/system/files/2023-05/COM_2023_623_1_EN.pdf.

European Commission. (2023d). *The impact of demographic changes in a changing environment.* Publication Office of the European Union, https://commission.europa.eu/system/files/2023-01/the_impact_of_demographic_change_in_a_changing_environment_2023.PDF.

Fanti, L., & Gori, L. (2009). Population and neoclassical economic growth: A new child policy perspective. *Economics Letters, 104*(1), 27–30.

Fougère, M., & Mérette, M. (1999). Population ageing and economic growth in seven OECD countries. *Economic Modelling, 16*(3), 411–427.

Garcia-Lazaro, A., & Pearce, N. (2023). Intangible capital, the labour share and national 'growth regimes'. *Journal of Comparative Economics, 51*(2), 674–695.

Harnphattananusorn, S., & Puttitanun, T. (2021). Generation gap and its impact on economic growth. *Heliyon, 7*(6), e07160.

Jie, H., Khan, I., Alharthi, M., Zafar, M. W., & Saeed, A. (2023). Sustainable energy policy, socio-economic development, and ecological footprint: The economic significance of natural resources, population growth, and industrial development. *Utilities Policy, 81*, 101490.

Malthus, T. R. (1798). *An essay on the principle of population* (History of Economic Thought Books). McMaster University Archive for the History of Economic Thought.

Ministry of Finance. (2023, December 31). *Evolution of financial flows between Romania and the European Union.* Ministry of Finance, https://mfinante.gov.ro/evolutia-fluxurilor-financiare-dintre-romania-si-ue.

National Bank of Romania. (2022, December). *Report on financial stability.* NBR, https://www.bnr.ro/PublicationDocuments.aspx?icid=19968.

Oxford Economics. (2023). *Human capital and productive employment creation.* Retrieved March 10, 2023, from https://www.oxfordeconomics.com/resource/human-capital-and-productive-employment-creation/

Peterson, E. (2017). The role of population in economic growth. *SAGE Open, 7*(4), 1–15.

Pilli, R., & Grassi, G. (2021). *Provision of technical and scientific support to DG ESTAT in relation to EU land footprint estimates and gap-filling techniques for European forest accounts (LAFO)*. Publications Office of the European Union.

Polyzos, E., Kuck, S., & Khadija, A. (2022). Demographic change and economic growth: The role of natural resources in the MENA region. *Research in Economics, 76*, 1–13.

Prato, T. (2012). Increasing resilience of natural protected areas to future climate change: A fuzzy adaptive management approach. *Ecological Modelling, 242*, 46–53.

Romanian Government. (2020). *National integrated plan for energy and climate change over the period 2021–2030*. Romanian Government, https://climate-laws.org/document/ romania-s-2021-2030-integrated-national-energy-and-climate-plan_20f8.

Romanian Government. (2021). *National strategy for employment 2021–2027 and action plan for the implementation of the strategy*. Romanian Government, https://mmun-cii.ro/j33/images/Documente/MMPS/SNOFM_2021-2027.pdf.

Roubini, N., & Bundy, R. (2023). *What climate finance needs*. Retrieved September 20, 2023, from https://www.project-syndicate.org/commentary/climate-finance-private-capital-new-financial-instruments-by-nouriel-roubini-and-reza-bundy-2023-09

Škare, M., & Lacmanović, S. (2015). Human capital and economic growth: A review essay. *Amfiteatru Economic Journal, 17*(39), 735–760.

Social Progress Imperative. (2023). *2022 Social Progress index*. Retrieved September 10, 2023, from https://www.socialprogress.org/global-index-2022-results/

Tanzila, S., Sima, R. D., & Tareque, M. (2022). Exploring the linkage between human capital and economic growth: A look at 141 developing and developed countries. *Economic Systems, 46*(3), 101017.

Temsumrit, N. (2023). Can aging population affect economic growth through the channel of government spending? *Heliyon, 9*(9), e19521.

UNCTAD. (2022). *World investment report*. UNCTAD, https://unctad.org/system/files/ official-document/wir2022_overview_en.pdf.

Vandeplas, A., Vanyolos, I., Vigani, M., & Vogel, L. (2022). *The possible implications of the green transition for the EU labour market*. EC DG ECFIN.

World Bank. (2020). *Markets and people. Romania country economic memorandum*. The World Bank Group, https://documents1.worldbank.org/curated/en/294831583173658317/ pdf/Markets-and-People-Romania-Country-Economic-Memorandum.pdf.

World Bank. (2023). *Diagnostic sistematic de țară actualizat – România*. The World Bank Group, https://www.worldbank.org/ro/country/romania/brief/consultations-roma-nia-systematic-country-diagnostic-update-2023.

World Economic Forum. (2023). *Future of jobs report 2023* [WEF Insight Report], https:// www3.weforum.org/docs/WEF_Future_of_Jobs_2023.pdf.

Zwysen, W. (2023, March). *Labour shortages – Turning away from bad jobs*. ETUI.

Appendix. Indicators for SWOT Analyses of Human Resources and Green Transition, 2007–2022.

No.	Indicators	UM	Year	Romania		EU 27 Levels		
				Level	Rank in EU 27	Minimum	Medium	Maximum
1	GDP per capita	Euro	2022	15,010	26	12,400 Bulgaria	35,210	119,230 Luxembourg
			2007	6,110	26	4,240 Bulgaria	24,550	78,310 Luxembourg
2	GDP per capita	Euro PPS	2022	27,138	23	20,683 Bulgaria	35,210	92,020 Luxembourg
			2007	10,817	26	9,964 Bulgaria	24,553	67,097 Luxembourg
3	Social Progress Index (2014, without Cyprus, Malta and Luxembourg)	Score (0–100)	2022	76.89	26	76.81 Bulgaria	84.76	90.54 Denmark
			2014	67.72	24	67.72 Romania-		87.37 Netherlands
4	Human Development Index	Score (0–1,000)	2021	0.821	26	0.795 Bulgaria	–	0.948 Denmark
			2007	0.837	27	0.837 Romania	–	0.965 Ireland
5	Government effectiveness	Score (0–100)	2021	47.60	26	47.12 Bulgaria		99.04 Denmark
			2007	44.17	27	44.17 Romania		99.51 Denmark
6	Corruption Perception Index	Score (0–100)	2022	46	25	42 Hungary	–	90 Denmark
			2007	37	27	37 Romania	–	94 Denmark

#	Indicator	Unit	Year	Value				
7	Total population	Million persons	2021	19.12	6	0.52 Malta	16.55	83.20 Germania
			2007	20.88	6	0.41 Malta	16.22	82.27 Germania
8	Population natural increase	Thousand persons	2021	−142.3	24	−301.1 Italy	−44.8	80.8 France
			2007	−37.2	25	−142.3 Germany	10.4	288.3 France
9	Net migration	Thousand persons	2021	−16.9	25	−160.3 Greece	32.2	310.3 Germany
			2007	−457.8	27	−457.8 Romania	45.7	776.4 Spain
10	Demographic dependency ratio (0–14 years) + (65 years and above)/(15–64 years)*100	%	2021	55.5	16	44.2 Luxembourg	56.5	62.5 France
			2007	46.2	12	39.3 Slovakia	48.7	53.5 France
11	Life expectancy at birth	Years	2021	72.8	26	71.4 Bulgaria	80.1	83.3 Spain
			2007	73.1	24	70.7 Lithuania	79.1	81.6 Italy
12	Active population (15–64 years)	Million persons	2022	8.19	7	0.29 Malta	7.79	42.35 Germany
			2007	9.48	6	0.17 Malta	7.52	40.99 Germany
13	Employed population (15–64 years)	Million persons	2022	8.19	7	0.29 Malta	7.79	42.35 Germany
			2007	8.84	6	0.16 Malta	6.95	37.40 Germany

(Continued)

Appendix   (*Continued*)

No.	Indicators	UM	Year	Romania		EU 27 Levels		
				Level	Rank in EU 27	Minimum	Medium	Maximum
14	Labor productivity (% of EU 27 average = 100.0)	%	2020	75.2	20	50.8 Bulgaria	100.0	213.7 Ireland
			2007	44.2	26	38.0 Bulgaria	100.0	179.7 Luxembourg
15	Employment rate (15–64 years)	%	2022	63.1	25	60.1 Italy	67.5	81.8 Netherlands
			2007	58.8	23	55.0 Malta	64.3	77.0 Denmark
16	Activity rate (15–64 years)	% in total population	2022	66.8	27	66.8 Romania	72.3	84.7 Netherlands
			2009	54.1	27	54.1 Romania	69.2	78.9 Sweden
17	Economic dependency (inactive population + unemployed)/(employed population)*100	%	2020	1.26	20	0.94 Netherlands	1.27	1.76 Greece
			2007	1.23	16	0.95 Denmark	1.29	1.62 Malta
18	Share of agriculture, forestry and fishery in total employed population	%	2022	21.1	27	0.7 Luxembourg	4.3	21.1 Romania
			2007	31.7	27	1.2 Luxembourg	6.2	31.7 Romania
19	Share of employees in total employed population (15 years and above)	%	2022	85.8	18	70.7 Greece	86.3	92.2 Denmark
			2007	66.3	26	64.7 Greece	82.5	92.8 Luxembourg

No	Indicator	Unit	Year					
20	Share of unpaid family workers in employed population* (15 years and above)	%	2022	2.7	26	0.0 Slovakia	1.0	2.9 Greece
			2007	1.6	27	0.0 Malta	2.0	12.6 Romania
21	Share of self-employed in total employed population (15 years and above)	%	2022	11.5	18	7.6 Denmark	13.1	26.3 Greece
			2007	21.2	24	7.0 Luxembourg	15.4	29.0 Greece
22	R&D personnel	Number (full-time equivalent)	2021	34,270	17	1,881 Malta	115,735	752,219 Germany
			2007	28,977	15	862 Malta	75,049	506,450 Germany
23	Share of R&D personnel in total employment	% (full-time equivalent)	2021	0.45	27	0.45 Romania	1.62	2.49 Austria
			2007	0.33	27	0.33 Romania	1.08	2.29 Finland
24	Minimum wage (in effect in 19 MS in 2007 and in 22 MS in 2023)	Euro	S1 2023	606.12	20	398.81 Bulgaria	1,108.0	2,387.4 Luxembourg
			S1 2007	115.27	18	92.03 Bulgaria	–	1,570.28 Luxembourg
25	Minimum wage	Euro PPS	S2-2022	943	18	653 Bulgaria	–	1,695 Luxembourg
			S2-2007	184	27	184 Romania	–	1,620 Luxembourg

(Continued)

Appendix   (*Continued*)

No.	Indicators	UM	Year	Romania		EU 27 Levels		
				Level	Rank in EU 27	Minimum	Medium	Maximum
26	Net income estimated on active life (45 years, own estimations based on net incomes of a single person, without children, earning an average net income of the economy)	Euro	2022	402,604	26	378,529 Bulgaria	1,176,098	2,143,784 Luxembourg
			2007	178,222	26	117,624 Bulgaria	687,123	1,472,740 Luxembourg
27	Average hourly labor cost in industry, constructions and services	Euro	2022	9.5	2	50.7 Luxembourg	30.5	8.2 Bulgaria
			2008	4.2	2	34.6 Denmark	21.6	2.6 Bulgaria
28	Support ratio for the public pension system (number of taxpayers for a pensioner)	Persons	2020	1.21	25	0.24 Denmark	1.59	2.78 Cyprus
29	Support ratio for the public pension system (number of taxpayers for a pensioner)	Persons	2040	0.86	26	0.10 Denmark	1.28	2.33 Cyprus

No	Indicator	Unit	Year	Value				
30	Unemployment rate (% of active population, 15–74 years)	%	2022	5.6	15	12.9 Spain	6.2	2.2 Czech Republic
			2007	6.4	14	11.1 Slovakia	7.5	3.8 Denmark
31	Long-term unemployment rate (% of active population, 15–74 years)*	%	2022	2.2	20	0.5 Denmark	2.4	7.7 Greece
			2007	3.2	18	0.6 Denmark	3.2	8.3 Slovakia
32	Youth unemployment rate (% of active population, 15–24 years)	%	2022	20.8	24	31.4 Greece	14.5	6.0 Germany
			2007	20.1	22	25.2 Croatia	16.0	7.5 Denmark
33	Personal remittances (between resident and non-resident households) (2020 – data for 23 MS, without Denmark, Germany, Malta, Portugal; 2007 – data for 24 MS, without Denmark, Spain, Portugal)	Million euro	2020	3,421.7	1	0 Ireland	–	3,421.7 Romania
			2012	2,286.7	2	0 Germany, Malta, Ireland	–	2,933.0 Spain

(Continued)

Appendix (*Continued*)

No.	Indicators	UM	Year	Romania		EU 27 Levels		
				Level	Rank in EU 27	Minimum	Medium	Maximum
34	Employed population in foreign-controlled enterprises (% in total employment)	%	2020	28.94	3	6.88 Cyprus	–	37.77 Luxembourg
			2008	22.22	6	4.65 Cyprus	–	35.25 Estonia
35	National wealth – human capital	Billion USD	2018	1,446	15	97 Malta	4,359	31,650 Germany
			2014	1,075	15	94 Malta	4,924	37,873 Germany
36	Average national wealth per capita – human capital	USD/per capita	2018	74,282	25	62,575 Bulgaria	231,363	448,126 Luxembourg
			2014	54,014	24	47,593 Bulgaria	290,421	881,629 Luxembourg
37	Share of human capital in intangible assets	%	2018	108	10	88 Luxembourg	–	155 Ireland
			2014	50	23	46 Greece	–	76 Ireland
38	Social protection expenditures	Euro/inhabitant	2020	2,027	26	1,661 Bulgaria	9,536	24,823 Luxembourg
			2007	811	26	577 Bulgaria	6,211	15,046 Luxembourg
39	People in extreme poverty (% in total population)*	%	2020	15.2	25	1.7 Luxembourg	–	19.4 Bulgaria
			2007	38.0	26	0.8 Luxembourg	–	57.6 Bulgaria

		Unit	Year				
40	People at risk of poverty and social exclusion (% in total population)*	%	2020	30.4	11.9 Czech Republic	—	32.1 Bulgaria
			2007	47.0	13.9 Sweden		60.7 Bulgaria
41	In-work poverty (persons aged 18 years and above)*	%	2020	14.9	3.1 Finland	9.4	14.9 Romania
			2007	17.4	3.3 Czech Republic		17.4 Romania
42	Percentage of incomes earned by the poorest 40% of households	%	2021	17.8	17.0 Bulgaria	21.3	25.5 Slovakia
			2007	16.5	16.5 Romania	—	25.3 Slovenia
43	Average health expenditures per capita	Euro/inhabitant	2021	690	603 Bulgaria	2,637	6,124 Luxembourg
			2007	223	174 Bulgaria	1,595	3,686 Luxembourg
44	Average pension expenditures per capita	Euro/inhabitant	2020	859	580 Bulgaria	3,658	8,580 Luxembourg
			2007	374	312 Bulgaria	—	6,840 Luxembourg
45	NEETs – share of young people aged 15–29 years who are neither in employment nor in education or training	%	2022	19.8	4.2 Netherlands	11.7	19.8 Romania
			2007	14.8	5.3 Denmark	13.2	20.3 Bulgaria

(Continued)

Appendix *(Continued)*

No.	Indicators	UM	Year	Romania		EU 27 Levels		
				Level	Rank in EU 27	Minimum	Medium	Maximum
46	Early school leaving (% of people aged 18–24 years)*	%	2022	15.6	27	2.3 Croatia	9.6	15.6 Romania
			2007	17.3	23	4.1 Slovenia	14.7	36.5 Portugal
47	Graduates in tertiary education (% of people aged 18–74 years)	%	2022	16.2	27	16.2 Romania	30.0	46.3 Luxembourg
			2007	9.8	27	9.8 Romania	19.3	30.4 Finland
48	Hiring rate of recent graduates (aged 20–34 years graduating the education system one to three years before the reference year) ISCED 3–8 (total)	%	2022	69.6	25	65.0 Italy	81.5	92.6 Luxembourg
			2007	79.2	21	65.9 Italy	79.3	93.0 Malta
49	Adult participation in long life learning (25–64 years)	%	2022	5.4	24	1.7 Bulgaria	11.9	36.2 Sweden
			2007	1.5	27	1.5 Romania	7.9	29.1 Denmark
50	Public expenditure for education	% of GDP	2021	3.2	26	3.0 Ireland	4.8	6.7 Sweden
			2007	3.9	24	3.6 Greece	4.7	6.3 Sweden

51	Public and private expenditures per student – ISCED 0 (2012 – without Greece; 2019 – without Estonia, Ireland, Slovenia and Greece)	Euro	2019	2,007	23	2,007 Romania	7,797	21,247 Luxembourg
			2012	617	26	617 Romania	5,164	17,880 Denmark
52	Public and private expenditures per student – ISCED 1–2 (2012 – without Croatia and Slovakia; 2019 – without Slovakia and Ireland)	Euro	2019	1,642	25	1,642 Romania	6,911	20,139 Luxembourg
			2012	774	25	774 Romania	6,039	18,063 Luxembourg
53	Public and private expenditures per student – ISCED 3–4 (2012 – without Greece and Italy; 2019 – without Ireland, Greece and Slovakia)	Euro	2019	2,065	23	1,745 Bulgaria	8,163	20,942 Luxembourg
			2012	821	25	821 Romania	–	18,206 Luxembourg

(Continued)

Appendix   (*Continued*)

| No. | Indicators | UM | Year | Romania | | EU 27 Levels | | |
				Level	Rank in EU 27	Minimum	Medium	Maximum
54	Public and private expenditures per student – ISCED 5–8 (2012 – without Denmark, Luxembourg, Croatia, Slovakia; 2019 – without Ireland and Slovakia)	Euro	2019	3,470	24	2,361 Greece	10,743	39,897 Luxembourg
			2012	1,873	22	1,790 Bulgaria	9,489	22,844 Sweden
55	Share of ICT sector in GDP (data missing for: 2008 – Belgium, Czech Rep., Ireland, Cyprus, Luxembourg, Netherlands, Poland and Sweden; 2020 – Ireland, Spain, Italy, Cyprus, Luxembourg and Netherlands)	%	2020	4.25	15	3.23 Greece	5.23	8.14 Malta
			2008	3.16	17	2.16 Lithuania	–	6.68 Malta
56	Share of households with internet access in total households	%	2022	89	23	85 Croatia	92	98 Netherlands
			2007	22	26	19 Bulgaria	53	83 Netherlands

No.	Indicator	Unit	Year					
57	Share of individuals using internet in the last year in total population	%	2022	77	25	64 Croatia	86	98 Netherlands
			2007	28	27	28 Romania	58	86 Netherlands
58	Internet broadband speed (download)	Mbps	2023	170	2	40 Cyprus		188 Denmark
			2016	55.7	1	7.3 Croatia		55.7 Romania
59	Share of ICT professionals in total employment	%	2020	2.7	26	1.7 Greece	3.1	4.9 Finland
			2007	2.1	26	1.2 Greece	2.4	4.1 Sweden
60	FDI (inland stock)	Billion USD	2021	108.7	17	20.2 Slovenia	429.3	2,576.2 Netherlands
			2007	60.9	15	10.9 Slovenia	229.3	952.2 Germany
61	Resources productivity (GDP/inland material consumption)	Euro/kg	2021	0.434	27	0.434 Romania	2.29	6.59 Netherlands
			2007	0.298	26	0.228 Bulgaria	1.42	3.22 Netherlands
62	Material import dependency (% of total inland material consumption)	%	2021	10.0	1	10.0 Romania	22.9	91.4 Luxembourg
			2007	11.1	1	11.1 Romania	21.8	87.2 Luxembourg
63	GHG emissions	Million tons	2021	67.2	18	2.4 Malta	122.7	781.7 Germany
			2007	120.8	18	3.1 Malta	156.3	974.5 Germany

(Continued)

Appendix (Continued)

No.	Indicators	UM	Year	Romania		EU 27 Levels		
				Level	Rank in EU 27	Minimum	Medium	Maximum
64	Average GHG emissions per capita	Tons/inhabitant	2021	3.5	2	0.7 Sweden	7.4	16.7 Luxembourg
			2007	5.9	2	5.5 Letonia	9.8	27.4 Luxembourg
65	Energy dependency (net imports/energy inland consumption)	%	2020	28.2	2	97.5 Malta	57.5	10.5 Estonia
			2007	31.5	4	99.9 Malta	57.2	24.3 Estonia
66	Share of renewable energy in energy final consumption	%	2021	23.6	11	12.2 Malta	21.8	62.6 Sweden
			2007	18.2	8	0.2 Malta	11.7	43.2 Sweden
67	Energy productivity (GDP/energy consumption)	Euro/kg oil equivalent	2021	5.3	18	2.4 Bulgaria	8.5	24.4 Ireland
			2007	3.2	25	1.8 Bulgaria	6.7	11.6 Denmark
68	Forests wood timber (without bark)	Million cm	2020	2,355	6	12 Cyprus	–	3,663 Germany
			2007	2,121	6	9 Cyprus	–	3,509 Germany
69	Recycling rate (waste recycled/total waste generated)	%	2021	1.4	27	1.4 Romania	11.7	33.8 Netherlands
			2010	3.5	20	1.2 Letonia	10.8	25.3 Netherlands
70	Total waste generated per capita	Tons/inhabitant	2020	7.4	21	1.5 Letonia	4.7	20.9 Finland
			2008	9.2	22	1.5 Letonia	4.9	22.4 Bulgaria

No	Indicator	Unit	Year					
71	Share of forested area in total country surface	%	2018	34.1	19		3.9 Malta	65.2 Finland
			2009	34.1	12		3.9 Malta	65.6 Finland
72	E governance – Individuals using Internet in interaction with public authorities (2020, without France)	% in total population	2021	11	27	47	11 Romania	91 Denmark
			2009	7	27	36	7 Romania	73 Denmark

Source: Based on Eurostat data and other reports or databases of international organizations (UNCTAD, World Bank, European Commission and International Labour Organization).

Chapter 4

Integration of the Foreign Workforce in Tirolean Companies

Sergej Vasic[a] and Jean Vasile Andrei[b,c]

[a]*MCI Innsbruck, Austria*
[b]*Petroleum-Gas University of Ploiesti, Romania*
[c]*National Institute for Economic Research "Costin C. Kiriţescu" –
Romanian Academy, Romania*

Abstract

This research aims to examine how decision-makers' demographic traits affect the integration of foreign workforce into Tirolean (Austria) companies. With continuous world migrations, Tirol experiences a great inflow of foreign workforce. While integrating into the workforce, the foreign workers interact with various decision-makers whose demographic traits (e.g., age, gender, nationality) potentially influence the success of the integration process. To gather data on the integration levels of a foreign workforce, the author conducted a questionnaire. Furthermore, several statistical analyses were run to determine if the relationship between demographic characteristics and integration success exists. The study reveals that demographic characteristics influence decision-makers' acceptance of expatriates, as well as their recruitment, integration, and training and development outcomes. The empirical results indicate the strength of relationships identified through analyses. The study is limited to geographical, as well as the scope of the sample size, as the data are obtained from Tirol only. In addition, the results from the study serve as a basis for future discussions and research.

Keywords: Workforce integration; foreign workforce; demographic characteristics; decision-makers; Tirol (Austria)

Entrepreneurship and Development for a Green Resilient Economy, 85–130
Copyright © 2024 by Sergej Vasic and Jean Vasile Andrei
Published under exclusive licence by Emerald Publishing Limited
doi:10.1108/978-1-83797-088-920241004

1. Introduction

The integration of migrant workers into local communities is a topic of growing importance in modern literature. Demographic factors of a national population often shape attitudes and behaviors toward foreign workers. Understanding the relationship between these factors and the integration process is critical for decision-makers who are seeking to promote inclusivity and diversity in domestic companies. This chapter aims to examine how the demographic factors of decision-makers from the Austrian region of Tirol impact the integration of migrant workers.

Migrations are common and ever-happening occurrences that represent the movements of people from one operating geographical area to another, better one, usually fostered by security threats, lack of job availability, or need for prosperity (Dubey & Mallah, 2015, p. 228). In the paper published in 2016, Carling and Talleraas (p. 6) offered a detailed elaboration on the root causes, drivers, and determinants of migration. The authors found the root causes of migration to be social and political conditions of the states that foster people's desire to move away (e.g., conflicts, repression, and poverty). Drivers of migration, on the other hand, as suggested by the authors, are the mechanisms that would eventually result in migration to happen (such as access to information), while the determinants are the ones that serve as explanations and predictions of the migration patterns (e.g., the difference in net incomes) (Carling & Talleraas, 2016, p. 6; Simpson, 2022, p. 3). Further research suggests that, apart from social and political reasons, causes of migrations can similarly be found in environmental occurrences (for instance, rises of the sea) (Hauer et al., 2019, p. 35). Hauer et al. (2019) suggest that due to the climate changes – fostered by the increase in the emission of greenhouse gases – sea levels rise hazardously creating a direct threat to humans, resulting in so-called climate migrations (p. 35). Whether voluntary – people willingly moving to seek prosperity in other geographical areas – or forced – people were given no other choice but to leave their domicile – migrations are a heated topic and are of great research interest to scholars worldwide (De Haas, 2021, p. 32).

Research carried out by the United Nations (UN) provided a comparison between the international migrant stock data and revealed that, historically, Europe was the continent that experienced one of the greatest increases in migration levels (United Nations, 2020). The complete summary of findings by the UN is presented in Table 4.1 which offers a numerical representation of how the number of expatriates worldwide was varying from 1990 to 2020. The table also breaks the overall world estimates into smaller geographical units enabling supplementary comparisons. As observed in the table, the greatest inflow of refugees in the period between the final decade of the previous century and 2020 was in Asia and Europe (both more than 30 million). Less significant increases were noted in regions of Latin America and Caribbeans (slightly less than 7.7 million) and Oceania (slightly less than 5 million).

As reported by the International Labor Organization (ILO), the overall number of expatriates worldwide surpassed 280 million in 2020. Out of this number, 245 million people were of working age (15 years of age and older). Moreover,

Table 4.1.   International Migration Stock at Area of Destination, 1990–2020.

Region	1990	1995	2000	2005	2010	2015	2020
Africa	15,689,666	16,357,077	15,051,677	16,040,087	17,806,677	22,860,792	25,389,464
Asia	48,209,949	46,418,044	49,066,986	53,249,787	66,123,640	77,191,249	85,618,502
Europe	49,608,225	53,489,827	56,858,793	63,585,731	70,627,160	74,759,083	86,706,068
Latin America and Caribbean	7,135,971	6,661,553	6,539,738	7,184,113	8,326,588	9,441,503	14,794,623
Northern America	27,610,408	33,340,948	40,351,710	45,363,089	50,970,524	55,633,741	58,708,795
Oceania	4,731,938	5,022,527	5,361,681	6,024,021	7,128,598	8,072,276	9,380,653
World	152,986,157	161,289,976	173,230,585	191,446,828	220,983,187	247,958,644	280,598,105

Note. Reprinted from *International Migrant Stock 2020* by United Nations Department of Economic and Social Affairs, Population Division (2020). Copyright © 2020 by UN, made available under a Creative Commons license CC BY 3.0 IGO.

it is estimated that most international foreign workers – approximately 63.8 million or 37.7% – still found their haven in Europe (ILO, 2021). One of the most prominent reasons why expatriates choose Europe over the other continents is the open borders of the Schengen area (Geddes et al., 2020, p. 1). According to Votoupalová (2018, pp. 415–416), Schengen is presented as a project of the European Union (EU), which enables the borderless movement of individuals and goods within the EU member states. Therefore, it comes as no surprise that the member countries of the EU are experiencing a constant inflow of third-country nationals (TCNs) (EUROSTAT, 2021). Out of the total number of expatriates in Europe, roughly 61.2 million foreigners – out of which 23.7 million were non-EU citizens and the other 37.5 million people were born outside of the union – decided to seek habitat in one of the EU member states (European Commission, 2022). The Statistical Office of the EU further reports that, on the first of January 2021, EU and Norway were hosting 23.9 million TCNs, which represented 5.3% of the total population (EUROSTAT, 2021, p. 9). The holders of valid residence permits stated that the main reasons for applying for the EU permits were due to family reasons (39%), work opportunities (17%), asylum (9%), education (3%), or other (32%) (European Commission, 2022).

Once in the country, expatriates start the process of integration into the new environment. According to De Haas et al. (as cited in van Riemsdijk & Basford, 2022, p. 634), integration consists of the successful adoption of social and cultural norms which would enable the newcomers to completely "blend into" but not change the host society. A study carried out among Chinese adult migrants showed that successful foreigner integration is positively related to life satisfaction and psychological well-being (Xia & Ma, 2020, pp. 14–15). As life satisfaction is in direct relationship with the job performance of a worker (Kumar et al., 2021, pp. 6318–6319), there is a strong need for the effective incorporation of foreigners into society, creating a positive impact on their life satisfaction and, thus, job performance. That the incorporation of expatriates must not be just effective but also quick is best seen through the phenomenon of the aging population that Europe is currently facing. The study carried out by Jakovljevic et al. (2018, p. 3) predicted that the median age of the population in the EU will rise from 31.4 back in 1950, to 48.0 in 2050. At the same time, the overall number of expatriates is expected to grow by more than four times. Therefore, the rising demographic need for expatriates in Europe is notable. Although necessary, the integration of expatriates into the workforce must be executed with great care. The study carried out by Marois et al. (2020, pp. 7694–7695) showed that, without assuring a proper education, the integration of a foreign workforce could have a destructive effect and result in increased economic dependency. Therefore, one could argue that well-educated foreign workers are at a great advantage while undertaking the process of integration in Europe.

However, when it comes to successful integration into the workforce, foreign workers are not the only parties involved in this process. A significant role in their integration plays the decision-makers whose tasks range from selecting and training the candidates, aiming toward sustainable competitiveness of the company, to developing and maintaining the mental and physical well-being of employees (Peiris, 2021, pp. 72–73). Just like any human being, decision-makers – in this paper defined as "all parties involved in the integration processes of the newcomers in the companies" – are prone to bias and can be affected by certain traits of their personas. Research conducted by Zhang et al. (2022, p. 12) shows that social attitudes and the perception of fairness of Chinese decision-makers can significantly impact the integration of expatriates in rural areas of that country. Furthermore, Farashah and Blomquist (2019) observed that the demographic/individual traits of decision-makers are directly affecting their attitudes toward the expatriates while undertaking the process of integration. Therefore, according to the authors, apart from fulfilling the necessary criteria for unhindered inclusion into the working environment (i.e., language requirements or job techniques), expatriates furthermore need to discern the culture and demographical traits of their superiors (Farashah & Blomquist, 2019, p. 30). Keeping in mind the findings of the mentioned paper, consequently, this chapter aims to further investigate demographic factors and inspect how they affect the foreign workforce integration process in companies.

According to the data from Statistics Austria, in the final quarter of 2022, around 2.35 million people with a migration background lived in Austria. At this time, this number accounted for 26.1% of the total Austrian population, which further represented an increase of 4.9% in immigration levels between 2021 and 2022 (Statistik.at, 2023). The report shows that the majority of expatriates originate from European – Germany, Turkey, or the Balkans – or Middle Eastern regions (Syria) (Statistik.at, 2022). As of mid-2022, the estimates were that the Austrian capital – Vienna – alone hosted more than 73,000 refugees from Ukraine who fled their homeland due to ongoing conflicts (Kohlenberger et al., 2022). That Vienna is not merely a haven for Ukrainian, but the expatriates from other nations as well, shows the reports according to which, at the end of 2022, out of 2.35 million foreigners in Austria, the region of Vienna (including the capital city) hosted nearly 678,866 foreigners (roughly 34.2% of the total foreign population) out of which, only 5.1% were born in Austria (City of Vienna, 2023). After Vienna, on the list of the most desired regions in Austria, their place found Upper Austria (310,000 or 13.9%), Lower Austria (283,200 or 12.6%), and Styria (191,500 or 8.5%). With the steady annual rise of foreigners (Table 4.2), Tirol region ranks fifth in the number of foreigners with 139,700 people being of non-Austrian origin (18.1% of the entire population of Tirol) (Mohr, 2023). This number may come as a surprise to some, as the region of Tirol has been one of the top European destinations for both winter and summer tourism in Europe. With more than 5,600 hotels only, Tirol represents an important contributor to the Austrian economy, as well as a splendid provider of jobs in areas of hospitality and tourism (WKO.at, 2021, p. 30). Apart from the two mentioned industries, a substantial proportion of the Tirolean population is employed in financial sectors, the food industry, real estate, mechanical engineering, and other branches (WKO.at, 2023). Due to the vast variety of available industries, and its openness to expatriates, the region of Tirol will be further investigated in this chapter.

Table 4.2. Number of Foreigners in Tirol from 2015 to 2023.

	2015	2016	2017	2018	2019	2020	2021	2022	2023
N	95.776	105.402	111.626	116.445	120.322	123.887	127.214	131.287	139.700
%	13.1	14.3	15	15.5	15.9	16.4	16.7	17.2	18.1

Note. Percentual and numerical visualization of proportion of expatriates living in Tirol between 2015 and 2023. Numerical data from *Demografische Daten Tirol 2021* (p. 26) by Amt der Tiroler Landesregierung, 2022 . Copyright 2022 by Amt der Tiroler Landesregierung. Percentual data from *Anteil der Ausländer an der Bevölkerung in Tirol von 2013 bis 2023* by Statistik Austria (2023). Copyright 2023 by Statistik Austria.

As mentioned previously, most foreigners in Tirol are originating from non-EU and/or countries whose native language is other than German. Hence, the language barrier represents the first obstacle to successful integration into the working force (Risberg & Romani, 2022, p. 12). Moreover, the lack of business and industry knowledge of expatriates may cause hurdles while undergoing the integration process (Enderwick, 2011, p. 91). Furthermore, scarcity of bureaucratic awareness, legal, and cultural norms can stand in the expatriates' way toward successful integration (Tanrıkulu, 2020, p. 375). However, keeping in mind the findings from the previously mentioned paper by Farashah and Blomquist (2019), the greatest obstacle, as well as the opportunity that dictates the triumph of the integration processes, is the decision-makers' attitudes toward the foreign workforce. Consequently, with the focus on this specific geographic region, the research question follows: "How do different demographic factors of Tirolean[1] decision-makers affect the integration of the foreign workforce in that region?"

This chapter starts with an introduction to the topic followed by an explanation of the theoretical and managerial contributions of the findings. This chapter continues with the summary of the information already provided in the existing literature and is followed by the methodology section which describes the data collection process as well as the models applied in the study. The results section relates to data description and analysis, while the discussion serves to draw comparisons between the findings of this study and the studies carried out by other scholars. Moreover, it offers suggestions for future analyses as well as outlines the limitations of this chapter. This chapter ends with the conclusions on the findings, as well as the additional research-relevant materials indicated in the appendices.

2. Contributions and Aims of the Research

The main purpose of this chapter is to identify and discuss how different demographic characteristics affect the integration of foreign workers into the Tirolean workforce. As mentioned previously, demographic traits of decision-makers tend to influence decision-makers' expectations of the values expatriates should possess, making the whole integration process additionally perplexing (Farashah &

---

[1]The Austrian region of Tirol.

Blomquist, 2019, p. 31). Therefore, there is a strong need for additional research on this topic, and shedding light on the obstacles that may occur unintentionally due to the lack of awareness of one's demographic influences. The Austrian region of Tirol is chosen due to its openness to foreign workers, as well as the lack of research available for that region. The findings contribute to the science of Tirolean-based companies and emphasize the importance that must be attached to the issue of integration of expatriates, bearing in mind the increasing influx of both economic migrants and refugees in that country.

2.1. Managerial Contributions

The managerial relevance of the proposed chapter is in the clear elaboration of the ways demographic traits influence the decision-making process while assisting the integration of foreigners. As demographic characteristics are universal but person specific and tend to impact one's preferences and choices (Biresselioglu et al., 2018, p. 9), it is important to emphasize that the results of this chapter are not intended to criticize mentalities. They should, however, enable decision-makers to gain insight into how their demographic traits affect their performance while working in a multi-diverse environment, as well as provide an understanding of how demographic traits affect the effectiveness of the integration outcomes in their company. As most of the studies focus on the demographic traits of expatriates themself neglecting the others involved in the integration process (Farashah & Blomquist, 2019, p. 18), throughout this study, managers will gain an insight into how their traits affect their way of operating in a business environment. As mentioned previously, due to the different backgrounds they come from, foreign workers need quick and effective onboarding processes. Throughout this chapter, the examination of the effectiveness of onboarding processes from a managerial point of view takes place and aims for discovering – as well as clarifying – the trends that arose from the meticulous inputs of decision-makers. Through those trends, decision-makers are enabled to improve their learning curve and develop abilities that could not just shape the business environment of the expatriates but offer great job satisfaction for the workforce as well. Thus, this study contributes to the awareness of decision-makers and supports them further in taking the necessary means to establish effectiveness and speed while onboarding, yet not hindering the satisfaction of the workers.

2.2. Theoretical Contributions

Although the topic of factors affecting foreign workforce integrations in the workforce has already been explored to some extent, there is still a significant research gap when it comes to offering and exploring the organizational and managerial perspective on the topic (Farashah & Blomquist, 2019, p. 18). As stated previously, the existing literature on the topic mostly focuses on discussion and identifying the expatriates' demographic traits, often ignoring the decision-makers' (Farashah & Blomquist, 2019, p. 18). Therefore, as they are key to successful integration, it is vital to emphasize and elaborate on the influence of demographic characteristics of decision-makers – for example, CEOs, general managers, human resource managers, etc. – on decision-making processes. By offering a novel perspective on the topic, this chapter supports the enrichment of the existing theory and inspires future research. Moreover, the research gap in investigating the geographical area of the study was identified. As the focus of this chapter is on Tirol – which is a region largely interested in R&D practices (Ecker et al., 2022, pp. 47–48) – findings of this chapter will enable researchers and scholars to draw conclusions and make comparisons between different European regions/countries which could further enhance the future studies of the topic. The author believes that, by offering an original viewpoint on the region, Tirol may become an inspiring geographical region for further research. Therefore, this chapter does not just offer valuable managerial insights and literature inputs to the topic but serves as a valuable foundation for the future continuation of the research and development of existing literature associated not just with the topic of foreign workforce integration, but also the region investigated.

3. Literature Review

3.1. Identification of Factors

To support workforce integration, companies invest greatly in the provision of intercultural and language training to develop and promote cultural awareness and empathy between native-born and foreign workers (Malik & Manroop, 2017, p. 394). As foreigners are a part of the workforce striving toward the success of the business, it is of vital importance not just to create a sense of belonging among them but also reduce uncertainties of any kind and enhance their self-esteem (Grosskopf et al., 2021, p. 1896). Various studies show that, by experiencing a strong sense of affinity, expatriates are not only motivated to remain in their job positions but also encouraged to show their full potential and progress faster (Grosskopf et al., 2021, p. 1896; Ortlieb & Ressi, 2022, p. 198). Additionally, Hafsi and Turgut (2012, p. 475) claim that foreign workers bring novel perspectives and ideas to the team, care about the environment, and strive toward the reduction of ineffective transport, while Tihanyi et al. (2005, p. 279) report that foreign board members support the greater access to social networks, nurture international competencies, and cultural diversity (as cited in Beji et al., 2020, p. 143). However, for expatriates to become a part of the team in the first place – and later further progress – studies suggest that the responsibility is on decision-makers to pay close attention to encouraging the workers to apply their knowledge in driving their performance, as much as the business one (Ibidunni, 2020, p. 89). Even though the support of foreign workers in their successful integration and further self- and business development may come across as common sense, it is not always the case.

According to the research conducted by van Riemsdijk and Basford (2022), it is not unusual that integration measures often lack regulatory standards, creating the integration processes unevenly. Authors suggest that a lack of assistance with housing, bureaucratic, and personal issues can be a major cause of the early departure of international hires (van Riemsdijk & Basford, 2022, pp. 645–646). However, despite being common, language and regulatory barriers are not the most arduous ones expatriates face. Research suggests that one of the greatest obstacles to the successful integration of foreigners into the domestic force lies in those who are directly responsible and have the power to influence the integration outcomes – the decision-makers (Basford & van Riemsdijk, 2015, p. 11). In their study on the barrier to inclusion in Dutch companies, Knappert et al. (2019, pp. 42–43) depict managers' bias and stereotypes toward refugees, as well as the never-diminishing "refugee" label as the main issue toward the integration. Bias and stereotypes are considered destructive occurrences that tend to influence humans in exhibiting unrealistic behaviors toward their associates (Hristov et al., 2022, p. 1129). Therefore, in such a combination of unrealistic behaviors and labeling, expatriates would not only be disabled to receive a sense of equality with the rest of the workers but would likewise be under constant anguish knowing that they are considered "different." Hence, it comes as no surprise that certain business environments implicitly depict refugees as a threat to the organizations they are working in and choose not to engage with them at all (Risberg & Romani, 2022, p. 20).

To get to the heart of the matter, scholars join forces to investigate the causes of bias occurring in managers' decision-making processes which ultimately affect their business actions and attitudes (Mehrabi et al., 2021, p. 26). Various studies revealed that one of the main reasons for the occurrence of bias – which, as stated previously, lead to unsuccessful integration processes – lies in decision-makers' demographic traits that are in direct relationship with their decision-making processes (Ashikali & Groeneveld, 2013; Yadav & Lenka, 2020; Zikic, 2014). As suggested by Bleijenbergh et al. (2010, p. 417), demographic characteristics are those that make individuals perceive themselves as similar or different. Authors further claim that associating oneself differently from others leads to a lack of trust and synergy in the workplace while fostering the creation of subgroups of "alike" individuals. The creation of subgroups, according to the study, finally results in a paucity of effectiveness in the workplace, as these groups withdraw themselves from cooperation despite being in the same team (Bleijenbergh et al., 2010, p. 417). Similar can be concluded in the case of decision-makers' attitudes to migrant integration – namely, due to being treated as a part of the subgroup, the laborious integration processes result in unpleasing outcomes for expatriates (Hristov et al., 2022, p. 1129). Conclusively, the root causes of the above-mentioned intricating relationships are nothing more than the bias and stereotypes that are directly affecting the behavioral and decision-making processes of those in charge of expatriates' integration.

Despite triggering the creation of bias, not all demographic characteristics are in a direct relationship with the decision-making processes (Bulog, 2016, p. 399). As the most common demographic factors affecting one's behavior and decisions, researchers often list and explore gender, origin, and age, while regularly excluding factors such as sexual orientation, religion, disabilities, education, and others (Yadav & Lenka, 2020, p. 15). Following the findings of previous studies, the author used *age*, *gender*, and *origin* as the focus of this chapter and investigates how these three demographic characteristics affect Tirolean decision-makers while integrating foreign workforce into their companies. More specifically, variables *recruitment, integration*, as well as *training and development* of expatriates served as the main determinants of expatriates' overall (un)successful integration and investigated the influence of the above-mentioned demographic characteristics on them.

3.2. Gender

Following the assumption that female decision-makers behave differently from male ones (Adams & Ferreira, 2009, p. 307), it comes as no surprise that the gender of the decision-makers is one of the most widely explored demographic traits in literature. Various studies investigated the relationship between the gender of the decision-makers and the performance of their companies, frequently finding a link between the two variables (Adams & Ferreira, 2009; Liu et al., 2014). The focus of the researchers was not only on emphasizing the positive impact that female decision-makers have on business performance (Moreno-Gómez et al., 2018, p. 116) but also on praising the benefits of gender-diverse boards and their positive effect on the overall firms' effectiveness (Adams & Ferreira, 2009, p. 307).

Despite the positive impact female decision-makers create on the company's performance, their engagement in the boardroom is still a topic of constant discussion among researchers. Studies carried out at the end of the last century revealed that female decision-makers were mostly unsuccessful in attempts to take a part of the boardrooms of large enterprises, having to satisfy themselves with engagement in mostly small- or medium-sized companies (Nakamura, 1996, p. 77). Regardless of the significant progress created – and is still being created – in that sense over the last decade (Kılıç & Kuzey, 2016, p. 450), gender-discriminatory practices remain prevalent in the boardrooms of certain European-based companies (Sekkat et al., 2015, p. 20).

Evidence from companies that do not tolerate gender discrimination has shown that female decision-makers contribute greatly to the financial, social, and environmental outcomes of their businesses (Galletta et al., 2021, p. 170). Galletta et al. (2021, p. 171) further suggest that those contributions arise from the great business efficiency of female decision-makers directly attributable to the excellence in their soft skills (namely, socialization, communication, networking, and others) as well as emotional intelligence. Research carried out by Cabello et al. (2016, p. 1489) revealed that emotional intelligence abilities – often referred to as an "ability to reason about emotion" and linked to motivation, delight, or pride (Mayer et al., 2008, p. 509) – prevail in female decision-makers, meaning that female decision-makers tend to have a greater awareness and control of their emotions, as well as the emotions of others. The study by Graves and Powell (1996, pp. 254–256) suggests that, due to their greater emotional abilities, female recruiters often receive better outcomes during interviews and communication with employees, than male ones do. Moreover, research has shown that female decision-makers exercise stronger collegial support for work–life integration which leads to greater career satisfaction (Johnson et al., 2020, pp. 747–749). Apart from collegial support, females – oppositely to males – exhibit a greater amount of sympathy and solidarity toward one another (Crowder-Meyer, 2013, p. 409). Additionally, the diversity of decision-makers nurtures support and encourages work motivation, which further plays a significant role in the recruitment and integration of the workforce and positively contributes to the workforce's training and development processes (Bae et al., 2019, p. 579; Haque & Oino, 2019, p. 179).

Although research on the topic is scarce for both genders (Ortlieb & Ressi, 2022, p. 14), some indicators of gender affecting the attitudes toward the foreign workforce have been identified but not yet in-depth explored (Farashah & Blomquist, 2019, p. 29). Despite the findings of Farashah and Blomquist (2019, pp. 27–29) that female managers – in comparison to male ones – are displaying more negative attitudes toward the migrant workforce, the current literature does not provide enough evidence on the role of decision-makers in employee assessment and the characteristics of decision-makers that would further impact those assessments (Castilla, 2011, p. 686). One of the possible reasons for hurdles in concluding those remarks may be due to the values and conservation levels of gender-diverse managers. The study carried out by Schwartz and Rubel (2005, p. 1020) revealed that the conservation levels are prevalent in female decision-makers (in comparison to male ones), as females tend to put a greater emphasis on tradition, security, and conformity. However, the literature remains limited beyond the mentioned findings. Throughout the research process, several research gaps ranging from the attitudes of gender-diverse decision-makers toward recruitment of expatriates, expatriates' integration into the domestic workforce, and training and development opportunities for newcomers were identified. Considering the scarcity of the data provided, and the results of the previous studies, the first hypothesis follows: "*H1*: There is a relationship between the gender of the decision-makers and the foreign workforce integration." Consequently, the null hypothesis states that there is no relationship between the gender of decision-makers and foreign workforce integration.

3.3. Age

Throughout the studies, age appears as one of the factors that is most likely to impact the emotional and intelligence quotient of an individual (Cabello et al., 2016, pp. 1486–1492; Kim, 2020, p. 15). Studies on the topic do not only aim to draw a line between different generations of decision-makers but also to explain how age differences affect their business performance. Among the other researchers, Prufeta (2017) and Ackert et al. (2020) (as cited in Kim, 2020, p. 7), prove that age, together with emotional and intelligence quotients, has a direct effect on the performance of an individual. Consequently, research reveals that the emotional and intelligence quotient – often described as a set of principles enabling rational and logical thinking as well as problem-solving (Selman et al., 2011, p. 24) – impact various aspects of decision-makers' tasks, ranging from recruitment, all the way to change adoption and decision-making (Kim, 2020, pp. 15–16).

As emotional capabilities develop over time, middle-aged adults (Generation X) score higher in the evaluation of emotional intelligence but score lower in a general understanding of emotions (Cabello et al., 2016, pp. 1486–1492). Various papers published on this topic revealed that Generation X (group between 41 and 56 years of age) tends to be more motivated by their beliefs in comparison to 'Baby Boomers' and Generation Y (Ali et al., 2022, p. 9; Kump, 2021, p. 8). In other words, middle-aged decision-makers tend to stay stronger in containing emotions while carrying out business tasks but fail to identify them properly. Furthermore, Severo et al. (2018, p. 98) suggest that 'Baby Boomers' tend to be more conservative and pay closer attention to the quality of life (as cited in Severo et al., 2021, p. 11). In terms of the change adoption, studies have shown that companies run by younger managers tend to exhibit greater acceptance of the change to their strategies, while the companies managed by 'Baby Boomers' undergo minimal to no change at all (Wiersema & Bantel, 1992, pp. 1991–1992). One of the potential explanations for this phenomenon lies in the effectiveness of decision-making processes. Evidence from the last century indicates that the age of decision-makers is in direct association with their tendency to seek further information while deciding (Taylor, 1975, p. 1974). Consequently, research suggests that, due to these reasons, senior managers require more time to evaluate aspects necessary and reach a decision. On the contrary, younger managers seldom exhibit such behavior as they generally spend less time evaluating the options, which results in faster decision-making. Taylor (1975, p. 1974) further suggests that confidence and personal bias could potentially be the main triggers causing the uneven pace of the decision-making process.

The pace of overcoming and effectiveness of dealing with personal bias changes with age (Gonsalkorale et al., 2009, p. 413). Gonsalkorale et al. (2009, p. 413) suggest that the prejudices in senior decision-makers tend to have a greater impact on their business performance than is the case with the younger generation of decision-makers. Younger decision-makers are often perceived as more motivated and enabling, not just for the greater engagement with their team members frequently but also for acceptance and encouragement of the changes (Weiss & Weiss, 2019, p. 276). Consequently, the level of bias and prejudice toward novelty is prevalent among the senior, while exceptional among the younger decision-makers. Research on the age-related differences across the adult lifespan carried out by Grühn et al. (2010, pp. 496–497) further reveals that younger decision-makers characterize happiness and a positive mindset – in comparison to the senior ones – which results in lower selectivity of business and private associates. Thus, due to the high conservation values, and bias, it is expected that less favorable attitudes among the senior generation concerning the acceptance and support of foreign workers arise (Farashah & Blomquist, 2019, p. 12).

Despite a research gap on the topic, some studies examined how the age of the decision-makers affects the attitudes toward integration and acceptance of the migrant workforce. The study carried out among Anglo-Australian decision-makers revealed that the concern about expatriates' integration into the workforce rises as the decision-maker matures (Fernando et al., 2016, p. 18). This attitude may be attributable to the tendency of senior decision-makers to be more reluctant to change and novelty-acceptance. This claim is further supported by the findings of Farashah and Blomquist (2019, p. 30) who suggest that the more senior decision-makers – contrary to the younger ones – pay more attention to the language proficiency of newcomers, their lifestyle commitments, as well as tend to demand higher human capital. Over and beyond, the theoretical and empirical literature remains scarce on the topic on both global and Austrian levels (Goll & Rasheed, 2005, p. 1017). As already mentioned, despite evidence that age is in direct relationship with the level of bias, which further influences the way a person believes and makes decisions (Farashah & Blomquist, 2019; Fernando et al., 2016; Kim, 2020), there is still a strong need for further research. Therefore, the second hypothesis follows: "*H2*: There is a relationship between the age of a decision-maker and foreign workforce integration." The second null hypothesis disapproves of the existence of relationships between the respective variables.

3.4. Origin

Upon arrival in their country of choice, expatriates encounter novel living and working conditions which, if perceived negatively, may leave acute consequences on their future work and integration into domestic companies (Xypolytas, 2018, p. 646). Despite the assumption that the highly skilled foreign workforce is generally welcomed into domestic companies (Hainmueller & Hiscox, 2010, p. 79), research reveals that there are still high levels of discrimination against expatriates while attempting integration. To avoid the escalation of far greater integration challenges, decision-makers – whose responsibilities range from identifying the causes of the tensions, and understanding their consequences, to valuing and nurturing diversity – oftentimes invest greatly into fostering the acceptance of the foreign workforce (van Riemsdijk & Basford, 2022, p. 648). Despite the efforts, a considerable portion of integration measures fails to be established successfully. Hainmueller and Hiscox (2010) reveal that among the other triggers for discrimination – such as bias, prejudice, and stereotypes – injustice toward foreigners is often rooted in the specific demographic trait of decision-makers and associates of the workforce – the origin (p. 79). Research carried out by Li and Frenkel (2016) further revealed that the origin of the decision-maker influences not just human resource practices toward the foreign workforce but also the interactions between the supervisors and subordinates, as well as subordinates' engagement in the workplace (pp. 2386–2387). Therefore, it is logical to assume that the success of expatriates lies in whether the decision-maker is likewise of foreign roots or belongs to the domestic population.

Most of the time, foreigners first bond with the people of their origin. Research carried out by Ryan and Mulholland (2013) (as cited in Wessendorf & Phillimore, 2018, p. 135), showed that the high-skilled French researchers living in Great Britain tend to have difficulties bonding with the native population and choose to make acquaintances with the French natives instead. Apart from the obvious reasons for the social exclusion of highly skilled expatriates – that is, language barriers, discrimination, etc. – Horverak et al. (2013, p. 273) revealed that decision-makers tend to associate expatriates with threats to the company, either linked to one's security or the fear of expatriates replacing the domestic workers in the workforce. Therefore, expatriates tend to remain closer to people of their origin, frequently completely disengaging with the domestic population. As the main source of income for the foreign workforce are the given jobs, to diminish the risk of poverty and social exclusion (McGinnity et al., 2020, p. viii), foreigners tend to behave similarly while searching for/offering employment.

However, studies by van Riemsdijk and Basford (2022, p. 648) reveal that this level of social exclusion accompanied by the fear of foreigners is mostly discerned in companies under the supervision of a non-foreign decision-maker. Research suggests that foreign-born decision-makers do not merely exhibit a positive attitude toward the foreign workforce but also invest in expatriates' adaptation more than the domestic-born ones do (Farashah & Blomquist, 2019, p. 27; van Riemsdijk & Basford, 2022, p. 649). Moreover, Åslund et al. (2014) have shown that foreign-born managers tend to easily bond to and recruit foreign-born workers. Furthermore, the authors claim that, on average, foreign-born managers hire 21% of foreign workers while, in comparison, natives hire only 6% (p. 408). Evidence from Turkey suggests that Turkish native managers are more likely to hire native Turkish candidates over foreign ones, even if the Turkish candidate may be of a lower skill set than the foreign one (Horverak et al., 2013, p. 272). However, for migrants' integration to be successful, even though advantageous, both supervisor and subordinate do not need to be from the same country of origin. Interestingly, the researchers found that more than half of the foreign workforce in Sweden hired by foreign-born managers do not originate from the same country as their managers (Åslund et al., 2014, p. 413). Therefore, by purely sharing the mutual experiences with expatriates, or simply having interacted with the foreign workforce during their professional career (Åslund et al., 2014, pp. 421–424), decision-makers abolish the sense of threat and embrace expatriates into their working force, even if the discrepancies between the skill sets of foreign and domestic workers prevail.

Throughout the research, it became obvious that the acceptance of foreign-born workers is positively associated with foreign-born decision-makers (Farashah & Blomquist, 2019, p. 27) who recruit, hire, and support expatriates more frequently than the natives do. However, current literature, even though scarce, imposes criticism of the effects these acceptance practices have. In their research on drivers of recruitment of foreigners into business organizations, Lämsä et al. (2019) stressed the importance of awareness foreign-born managers must possess while promoting the employment of foreign-born workers in their companies (p. 671). The study carried out by Den Butter et al. (2004) revealed that foreign-born workers deploy greater levels of productivity when employed by foreign-born managers. The authors do not only support the concept of easy access of expatriates to the organization managed by foreigners but also identify higher rewards and lack of often-mandatory quality verifications, which as a result have decreased poverty and greater life satisfaction (p. 21). However, the authors further claim that, by being surrounded by people of their origin, the development of expatriates stagnates (especially the adoption of the language of the nation they work in) and lacks native work ethics and networking which, as a result, can negatively influence the company they work in (Den Butter et al., 2004, pp. 22–23).

Despite continuous battles of scholars and researchers to examine and explain the relationship between the origin of decision-makers and expatriates' integration outcomes, the egocentricity of the existing literature requires future research to be carried out on the topic. Namely, the already-scarce literature sets its focus solely on migrants' origins while neglecting the decision-makers'. Also, it excludes the evaluation of remaining human resource practices apart from the integration (e.g., training and development, recruitment, etc.) (van Riemsdijk & Basford, 2022, p. 32). Thus, to tackle the mentioned segments avoided in the existing literature, the third hypothesis follows: "*H3*: There is a relationship between the origin of the decision-makers and the foreign workforce integration." Respectively, the third null hypothesis supports no relationship between the two variables.

4. Methodology

4.1. Sample Selection

As the Austrian region Tirol experienced a great influx of migrant workforce in the period between 2020 and 2023, this region served as the focus of this study. The process of reaching out to the decision-makers with the purpose of data collection started by browsing online data platforms – such as LinkedIn, karriere. at, and firmenabc.at. Great care was given in choosing the population size – and sample size, respectively – as too narrow size may impact the reliability of the study, as well as shrink the number of statistical analyses that could be carried out (Fok et al., 2015, p. 944). Therefore, this chapter does not differentiate between "decision-makers" – for example, general managers, human resource managers, CEOs, etc. – as such differentiation would further narrow the already limited population size. With identical reasoning, this chapter also does not differentiate between the industries in which decision-makers operate. These two aspects exempted in this study could serve as a profound inspiration for future research.

Out of the population of 10,000 decision-makers – whose contact information was publicly listed on online channels and could, in theory, be reached – the questionnaires were distributed to 500 randomly selected decision-makers. It is important to emphasize that the exclusion criteria for the sampling were in correspondence to the companies those decision-makers work in. Namely, each decision-maker represented one company only. Therefore, all decision-makers sitting on the board of two or more companies were automatically excluded. Moreover, should a company be managed by multiple people whose contacts are obtainable online, the survey would have been distributed to only one of them. The aim of applying those exclusion principles was to avoid the possibility of over-representation and duplication of the research results (Ball, 2019, p. 414), which could further negatively affect the reliability of findings.

4.2. Research Approach

To answer the research question, for this cross-sectional deductive study, the quantitative method was chosen. More specifically, as the goal of this chapter is to identify and research the relationships between the variables allowing the possibility for future research (Lietz, 2010, p. 266), the quantitative data were obtained through online questionnaires previously distributed to Tirolean decision-makers. The inspiration for the questionnaire came from a detailed revision of the existing literature and identifying aspects and variables of interest to the research. Therefore, the survey begins with basic demographic questions about the decision-makers' age, gender, and origin. The remaining questions reflect on the challenges and experiences decision-makers encountered with the foreign workforce in the process of their recruitment, integration, training, and development. Demographic questions are presented in the form of single-choice questions, while the remaining questions are in the form of a Likert scale. The use of the Likert scale enables the acquisition of a profound understanding of the different opinions and perceptions of participants in the questionnaire (Joshi et al., 2015, p. 398). The scale consists of five points, which range from 1 ("Strongly Disagree") to 5 ("Strongly Agree") to allow respondents to express the level of (dis)agreement on a particular question.

The questionnaires were distributed via email and LinkedIn profiles to respective decision-makers. Each email contained a message explaining the motivation, purpose, and background of the study, as well as the link to the online survey. As the online links may not be eminently welcomed by the potential respondents – due to the great fear of cyber-attacks occurring mostly due to the malicious links (Dacorogna & Kratz, 2023, p. 15) – personal information (LinkedIn profile, email address, name, and the email address) of the author of this chapter were sent along with the survey to foster trust among respondents. It is crucial to mention that, to avoid invalidity and inaccuracy of the results, once the respondents decided to take a survey, all the question fields were mandatory to respond to. Likewise, according to the research on the adequate response rate of online surveys, the goal was to receive responses from at least 40% of distributed surveys (Story & Tait, 2019, p. 194). Therefore, given that 500 surveys were distributed, the minimum response number that had to be collected to satisfy this criterion was 200 (by obtaining 205 responses, the minimum response rate was satisfied).

4.3. Variables

Based on the literature research conducted, it was found that demographic characteristics have a strong impact on the choices to *recruit* migrant workforce, support their *integration* into the workforce, as well as allowance for further *training and development* (e.g., Åslund et al., 2014; Farashah & Blomquist, 2019; Kim, 2020). Based on the findings, the expectation was that foreign-born decision-makers would exhibit greater openness to expatriate workers. Furthermore, it would be expected that females, as well as senior decision-makers, exhibit negative attitudes toward foreigners. Respectively, lower acceptance rates among native-born, lower conservation rate among younger, and more positive attitudes among male decision-makers were assumed.

Several survey questions were assigned to each dependent variable. All the questions were designed in a way to explore a dependent variable from angles that have not yet been explored in the literature. For instance, while asking about the recruitment of foreigners, the intention was to detect the extent to which decision-makers value the importance of the origin of expatriates and their experience in the international environment influences the recruiting outcomes. Moreover, the author sought to discover if the language and cultural barriers affect integration, and what the proportion of the companies offering additional support to integration is. Lastly, it is of vital importance to find out if the companies enable foreigners to further train and develop – hence, progress – and if there is a presence of foreigners among decision-makers themselves. Table 4.3 provides an overview of each variable with their corresponding survey questions.

4.4. Regression Model

Upon the data reception, the statistical analysis comes into place. After the data were extracted from the survey, the first step was to check its validity and reliability. To ensure the validity of data, Cronbach's alpha was run in SPSS. Cronbach's alpha is a measure of internal consistency and is expressed as a number between 0 and 1. For alpha to be accepted, it must range from 0.70 to 0.95 (Tavakol & Dennick, 2011, pp. 53–54). After calculating the alpha, a descriptive statistics frequency table (Table 4.4) was created to list the results obtained through the questionnaire numerically as well as in percentages. Table 4.4 also includes cumulative and valid percent attributable to the survey responses. With the frequency table, the descriptive statistics part was concluded, and the research proceeded with the analysis of results.

For the first step in result analysis, the examination of how significant – if existent – the dependence between the variables is (Kim, 2017, p. 152) took place. For that part of the data analysis, the chi-square test was used. The chi-square test is frequently adopted to provide evidence of association without predicting estimates or effects of the outcomes (Connelly, 2019, p. 127; Pandis, 2016, p. 898). For the successful rejection of the null hypotheses – stating that there are no relationships between the variables – the test would need to produce a p-value lower than 0.05 (Pandis, 2016, p. 898). In other words, for the p-value > 0.05, no significant difference between variables would be identified, and the null hypothesis would be accepted, meaning that the tested variables would be independent of one another. Table 4.6 lists the chi-square test values, as well as their corresponding p-values.

Finally, upon successful establishment of the variable dependencies, the final step of the data analysis process began – namely, the analysis and description of the relationships between variables. The Spearman correlation coefficient was used to determine how strong the relationship between variables is (Hauke & Kossowski, 2011, p. 89). The coefficient ranges from −1 and +1, and the strength of the relationship between variables increases from 0 to 1 (Alsaqr, 2021, p. 2).

Table 4.3.   Dependent and Independent Variables With Corresponding Questions.

Variable	Label	Corresponding Question
Independent Variables:		
Age		*"Please indicate your age."*
Gender		*"Please specify your gender."*
Origin		*"Please specify your origin."*
Dependent Variables:		
Recruitment	*Re1*	*"I believe that the applicant's origin country is an important factor for the recruitment outcome."*
	Re2	*"I believe that the expertise in the work in the international environment of an applicant is an important factor for the recruitment outcome."*
	Re3	*"Throughout my career, I have recruited more foreign applicants than domestic ones."*
	Re4	*"I have observed that my colleagues are more compliant with candidates from their own country."*
Integration	*Int1*	*"The greatest hurdle foreign workforce faces while integrating is a language barrier."*
	Int2	*"I think that cultural differences are not barriers to employee integration."*
	Int3	*"Austrian workers are happy to assist foreigners throughout the integration processes."*
	Int4	*"It often happens that the foreign workers register difficulties in successful integration in our company."*
	Int5	*"Our company provides socialization and orientation programs for newcomers."*
Training and development	*TD1*	*"Foreign workers are passionate about learning and carrying out job-specific tasks."*
	TD2	*"Board of our company consists of members of foreign origin, too."*
	TD3	*"In our company, foreigners are enabled to progress to higher levels."*
	TD4	*"During my career, I have come across a company that improperly implemented the training process for the foreign workforce."*

Note. This table lists all dependent and independent variables examined in this chapter. Created by the author and distributed to decision-makers, it delivers the findings crucial to conclude the topic.

Table 4.4.   Summary Statistics for Independent Variables.

Variable	Frequency	Percentage	Valid Percentage	Cumulative Percentage
Age				
25 or younger	4	2.0	2.0	2.0
26–41	49	23.9	23.9	25.9
42–57	99	48.3	48.3	74.1
58–67	46	22.4	22.4	96.6
68 or older	7	3.4	3.4	100.0
Total	**205**	**100.0**	**100.0**	
Gender				
Male	140	68.3	68.3	68.3
Female	65	31.7	31.7	100.0
Divers	0	0	0	100.0
Total	**205**	**100.0**	**100.0**	
Origin				
Austrian-Born	178	86.8	86.8	86.8
Foreign-Born	27	13.2	13.2	100.0
Total	**205**	**100.0**	**100.0**	

Note. This table displays the summary statistics of all three independent variables examined in this chapter. Created by the author and obtained from decision-makers via the online survey, it delivers the findings crucial for further analyses.

In other words, the closer the coefficient to 1 is, the stronger the relationship between variables is. At the end of the data analysis, the calculations of the relationship between each variable were undertaken to draw general conclusions and discover if the findings are in line with the previous research. The Spearman correlation coefficient is presented in Table 4.7.

5. Results

5.1. Descriptive Statistics

A total of 205 responses were obtained through the online questionnaire. This number of responses surpassed the established response rate goal and, therefore, satisfied the criterion for further data analysis. Before the data analysis, the sample was examined and described. Important to note is that, as all answer fields of the survey were mandatory, no invalid or missing data were obtained. Table 4.4 displays the results of the demographic survey questions as well as the corresponding percentages of each independent variable ("age," "gender," "origin"). Moreover, cumulative percentages are displayed for each variable.

Based on the summary, it is notable that the age of the majority of respondents ranged between 42 and 57. Therefore, most of the respondents – almost half – belong to the so-called Generation X. Contrary, but not surprisingly, with only 2%, the lowest number of respondents were aged 20 or less (Generation Z). In terms of gender, the questionnaire results reveal that the great majority of respondents were male (68.3%), while the rest were female (31.7%). Surprisingly, no manager identified himself/herself as diverse. Moreover, in terms of the origin of decision-makers, the majority – 86.8% – claimed to be of Austrian roots, while only 13.2% belonged to the foreign-born population.

5.2. Analysis of Results and Hypotheses Testing

The second part of the data analysis consisted of data validity and reliability testing. To test the validity of the results, the analysis of Cronbach's alpha was used in SPSS. Table 4.5 offers the results of the test.

Given that the value of Cronbach's alpha is 0.368 – significantly lower than the acceptance threshold of 0.70–0.95 – the sample possessed a low level of internal consistency. The low levels of internal consistency are often attributable to the surveys with the low number of questions or poor interrelation between variables (Tavakol & Dennick, 2011, p. 54). For future work, the author could attempt to avoid low alpha by including more questions in the survey or removing some of the data. For this chapter, however, no data were removed as – according to the Item – Total Statistics table in Appendix 2, Table AII – the removal of the data with the lowest consistencies (e.g., 3, 9, 10, 11, 12, 13) would not change the alpha significantly.

Following the validity tests, the establishment of the dependencies and examination of the correlations between dependent and independent variables took place. The results have been obtained through chi-square test and the Spearman correlation coefficient in SPSS to find out if – and to what extent – "age," "gender," and "origin," affect the recruitment, integration, training, and development of foreign newcomers. Table 4.6 lists the findings of the chi-square test. Finally, the result analysis was concluded by calculating the Spearman correlation coefficient. The results for the Spearman correlation coefficient are listed in Table 4.7. The findings are further interpreted in terms of the hypotheses to allow for an upcoming discussion of the results. In the tables, each dependent variable, as explained previously, carries a certain number of questions labeled as "Re 1-4"

Table 4.5.   Summary of Results: Cronbach's Alpha.

Cronbach's Alpha	Cronbach's Alpha Based on Standardized Items	No. of Items
0.377	0.368	13

Note. This table displays the value obtained for Cronbach's alpha and reveals the low level of internal consistency for the sample. The elaboration on possible causes of such low value follows.

Table 4.6. Summary of Results: Chi-Square Test.

Dependent Variables	Age			Gender			Origin		
	Value	df	Asymp. Sig. (Two-sided)	Value	df	Asymp. Sig. (Two-sided)	Value	df	Asymp. Sig. (Two-sided)
Recruitment									
Re1	12.480[a]	16	0.710	3.530[a]	4	0.473	4.997[a]	4	0.288
Re2	20.389[a1]	16	0.203	9.515[a1]	4	0.049	5.206[a1]	4	0.267
Re3	23.844[a2]	16	0.093	6.276[a2]	4	0.179	12.175[a2]	4	0.016
Re4	14.834[a3]	16	0.537	4.613[a3]	4	0.329	4.440[a3]	4	0.350
Integration									
Int1	33.991[a]	16	0.005	4.369[a]	4	0.358	0.408[a]	4	0.982
Int2	15.554[a2]	16	0.485	1.251[a1]	4	0.870	7.074[a1]	4	0.132
Int3	6.952[a3]	16	0.974	5.557[a2]	4	0.235	9.869[a2]	4	0.043
Int4	8.316[a4]	16	0.939	2.329[a3]	4	0.676	3.160[a3]	4	0.531
Int5	31.801[a5]	16	0.011	2.878[a4]	4	0.579	2.674[a4]	4	0.614
Training and development									
TD1	14.852[a]	16	0.535	2.584[a]	4	0.630	2.745[a]	4	0.601
TD2	13.016[a1]	16	0.672	1.099[a1]	4	0.894	43.970[a1]	4	0.000
TD3	8.137[a2]	16	0.945	7.195[a2]	4	0.126	10.108[a2]	4	0.039
TD4	18.133[a3]	16	0.316	4.382[a3]	4	0.357	8.473[a3]	4	0.076

Note. This table displays the summary of results obtained while running the chi-square test between independent and dependent variables. The table offers an overview of (in)dependencies and serves as a valuable addition to the previous findings and enables the author to conclude the topic. Notes to the chi-square results are displayed in Appendix 3, Table AIII.

Table 4.7. Summary of Results: Spearman Correlation Coefficient.

Variables	Recruitment				Integration					Training and Development			
	Re1	Re2	Re3	Re4	Int1	Int2	Int3	Int4	Int5	TD1	TD2	TD3	TD4
Gender	0.012	−0.075	−0.110	−0.009	−0.038	0.013	0.117	0.037	−0.002	0.090	−0.045	0.039	0.043
Age	−0.016	−0.132	0.003	0.017	−0.163*	−0.042	−0.025	−0.095	−0.070	−0.086	0.019	0.081	−0.012
Origin	−0.109	0.041	−0.207**	−0.139*	0.027	0.099	0.054	−0.102	−0.064	−0.018	−0.366**	0.063	−0.121

* Correlation is significant at the 0.05 level (two-tailed).
** Correlation is significant at the 0.01 level (two-tailed).

Note. This table displays the summary of results obtained while running the Spearman correlation coefficient between independent and dependent variables in SPSS. The table offers a valuable addition to the previous findings and enables the author to draw conclusions on the topic.

(*recruitment*), "Int 1-5" (*integration*), and "TD 1-4" (*training and development*). To learn which label corresponds to which survey question, refer to the codebook in Appendix 1, Table AI.

For the dependencies to be established, the p-value of the chi-square test (as mentioned previously) should be lower than 0.05. The research suggested that the acceptance threshold of the p-value equals or exceeds the values for variables *Int1* (0.05) and *Int5* (0.011). Therefore, as chi-square results indicated strong-enough evidence of a significant association between these two variables and the age of decision-makers, the null hypothesis was rejected. However, the null hypothesis could not be rejected for any other integration variable, as the values of *Int2*, *Int3*, as well as *Int4*, exceeded the acceptance threshold of 0.05. In other words, the chi-square test provided no evidence for a significant relationship between "age" and the mentioned integration variable. Furthermore, results of the chi-square test provided no evidence of a significant relationship between the age of decision-maker and any of the recruitment (*Re1–Re4*) and training and development (*TD1–TD4*) variables.

Similar to the previous scenario, the results of the chi-square test for the gender of decision-makers provided evidence of dependencies to only one dependent variable – *Re2* ($p = 0.049$). Hence, the null hypothesis was exclusively rejected for this variable. For all the remaining recruitment, integration, training, and development variables, the null hypothesis was accepted, concluding that – based on the results of the test – there was no evidence to claim that there is a significant relationship between the variables and the gender of the decision-maker.

On the contrary, the greatest number of interdependencies was identified for the origin of decision-makers (*Re3* (0.016), *Int 3* (0.043), *TD2* (0.000), and *TD3* (0.039)). Interestingly, the p-value for *TD2* was precisely zero, meaning that there was strong evidence to reject the null hypothesis in that value. From that observed value, the existence of a significant association between the origin of the decision-maker and the *TD2* was noted. For the remaining variables in which p-values remained greater than the acceptance threshold, no statistical significance was identified, hence the evidence for rejecting the null hypothesis was sufficiently weak.

According to the results displayed in Table 4.7, the recruitment variables *Re2*, *Re3*, and *Re4* demonstrated a significant negative weak relationship to the gender of decision-makers. Consequently, the results of Spearman suggested that, as the relationship was significantly weak, there was little to no evidence available that the increase in one variable may result in a decrease in another one (Akoglu, 2018, p. 92). Furthermore, results for recruitment revealed only one very weak positive relationship to the gender of decision-makers (*Re1*). Moreover, the "strongest" positive relationship – despite being weak – was displayed by variable *Int3*. On the contrary, variable *Int1* displayed a very weak negative, while *Int4* and *Int2* demonstrated a very low positive relationship to "gender." Finally, findings revealed that the relationship between "gender" and *Int5* may be nonexistent at all, as the value of Spearman was too close to zero. In terms of the results for training and development, the most significant correlation – even though weak positive – was obtained with *TD1*. The remaining results remained weak, with *TD2* being the only negative one.

Similar to the "gender," Spearman revealed a variety of correlations between "age" and the remaining dependent variables. In terms of variables associated with the recruitment of foreign newcomers, "age" displayed a negligibly low negative correlation to variables *Re1*, *Re3*, and *Re4*. In other words, the results were not significant enough to establish a relationship between variables. A slightly more significant result was noted for the variable *Re2*. However, the result remained very weak and negative. Furthermore, Spearman revealed a weak negative relationship to *Int4* and *Int5*, while a moderate negative relationship to variable *Int1*. Spearman, however, failed to recognize the existence of a relationship between the "age" and *Int2* and *Int3*, as the correlations of these variables were – once again – too adjacent to zero. For the variable *Int1*, it may be of interest to note that the value came with the asterisk. Namely, the asterisk indicates that the observed relationship between two variables may indeed be meaningful rather than random, but there is no absolute certainty for such a claim (Kozak et al., 2012, p. 1152). Finally, results indicated a very weak negative relationship between "age" and *TD1*, as well as a very weak positive relationship to *TD3*. For the remaining training and development variables, no correlation to the age of decision-makers was established.

To the author's delight, the third variable – "origin" – obtained the greatest number of significant correlations to the dependent variables (in comparison to "age" and "gender"). For the recruitment of the foreign workforce, Spearman established a significant and moderate negative relationship between the "origin" and *Re3* and *Re4*. The asterisk at the *Re4*'s value – as already explained – indicated a possibility of a significant relationship. On the contrary, two asterisks on the *Re3*'s value suggested that the significance exists and did not occur due to the chance (Han et al., 2018, p. 4). Consecutively, for *Re1*, Spearman indicated a weak negative relationship, while a weak positive relationship for *Re2*. Furthermore, for variables *Int1*, *Int2*, and *Int3*, Spearman discovered a very weak positive relationship, while a very weak negative correlation for variables *Int4* and *Int5*. Ultimately, in terms of training and development of the expatriates, results for *TD2* indicated a moderately strong negative correlation to "origin" which, according to the asterisks, did not happen by chance. Besides, compared to the outcomes of correlations between training and development with "age" and "gender," the correlation between origin and *TD2* displayed the greatest significance among all the results for that dependent variable. Finally, the remaining values displayed a very weak positive (*TD3*) relationship and a weak negative (*TD4*) relationship to training and development, while no relationship was identified for *TD1*. The correlation results obtained for the origin of decision-makers – as well as their "age" and "gender" – serve as a valuable foundation, not just for further discussion of this chapter but also for future research.

6. Discussion

The purpose of this chapter was to describe the relationship between the demographic traits of decision-makers and the way those influence the integration of migrant workers into Tirolean companies. To guide the research process, the three hypotheses attributable to the research question were created. Namely, with the focus on discovering *how different demographic factors of Tirolean decision-makers affect the integration of the foreign workforce in that region*, the author differentiated between three demographic traits and hypothesized:

H1. There is a relationship between the gender of the decision-makers and the foreign workforce integration.

H2. There is a relationship between the age of a decision-maker and the foreign workforce integration.

H3. There is a relationship between the origin of the decision-makers and the foreign workforce integration.

The data were obtained through the online survey and distributed to Tirolean decision-makers. The survey consisted of 19 questions in total. The focus of the survey was on collecting quantitative data based on which the relationships between variables would be established. The chosen independent variables (the demographic traits) were "age," "gender," and "origin," while the dependent variables were "recruitment," "integration," and "training and development." Therefore, based on the research question, the research went beyond the scope of exclusively examining the relationships to integration and explored deeper into topics of training and development and recruitment of expatriates. Also, in terms of the questionnaire, each dependent variable carried a certain number of questions attributable to each. The meaning of each "sub-variable" can be seen in Table 4.3. Providing a variety of "sub-variables" in the questionnaire enabled the researcher to explore different paths related to migrant integration in the workplace and offer a solid foundation for future research.

6.1. Hypothesis 1

According to the previously carried statistical analyses, the variable "gender" yielded no evidence for the existence of a significant association with any of the independent variables. The exception to this statement was the variable *Re2* for which the value of the chi-square test failed to surpass the acceptance threshold ($p = 0.049$), hence resulting in the rejection of the null hypothesis. In other words, throughout the research process, the mutual dependencies were identified between the gender of decision-makers and the managers' attitude that the applicants' work in the international environment is an important factor for the recruitment outcome (*Re2*). In simpler terms, the attitude toward a workforce with international experience – resulting in recruitment outcomes – may vary depending on the gender of the decision-makers. Furthermore, based on the results of Spearman analysis, it is possible to conclude that – as the weak and positive relationship between two respective variables were identified – the gender of decision-makers may only play a small role in determining the attitudes toward international experience in recruitment but is not the most prevalent one. In terms of the results for remaining recruitment variables, the results indicated no association between either *Re1*, *Re3*, or *Re4*, and the gender of decision-makers. Moreover, the only variable in which the correlation coefficient was weak and positive was related to the perception of applicants' origin (*Re1*). This would mean that, despite displaying no dependency, the applicants' origin may be perceived differently by a different gender of decision-makers as one of the important factors toward the recruitment outcomes. However, according to the results, the strength of this perception remains insignificant. These claims support the findings of Farashah and Blomquist (2019, pp. 27–29) who suggested that female managers tend to display a greater bias toward foreign applicants than male ones do. Finally, for the remaining recruitment variables, the gender of decision-makers yielded no significant impact on whether the organization recruits more foreign or domestic applicants (*Re3*), nor lead to the realization of whether colleagues are more compliant with candidates from their own country or not (*Re4*).

In terms of the decision-makers' gender affecting the integration outcomes of the foreign workforce, no association was established. Furthermore, Spearman revealed that the decision-makers do not perceive issues like language barriers (*Int1*), or general adaptation difficulties (*Int4*), any differently based on their genders. This comes as a surprise as the literature suggests that female managers tend to display greater empathy and aim toward the enhancement of collegial support (Johnson et al., 2020, pp. 747–749). Further opposing the findings of the study (and supporting the literature), the results of this chapter suggested that gender affects tolerance toward the obstacles caused by cultural differences (*Int2*). Similarly, the results of the study revealed that the provision of socialization and orientation programs for newcomers (*Int5*) is in no relationship to decision-makers' gender. In other words, the decision of the company to provide orientation programs for expatriates is entirely unrelated to the gender of the actor making such a decision. Finally, "gender" has proven itself to be positively related (despite being independent and insignificant) to the perception of the willingness of Austrian colleagues to assist foreigners with the integration process (*Int3*). Past research further supports this claim, as it identified colleagues as one of the main actors in the successful integration of expatriates (van Riemsdijk & Basford, 2022, p. 648).

Finally, in terms of training and development, the results of this study provided no evidence for the dependency of any of the training and development factors on the gender of decision-makers. Results have shown a negative relationship between migrants being on the board of the company and the gender of the remaining board members (*TD2*). Hence, the decision on whether to include foreigners on the board depends on factors different from the gender of decision-makers. This may go in line with the idea that, once in the country, expatriates seek lower-qualified jobs, such as in accommodation and food service industries, construction, domestic work, or administrative and support activities (EUROSTAT, 2021). In addition, despite the fear of being excluded from their participation in the board of directors, according to results, expatriates are still encouraged to progress and self-develop, and this encouragement is further related to the gender of decision-makers (*TD3*). Finally, the remaining results indicated that the gender of decision-makers may have some impact on the recognition of the expatriates' learning passion (*TD1*), as well as the awareness of the existence of improper training for newcomers (*TD4*), but those impacts are not significantly strong. As literature is scarce on these topics, the results of this chapter could be linked to the general discussion on the different empathy levels among different genders and open for future discussions.

6.2. Hypothesis 2

The second hypothesis dealt with the age of decision-makers. According to the results of the chi-square test, no dependencies were established between the "age" and any of the recruitment factors. Furthermore, Spearman revealed no relationship between "age" and perception of the importance of the applicant's country of origin (*Re1*), nor the number of foreigners recruited in comparison to domestic applicants (*Re3*). This may come as a surprise knowing that the senior decision-makers tend to display more stereotypical attitudes toward foreigners (Farashah & Blomquist, 2019, p. 12); hence, it would be expected that they pay closer attention to the applicant's origin. Furthermore, Spearman observed no relationship between "age" and the awareness of compliance toward applicants of the same origin (*Re4*). The only – low negative – relationship was noted in the attitude toward expatriates' international orientation (*Re2*). Namely, the tendency of decision-makers to differently value the international orientation of expatriates based on their age exists, but those are not strongly associated.

Surprisingly, in terms of the integration of expatriates, the results yielded a dependency between the age of decision-makers and recognition of language barriers (*Int1*), as well as the provision of training programs for expatriates (*Int5*). Based on the results from the Spearman correlation, the age of decision-makers is in direct relationship to both integration variables. Therefore, based on the literature and data findings, it is possible to conclude that younger decision-makers support the overcoming of language barriers, as well as assist newcomers through further integration programs more than senior ones (Farashah & Blomquist, 2019, p. 30). Similarly, the overall recognition of expatriates' hurdles tends to progress with age (*Int4*). Finally, Spearman gave no evidence that the age of decision-makers in any way affects the recognition of obstacles caused by cultural differences (*Int3*), nor general adaptation issues (*Int2*), which is directly opposing the findings from *Int1* and *Int5*.

Lastly, results for training and development processes yielded independence of the decision-makers' age. Spearman identified that the age of decision-makers does not affect a decision to employ an expatriate to the board of a company (*TD2*). Furthermore, no relationship was found to encounter improper training processes (*TD4*). Despite there being no supporting literature available, the author believed that, with the increase in the age of decision-makers, their experiences would broaden; hence, the awareness of the existence of inaccurate training programs would boost. This means that the age of decision-makers may have some influence on whether the foreign workers are perceived as passionate or not (*TD1*), and whether the foreigners are supported to progress further (*TD3*), but that influence is not significant. This claim opposes the findings from the literature, in which age is commonly considered an influencing factor in the perception, selectivity, and support of foreign newcomers (Gonsalkorale et al., 2009; Grühn et al., 2010).

6.3. Hypothesis 3

The third hypothesis was related to the origin of decision-makers. As stated previously, the "origin" variable was of great importance for this chapter, as it yielded the most plentiful results. Namely, the dependency between the origin of decision-makers and their tendency to recruit more foreign than domestic workers in their companies (*Re3*) was discovered. In other words (based on the results from Spearman), a decision on whether to employ a foreigner is in a direct relationship to whether the decision-maker himself/herself is a foreigner or not. This finding is fully supported by the research carried out by Åslund et al. (2014, p. 413), who likewise identified that foreign workers have greater chances to be recruited by a foreign decision-maker. Spearman further identified that the origin may be related to the awareness of compliance of foreign decision-makers toward the acceptance of expatriates (*Re4*). Furthermore, despite no identified dependency, data suggested that the origin of decision-makers may impact the belief that the applicant's origin country is an important factor for the recruitment outcome (*Re1*), but this impact is not very strong, and the tendency is toward lower compliance. This statement opposes the findings of Horverak et al. (2013) who discovered that Turkish decision-makers tend to display strong compliance toward Turkish applicants even if their skill set may be low. Finally, the origin of decision-makers may additionally have some impact on whether the international expertise of foreigners is a crucial factor for recruitment outcome (*Re2*). However, the impact of this claim remained rather weak.

In terms of the integration variables, the dependency on the origin of decision-makers was established for the perception that the Austrian workers gladly assist foreigners throughout the integration processes (*Int3*). It may be of interest to research deeper into the respective topic, as such claims could easily be biased, hence inaccurate. However, for this research, despite the impact that may have occurred, it remained weak. Further research suggested that the origin of decision-makers may have had some impact on the perception of the language barriers (*Int1*), but this impact was likewise infirm. Furthermore, data suggested that the origin of decision-makers may have some influence on the provision of socialization programs for foreign workers (*Int5*) as well as the awareness of the general integration obstacles (*Int4*), but the respective influence tended toward lower compliance. These findings opposed the findings from the literature, in which the foreign decision-makers tend to exhibit great levels of tolerance toward foreign applicants, as well as the provision of assistance in integration processes (van Riemsdijk & Basford, 2022, p. 649). Finally, based on the data, the origin of decision-makers may have some impact on the perception of whether an applicant's cultural differences are barriers to employee integration, but this impact is likewise weak.

Finally, the results have shown the dependency between the origin of decision-makers and origin-diverse boards (*TD2*) as well as the opportunity for further development of expatriates (*TD3*). Despite those claims may come across as purely logical, Spearman suggested the weak impact of the origin of decision-makers on the development opportunities, and the strong significance to the origin-diverse boards and the foreign decision-makers. This opposes the findings of Farashah and Blomquist (2019) and van Riemsdijk and Basford (2022) who suggested that the foreign-born decision-makers exhibit a positive attitude toward expatriates, and – in comparison to domestic-born ones – dedicate a great number of resources to expatriates' adaptation. Furthermore, results from this chapter suggested that the origin of decision-makers may have some impact on the awareness of improper training processes (*TD4*), but such impact remains weak. Finally, the results indicated that decision-makers of different origins do not differ while perceiving the passion of foreigners toward learning (*TD1*), as no relationship was established for these two variables.

6.4. Limitations

As stated previously, the sample of this chapter exhibited a low level of internal consistency. One of the major limitations of this chapter – which is directly attributable to the internal consistency – was the size of the sample. Despite being large enough for the chapter itself, more enhanced size of the sample would enable more accurate statistical analyses. More specifically, as some of the results tend to oppose the findings from existing literature, the broader sample would allow for a greater elaboration of whether and why the discrepancies have occurred. Another limitation can be attributable to the chosen geographical area of the study. As Tirol is geographically narrow, and scientifically considered a knowledge transfer region (Ecker et al., 2022, p. 30), the amount of available literature related to the topic was scarce. Therefore, the comparisons drawn in this chapter were mostly in correspondence to world literature. Hence, by broadening the region to the whole of Austria (for example), the potential author would not only be able to discuss if the trends discovered in the world literature differ anyhow from the regional ones discovered in this chapter but also would contribute to the sample size and the accuracy of the results. Finally, the third limitation of this chapter was the strict word count limit. Despite 12,000 words being – theoretically – sufficient for the basic conclusions to be drawn, certain parts of this chapter that would explore the topic in greater detail were excluded as they would have caused an excess of the words, respectively. Hence, in the future, the preclusion of the limitations to the word count – aiming to broaden scientific research – would comprise additional discussions.

7. Conclusion

The EU experiences constant inflows of expatriates looking for enhancement of living conditions (United Nations, 2020). Out of the total number of inhabitants, expatriates accounted for 25.4% of the total population of Austria (Statistik.at, 2022).

Among the other Austrian regions, region Tirol represented a haven for nearly 140,000 foreigners which accounted for 18.1% of the entire population of this region (Table 4.2) (Mohr, 2023). Despite the increase in global migration rates becoming a common topic in current literature, no migrant-related research focused specifically on the region of Tirol. Various researchers, however, invested their efforts into examining the causes and the consequences of this phenomenon on a global scale. At the same time, another portion of the literature revolved around the treatment of the expatriates upon arrival to the novel living environment. Farashah and Blomquist (2019) examined expatriates as workers and aimed to determine what affects their successful integration into the foreign workplace. The authors focused on the decision-makers and found their tendency to react under the influence of their demographic traits, which shape the way they make decisions (Farashah & Blomquist, 2019, p. 30). In other words, the demographic traits of decision-makers tend to be in direct relationship with their attitudes toward the foreign workforce. Hence, with a focus on the specific demographic traits of decision-makers (age, gender, and origin), this chapter explains how different demographic factors of Tirolean decision-makers affect the integration of the foreign workforce in that region.

By analyzing the dependencies and relationships of the variables in the sample, it was noted that the gender of decision-makers is not just directly related to the perception of the expatriates' origin but also further affects the way decision-makers react toward the obstacles caused by the cultural differences. Results also prove that the gender of decision-makers affects the support toward expatriates' self-development procedures. Moreover, results reveal the relationship between the age of decision-makers and the provision of training programs for expatriates. Also, age is related to the recognition of language barriers as well as the provision of support for migrants. Finally, the origin of decision-makers yielded the most fruitful results. Results suggest that foreign decision-makers tend to display greater levels of compliance toward foreign workers, as well as directly affecting the decision of whether to recruit a foreigner or not. Moreover, there may be evidence of decision-makers' origin affecting the tolerance toward language barriers, as well as the support of expatriates' self-development.

The contributions of this chapter are seen from both a business and theoretical standpoint. By creating awareness of the impacts of demographic traits on individual behaviors, decision-makers would be able to establish an effective path toward unbiased decision-making processes, especially concerning their openness to the foreign workforce. Moreover, this chapter enhances the science of Tirolean-based companies by offering a yet-unexplored view of this geographical region. Furthermore, this chapter serves as a solid foundation for future research of Tirolean scholars. Future research could, likewise, include the inter-Austrian comparison and discover what are the main differences and similarities between the regions in this country while executing the onboarding processes. It may also be of interest for future scholars to undertake regional comparisons of Austria and investigate how – and if – the decision-makers from different regions tend to handle the topic of migrations. Finally, similar to the differentiation of the regions, the differentiation between different decision-makers (i.e., managers, human resource departments, CEOs, etc.) could be of great interest to future studies. However, for such research to be possible, a future author must ensure that not just the sample is broad enough but also not limited to the geographical location or the word counts. Lastly, given the variety of topics to be yet explored, and the ongoing influx of migrant workers, the author is convinced that the future of Tirol will be interlaced with the abundance of prominent scientific literature as well as the strength of domestic and foreign workforce working toward the common goal – unity.

References and Further Reading

Aburumman, O., Salleh, A., Omar, K., & Abadi, M. (2020). The impact of human resource management practices and career satisfaction on employee's turnover intention. *Management Science Letters*, *10*(3), 641–652. https://doi.org/10.5267/j.msl.2019.9.015

Ackert, L. F., Deaves, R., Miele, J., & Nguyen, Q. (2020). Are time preference and risk preference associated with cognitive intelligence and emotional intelligence? *Journal of Behavioral Finance*, *21*(2), 1–21. https://doi.org/10.1080/15427560.2019.1663850

Adams, R. B., & Ferreira, D. (2009). Women in the boardroom and their impact on governance and performance☆. *Journal of Financial Economics*, *94*(2), 291–309. https://doi.org/10.1016/j.jfineco.2008.10.007

Akoglu, H. (2018). User's guide to correlation coefficients. *Turkish Journal of Emergency Medicine*, *18*(3), 91–93. https://doi.org/10.1016/j.tjem.2018.08.001

Ali, Q., Parveen, S., Yaacob, H., Rani, A. N., & Zaini, Z. (2022). Environmental beliefs and the adoption of circular economy among bank managers: Do gender, age and knowledge act as the moderators? *Journal of Cleaner Production*, *361*, 132276. https://doi.org/10.1016/j.jclepro.2022.132276

Ali, Q., Parveen, S., Yaacob, H., Zaini, Z., & Sarbini, N. A. (2021). Covid-19 and dynamics of environmental awareness, sustainable consumption and social responsibility in Malaysia. *Environmental Science and Pollution Research*, *28*(40), 56199–56218. https://doi.org/10.1007/s11356-021-14612-z

Alsaqr, A. M. (2021). Remarks on the use of Pearson's and Spearman's correlation coefficients in assessing relationships in ophthalmic data. *African Vision and Eye Health*, *80*(1), a612. https://doi.org/10.4102/aveh.v80i1.612

Aman-Ullah, A., Aziz, A., Ibrahim, H., Mehmood, W., & Abdullah Abbas, Y. (2021). The impact of job security, job satisfaction and job embeddedness on employee retention: An empirical investigation of Pakistan's health-care industry. *Journal of Asia Business Studies*, *16*(6), 904–922. https://doi.org/10.1108/jabs-12-2020-0480

Ashikali, T., & Groeneveld, S. (2013). Diversity management in public organizations and its effect on employees' affective commitment. *Review of Public Personnel Administration*, *35*(2), 146–168. https://doi.org/10.1177/0734371x13511088

Åslund, O., Hensvik, L., & Skans, O. N. (2014). Seeking similarity: How immigrants and natives manage in the labor market. *Journal of Labor Economics*, *32*(3), 405–441. https://doi.org/10.1086/674985

Bae, K. B., Lee, D., & Sohn, H. (2019). How to increase participation in telework programs in U.S. federal agencies: Examining the effects of being a female supervisor, supportive leadership, and diversity management. *Public Personnel Management*, *48*(4), 565–583. https://doi.org/10.1177/0091026019832920

Ball, H. L. (2019). Conducting online surveys. *Journal of Human Lactation*, *35*(3), 413–417. https://doi.org/10.1177/0890334419848734

Basford, S., & van Riemsdijk, M. (2015). The role of institutions in the student migrant experience: Norway's quota scheme. *Population, Space and Place, 23*(3), e2005. https://doi.org/10.1002/psp.2005

Beji, R., Yousfi, O., Loukil, N., & Omri, A. (2020). Board diversity and corporate social responsibility: Empirical evidence from France. *Journal of Business Ethics, 173*(1), 133–155. https://doi.org/10.1007/s10551-020-04522-4

Biresselioglu, M. E., Demirbag Kaplan, M., & Yilmaz, B. K. (2018). Electric mobility in Europe: A comprehensive review of motivators and barriers in decision making processes. *Transportation Research Part A: Policy and Practice, 109*, 1–13. https://doi.org/10.1016/j.tra.2018.01.017

Bleijenbergh, I., Peters, P., & Poutsma, E. (2010). Diversity management beyond the business case. *Equality, Diversity and Inclusion: An International Journal, 29*(5), 413–421. https://doi.org/10.1108/02610151011052744

Bulog, I. (2016). The influence of top management demographic characteristics on decision making approaches. *Ekonomski Vjesnik/Econviews – Review of Contemporary Business, Entrepreneurship and Economic Issues, 29*(2), 393–403.

Cabello, R., Sorrel, M. A., Fernández-Pinto, I., Extremera, N., & Fernández-Berrocal, P. (2016). Age and gender differences in ability emotional intelligence in adults: A cross-sectional study. *Developmental Psychology, 52*(9), 1486–1492. https://doi.org/10.1037/dev0000191

Carling, J., & Talleraas, C. (2016). *Root causes and drivers of migration* (pp. 1–44). Peace Research Institute Oslo (PRIO).

Carlsson, M., & Eriksson, S. (2019). In-group gender bias in hiring: Real-world evidence. *Economics Letters, 185*, 108686. https://doi.org/10.1016/j.econlet.2019.108686

Castilla, E. J. (2011). Bringing managers back in. *American Sociological Review, 76*(5), 667–694. https://doi.org/10.1177/0003122411420814

City of Vienna. (2023). *Facts and figures on migration 2023 – Viennese population*. https://www.wien.gv.at/english/social/integration/facts-figures/population-migration.html#::text=At%20the%20beginning%20of%202023%2C%2034.2%20per%20cent,foreign%20citizenship%20or%20were%20Austrian%20nationals%20born%20abroad

Colakoglu, N., Eryilmaz, M., & Martínez-Ferrero, J. (2020). Is board diversity an antecedent of corporate social responsibility performance in firms? A research on the 500 biggest Turkish companies. *Social Responsibility Journal, 17*(2), 243–262. https://doi.org/10.1108/srj-07-2019-0251

Cole, M. S., Feild, H. S., & Giles, W. F. (2004). Interaction of recruiter and applicant gender in resume evaluation: A field study. *Sex Roles, 51*(9–10), 597–608. https://doi.org/10.1007/s11199-004-5469-1

Connelly, L. (2019). Chi-square test. *Medsurg Nursing, 28*(2), 127–127.

Crowder-Meyer, M. (2013). Gendered recruitment without trying: How local party recruiters affect women's representation. *Politics & Gender, 9*(4), 390–413. https://doi.org/10.1017/s1743923x13000391

Dacorogna, M. M., & Kratz, M. (2023). Managing cyber risk, a science in the making. *SSRN Electronic Journal*. https://doi.org/10.2139/ssrn.4356389

De Haas, H. (2021). A theory of migration: The aspirations-capabilities framework. *Comparative Migration Studies, 9*(1), 1–35. https://doi.org/10.1186/s40878-020-00210-4

De Haas, H., Miller, M. J., & Castles, S. (2019). *The age of migration: International population movements in the modern world*. Macmillan Education.

Den Butter, F. A., Masurel, E., & Mosch, R. H. (2004). The economics of co-ethnic employment: Incentives, welfare effects and policy options. *SSRN Electronic Journal*. https://doi.org/10.2139/ssrn.514222

Dubey, S., & Mallah, V. (2015). Migration: Causes and effects. *The Business & Management Review, 5*(4), 228.

Ecker, B., Brunner, P., Dick, N., Hartmann, E., Heckenberg, D., Johs, J., Kasneci, G., Marcher, A., Philipp, S., Régent, V., Sardadvar, S., Schneider, H., Schuch, K., Steyer, M., Sturn, D., Warta, K., Wagner, V., & Wieser, H. (2022). *Austrian research and technology report 2022*, 1–241. https://doi.org/10.22163/fteval.2022.575

Enderwick, P. (2011). Acquiring overseas market knowledge: A comparison of strategies of expatriate and immigrant employees. *Journal of Asia Business Studies, 5*(1), 77–97. https://doi.org/10.1108/15587891111100813

Erlandsson, A. (2019). Do men favor men in recruitment? A field experiment in the Swedish labor market. *Work and Occupations, 46*(3), 239–264. https://doi.org/10.1177/0730888419849467

EUMMAS – European Marketing and Management Association. (n.d.). Retrieved January 7, 2023, from https://eummas.net/

European Commission. (2022). *Statistics on migration to Europe.* Retrieved June 4, 2022, from https://ec.europa.eu/info/strategy/priorities-2019-2024/promoting-our-european-way-life/statistics-migration-europe_en#::text=or%20work%20reasons.-, Employment%20of%20immigrants,to%204.6%25%20of%20the%20total

EUROSTAT. (2021). *Population on 1 January by age group, sex and citizenship.* European Commission. Retrieved October 13, 2022, from https://ec.europa.eu/eurostat/databrowser/view/MIGR_POP1CTZ__custom_2721297/bookmark/map?lang=en&bookmarkId=0bb119b2-ef52-405a-a4cc-96c5c1ab95fa

Farashah, A. D., & Blomquist, T. (2019). Exploring employer attitude towards migrant workers. *Evidence-based HRM: A Global Forum for Empirical Scholarship, 8*(1), 18–37. https://doi.org/10.1108/ebhrm-04-2019-0040

Fernandez-Mateo, I., & Kaplan, S. (2018). Gender and organization science: Introduction to a virtual special issue. *Organization Science, 29*(6), 1229–1236. https://doi.org/10.1287/orsc.2018.1249

Fernando, M., Almeida, S., & Dharmage, S. C. (2016). Employer perceptions of migrant candidates' suitability: The influence of decision-maker and organisational characteristics. *Asia Pacific Journal of Human Resources, 54*(4), 445–464. https://doi.org/10.1111/1744-7941.12091

Fok, C. C., Henry, D., & Allen, J. (2015). Maybe small is too small a term: Introduction to advancing small sample prevention science. *Prevention Science, 16*(7), 943–949. https://doi.org/10.1007/s11121-015-0584-5

Galletta, S., Mazzù, S., Naciti, V., & Vermiglio, C. (2021). Gender diversity and sustainability performance in the banking industry. *Corporate Social Responsibility and Environmental Management, 29*(1), 161–174. https://doi.org/10.1002/csr.2191

Geddes, A., Hadj-Abdou, L., & Brumat, L. (2020). *Migration and mobility in the European Union.* Red Globe Press.

Ghani, B., Zada, M., Memon, K. R., Ullah, R., Khattak, A., Han, H., Ariza-Montes, A., & Araya-Castillo, L. (2022). Challenges and strategies for employee retention in the hospitality industry: A review. *Sustainability, 14*(5), 2885. https://doi.org/10.3390/su14052885

Goll, I., & Rasheed, A. A. (2005). The relationships between top management demographic characteristics, rational decision making, environmental munificence, and firm performance. *Organization Studies, 26*(7), 999–1023. https://doi.org/10.1177/0170840605053538

Gomez, L. E., & Bernet, P. (2019). Diversity improves performance and outcomes. *Journal of the National Medical Association, 111*(4), 383–392. https://doi.org/10.1016/j.jnma.2019.01.006

Gonsalkorale, K., Sherman, J. W., & Klauer, K. C. (2009). Aging and prejudice: Diminished regulation of automatic race bias among older adults. *Journal of Experimental Social Psychology, 45*(2), 410–414. https://doi.org/10.1016/j.jesp.2008.11.004

Grand, C. l., & Szulkin, R. (2002). Permanent disadvantage or gradual integration: Explaining the immigrant-native earnings gap in Sweden. *Labour*, *16*(1), 37–64. https://doi.org/10.1111/1467-9914.00186

Graves, L. M., & Powell, G. N. (1996). Sex similarity, quality of the employment interview and recruiters' evaluation of actual applicants. *Journal of Occupational and Organizational Psychology*, *69*(3), 243–261. https://doi.org/10.1111/j.2044-8325.1996.tb00613.x

Grosskopf, S., Landes, A., & Barmeyer, C. (2021). A black-box yet to be opened: Multi-level processes during migrants' organizational socialization. *Journal of International Migration and Integration*, *23*(4), 1875–1902. https://doi.org/10.1007/s12134-021-00906-1

Grühn, D., Kotter-Grühn, D., & Röcke, C. (2010). Discrete affects across the adult lifespan: Evidence for multidimensionality and multidirectionality of affective experiences in young, middle-aged and older adults. *Journal of Research in Personality*, *44*(4), 492–500. https://doi.org/10.1016/j.jrp.2010.06.003

Hafsi, T., & Turgut, G. (2012). Boardroom diversity and its effect on social performance: Conceptualization and empirical evidence. *Journal of Business Ethics*, *112*(3), 463–479. https://doi.org/10.1007/s10551-012-1272-z

Hainmueller, J. E. N. S., & Hiscox, M. I. C. H. A. E. L. J. (2010). Attitudes toward highly skilled and low-skilled immigration: Evidence from a survey experiment. *American Political Science Review*, *104*(1), 61–84. https://doi.org/10.1017/s00030 55409990372

Han, M., Hao, L., Lin, Y., Li, F., Wang, J., Yang, H., Xiao, L., Kristiansen, K., Jia, H., & Li, J. (2018). A novel affordable reagent for room temperature storage and transport of fecal samples for metagenomic analyses. *Microbiome*, *6*(1), 1–7. https://doi.org/10.1186/s40168-018-0429-0

Haque, A. u., & Oino, I. (2019). Managerial challenges for software house related to work, worker and workplace: Stress reduction and sustenance of human capital. *Polish Journal of Management Studies*, *19*(1), 170–189. https://doi.org/10.17512/pjms.2019.19.1.13

Hauer, M. E., Fussell, E., Mueller, V., Burkett, M., Call, M., Abel, K., McLeman, R., & Wrathall, D. (2019). Sea-level rise and human migration. *Nature Reviews Earth & Environment*, *1*(1), 28–39. https://doi.org/10.1038/s43017-019-0002-9

Hauke, J., & Kossowski, T. (2011). Comparison of values of Pearson's and Spearman's correlation coefficients on the same sets of data. *QUAGEO*, *30*(2), 87–93. https://doi.org/10.2478/v10117-011-0021-1

Horverak, J. G., Sandal, G. M., Bye, H. H., & Pallesen, S. (2013). Managers' selection preferences: The role of prejudice and multicultural personality traits in the assessment of native and immigrant job candidates. *European Review of Applied Psychology*, *63*(5), 267–275. https://doi.org/10.1016/j.erap.2013.07.003

Hristov, I., Camilli, R., & Mechelli, A. (2022). Cognitive biases in implementing a performance management system: Behavioral strategy for supporting managers' decision-making processes. *Management Research Review*, *45*(9), 1110–1136. https://doi.org/10.1108/mrr-11-2021-0777

Ibidunni, A. S. (2020). Exploring knowledge dimensions for improving performance in organizations. *Journal of Workplace Learning*, *32*(1), 76–93. https://doi.org/10.1108/jwl-01-2019-0013

ILO. (2021). *ILO global estimates on international migrant workers, results and methodology*. Retrieved March 28, 2021, from https://www.ilo.org/wcmsp5/groups/public/@dgreports/@dcomm/@publ/documents/publication/wcms_808935.pdf

Jakovljevic, M. M., Netz, Y., Buttigieg, S. C., Adany, R., Laaser, U., & Varjacic, M. (2018). Population aging and migration – History and UN forecasts in the EU-28 and its east and south near neighborhood – One century perspective 1950–2050. *Globalization and Health*, *14*(1), 1–6. https://doi.org/10.1186/s12992-018-0348-7

Johnson, H. M., Irish, W., Strassle, P. D., Mahoney, S. T., Schroen, A. T., Josef, A. P., Freischlag, J. A., Tuttle, J. E., & Brownstein, M. R. (2020). Associations between career satisfaction, personal life factors, and work–life integration practices among US surgeons by gender. *JAMA Surgery*, *155*(8), 742. https://doi.org/10.1001/jama-surg.2020.1332

Jøranli, I. (2018). Managing organisational knowledge through recruitment: Searching and selecting embodied competencies. *Journal of Knowledge Management*, *22*(1), 183–200. https://doi.org/10.1108/jkm-12-2016-0541

Joshi, A., Kale, S., Chandel, S., & Pal, D. (2015). Likert scale: Explored and explained. *British Journal of Applied Science & Technology*, *7*(4), 396–403. https://doi.org/10.9734/bjast/2015/14975

Kılıç, M., & Kuzey, C. (2016). The effect of board gender diversity on firm performance: Evidence from Turkey. *Gender in Management: An International Journal*, *31*(7), 434–455. https://doi.org/10.1108/gm-10-2015-0088

Kim, H. T. (2020). Linking managers' emotional intelligence, cognitive ability and firm performance: Insights from Vietnamese firms. *Cogent Business & Management*, *7*(1), 1829272. https://doi.org/10.1080/23311975.2020.1829272

Kim, H.-Y. (2017). Statistical notes for clinical researchers: Chi-squared test and Fisher's exact test. *Restorative Dentistry & Endodontics*, *42*(2), 152. https://doi.org/10.5395/rde.2017.42.2.152

Knappert, L., van Dijk, H., & Ross, V. (2019). Refugees' inclusion at work: A qualitative cross-level analysis. *Career Development International*, *25*(1), 32–48. https://doi.org/10.1108/cdi-01-2018-0021

Koellen, T. (2021). Diversity management: A critical review and agenda for the future. *Journal of Management Inquiry*, *30*(3), 259–272. https://doi.org/10.1177/1056492619868025

Kohlenberger, J., Pędziwiatr, K., Rengs, B., Riederer, B., Setz, I., Buber-Ennser, I., Brzozowski, J., & Nahorniuk, O. (2022, September 7). *What the self-selection of Ukrainian refugees means for support in host countries*. Retrieved March 5, 2023, from https://blogs.lse.ac.uk/europpblog/2022/09/07/what-the-self-selection-of-ukrainian-refugees-means-for-support-in-host-countries/.

Kozak, M., Krzanowski, W., & Tartanus, M. Ł. (2012). Use of the correlation coefficient in agricultural sciences: Problems, pitfalls and how to deal with them. *Anais Da Academia Brasileira De Ciências*, *84*(4), 1147–1156. https://doi.org/10.1590/s0001-37652012000400029

Kumar, P., Kumar, N., Aggarwal, P., & Yeap, J. A. L. (2021). Working in lockdown: The relationship between COVID-19 induced work stressors, job performance, distress, and life satisfaction. *Current Psychology*, *40*(12), 6308–6323. https://doi.org/10.1007/s12144-021-01567-0

Kump, B. (2021). When do threats mobilize managers for organizational change toward sustainability? An environmental belief model. *Business Strategy and the Environment*, *30*(5), 2713–2726. https://doi.org/10.1002/bse.2773

Kurdi, B. A., Alshurideh, M., & afaishat, T. A. (2020). Employee retention and organizational performance: Evidence from banking industry. *Management Science Letters*, *10*, 3981–3990. https://doi.org/10.5267/j.msl.2020.7.011

Lämsä, A.-M., Mattila, M., Lähdesmäki, M., & Suutari, T. (2019). Company values guiding the recruitment of employees with a foreign background. *Baltic Journal of Management*, *14*(4), 658–675. https://doi.org/10.1108/bjm-04-2019-0112

Landesregierung, A. d. T. (2022, December). *Landesstatistik*. Land Tirol. Retrieved April 12, 2023, from https://www.tirol.gv.at/statistik-budget/statistik/

Li, X., & Frenkel, S. (2016). Where *hukou* status matters: Analyzing the linkage between supervisor perceptions of HR practices and employee work engagement. *The International Journal of Human Resource Management*, *28*(17), 2375–2402. https://doi.org/10.1080/09585192.2015.1137613

Lietz, P. (2010). Research into questionnaire design: A summary of the literature. *International Journal of Market Research, 52*(2), 249–272. https://doi.org/10.2501/s147078530920120x

Liu, Y., Wei, Z., & Xie, F. (2014). Do women directors improve firm performance in China? *Journal of Corporate Finance, 28*, 169–184. https://doi.org/10.1016/j.jcorp-fin.2013.11.016

Malik, A., & Manroop, L. (2017). Recent immigrant newcomers' socialization in the workplace. *Equality, Diversity and Inclusion: An International Journal, 36*(5), 382–400. https://doi.org/10.1108/edi-11-2016-0083

Marois, G., Bélanger, A., & Lutz, W. (2020). Population aging, migration, and productivity in Europe. *Proceedings of the National Academy of Sciences, 117*(14), 7690–7695. https://doi.org/10.1073/pnas.1918988117

Mayer, J. D., Roberts, R. D., & Barsade, S. G. (2008). Human abilities: Emotional intelligence. *Annual Review of Psychology, 59*(1), 507–536. https://doi.org/10.1146/annurev.psych.59.103006.093646

McGinnity, F., Privalko, I., Fahey, É., O'Brien, D., & Enright, S. (2020). *Origin and integration: A study of migrants in the 2016 Irish census.* https://doi.org/10.26504/bkm-next392

Mehrabi, N., Morstatter, F., Saxena, N., Lerman, K., & Galstyan, A. (2021). A survey on bias and fairness in machine learning. *ACM Computing Surveys, 54*(6), 1–35. https://doi.org/10.1145/3457607

Mohr, V. v. M. (2023). *Tirol – Ausländeranteil 2023.* Statista. Retrieved March 5, 2023, from https://de.statista.com/statistik/daten/studie/1269500/umfrage/auslaenderanteil-in-tirol/

Moreno-Gómez, J., Lafuente, E., & Vaillant, Y. (2018). Gender diversity in the board, women's leadership and business performance. *Gender in Management: An International Journal, 33*(2), 104–122. https://doi.org/10.1108/gm-05-2017-0058

Nakamura, M. (1996). Development of female managers and the *sôgôshoku* in Japan. *Journal of Management Development, 15*(8), 65–78. https://doi.org/10.1108/02621719610145915

Nguyen, N. T., Yadav, M., Pande, S., Bhanot, A., & Hasan, M. F. (2021). Impact of diversity management on organizational performance in hotel organizations: A conceptual framework. *International Journal of System Assurance Engineering and Management, 13*(S1), 186–196. https://doi.org/10.1007/s13198-021-01358-7

Ortlieb, R., & Ressi, E. (2022). From refugee to manager? Organisational socialisation practices, refugees' experiences and polyrhythmic socialisation. *European Management Review, 19*(2), 185–206. https://doi.org/10.1111/emre.12500

Pandis, N. (2016). The chi-square test. *American Journal of Orthodontics and Dentofacial Orthopedics, 150*(5), 898–899. https://doi.org/10.1016/j.ajodo.2016.08.009

Peiris, J. M. (2021). HR department's compelling new role in workplace transition in response to the coronavirus. *Kelaniya Journal of Human Resource Management, 16*(1), 58. https://doi.org/10.4038/kjhrm.v16i1.87

Prufeta, P. (2017). Emotional intelligence of nurse managers: An exploratory study. *JONA: The Journal of Nursing Administration, 471*, 134–139. https://doi.org/10.1097/NNA.0000000000000455

Quality report on European statistics on international trade in goods. (2021). *Eurostat*, 1–119. https://doi.org/10.2785/302391

Risberg, A., & Romani, L. (2022). Underemploying highly skilled migrants: An organizational logic protecting corporate 'normality.' *Human Relations, 75*(4), 655–680. https://doi.org/10.1177/0018726721992854

Roberson, Q. M. (2019). Diversity in the workplace: A review, synthesis, and future research agenda. *Annual Review of Organizational Psychology and Organizational Behavior, 6*(1), 69–88. https://doi.org/10.1146/annurev-orgpsych-012218-015243

Ryan, L., & Mulholland, J. (2013). French connections: The networking strategies of French highly skilled migrants in London. *Global Networks*, *14*(2), 148–166. https://doi.org/10.1111/glob.12038

Schmidt, W., & Müller, A. (2021). Workplace universalism and the integration of migrant workers and refugees in Germany. *Industrial Relations Journal*, *52*(2), 145–160. https://doi.org/10.1111/irj.12320

Schwartz, S. H., & Rubel, T. (2005). Sex differences in value priorities: Cross-cultural and multimethod studies. *Journal of Personality and Social Psychology*, *89*(6), 1010–1028. https://doi.org/10.1037/0022-3514.89.6.1010

Sekkat, K., Szafarz, A., & Tojerow, I. (2015). Women at the top in developing countries: Evidence from firm-level data. *SSRN Electronic Journal*. https://doi.org/10.2139/ssrn.2699433

Selman, V., Selman, R. C., Selman, J., & Selman, E. (2011). Spiritual-intelligence/-quotient. *College Teaching Methods & Styles Journal (CTMS)*, *1*(3), 23. https://doi.org/10.19030/ctms.v1i3.5236

Severo, E. A., de Guimarães, J. C., & Henri Dorion, E. C. (2018). Cleaner production, social responsibility and eco-innovation: Generations' perception for a sustainable future. *Journal of Cleaner Production*, *186*, 91–103. https://doi.org/10.1016/j.jclepro.2018.03.129

Severo, E. A., de Guimarães, J. C., & Dellarmelin, M. L. (2021). Impact of the COVID-19 pandemic on environmental awareness, sustainable consumption and social responsibility: Evidence from generations in Brazil and Portugal. *Journal of Cleaner Production*, *286*, 124947. https://doi.org/10.1016/j.jclepro.2020.124947

Simpson, N. B. (2022). Demographic and economic determinants of migration. *IZA World of Labor*, *3*, 373. https://doi.org/10.15185/izawol.373.v2

Singh, D. (2019). A literature review on employee retention with focus on recent trends. *International Journal of Scientific Research in Science, Engineering and Technology*, *6*, 425–431. https://doi.org/10.32628/ijsrst195463

Statistik.at. (2022). *More than a quarter of the total Austrian population has a ….* Retrieved October 14, 2022, from https://www.statistik.at/fileadmin/announcement/2022/07/20220725MigrationIntegration2022EN.pdf

Statistik.at. (2023). *Mehr als ein Viertel der Bevölkerung hat Wurzeln im Ausland.* https://www.statistik.at/fileadmin/announcement/2023/08/20230824MigrationIntegration2023.pdf.

Story, D. A., & Tait, A. R. (2019). Survey research. *Anesthesiology*, *130*(2), 192–202. https://doi.org/10.1097/aln.0000000000002436

Tanrıkulu, F. (2020). The political economy of migration and integration: Effects of immigrants on the economy in Turkey. *Journal of Immigrant & Refugee Studies*, *19*(4), 364–377. https://doi.org/10.1080/15562948.2020.1810840

Tavakol, M., & Dennick, R. (2011). Making sense of Cronbach's alpha. *International Journal of Medical Education*, *2*, 53–55. https://doi.org/10.5116/ijme.4dfb.8dfd

Taylor, R. N. (1975). Age and experience as determinants of managerial information processing and decision making performance. *Academy of Management Journal*, *18*(1), 74–81. https://doi.org/10.5465/255626

The University of Akron, Ohio. (2021, September 24). *Office of research administration.* The University of Akron, Ohio. Retrieved November 19, 2022, from https://www.uakron.edu/research/ora/

Tihanyi, L., Griffith, D. A., & Russell, C. J. (2005). The effect of cultural distance on entry mode choice, international diversification, and MNE performance: A meta-analysis. *Journal of International Business Studies*, *36*(3), 270–283. https://doi.org/10.1057/palgrave.jibs.8400136

United Nations. (2020). *International migrant stock\population division.* United Nations. Retrieved March 3, 2023, from https://www.un.org/development/desa/pd/content/international-migrant-stock

van Knippenberg, D., Dawson, J. F., West, M. A., & Homan, A. C. (2010). Diversity fault-lines, shared objectives, and top management team performance. *Human Relations*, *64*(3), 307–336. https://doi.org/10.1177/0018726710378384

van Riemsdijk, M., & Basford, S. (2022). Integration of highly skilled migrants in the work-place: A multi-level framework. *Journal of International Migration and Integration*, *23*(2), 633–654. https://doi.org/10.1007/s12134-021-00845-x

Votoupalová, M. (2018). Schengen cooperation: What scholars make of it. *Journal of Borderlands Studies*, *35*(3), 403–423. https://doi.org/10.1080/08865655.2018.1457974

Weiss, D., & Weiss, M. (2019). Why people feel younger: Motivational and social-cognitive mechanisms of the subjective age bias and its implications for work and organiza-tions. *Work, Aging and Retirement*, *5*(4), 273–280. https://doi.org/10.1093/workar/waz016

Wessendorf, S., & Phillimore, J. (2018). New migrants' social integration, embedding and emplacement in superdiverse contexts. *Sociology*, *53*(1), 123–138. https://doi.org/10.1177/0038038518771843

Wiersema, M. F., & Bantel, K. A. (1992). Top management team demography and cor-porate strategic change. *Academy of Management Journal*, *35*(1), 91–121. https://doi.org/10.5465/256474

WKO.at. (2021). *Tourismus Freizeitwirtschaft in Zahlen 2021*. Retrieved March 5, 2023, from https://www.wko.at/branchen/tourismus-freizeitwirtschaft/tourismus-freizeitwirtschaft-in-zahlen-2021.pdf

WKO.at. (2023). *Das Portal der Wirtschaftskammern – Service*. Retrieved March 5, 2023, from https://www.wko.at/

Xia, Y., & Ma, Z. (2020). Social integration, perceived stress, locus of control, and psy-chological wellbeing among Chinese emerging adult migrants: A conditional pro-cess analysis. *Journal of Affective Disorders*, *267*, 9–16. https://doi.org/10.1016/j.jad.2020.02.016

Xypolytas, N. (2018). The refugee crisis as a preparation stage for future exclusion. *International Journal of Sociology and Social Policy*, *38*(7–8), 637–650. https://doi.org/10.1108/ijssp-11-2017-0149

Yadav, S., & Lenka, U. (2020). Diversity management: A systematic review. *Equality, Diversity and Inclusion: An International Journal*, *39*(8), 901–929. https://doi.org/10.1108/edi-07-2019-0197

Zhang, Y., Jiang, T., Sun, J., Fu, Z., & Yu, Y. (2022). Sustainable development of urbani-zation: From the perspective of social security and social attitude for migration. *Sustainability*, *14*(17), 10777. https://doi.org/10.3390/su141710777

Zikic, J. (2014). Skilled migrants' career capital as a source of competitive advantage: Implications for strategic HRM. *The International Journal of Human Resource Management*, *26*(10), 1360–1381. https://doi.org/10.1080/09585192.2014.981199

Appendix 1

Table AI.   Codebook.

Variable	Position	Label	Measurement Level
ID	1.	Identification number	NA
DATE	2.	Date of completion of the questionnaire	NA
AGE		"Please indicate your age." 1 – 25 or younger 2 – 26–41 3 – 42–57 4 – 58–67 5 – 68 or older	Ratio
GEN		"Please specify your gender." 1 – Male 2 – Female 3 – Diverse	Nominal
OR		"Please specify your origin." 1 – Austrian-born 2 – Foreign-born	Nominal
ET		"Please indicate your average employee turnover." 1 – 10% or less 2 – 11–20% 3 – 21–30% 4 – 31–40% 5 – 41–50% 6 – 51% or more	Ratio
NO		"Indicate the number of employees in your company." 1 – Fewer than 10 employees 2 – 10–49 employees 3 – 50–249 employees 4 – 250 or more employees	Ratio

(*Continued*)

Table AI.   (*Continued*)

Variable	Position	Label	Measurement Level
IND		"Indicate the industry you are operating in."	Nominal
		1 – Banking, finance, and insurance	
		2 – Construction, real estate, and home automation	
		3 – Hospitality and tourism	
		4 – The food industry	
		5 – Wood processing	
		6 – Mechanical engineering	
		7 – Other	
Re1		"I believe that the applicant's origin country is an important factor for the recruitment outcome."	Ordinal
		1 – I strongly agree	
		2 – I agree	
		3 – Neutral	
		4 – I disagree	
		5 – I strongly disagree	
Re2		"I believe that the expertise in the work in the international environment of an applicant is an important factor for the recruitment outcome."	Ordinal
		1 – I strongly agree	
		2 – I agree	
		3 – Neutral	
		4 – I disagree	
		5 – I strongly disagree	
Re3		"Throughout my career, I have recruited more foreign applicants than domestic ones."	Ordinal
		1 – I strongly agree	
		2 – I agree	
		3 – Neutral	
		4 – I disagree	
		5 – I strongly disagree	

Table AI. (*Continued*)

Variable	Position	Label	Measurement Level
Re4		"I have observed that my colleagues are more compliant with candidates from their own country."	Ordinal
		1 – I strongly agree	
		2 – I agree	
		3 – Neutral	
		4 – I disagree	
		5 – I strongly disagree	
Int1		"The greatest hurdle foreign workforce faces while integrating is a language barrier."	Ordinal
		1 – I strongly agree.	
		2 – I agree	
		3 – Neutral	
		4 – I disagree	
		5 – I strongly disagree	
Int2		"I think that cultural differences are not barriers to employee integration."	Ordinal
		1 – I strongly agree	
		2 – I agree	
		3 – Neutral	
		4 – I disagree	
		5 – I strongly disagree	
Int3		"Austrian workers are happy to assist foreigners throughout the integration processes."	Ordinal
		1 – I strongly agree	
		2 – I agree	
		3 – Neutral	
		4 – I disagree	
		5 – I strongly disagree	

(*Continued*)

Table AI.   (*Continued*)

Variable	Position	Label	Measurement Level
Int4		"It often happens that the foreign workers register difficulties in successful integration in our company."	Ordinal
		1 – I strongly agree	
		2 – I agree	
		3 – Neutral	
		4 – I disagree	
		5 – I strongly disagree	
Int5		"Our company provides socialization and orientation programs for newcomers."	Ordinal
		1 – I strongly agree	
		2 – I agree	
		3 – Neutral	
		4 – I disagree	
		5 – I strongly disagree	
TD1		"Foreign workers are passionate about learning and carrying out job–specific tasks."	Ordinal
		1 – I strongly agree	
		2 – I agree	
		3 – Neutral	
		4 – I disagree	
		5 – I strongly disagree	
TD2		"Board of our company consists of members of foreign origin, too."	Ordinal
		1 – I strongly agree	
		2 – I agree	
		3 – Neutral	
		4 – I disagree	
		5 – I strongly disagree	

Table AI. (*Continued*)

Variable	Position	Label	Measurement Level
TD3		"In our company, foreigners are enabled to progress to higher levels."	Ordinal
		1 – I strongly agree	
		2 – I agree	
		3 – Neutral	
		4 – I disagree	
		5 – I strongly disagree	
TD4		"During my career, I have come across a company that improperly implemented the training process for the foreign workforce."	Ordinal
		1 – I strongly agree	
		2 – I agree	
		3 – Neutral	
		4 – I disagree	
		5 – I strongly disagree	

Note. After the acceptance of paper proposal, the author distributed the survey among the Tirolean companies. The data obtained from the survey responses enabled statistical analyses and for drawing the conclusions of the research.

Appendix 2

Table AII.   Item – Total Statistics Table.

	Item – Total Statistics Table				
	Scale Mean if Item Deleted	Scale Variance if Item Deleted	Corrected Item–Total Correlation	Squared Multiple Correlation	Cronbach's Alpha If Item Deleted
Q1	35.28	23.753	−0.127	0.192	0.450
Q2	36.05	22.188	0.077	0.051	0.373
Q3	34.81	19.318	0.275	0.202	0.301
Q4	35.45	22.376	0.024	0.161	0.391
Q5	36.40	22.605	0.027	0.117	0.388
Q6	35.64	21.113	0.083	0.233	0.377
Q7	35.66	22.960	0.008	0.105	0.390
Q8	34.96	22.944	−0.013	0.144	0.399
Q9	35.00	19.373	0.293	0.180	0.296
Q10	35.54	20.651	0.297	0.328	0.313
Q11	34.23	18.974	0.275	0.198	0.297
Q12	36.33	21.007	0.214	0.173	0.333
Q13	34.84	19.449	0.248	0.194	0.311

Note. Table AII serves as an addition to the results obtained by the Cronbach's alpha. The numbers from the table suggest the improvements in validity of the alpha, in case a variable – or multiple ones – gets removed from the dataset. The results in the table suggest that, by removing the data with the lowest consistencies – 3, 9, 10, 11, 12, and 13 – the validity of the data would not change significantly.

Appendix 3

Table AIII. Notes to Chi-Square Test.

Dependent Variables	Age Notes	Gender Notes	Origin Notes
Recruitment			
Re1	a – 10 cells (40.0%) have expected count less than 5. The minimum expected count is 0.45	a1 – 0 cell (0.0%) has expected count less than 5. The minimum expected count is 7.29	a – 3 cells (30.0%) have expected count less than 5. The minimum expected count is 3.03
Re2	a1 – 15 cells (60.0%) have expected count less than 5. The minimum expected count is 0.08	a1 – 3 cells (30.0%) have expected count less than 5. The minimum expected count is 1.27	a1 – 3 cells (30.0%) have expected count less than 5. The minimum expected count is 0.53
Re3	a2 – 12 cells (48.0%) have expected count less than 5. The minimum expected count is 0.29	a2 – 1 cell (10.0%) has expected count less than 5. The minimum expected count is 4.76	a2 – 2 cells (20.0%) have expected count less than 5. The minimum expected count is 1.98
Re4	a3 – 14 cells (56.0%) have expected count less than 5. The minimum expected count is 0.31	a3 – 0 cell (0.0%) has expected count less than 5. The minimum expected count is 5.07	a3 – 2 cells (20.0%) have expected count less than 5. The minimum expected count is 2.11
Integration			
Int1	a – 16 cells (64.0%) have expected count less than 5. The minimum expected count is 0.10	a – 3 cells (30.0%) have expected count less than 5. The minimum expected count is 1.59	a – 4 cells (40.0%) have expected count less than 5. The minimum expected count is 0.66
Int2	a2 – 12 cells (48.0%) have expected count less than 5. The minimum expected count is 0.39	a1 – 0 cell (0.0%) has expected count less than 5. The minimum expected count is 6.34	a1 – 2 cells (20.0%) have expected count less than 5. The minimum expected count is 2.63

(Continued)

Table AIII.   (*Continued*)

Dependent Variables	Age Notes	Gender Notes	Origin Notes
Int3	a3 – 16 cells (64.0%) have expected count less than 5. The minimum expected count is 0.08	a2 – 3 cells (30.0%) have expected count less than 5. The minimum expected count is 1.27	a2 – 4 cells (40.0%) have expected count less than 5. The minimum expected count is 0.53
Int4	a4 – 13 cells (52.0%) have expected count less than 5. The minimum expected count is 0.04	a3 – 2 cells (20.0%) have expected count less than 5. The minimum expected count is 0.63	a3 – 4 cells (40.0%) have expected count less than 5. The minimum expected count is 0.26
Int5	a5 – 12 cells (48.0%) have expected count less than 5. The minimum expected count is 0.21	a4 – 1 cell (10.0%) has expected count less than 5. The minimum expected count is 3.49	a4 – 3 cells (30.0%) have expected count less than 5. The minimum expected count is 1.45
Training and development			
TD1	a – 15 cells (60.0%) have expected count less than 5. The minimum expected count is 0.16	a – 2 cells (20.0%) have expected count less than 5. The minimum expected count is 2.54	a – 3 cells (30.0%) have expected count less than 5. The minimum expected count is 1.05
TD2	a1 – 16 cells (64.0%) have expected count less than 5. The minimum expected count is 0.27	a1 – 3 cells (30.0%) have expected count less than 5. The minimum expected count is 4.44	a1 – 4 cells (40.0%) have expected count less than 5. The minimum expected count is 1.84
TD3	a2 – 16 cells (64.0%) have expected count less than 5. The minimum expected count is 0.06	a2 – 4 cells (40.0%) have expected count less than 5. The minimum expected count is 0.95	a2 – 3 cells (30.0%) have expected count less than 5. The minimum expected count is 0.40
TD4	a3 – 12 cells (48.0%) have expected count less than 5. The minimum expected count is 0.31	a3 – 0 cell (0.0%) has expected count less than 5. The minimum expected count is 5.07	a3 – 2 cells (20.0%) have expected count less than 5. The minimum expected count is 2.11

Note. Table AIII includes the list of the notes received from obtaining the chi-square test. Data displayed in the table are the additions to the dependencies as well as expected counts for each variable.

Chapter 5

Social Challenges of the Green Transition: A Focus on the Employment Gender Gap in Romania

Gheorghe Dan Isbăşoiu[a], Dana Volosevici[a] and Adriana Grigorescu[b–d]

[a]*Petroleum-Gas University Ploiesti, Romania*
[b]*National University of Political Studies and Public Administration, Romania*
[c]*National Institute for Economic Research "Costin C. Kiritescu" – Romanian Academy, Romania*
[d]*Academy of Romanian Scientists, Romania*

Abstract

The European growth model set out by the European Commission is founded on a dual transition, to green and digital. Although the transition to the new growth model requires an in-depth analysis of the transformations that will affect industry in its main branches and the energy system in particular, the social and employment aspects must not be ignored, in order to ensure that the twin transitions are fair and inclusive and have a substantive contribution to strengthening the Union's social resilience and the prosperity of all citizens. Taking as a starting point the fact that the green transition will have direct impacts on the labor market, affecting, as emphasized by the European institutions, primarily workers who already have a vulnerable status, this chapter aims to analyze the topic of employment gender gap, highlighting those aspects that could be aggravated during the green transition. The analysis was carried out on relevant statistical data for the Romanian labor market, which were projected on EU27 data.

Keywords: Gender gap; green transition; education; gender pay gap; labor

Entrepreneurship and Development for a Green Resilient Economy, 131–163
Copyright © 2024 by Gheorghe Dan Isbăşoiu, Dana Volosevici and Adriana Grigorescu
Published under exclusive licence by Emerald Publishing Limited
doi:10.1108/978-1-83797-088-920241005

Introduction

The European growth model set out by the European Commission is founded on a dual transition, to green and digital, intended to bolster the economic and social resilience of the European Union (EU; European Commission, 2022). The primary objective of this transition is to address the intricate challenges within the European region and solidify the EU's standing in the economic and geopolitical arenas. The European Green Deal, having the ultimate goal of reaching climate neutrality by 2050, will bring potential for economic growth, for new business models and markets, for new jobs and technological development (European Council, 2019). On a wider level, the EU institutions have stressed that achieving climate neutrality will require overcoming serious challenges, from those related to the need for public and private investments to the imperative to ensure the fairness of the new economic model (Chen et al., 2022; Wolf et al., 2021). Although the transition to the new growth model requires an in-depth analysis of the transformations that will affect industry in its main branches and the energy system in particular, the social and employment aspects must not be ignored (Brătianu et al., 2020). Therefore, the European growth model addressed the need for a strong political response in order to ensure that the twin transitions are fair and inclusive and have a substantive contribution to strengthening the Union's social resilience and the prosperity of all citizens.

In this regard, the European green legislation, such as the European Climate Law (2021), for example, expressly states "the need to ensure a just and socially fair transition for all." In the same vein, the Fit for 55 package, a set of proposals to revise and complete the EU legislation related to climate, energy and transport, aims at providing a coherent framework for reaching the EU's climate goals but, at the same time, integrates principles that go beyond the climatic framework, in order to ensure a just and socially fair transition (Jenkins et al., 2018; Velicu & Barca, 2020; Wang & Lo, 2021).

Similarly, the 20 principles of the European Pillar of Social Rights proclaimed at the Gothenburg Summit in November 2017 express the transposition of the will of the European institutions to integrate the "social rulebook" for fair and well-functioning labor markets in the implementation of the fair transition toward a strong, climate-neutral Social Europe. The 20 principles were turned into concrete action through the European Pillar of Social Rights Action Plan (European Commission, 2021), which established three EU headline targets to be achieved by the end of 2030, in the areas of employment, skills and social protection (Lewis, 2018). In the area of employment, as regards the employment rate for the 20–64 age group, the European target is to reach 78% by 2030. In the area of skills, the action plan proposed to increase adult participation in training to 60%, up from a much more modest rate of 37% in 2017, with only 18% for the low-qualified adults. In the area of social protection, the target pointed to reduce by at least 15 million the number of people at risk of poverty or social exclusion, knowing that in 2019, around 91 million people were at such risk in the EU.

At the international level, Member States have endorsed the Paris Agreement, which refers to "the imperatives of a just transition of the workforce and the creation of decent work and quality jobs" (UN, 2015). The International Labor Organization's (ILO) *guidelines for a just transition toward environmentally sustainable economies and societies for all* are also focused on topics such as the strong gender dimension of the climate transition, the need to anticipate impacts on labor market, securing sufficient and sustainable safeguards for job losses, displacement, or skills enhancement (Grigorescu et al., 2022; Pirciog et al., 2023). Moreover, the guidelines stress that there is no "one size fits all"; therefore, the policies and programs should be tailored to the unique conditions of each country (ILO, 2015).

Taking as a starting point the fact that the green transition will have direct impacts on the labor market, affecting, as emphasized by the European institutions, primarily workers who already have a vulnerable status, this chapter aims to analyze the topic of the employment gender gap, highlighting those aspects that could be aggravated during the green transition. The analysis was conducted through time series with comparable data, as well as stationary at the level of year 2022, for the population in Romania, using the average European level as a reference. At times, reporting was done at the minimum and maximum levels of the range, depending on the objectives pursued.

Gender Equality

Gender equality is one of the objectives of the EU, as pointed out in Articles 2 and 3(3) of the Treaty of European Union (TEU), as well as in Articles 8, 10, 19 and 157 of the Treaty on the Functioning of the European Union (TFEU) and a fundamental right, expressly provided by Articles 21 and 23 of the EU Charter of Fundamental Rights. The EU legislation covers a number of important gender equality issues, such as equality between women and men in the workplace, in self-employment or related to access to goods and services, social security, pregnancy and maternity and on family-related leave and flexible working arrangements for parents and carers. Moreover, gender equality constitutes one of the 17 sustainable development goals (SDGs), part of the 2030 Agenda for Sustainable Development, adopted by the United Nations (UN) in September 2015. The EU upholds the 2030 Agenda, with the SDGs forming the central focus of Commission policymaking, influencing both internal and external actions across various sectors. As demonstrated by the doctrine, gender equality – "Achieve gender equality and empower all women and girls" (SDG 5) – can be regarded as cross-cutting issue in the implementation of the SDGs, spanning all the other 16 SDGs, with a total of 45 targets and 54 gender-related indicators (Filho, 2022). This pervasion demonstrates that gender equality has a catalytic effect on human development (Odera & Mulusa, 2020). SDG 5 brings forward issues of gender-based discrimination such as unpaid work, sexual and reproductive rights and gender-based violence (Hirsu et al., 2019), mirroring the ongoing and growing endeavors by the UN to promote gender equality, highlighted by the creation of the Commission on the Status of Women in 1946 (UN Women, 2020) and the adoption of landmark agreements such as the Convention on the Elimination of All Forms of Discrimination Against Women in 1979 (OHCHR, 2020), the Beijing Declaration and Platform for Action in 1995 (UN, 1995) and the establishment of UN Women in 2010 (UN, 2012). Despite all the UN actions, the 2023 Report on SDGs (UN, 2023) pointed out that, as regards SDG 5, progress has been too slow. At the present pace, it will require 286 years to eliminate disparities in legal protection and eradicate discriminatory laws, and it will take 140 years for women to achieve equal representation in positions of power and leadership in the workplace (Bell, 2021).

SDG 5 is also monitored in an EU context, being focused on the topics of gender-based violence, access to quality education, participation in employment, equal payment and a balanced representation in leadership positions. SDG 5 data are to be corroborated with targets and indicators of SDG 8, decent work and economic growth. In accordance with the Eurostat (2023) Report, women are still less likely to be employed than men, and the EU is not on track to halve its gender employment gap by 2030, as established by the European Pillar of Social Rights Action Plan. Women's gross hourly earnings in the EU were still on average 12.7% below those of men, because of the sectorial and occupational gender gap (Cortes & Pan, 2018; Fodor & Glass, 2018).

Gender Equality Index

Gender equality is a criterion that is analyzed homogeneously across all EU countries. In principle, it is useful to aggregate all sub-criteria by which gender equality can be analyzed into a single statistical indicator (Dilli et al., 2019). The European Institute for Gender Equality (EIGE) has done this by developing the Gender Index. The index measures gender equality through a selection of 31 indicators divided into six core domains (work, money, knowledge, time, power, health) and two additional domains – violence against women and intersecting inequalities (Barnat et al., 2019; Nguyen, 2021).

The Gender Equality Index indicates that Member States on average scored 68.6 out of 100, a score which has improved only by 6.6 points since 2005. Moreover, as a consequence of COVID-19, for the first time in a decade, gender inequalities in employment (full-time equivalent employment rate (FTE) and duration of working life), education (tertiary graduation and participation in formal or informal education and training), health status and access to health services have grown (EIGE, 2022).

In view of the objectives pursued, it seems necessary to present the values of the gender index recorded in the countries of the EU, thus providing a general picture of gender equality. The maximum level of 100 points means perfect gender equality in relation to all domains which are covered by the index; therefore, a level of 50 points, as obtained by a number of EU Member States, indicates significant gaps between genders. A low value of the gender index could be due to the fact that women devote a significant part of their time to activities related to child care and household work.

The values of the Gender Equality Index for 2002, for each EU Member State and the European average are presented in Table 5.1 and Fig. 5.1.

An analysis of the European gender index's values and of their evolution shows significant differences between countries. In addition, the shock provoked

Table 5.1.   Gender Equality Index (2020).

Country	Gender Equality Index	Country	Gender Equality Index	Country	Gender Equality Index	Country	Gender Equality Index
SE	83.9	BE	74.2	IT	65.0	PL	57.7
DK	77.8	LU	73.5	PT	62.8	CY	57.3
NL	77.3	AT	68.8	LV	61.4	CZ	57.2
BE	75.4	DE	68.7	EE	61.0	SK	56.0
FR	75.1	EU27	68.6	BG	60.7	HU	54.2
ES	74.6	SI	67.5	HR	60.7	RO	53.7
IE	74.3	MT	65.6	LT	60.6	EL	53.4

Source: Database Eurostat.

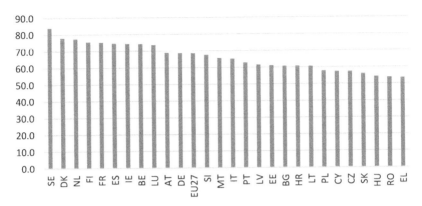

Fig. 5.1.   Gender Equality Index (2020). *Source*: Database Eurostat.

to economies by the COVID-19 pandemic has had a strong impact on gender equality, which is expected to continue in the longer term. At the level of 2022, the gender index values are heterogeneous across the EU. The difference between the high of 83.9 points for Sweden and the low of 53.4 points for Greece, compared to the European average level of 68.6 points, indicates a relative level of breadth of 44.46%.

The data clearly demonstrate that across the EU women continue to experience gender gaps in employment, pay, type of employment contract or level of education, which together with interruptions due to childbirth or household activities, for example, lead to much lower opportunities for career development. Other factors that may have an impact on women's career development are related to their status as sole income earner or migrant workers or to their rural background.

The gender gaps resulting from the statistical data relative to Romania occur despite the existence of a legislative framework that creates the legal premises for ensuring equality on the labor market between men and women and which represents the transposition into domestic law of the relevant European rules in the matter. Thus, the law on equal opportunities and treatment between women and men (Law 202/2002, 2013) provides non-discriminatory access to the choice or free exercise of a profession or activity, to employment in all vacant positions and at all levels of the professional hierarchy, as well as to promotion at any hierarchical and professional level (Article 7, Para. (1), Lett. (a), (b), (e)). In order to ensure the implementation of the legal provisions, the law, which partially transposes Directive 2006/54/EC and Directive 2010/41/EU, establishes for the employer the obligation to ensure equal opportunities and treatment between employees, women and men, in the framework of labor relations of any kind, including by introducing provisions for the prohibition of discrimination based on the criterion of gender in the organization and functioning regulations and in the internal regulations of the company (Article 8, Lett. (a)).

Also, the employer is obliged to permanently inform the employees, including by displaying in visible places, about the rights they have in terms of respect for equal opportunities and treatment between women and men in labor relations (Article 8, Lett. (c)).

The Labor Code, which constitutes the general law in the matter of labor relations, prohibits any direct or indirect discrimination against an employee, discrimination by association, harassment or act of victimization, based on a series of criteria, including the one regarding the sex of the person (Article 5, Para. (2)).

Government Emergency Ordinance No. 137/2000 on the prevention and combating of all forms of discrimination, transposing the provisions of the Council Directive 2000/43/EC of June 29, 2000 and of the Council Directive 2000/78/CE of November 27, 2000, establishes a series of contraventions that sanction the conditioning of a person's participation in an economic activity or the free choice or exercise of a profession of their gender (along with other expressly provided criteria) (Article 6). Also, it is considered a misdemeanor the action to discriminate against a person because of their gender, except for the cases provided by law, manifested in areas such as the conclusion, suspension, modification or termination of the employment relationship; establishment and modification of job duties, workplace or salary; training, improvement, reconversion and professional promotion (Article 7, Lett. (a), (b), (d)).

Article 8 of Government Ordinance 137/2000 expressly sanctions the refusal of a natural or legal person to employ a person because of their gender, except in the cases provided for by law, as well as the condition of occupying a position through an announcement or competition, launched by the employer or by its representative, by the gender of the candidates (Article 8, Para. (1), (2)).

In addition, natural and legal persons having duties related to mediation and job assignment are obliged to apply equal treatment to all those looking for a job, ensuring them free and equal access to consulting the demand and supply on the labor market, as well as to consultation regarding the possibilities of employment and obtaining a qualification (Article 8, Para. (3)).

The actuality of the problem of discrimination in labor relations is also demonstrated by the activity of the National Council for Combating Discrimination (CNCD). According to the CNCD (2022) Report, the distribution of petitions registered in the period 2011–2022 by areas of discrimination shows that access to employment and profession is constantly the main area of referral to the authority, as shown in bold values in Table 5.2.

Regarding the sanctions applied by the National Council for Combating Discrimination and the fines related to them, in 2022, the amount of fines applied in the field of access to training and profession represented 27.8% of the total amount, ranking second after the fines applied for discrimination. On discrimination based on gender, the amount of fines scored 29.7% of the total amount, representing the highest amount compared to all the other discrimination criteria.

Access to the Labor Market

The analysis of access to the labor market is based on the determination of resources, in this case labor resources. The analysis of resources only concerns the

Table 5.2.   Distribution of Petitions Registered With the National Council for Combating Discrimination in the Period 2011–2022 by Areas of Discrimination.

Areas	Years											
	2011	**2012**	**2013**	**2014**	**2015**	**2016**	**2017**	**2018**	**2019**	**2020**	**2021**	**2022**
Access to housing	8	2	2	2	7	10	6	0	4	4	9	15
Access to public places	15	12	14	10	11	22	27	22	21	45	90	20
Access to education	9	29	43	30	33	46	51	50	43	69	41	56
Dignity	76	115	123	105	92	149	144	177	163	364	263	239
Access to training and profession	**211**	**209**	**459**	**369**	**362**	**357**	**273**	**365**	**432**	**297**	**397**	**362**
Other	36	35	67	79	69	78	27	48	60	42	0	0
Access to public services	110	146	150	181	178	180	154	160	181	218	248	296
Total	465	548	858	776	752	842	682	822	904	1,039	1,048	998

Source: CNCD, Activity Report 2022.

situation in Romania, while other aspects, such as the employment rate or gender differences by the type of employment contract, will be analyzed by comparison with the European average. Labor resources for Romania are presented in Table 5.3 and Fig. 5.2. It is to be specified that the statistical data collected are after 2014, since the records made before have the mention of data incomparability.

The data above indicate an obvious decrease of the labor resource in Romania out of the total population, with a rate of −4.85%, the drop being smaller in the case of women (−3.46%), compared to that of men (−6.11%).

Regarding the employed population (Table 5.4), the values that have been recorded show a completely different picture. Thus, if for the total employed population there is a decrease of −9.37%, obviously lower than the rate of decrease of the labor resource, in the case of men the decrease is by −7.25% and in the case of women by −12.10%. Additional explanations for these differences in rates of evolution must be sought for this period. The causes should not be sought in the area of pensioners, as the number of pensioners decreased during this period by approximately 353,000 people, that is, a relative decrease of −6.59%.

In addition, the representation of the absolute changes recorded both for resources and for the employed population for the analyzed period provides a much clearer picture of the size of the drop in the labor market, as well as the evolution trend of the employed population in relation to the labor resource (Table 5.5).

Even in the hypothesis in which we admit that the natural decrease of the population, observed by the values corresponding to the labor resource, implicitly led to the decrease in absolute values of the employed population, it is obvious that in the case of women there are other causes that lead to the multiplication of more than two times the number of inactive people.

Even in conditions where labor resources are decreasing, as well as the employed population, as can be seen from the values presented in Table 5.6 and Fig. 5.3, the average number of employees in Romania is increasing. The growth rates, that is, 15.57% in total, 14.14% in the case of men and 17.16% in the case of women, can be considered to be completely opposite in trend, not only in terms of number of employees as a whole but also in terms of the rate of increase in employment between women and men. This growth should not be treated intrinsically but will have to be compared with the employment rate in the corresponding age category. Of course, the higher rate of increase in female employment is also important, but this has to be compared to the number of female employees in the total number of women compared to men.

The data regarding the employment should be seen against the background of existing European and national legislative regulations. Employment contracts of an indefinite duration are, in accordance with the EU legislation, mainly Directive 99/77/CE, and with the Romanian labor Code, the general form of employment. However, fixed-term employment contracts could respond, in certain circumstances, to the needs of both employers and workers. At a political level, Conclusions of the European Council meeting in Essen in 1994 called for measures aimed at "increasing the employment intensiveness of growth, in particular by more flexible organization of work in a way which fulfills both the wishes of employees and the requirements of competition." The concept of flexible

Table 5.3.   Labor Resources in Romania in the Period 2014–2022.

Sex	Years								
	2014	**2015**	**2016**	**2017**	**2018**	**2019**	**2020**	**2021**	**2022**
	Thousands of People								
Total	12,597.7	12,481.1	12,562	12,432.5	12,238.9	12,198.3	12,216.8	12,201.4	11,986.4
M	6,603.4	6,536.5	6,572.8	6,516.1	6,352.4	6,408.8	6,377.7	6,301.3	6,199.7
W	5,994.3	5,944.6	5,989.2	5,916.4	5,886.5	5,789.5	5,839.1	5,900.1	5,786.7

Source: Database Eurostat.

Table 5.4.   The Employed Population in Romania in the Period 2014–2022.

Sex	Years								
	2014	**2015**	**2016**	**2017**	**2018**	**2019**	**2020**	**2021**	**2022**
	Thousands of People								
Total	8,431.7	8,340.6	8,317.6	8,366.8	8,407.5	8,492.6	8,440.8	7,600.8	7,812.1
M	4,478.4	4,492.8	4,526.9	4,564.3	4,569.9	4,601.1	4,607.8	4,211.4	4,300.0
W	3,953.3	3,847.8	3,790.7	3,802.5	3,837.6	3,891.5	3,833.0	3,389.4	3,512.1

Source: Database Eurostat.

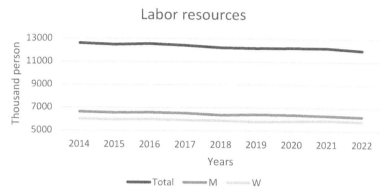

Fig. 5.2. The Evolution of the Labor Resource in Romania in the Period 2014–2022. *Source:* Database Eurostat.

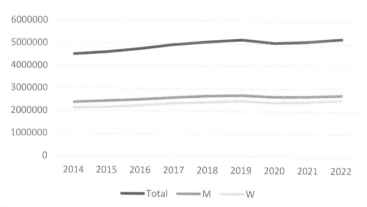

Fig. 5.3. Evolution of the Number of Employees in Romania From 2014 to 2022. *Source*: Database Eurostat.

Table 5.5. Absolute Differences in Human Resources and the Employed Population for the Period 2014–2022.

Gender	HR			Employed Population		
	Total	**M**	**W**	**Total**	**M**	**W**
Absolute differences between 2022 and 2014 (thousands of people)	−611.3	−403.7	−207.6	−807.3	−351.2	−456.1

Source: Database Eurostat.

organization of work has significantly evolved in recent years, and it holds significant importance because, among other benefits, it facilitates access to work for men and women in order to prepare for retirement, reconcile professional and

Table 5.6. Evolution of the Number of Employees in Romania.

	Years								
	2014	2015	2016	2017	2018	2019	2020	2021	2022
Total	4,507,729	4,611,395	4,759,419	4,945,868	5,068,063	5,164,471	5,031,767	5,094,288	5,209,493
M	2,375,452	2,442,469	2,508,302	2,599,249	2,670,984	2,704,275	2,644,032	2,664,339	2,711,398
W	2,132,277	2,168,926	2,251,117	2,346,619	2,397,079	2,460,196	2,387,735	2,429,949	2,498,095

Source: Database Eurostat.

family life or take up education and training opportunities to improve their skills and career opportunities.

According to the EIGE, access to flexible working arrangements is lower in Romania than in the EU, where 57% of women and 54% of men have no control over their working time arrangements, while in the Romanian private sector, 71% of women and 68% of men employees have no control over their working time. The situation is aggravated by the fact that there is a gender gap including in the matter of flexible organization of work, which has a significant impact on career management by women.

Regarding the access to a job, it can easily be noted that, apart from a permanent contract, part-time employment or those with a temporary employment contract have a particular impact. Therefore, participation in the employment rate is, on the one hand, positively influenced by contracts that are not for an indefinite period, but it is unanimously accepted that from the point of view of career management, this is not a favorable element. As can be seen from the data presented in Table 5.7, the European trend is that of increasing the number of employees with full-time contracts. As can be easily noted, the number of employees in this category has increased significantly more in Romania (11.6%) compared to the EU average (7.8%).

On the other hand, the global trend of the entire analyzed period should not be neglected. If in 2013, the difference between the total employed population regardless of the type of work commitment between the average of the EU and Romania was 28.5%, it was reduced in 2022 to 24.6%, an element that indicates some alignment of the labor force in Romania to the values and trends of the European workforce.

It should be noted that in Romania, 21% of women and 25.4% of men have more than one employment contract, as shown by the statistics that indicate a number of 9,650.2 employment contracts, out of a total employed population of 7,812.1. The absolute volumes for women are 4,257 employment contracts for 3,512.1 women in the employed population and 5,392 employment contracts for 4,300 men in the employed population.

In order to have an accurate picture of gender equality related to the rate for the employed population between 20 and 64 years old, we present in Table 5.8 the gender employment gap by the type of employment, in the EU and Romania, respectively. It should be noted that the gender gap in Romania is almost double than the European average in the category in which most of the employed population is found, that is, employed persons. On the contrary, in terms of part-time and temporary contracts, Romania ensures gender equality above the European average.

Another element that characterizes the labor market is given by the transition of the labor force from the unemployed to the employed status. As shown in the data presented in Table 5.9, the transition rate in Romania has a much lower trend than in Europe. While in 2014, the gap was around 10%, and it is now over 15%, which is 15.1% lower than the European average.

If for men the gap to the European average is −13.2%, for women it is −18.5%.

The duration of working life is an indicator that characterizes the level of development of the society to which people belong, as well as the standard of living. This can also be seen from the observation of the countries that are in the upper part of

Table 5.7. Employment Rate by Type of Contract From the Total Population in the 20–64 Age Group.

Employment		Time									
		2013	2014	2015	2016	2017	2018	2019	2020	2021	2022
Employed persons	EU	66.8	67.5	68.5	69.6	70.9	71.9	72.7	71.7	73.1	74.6
	Romania	56.9	58.0	59.2	60.3	62.7	63.9	65.1	65.2	67.1	68.5
Employed persons working part-time	EU	12.8	12.9	13.1	13.2	13.4	13.4	13.6	12.4	12.5	12.7
	Romania	3.2	3.2	3.3	2.8	2.6	2.5	2.3	2.3	2.4	2.3
Employed persons with temporary contract	EU	8.0	8.4	8.7	8,9	9.1	9.1	8.9	8.0	8.2	8.3
	Romania	0.6	0.7	0.7	0.7	0.6	0.6	0.8	0.7	1.3	1.2
Underemployed persons working part-time	EU	2.9	3.0	2.9	2.8	2.6	2.4	2.3	2.3	2.3	2.0
	Romania	1.1	1.2	1.2	1.0	1.0	1.0	0.9	0.8	1.0	1.0
Total	EU	90.4	91.7	93.2	94.5	96.1	96.9	97.4	94.4	96.1	97.6
	Romania	61.9	63.1	64.4	64.8	67.0	67.9	69.1	69.0	71.9	73.0

Source: Database Eurostat.

Table 5.8.   Gender Employment Gap by Type of Employment.

Gender Employment Gap, by Type of Employment (from 20 to 64 years, %)		Time								
		2014	2015	2016	2017	2018	2019	2020	2021	2022
Employed persons	EU	11.1	11.1	11.1	11.3	11.3	11.2	11.1	10.9	10.7
	Romania	17.5	17.7	17.7	17.3	18.5	19.2	19.3	20.1	18.6
Employed persons working part-time	EU	−23.6	−23.3	−23.2	−22.9	−22.7	−22.7	−21.1	−20.6	−20.2
	Romania	0.6	1.0	0.8	1.0	0.7	0.8	0.8	1.1	0.9
Employed persons with temporary contract	EU	−2.0	−1.9	−2.0	−2.1	−2.3	−2.0	−2.1	−2.3	−2.5
	Romania	0.3	0.4	0.5	0.3	0.2	0.5	0.5	1.7	1.6
Underemployed persons working part-time	EU	−3.8	−3.6	−3.2	−3.1	−2.9	−2.7	−2.7	−2.5	−2.2
	Romania	1.2	1.3	1.0	0.9	0.7	0.7	0.6	1.2	1.2

Source: Database Eurostat.

Table 5.9. Transition Unemployment–Employment.

Unemployment–Employment Transition		Time						
		2014	2015	2016	2017	2018	2019	2020
Total	EU	28.4	29.2	30.8	32.5	33.1	33.2	30.0
	Romania	17.7	:	20.3	23.6	18.1	16.6	14.9
Males	EU	28.9	30.1	31.9	33.5	34.2	34.5	30.4
	Romania	20.2	:	23.2	23.2	20.8	17.9	17.2
Females	EU	27.8	28.2	29.6	31.4	32.0	31.8	29.6
	Romania	13.8	:	15.5	24.4	13.1	14.4	11.1

Source: Database Eurostat.

the ranking (Sweden, Denmark, Holland, Germany and Finland) but also from the rate of growth that these countries have for this indicator. Regarding the effects of the analysis of this indicator, it should be remembered that the ratio of active life spans between Germany and Italy is approximately the same as that of the standard of living although many other economic indicators are different, such as that of the average working life where the difference is about seven years in favor of Germany. In Romania, in 2022, the duration of the working life was 31.5 years, compared to 36.6 years in the EU. Moreover, this value should be compared with that recorded in the Netherlands (42.5 years), Sweden (42.3 years) or Denmark (40.3 years). Romania ranks last in Europe, not far from Italy (31.6 years) and Greece (32.9 years). The evolution of the duration for the EU and Romania is presented in Table 5.10.

Another issue that should be pointed out is the gender gap in the matter of duration of working life, which, in Romania, is out of line with the trend in the EU. In the majority of EU Member States (except Lithuania, Estonia, Finland and Latvia), men are expected to work longer than women (4.4 years in the EU). The countries with the largest gender gaps in 2022 were Italy (8.9 years), Greece (7.0 years), Romania (6.9 years), Malta (6.8 years), Cyprus (6.3 years), Ireland and Czech (both 6.0 years).

It is important to point out that the indicator on duration of working life is an estimate of the number of years a person, currently aged 15, is expected to be in the labor force throughout his or her life. The indicator therefore allows, and should incentivize, the prompt taking of measures to remedy the identified deficiencies. These measures can, of course, consist of the introduction of new benefits but also of correcting those benefits or measures that have proven not to achieve their objective.

In Romania, for example, there is progress on the legislative level, imposed, in most cases, by European legislation, transposed directly or through jurisprudence. Thus, it should be pointed out that, starting from 2019, the Romanian Labor Code established the right of women who cumulatively meet the standard age conditions and the minimum contribution period for retirement to opt for the continuation of the individual employment contract, until reaching the age of 65 years old. Otherwise, the individual employment contract would cease by law, upon the cumulative fulfillment of the standard age conditions and the minimum contribution period. The employer cannot restrict or limit the employee's right to continue the activity, if she expresses her option in writing. The new legal provisions implement the decision of the Constitutional Court of Romania (CCR), which stated that the

> termination of a woman's employment at a younger age than a man can and must remain her option. The transformation of this legal benefit into a consequence of the termination of the individual employment contract arising *ope legis* acquires unconstitutional values, to the extent that it ignores the woman's will to be subjected to equal treatment with that applicable to men. (CCR, 2018)

A series of other legal provisions newly introduced in the Labor Code, transposing European directives, create a framework that allows women to ensure

Table 5.10. Duration of Working Life.

Duration of Working Life		Time								
		2013	2014	2015	2016	2017	2018	2019	2020	2021	2022
Total	EU	34.7	34.8	34.9	35.1	35.4	35.7	35.9	35.6	35.9	36.5
	Romania	32.6	32.8	32.8	32.4	33.3	33.5	33.8	33.7	31.1	31.5
Males	EU	37.2	37.3	37.4	37.6	37.9	38.1	38.3	37.9	38.1	38.6
	Romania	35.5	35.7	36.0	35.6	36.3	36.6	37.0	37.0	34.7	34.9
Females	EU	32.0	32.2	32.3	32.6	32.9	33.2	33.4	33.1	33.6	34.2
	Romania	29.5	29.7	29.4	29.0	30.1	30.2	30.3	30.3	27.2	28.0

Source: Database Eurostat.

continuity in work and provide the legal regime for carer's leave or days off for family emergencies. Policies aiming to achieve work–life balance should play a role in advancing gender equality by encouraging women's participation in the workforce and fostering an equal distribution of caring responsibilities between men and women. The significant challenge of reconciling work and family responsibilities is a key factor in the lower representation of women in the labor market. This is because women often work fewer hours in paid employment and allocate more time to unpaid caregiving duties. Statistics indicate that having children or caring for a sick or dependent relative negatively affects women's employment, sometimes leading them to exit the labor force altogether.

Thus, according to Article 152[1] of the Labor Code, the employer is obligated to grant caregiver leave to the employee for the purpose of providing care or personal support to a relative or a person living in the same household as the employee and who requires care or support due to a serious medical condition. The leave has a duration of five working days in a calendar year, duration that can be increased by special laws or by the applicable collective labor contract. During this period, employees have the right to paid days off, which are not included in the duration of the annual vacation and constitute seniority in work and in the specialty. In addition, the period of the carer's leave constitutes a contribution period for establishing the right to unemployment allowance and allowance for temporary incapacity for work granted in accordance with the legislation in force.

Another facility granted to employees, but which, given the role of women in the household and in providing care, can favor the continuity of the employment relationship, is the right to be absent from the workplace in unforeseen situations. In order to benefit from these provisions, the Labor Code imposes a series of cumulative conditions, likely to limit abuses by employees, but which could also constitute an obstacle in the exercise of the right. Thus, the unforeseen situations must have been determined by a family emergency, caused by illness or accident, which make the immediate presence of the employee indispensable. Before exercising the right, respectively, to be absent, the employee must inform the employer. In addition, the maximum duration of absence is 10 working days in a calendar year, and the absent period must be recovered until the full coverage of the normal duration of the employee's work schedule.

Finally, in the transposition of the same Directive 2019/1158, Article 118 et seq. of the Labor Code provide that the employer can establish individualized work programs for all employees, including those who benefit from carer's leave, with their consent or at their request, which may have a limited duration. Individualized work schedules presuppose a flexible way of organizing work time, thereby understanding the possibility for employees to adapt the work schedule, including through the use of remote work formulas, flexible work schedules, individualized work schedules or other programs of work with reduced working hours. Moreover, employees who support children aged up to 11 years benefit, upon request, from four days per month of work at home or telework, except in cases where the nature or type of work does not allow the activity in such conditions.

Even if the legal framework was created, it is necessary to monitor how these legislative instruments will be used in practice by employees and if there will be obstacles to the exercise of the related rights, obstacles that may be generated by the lack of information, the refusal of employers or the discouragement of such practices.

It should be emphasized that the inactivity rate for women is an indication of a country's social customs, attitudes toward women in the labor force and family structures in general (ILO, 2015, p. 17). Especially in light of the paradigm shifts in the economy driven by the transition to green and digital technologies, there is an imperative need for cohesive efforts from political stakeholders, employers and civil society to ensure a framework for integrating women into the labor market on an equal footing with men and for a working life duration that aligns with each woman's free choice.

Given the transition to a green economy, we consider that the workforce needs to acquire skills that enable them to adapt to new technologies and economic and industrial realities. The productivity of the new economic model is determined by specific skills, themselves constructed according to new societal values, through an educational system that needs to be reformed. Thus, an essential aspect of the transition to a sustainable economy is given by the existence of policies with a high degree of efficiency in the field of education, as well as actions in the field of professional training and improvement. These types of policies can also ensure integration and social inclusion. Piketty (2014) argues that "over the long run, education and technology are the decisive determinants of the wage levels" and that "in the long run, the best way to reduce inequalities with respect to labor as well as to increase the average productivity of the labor force and the overall growth of the economy is surely to invest in education" (p. 307).

In addition to keeping a job already accessed or also accessing a job, issues on the workforce are also related to understanding the themes of transition, which includes knowing another type of production or consumption. In addition, the population must become a component part of the transformations as stakeholders of the transition. Thus, the absence of the labor force from continuous learning programs leads to the reduction of personal development opportunities and also to the slowdown of economic growth. On average in the EU, women have higher educational attainment levels than men and lower rates of early leaving from education and training. Yet there is a persistent gender gap in some scientific fields of study, often those leading to better-paid jobs. Despite achieving greater digital literacy scores in ICILS education surveys, in 2018, women represented 26% of students in engineering, manufacturing and construction and only 18% in ICT studies (European Commission, 2020). As pointed out by the European Commission Reflection Paper "Towards a Sustainable Europe by 2030," the transition to an environmentally sustainable, circular and climate-neutral economy has significant employment and social impacts (European Commission, 2019). Europe can have a sustained economic recovery focused on green and digital transitions only with the right skills and education, ensured at an appropriate level of performance and without any form of discrimination.

As can be seen from Tables 5.11–5.13, the educational level influences the occupational status. The data relate to full-time employees. It is absolutely clear that an increase in educational level leads to a higher employment rate. For Level

1 or 2 education category (Table 5.11), about half of the population has full-time employment status. For this category of education, it should be noted that only about 25% of women in Romania are employed, and moreover, it is practically the only category that does not practically have an increasing trend as can be observed in the other cases. For this population category, we will have to see what exactly determines such a low employment rate, what are the causes that lead both to the abandonment of educational evolution and, respectively, the low degree of employment. For this, we will study the trend of the employment rate by degrees of urbanization and naturally in conjunction with the concern for household problems, raising children or caring for the elderly.

In the case of employees with a training level of 3–4, it can be observed that for all analyzed categories (Table 5.12), the trend is increasing, and more so for the analyzed period, all categories have an increase of 10%. And in this case of the population with an average level of training, the most difficult situation is for women in Romania where the lowest employment rate is recorded in 2022, namely 59.1%, which is practically 15% lower than the European average and 10% lower than the European average for women.

A completely different situation is in the case of the workforce with higher education. In this case, the employment rate is relatively the same in all categories (Table 5.13) and more so with approximately the same rate of growth. On the other hand, in the case of women in Romania, the highest increase is recorded with 7.6% more in 2022 compared to 2013.

The existence of an influence of the level of urbanization on the degree of employment is a first hypothesis that could explain the discrepancies between women and men. Table 5.14 shows the data on gender equality regarding the degree of employment at the level of the EU and Romania as a whole. Also, the data are broken down by the level of urbanization of the population.

At this moment, we can consider the level of urbanization in which the female population lives, a first factor that negatively influences the employment rate for women in Romania in a European context. The degree of urbanization from which the studied population comes can mean, from an economic point of view, the level of development in the different categories of settlements of the population but also the level of education or participation in household activities. If at the EU level relatively homogeneous values can be observed in a decreasing trend for all levels of urbanization, in Romania, the situation is different. At the urban level, it can be considered that the evolution is part of the European level of trends, but with the exit from the urban environment in Romania, the trend not only becomes downward but also registers alarming values of segregation. The differences between Romania and the EU, for the values of the employment rate in the situation of employed persons, for different levels of urbanization provide a clear picture of the lack of effect of the policies that concern this segment.

In order to have a clearer picture of the causes that determine gender segregation, we further analyze the structure of the employed population in Romania by gender and, respectively, education level (Table 5.15).

First of all, it can be found that 24.1% of the total population is at an educational level of grades 5–8. The majority population is women with 30.3%,

Table 5.11. Employment by Educational Levels 1–2.

		Years									
		2013	2014	2015	2016	2017	2018	2019	2020	2021	2022
Total	EU	49.6	50.0	50.9	51.9	53.2	54.4	55.1	54.0	55.0	57.2
	Romania	35.2	37.7	37.6	38.3	39.8	40.2	41.6	40.5	42.5	44.9
Males	EU	58.7	59.1	60.4	61.6	63.2	64.6	65.5	64.2	65.5	67.7
	Romania	48.1	50.6	52.1	53.4	55.2	55.9	58.3	57.2	61.4	63.3
Females	EU	40.5	40.8	41.2	41.8	42.8	43.5	44.0	42.8	43.5	45.6
	Romania	25.3	26.9	25.5	25.5	26.4	26.3	26.7	25.9	26.3	28.5

Source: Database Eurostat.

Table 5.12. Employment by Educational Levels 3–4.

		Years									
		2013	2014	2015	2016	2017	2018	2019	2020	2021	2022
Total	EU	67.9	68.7	69.4	70.5	71.5	72.4	73.0	71.5	72.7	74.2
	Romania	59.1	60.9	61.1	61.7	64.1	65.4	66.2	66.2	68.3	69.1
Males	EU	73.5	74.2	74.9	76.0	77.1	78.0	78.7	77.4	78.5	79.9
	Romania	66.7	68.8	68.8	69.4	72.0	74.1	75.4	75.4	77.8	78.0
Females	EU	62.1	62.9	63.6	64.7	65.6	66.4	66.9	65.2	66.5	68.0
	Romania	50.3	52.0	52.3	53.1	55.3	55.6	56.0	55.7	57.6	59.1

Source: Database Eurostat.

Table 5.13. Employment by Educational Levels 5–8.

| | | Years | | | | | | | | | |
		2013	2014	2015	2016	2017	2018	2019	2020	2021	2022
Total	EU	81.2	81.5	82.3	83.1	83.8	84.4	84.8	83.8	85.0	86.0
	Romania	82.3	82.2	85.0	86.0	87.7	88.1	88.9	88.6	88.4	89.5
Males	EU	84.6	84.8	85.6	86.3	87.1	87.7	87.9	86.7	87.9	88.9
	Romania	84.6	84.4	87.8	88.8	89.5	90.3	90.9	90.7	90.5	91.4
Females	EU	78.3	78.7	79.4	80.2	80.9	81.5	82.1	81.3	82.5	83.6
	Romania	80.2	80.0	82.6	83.4	86.1	86.1	87.1	86.7	86.7	87.8

Source: Database Eurostat.

Table 5.14.   The Employed Population According to the Level of Urbanization.

	2010	2011	2012	2013	2014	2015	2016	2017	2018	2019	2020	2021	2022
Total RO	17.5	16.7	17.2	17.2	17.5	17.7	17.7	17.3	18.5	19.2	19.3	20.1	18.6
Total EU	12.7	12.5	11.8	11.3	11.1	11.1	11.1	11.3	11.3	11.2	11.1	10.9	10.7
Cities RO	12.5	12.8	13.7	13.6	14.4	12.8	12.2	11.4	13.1	13.1	12.3	11	9.6
EU Cities	12	11.8	10.1	9.5	9.5	9.4	9.5	9.8	9.9	9.6	9.2	8.5	8,9
Town and suburbs RO	17	17.3	15.9	16.1	16.8	19.3	19.8	19.4	20.9	21.5	21.1	2. 3	21.6
Town and suburbs EU	14.6	14.2	13.6	13	12.7	12.8	13	12.9	13	13	12.8	12.5	12.1
Rural areas RO	19.5	17.1	18.4	18.8	18.6	20.7	21.4	21.2	21.6	23.3	25.2	28.2	26.8
EU rural areas	14.1	13.6	13.7	13.4	13.1	13.3	13.2	13.1	13.1	13.2	13.5	12.3	11.8

Source: Database Eurostat.

only 19.5% being the employment rate of men with higher education in the total employed population. It is not utopian to consider that a population with an education level below Level 4 can hardly face a transition to an economy based on other principles. In addition, in Romania, of the 75.9% in this situation, 29% are at Qualification Levels 1–2. Here we find 20% of the total female employed population in Romania. It is clear that for all those in Education Categories 1–2, additional programs will have to be developed to provide qualifications and skills appropriate to the society we are moving toward. Special attention must also be paid to those in Categories 3–4, as their training level can be a basis for other qualifications. Additionally, Table 5.16 provides data on education level and degree of urbanization, in order to point out the fact that the rural area is an important negative factor for employment, especially in the case of 5–8 qualification-level professions.

By grouping the employed population by gender and education level, the data from Table 5.17 and which are presented in Fig. 5.4 are obtained.

By grouping the degree of urbanization and the level of education, the data from Table 5.18 and which are presented in Fig. 5.4 are obtained.

The data clearly demonstrate that at this moment in Romania, the degree of urbanization influences the education level of the population. The more the population comes from the countryside, the lower the level of education. The reasons may be related to transport and generally to the level of mobility. Considering also the large number of rural women who have a low level of education, it can also be taken into account that a part of the rural female population is primarily involved in childcare and elderly care activities, as well as in household activities. A low level of employee education can automatically mean a low level of digitization or knowledge related to the use of new technologies.

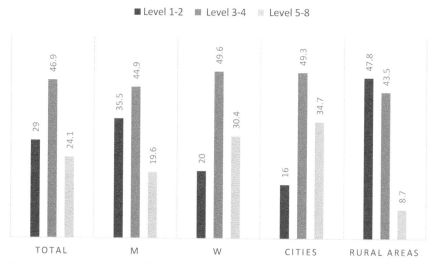

Fig. 5.4.   Employed Population by Level of Education, Degree of Urbanization and Sex. *Source*: Database Eurostat.

Table 5.15. Employed Population by Education Level and Gender 2022.

	Total	University	Specialized or Technical Post-Secondary School for Foremen	High School	Professional, Complementary or Apprentice	Secondary	Primary (Grades 1–4)	No Graduate School
Total	7,806,452	1,881,921	308,065	3,355,956	1,299,325	849,134	94,347	17,705
Male	4,492,654	877,375	99,378	1,919,521	961,118	553,457	68,713	13,092
Female	3,313,799	1,004,546	208,687	1,436,434	338,207	295,677	25,634	4,612

Source: Database Eurostat.

Table 5.16. Employed Population by Education Level and Degree of Urbanization 2022.

	Total	University	Specialized or Technical Post-Secondary School for Foremen	High School	Professional, Complementary or Apprentice	Secondary	Primary (Grades 1–4)	No Graduate School
Total	7,806,452	1,881,921	308,065	3,355,956	1,299,325	849,134	94,347	17,705
Urban	4,623,522	1,603,088	236,068	2,043,922	544,511	165,049	26,429	4,453
Rural	3,182,931	278,832	71,997	1,312,034	754,814	684,085	67,917	13,251

Source: Database Eurostat.

Table 5.17.   Employed Population by Education Level and Sex.

	Levels 1–2	**Levels 3–4**	**Levels 5–8**
Total	29	46.9	24.1
M	35.5	44.9	19.6
W	20	49.6	30.4

Source: Database Eurostat.

Table 5.18.   Employed Population by Level of Education and Degree of Urbanization.

	Levels 1–2	**Levels 3–4**	**Levels 5–8**
Total	29	46.9	24.1
Cities	16	49.3	34.7
Rural areas	47.8	43.5	8.7

Source: Database Eurostat.

To reintegrate the population into the education system, effective measures are needed that lead to real effects. Thus, it is possible to discuss the diversification of education systems, the establishment of performance indicators that are equivalent to the current evaluation system or even the use of financing programs that contribute to continuous professional training. These measures can lead to a reduction in school dropouts or even an increase in the number of graduates with a bachelor's degree.

Gender Pay Gap

The study of women's economic independence can also be done by analyzing gender pay equality. Disparities in terms of income lead to a high risk of poverty, both in the short term but especially in the long term, and we refer here to the time of retirement and living needs during retirement. The gender differences recorded in employment on the different types of contracts, especially in terms of part-time and fixed-term contracts, can be found both in terms of personal development, but especially in terms of salary or the social services available. Data recorded at the European level confirm that women represent a majority of low wages.

The level of pay is generally determined by family status (marriage, children), age, education, disability and even in some cases where they live. For example, at the European level, most women raising their children alone generally work part-time or on a temporary contract. Also, a lower level of education entails a lower salary. But in Romania, as shown by the data presented, the area in which women lead their lives has a negative influence on the level of education and implicitly on the level of salary.

Therefore, wage disparity is an indicator that reflects the state of gender equality in several categories.

The gender pay disparity in Romania is clearly lower than at the European level, the difference in Romania's favor being approximately 10%. The problem is that if at the European level, the trend is decreasing, then at the Romanian level, the trend is increasing in the last five years (Table 5.19). We believe that the upward trend of employment contracts could have a positive contribution to the achievement of gender equality in terms of wages.

From a legislative point of view, at the national level, a series of provisions ensure equality between women and men in the field of wages. Thus, Article 41, Para. (4) of the Romanian Constitution provides that for equal work, women have the same salary as men. The principle is taken over by Article 6, Para. (3) of the Labor Code, which states that for work of equal value or of equal value, any discrimination based on gender is prohibited with regard to all elements and conditions of remuneration. Moreover, the Labor Code prohibits any discrimination on the basis of gender both when determining and when granting wages (Article 159, Para. (3)). In the same vein, the Law No. 202 of April 19, 2002, regulates not only equal incomes for work of equal value but also non-discriminatory access to benefits, other than those of a salary nature, as well as to public systems and private social security.

The provisions of the Romanian legislation are in agreement with the European ones. Article 157 TFEU expressly states that each Member State shall ensure that the principle of equal pay for male and female workers for *equal work* or *work of equal value* is applied. As the European Court of Justice (ECJ) pointed out, the Treaty imposes, clearly and precisely, an obligation to achieve a particular result and is mandatory as regards both "equal work" and "work of equal value" (ECJ, 2021). "Pay" means the ordinary basic or minimum wage or salary and any other consideration, whether in cash or in kind, which the worker receives directly or indirectly, in respect of his employment, from his employer.

The Treaty goes beyond simply stating the principle and establishes the concrete content of the concept, thus expressly providing that

> equal pay without discrimination based on sex means: (a) that pay for the same work at piece rates shall be calculated on the basis of the same unit of measurement; (b) that pay for work at time rates shall be the same for the same job.

The new "EU Pay Transparency Directive" (Directive (EU) 2023/970) aims to implement concrete measures to close the gender pay gap. Thus, the directive gives employees the right to request and receive in writing information on their individual pay level and the average pay levels, broken down by sex, for categories of workers performing the same work as them or work of equal value to theirs. The directive also includes provisions on compensation for victims of pay discrimination and penalties, including fines.

In 2022, the percentage of people who engaged in learning activities after leaving initial education and training was 11.9% on average in the EU, 1.1 pp more than in 2021 (Table 5.20). However, the rates were stratified: 19.8% for those with tertiary education, 9.0% for individuals with upper secondary and

Table 5.19. Industry, Construction and Services (Except Public Administration, Defense, Compulsory Social Security).

	2013	2014	2015	2016	2017	2018	2019	2020	2021
					Time				
EU	16.0	15.7	15.5	15.1	14.6	14.4	13.7	12.9	12.7
Romania	4.9	4.5	5.6	4.8	2.9	2.2	3.3	2.4	3.6

Source: Database Eurostat.

Table 5.20. Participation Rate of Employees in Education and Training (Last Four Weeks) by Sex, Age and Occupation.

		2013	2014	2015	2016	2017	2018	2019	2020	2021	2022
							Time				
Total	EU	13.7	13.8	13.7	13.8	13.9	14.1	14.3	12.3	14.4	15.7
	Romania	2.5	2.0	1.8	1.5	1.4	1.2	1.6	1.1	7.5	8.1
Males	EU	12.2	12.4	12.2	12.3	12.4	12.5	12.7	11.0	12.9	14.1
	Romania	2.4	2.0	1.6	1.4	1.3	1.1	1.6	1.1	7.1	7.6
Females	EU	15.2	15.3	15.3	15.4	15.5	15.8	16.1	13.7	16.0	17.4
	Romania	2.7	1.9	2.1	1.6	1.5	1.3	1.7	1.2	7.9	8.6

Source: Database Eurostat.

post-secondary (non-tertiary) education and merely 4.7% for those with less than primary, primary and lower secondary education. This suggests that individuals who might benefit the most from training may not have adequate access (European Commission, 2023).

Conclusions

The differences that still exist in the way women and men access and are treated in the labor market must be a starting point when determining the concrete measures designed to move toward a green economy and, above all, when setting the course of action to ensure a just and socially fair transition. In today's increasingly global economy with continuous search for the introduction of new technologies, both employers and employees are confronted with the need to adapt. Although the process of structural changes has positive effects on growth and employment, it also entails disruptive transformations for certain workers and businesses. This requires new forms of work organization but also enhanced legal protection for those categories for employees who are, according to labor market data, in an adverse situation.

The European economy needs to improve its capacity to anticipate and absorb economic and social change, diminishing the gender gap, defined by the European Commission as the gap in any area between women and men in terms of their levels of participation, access to resources, rights, remuneration or benefits (European Commission, 1998).

In this chapter, specific indicators at the European level were examined and the data obtained for Romania were reported to the European average. The analysis showed that at the national level, there are still significant differences between women and men in terms of access to the labor market, as well as in terms of quality of the employment relationship. Romania's transposition of European legislation in the field of non-discrimination at work can contribute to an improvement in the status of women, but mere transposition of legislation cannot be sufficient. We argue that measures in the field of labor relations implemented by the national authorities must be complemented by programs that contribute to additional and sustained education of the population. We are referring both to the population that has already had a tertiary level of education, but which will have to be supported in order to face the challenges of the transition to green, but also to the population with a low level of education, which, as we have shown, has a vulnerable status on the labor market.

Future studies could look at the opportunity of implementing insertion programs for tertiary graduates, programs that develop skills related to climate, environment, circular economy or bioeconomy. Given that in Romania an important part of the employed population works in the traditional industries, such programs could contribute to the adaptation of the workforce to the new economic model, in a way that respects environmental and digitalization requirements, as well as non-discrimination and gender equality.

References

Barnat, N., MacFeely, S., & Peltola, A. (2019). Comparing global gender inequality indices: How well do they measure the economic dimension? *Journal of Sustainability Research, 1*, 1–33.

Bell, C. (2021). Power-sharing, conflict resolution, and women: A global reappraisal. In S. Byrne & A. McCulloch (Eds.), *Power-sharing pacts and the women, peace and security agenda* (pp. 13–32). Routledge.

Brătianu, C., Neştian, A. Ş., Tiţă, S. M., Vodă, A. I., & Guţă, A. L. (2020). The impact of knowledge risk on sustainability of firms. *Amfiteatru Economic, 22*(55), 639–652. https://doi.org/10.24818/EA/2020/55/639

CCR. (2018). *The Constitutional Court of Romania, decision no. 387 of June 5, 2018*. Official Gazette No. 642 of July 24, 2018.

Chen, L., Msigwa, G., Yang, M., Osman, A. I., Fawzy, S., Rooney, D. W., & Yap, P. S. (2022). Strategies to achieve a carbon neutral society: A review. *Environmental Chemistry Letters, 20*(4), 2277–2310.

CNCD. (2022). *The activity report of the institution for the year 2022*. National Council for Combating Discrimination. https://www.cncd.ro/rapoarte/

Cortes, P., & Pan, J. (2018). Occupation and gender. In S. Averett & L. M. Argys (Eds.), *The Oxford handbook of women and the economy* (pp. 425–452). Oxford.

Council Directive 2000/43/EC of June 29, 2000. On the implementation of the principle of equal treatment between persons, regardless of race or ethnic origin. Published in the *Official Journal of the European Communities (JOCE)*, series L, no. 180 of July 19, 2000.

Council Directive 2000/78/EC of November 27, 2000. Creating a general framework in favour of equal treatment, as regards employment and employment. *Official Journal of the European Communities (JOCE)*, series L, no. 303 of December 2, 2000.

Dilli, S., Carmichael, S. G., & Rijpma, A. (2019). Introducing the historical gender equality index. *Feminist Economics, 25*(1), 31–57.

Directive 2006/54/EC of the European Parliament and of the Council of July 5, 2006. On the implementation of the principle of equal opportunities and equal treatment between men and women in matters of employment and work (reform). Published in the *Official Journal of the European Union*, series L, no. 204 of July 26, 2006.

Directive 2010/41/EU of the European Parliament and the Council of July 7, 2010. Regarding the application of the principle of equal treatment between men and women who carry out an independent activity and repealing Directive 86/613/EEC of Council.

Directive (EU) 2019/1158 of the European Parliament and of the Council of 20 June 2019. On work–life balance for parents and carers and repealing Council Directive 2010/18/EU.

Directive (EU) 2023/970 of the European Parliament and of the Council of 10 May 2023. To strengthen the application of the principle of equal pay for equal work or work of equal value between men and women through pay transparency and enforcement mechanisms. *Official Journal of the European Union* L 132/21, May 17, 2023.

European Climate Law. (2021). Regulation (EU) 2021/1119 of the European Parliament and of the Council of 30 June 2021 establishing the framework for achieving climate neutrality and amending Regulations (EC) No. 401/2009 and (EU) 2018/1999 (OJ L 243, 9.7.2021, p. 1).

European Commission. (1998).. *One hundred words for equality – A glossary of terms on equality between women and men*. Directorate-General for Employment, Social Affairs and Inclusion, Publications Office.

European Commission. (2019). *Reflection paper: Towards a sustainable Europe by 2030.* https://commission.europa.eu/system/files/2019-02/rp_sustainable_europe_30-01_en_web.pdf

European Commission. (2020). *Communication on achieving the European education area by 2025* (COM/2020/625 final).

European Commission. (2021, March 4). *Communication from the Commission 'The European Pillar of Social Rights Action Plan'* (COM(2021) 102 final).

European Commission. (2022, March 2), *Communication from the Commission 'Towards a green digital and resilient economy: Our European growth model'* (COM(2022), 83 final).

European Commission. (2023). *Employment and social developments in Europe 2023* (p. 30). EC Directorate-General for Employment, Social Affairs and Inclusion.

European Council. (2019, December 12). *Conclusions* [Press release]. European Council.

European Court of Justice. (2021). *Case c -624/k and others v. Tesco Stores Ltd.* (request for a preliminary ruling from the Watford Employment Tribunal), judgment of the court (second chamber), 3 June 2021. Para 20.

European Institute for Gender Equality. (2022). *Gender Equality Index 2022. The COVID-19 pandemic and care* (p. 11). Publications Office.

Eurostat. (2023). *SDG 5 – Gender equality. Achieve gender equality and empower all women and girls.* https://ec.europa.eu/eurostat/statistics-explained/SEPDF/cache/63333.pdf

Filho, L. W., Kovaleva, M., Tsani, S., Ţîrcă, D.-M., Shiel, C., Dinis, M. A. P., Nicolau, M., Sima, M., Fritzen, B., Salvia, A. L., Minhas, A., Kozlova, V., Doni, F., Spiteri, J., Gupta, T., Wakunuma, K., Sharma, M., Barbir, J., Shulla, K., … Tripathi, S. (2022). Promoting gender equality across the sustainable development goals. *Environment, Development and Sustainability*, 25, 14177–14198. https://doi.org/10.1007/s10668-022-02656-1

Fodor, É., & Glass, C. (2018). Labor market context, economic development, and family policy arrangements: Explaining the gender gap in employment in Central and Eastern Europe. *Social Forces*, 96(3), 1275–1302.

Government Emergency Ordinance No. 137/2000. (2014, March 7). *On preventing and punishing all forms of discrimination.* Republished in the Official Gazette of Romania No. 166.

Grigorescu, A., Ion, A.-E., Lincaru, C., Pirciog, S. (2022). Synergy analysis of knowledge transfer for the energy sector within the framework of sustainable development of the European Countries. *Energies*, 15(1), 276. https://doi.org/10.3390/en15010276

Hirsu, L., Hashemi, L., & Quezada-Rayes, Z. (2019). *SDG 5: Achieve gender equality and empower all women and girls* [Jean Monnet Sustainable Development Goals Network Policy Brief Series]. RMIT University. https://www.rmitedu.au/content/dam/rmit/rmit-images/college-of-dsc-images/eu-center/sdg-5-policy-brief. pdf

International Labor Organization. (2015). *Key indicators on the labor market: Full report* (9th ed.). International Labor Office. https://www.ilo.org/wcmsp5/groups/public/@ed_emp/@emp_ent/documents/publication/wcms_432859.pdf

Jenkins, K., Sovacool, B. K., & McCauley, D. (2018). Humanizing sociotechnical transitions through energy justice: An ethical framework for global transformative change. *Energy Policy*, 117, 66–74.

Law 202/2002. (2013, June 5). *On equal opportunities and equal treatment of women and men.* Republished in the Official Gazette of Romania No. 326.

Lewis, J. (Ed.). (2018). *Gender, social care and welfare state restructuring in Europe.* Routledge.

Nguyen, C. P. (2021). Gender equality and economic complexity. *Economic Systems*, 45(4), 100921.

Odera, J. A., & Mulusa, J. (2020). SDGs, gender equality and women's empowerment: What prospects for delivery? In M. Kaltenborn, M. Krajewski, & H. Kuhn (Eds.), *Sustainable development goals and human rights. Interdisciplinary studies in human rights* (Vol. 5, pp. 95–118). Springer. https://doi.org/10.1007/978-3-030-30469-0_6

OHCHR. (2020). *Convention on the elimination of all forms of discrimination against women New York, 18 December 1979.* https://www.ohchr.org/en/professionalinterest/pages/cedaw.aspx

Piketty, T. (2014). *Capital in the 2nd century* (A. Goldhammer, Trans.). Harvard University Press.

Pirciog, S. C., Grigorescu, A., Lincaru, C., Popa, F. M., Lazarczyk Carlson, E., & Sigurdarson, H. T. (2023). Mapping European high-digital intensive sectors – Regional growth accelerator for the circular economy. *Frontiers in Environmental Science, 10*, 1061128. https://doi.org/10.3389/fenvs.2022.1061128

UN. (1995). *Beijing declaration and platform for action.* https://www.a.org/en/events/pastevents/pdfs/Beijing_Declaration_and_Platform_for_Action.Pdf

UN. (2012). *Resolution adopted by the General Assembly on 27 July 2012.* (A/RES/66/288). https://www.un.org/en/development/desa/population/migration/generalassembly/docs/globalcompact/A_RES_66_288.pdf

UN. (2015). *Paris Agreement.* https://unfccc.int/files/essential_background/convention/application/pdf/english_paris_agreement.pdf

UN. (2023). *The sustainable development goals report 2023: Special edition towards a rescue plan for people and planet.* https://unstats.un.org/sdgs/report/2023/

UN Women. (2020). *Commission on the status of women.* https://www.unwomen.org/en/csw

Velicu, I., & Barca, S. (2020). The just transition and its work of inequality. *Sustainability: Science, Practice and Policy, 16*(1), 263–273.

Wang, X., & Lo, K. (2021). Just transition: A conceptual review. *Energy Research & Social Science, 82*, 102291.

Wolf, S., Teitge, J., Mielke, J., Schütze, F., & Jaeger, C. (2021). The European green deal – More than climate neutrality. *Intereconomics, 56*, 99–107.

Chapter 6

Challenges of Developing a Green, Resilient Economy from the Perspective of Gender Equality in Female Entrepreneurship

Bianca-Florentina Nistoroiu[a], Alina Zaharia[a] and Predrag Vuković[b]

[a]*Bucharest University of Economic Studies, Romania*
[b]*Institute of Agricultural Economics Belgrade, RS Serbia*

Abstract

The current research provides an overview of the intersection between female entrepreneurship and development, with a specific focus on the catalyzing role of gender equality. The study delves into the manifold implications of empowering women in entrepreneurship and its contributions to socio-economic development. It emphasizes the importance of gender-inclusive policies, access to resources, and equitable opportunities as catalysts for fostering female entrepreneurship and driving sustainable development. By shedding light on the interplay between these critical factors, this research seeks to inform policies and strategies that can promote gender equality, female entrepreneurship, and economic growth.

Keywords: Sustainability; gender disparities; equal opportunities; social constraints; entrepreneurship; women; government

Introduction

One of our time's greatest challenges is the transition to a more sustainable lifestyle. In order to combat environmental deterioration and promote sustainable development in the European Union (EU), green entrepreneurship emerged as a crucial answer. It entails the development of companies that prioritize environmental protection while fostering economic growth. Innovation is the driving

Entrepreneurship and Development for a Green Resilient Economy, 165–179
Copyright © 2024 by Bianca-Florentina Nistoroiu, Alina Zaharia and Predrag Vuković
Published under exclusive licence by Emerald Publishing Limited
doi:10.1108/978-1-83797-088-920241006

force behind this transition. Innovative solutions hold the key to unlocking and discovering fresh approaches to this difficult and multifaceted problem. Because it has the greatest potential to influence economies and cultures, green entrepreneurship is crucial. Ensuring that this change combines inclusivity and sustainability is also essential.

As a result, encouraging gender equality in green entrepreneurship is essential for the EU's sustainable growth. Women tend to focus on social and environmental results in their enterprises, making them crucial change agents for environmental sustainability. Therefore, encouraging female green business owners may aid in the region's inclusive and long-term economic success (Radović-Marković & Živanović, 2019).

It is essential to understand the present situation of gender inequality in the EU's green industry and in entrepreneurship. For instance, despite major improvements in women's education, their job and business chances have not yet completely improved. In comparison to companies owned by men, women-owned micro-, small-, and medium-sized enterprises (MSMEs) have a more constrained reach and operate on a smaller scale (Sanchez-Riofrio et al., 2023).

As males predominately hold executive positions and get the majority of financing and resources throughout the EU area, women also encounter considerable entry-level obstacles in the green industry. In addition, women in green entrepreneurship confront difficulties that limit their involvement, including restricted access to markets and financing, a lack of technical expertise, education, and gender-based prejudice. As a result, while developing energy infrastructure, including renewable energy projects, their expertise, requirements, and preferences are frequently neglected (Lee & Huruta, 2022).

Surveys show that younger EU customers choose inclusive and sustainable goods and services, which is another cause for confidence. Therefore, it makes sense to assume that their purchasing habits will be a key factor in propelling the creation of sustainable and resilient company models. Therefore, specific policies and activities are needed to overcome the gender gap in entrepreneurship and the green industry. Women's access to markets, finance, education, and training must all be improved, and it is critical to fight employment discrimination based on gender. Enabling women to participate fully in green business not only boosts productivity and spurs innovation, but it also forms the basis for building more harmonious communities (Njuki, 2021). This demonstrates how important women's economic empowerment is to the transition to a resilient green economy (Grown et al., 2006).

Female entrepreneurship plays a pivotal role in fostering economic diversification and sustainability in economic, social, and environmental dimensions. Female entrepreneurs exhibit a greater proclivity for addressing societal issues through innovative approaches when compared to their male counterparts (Langowitz & Minniti, 2007). Within developing nations, women's entrepreneurship is regarded as an indispensable driver of economic growth, offering the potential to alleviate poverty, generate employment opportunities, and advance gender parity (Okeke-Uzodike, 2019). Women's profound familiarity with local contexts and their astute understanding of the environment are indispensable assets in the formulation and dissemination of adaptation strategies, with the potential for wide-scale adoption within their communities. Furthermore, female entrepreneurship assumes heightened significance as sectors traditionally led by women face increasing vulnerabilities due to climate change (Atahau et al., 2021).

To foster and facilitate female entrepreneurship and contribute to the establishment of a green, resilient economy, several recommended policies, and strategies are proposed. The enhancement of access to credit facilities, especially during the nascent and expansion phases, is deemed essential as female entrepreneurs often grapple with financial constraints. Policies aimed at ameliorating this access to credit can significantly bolster female entrepreneurship. Moreover, the provision of comprehensive training programs designed to impart new skills and knowledge is imperative, given the common challenges faced by women entrepreneurs in accessing education and training opportunities (Macías-Prada et al., 2023). The development of a Gender Data Network is a requisite step, enabling the collection, analysis, and evaluation of robust, gender-disaggregated data, thereby identifying gaps in gender data across all economic sectors, including women's entrepreneurship. As proposed by Lopez and Contreras (2020) for G20 member countries, progress in this endeavor should be systematically benchmarked, assessed, and reported on an annual basis.

Further, the establishment of a Women's Entrepreneurship Policy Framework is recommended by governments, and it is designed to comprehensively address the distinctive challenges encountered by women entrepreneurs, thereby promoting their growth and development. This framework should encompass policies targeting improved access to financial resources, training opportunities, and other vital resources. Finally, policies aimed at augmenting climate investment while incorporating gender sensitivity are imperative, as they can provide essential support to women entrepreneurs and workers navigating climate-vulnerable circumstances (Foss et al., 2019).

In summary, the sustenance and promotion of female entrepreneurship and development are integral components in the pursuit of a resilient, eco-friendly economy. Policies and strategies oriented toward enhancing credit accessibility, offering training programs, aggregating gender-disaggregated data, formulating a dedicated policy framework, and amplifying gender-sensitive climate investments are crucial in advancing female entrepreneurship and fostering its development.

Gender Statistics in the EU

This section contains indicators from a range of domains, such as education, the job market, and income inequality. When it comes to detecting gender gaps – differences in the ways that men and women perceive certain circumstances – these measurements are particularly crucial. Gender statistics goes beyond typical statistical categories to address basic issues such as identification, collecting, and transmission of data that accurately represents the daily lives of both men and women. Gender equality-related policy issues are also covered in the United Nations Economic Commission for Europe (UNECE) article "Developing Gender Statistics: A Practical Tool," which was published in 2010.

The indicators selected below highlight gender disparities while also presenting the overall levels obtained by the population as a whole, both within the EU and among its various Member States. For example, it examines the gender salary gap by accounting for employment rates. This method provides a comprehensive picture of gender disparities in terms of access to opportunities and assets within the larger context of their real availability. The proportion of people who complete tertiary education, which is the acquisition of university-level or higher education credentials, is a crucial variable in the field of educational statistics. A framework for determining gender inequalities in educational results is provided by this measure of "tertiary education attainment." It is particularly calculated as the gap between the proportion of men aged 30–34 who have finished their university degree and the corresponding figure for women. The gender gap in this area across the EU was −10.7 percentiles (pp) in 2021, meaning that there were 10.7% more women than males in this age group who had completed postsecondary education, as illustrated in Fig. 6.1.

Notably, in all EU Member States in 2021, there was a negative gender gap in higher educational attainment. The gender disparity in Germany was the smallest at −1.6 percentage points, while the gender gap in Slovenia was the biggest at −25.2 percentage points. In this regard, the Republic of Slovakia (−23.2 pp) and Lithuania (−22.9 pp) were also among the nations with significant gender disparities. In Luxembourg, 62.5% of adults between the ages of 30 and 34 have finished their higher education in 2021, compared to 24% in Romania. Slovenija's and Lithuania's tertiary degree holdings were higher (49.2% and 60.2%, respectively), while Slovakia's was lower than the EU average of 41.6% among the EU Member States with the most significant gender inequalities in absolute terms (above 22%). The proportion of people aged 30–34 with higher education, on the other hand, dipped below the EU norm for Romania (24.8%) and Germany (36.3%), while surpassing it for Austria (43.0%) and Ireland (62.0%)

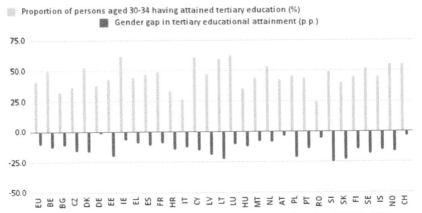

Fig. 6.1.   Tertiary Education Attainment and Gender Gap in EU-27, 2021.
Source: Based on Eurostat (2023a, 2023b, 2023c).

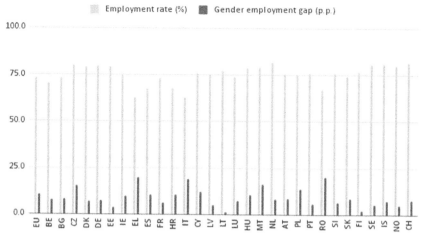

Fig. 6.2.   Employment Rate and Gender Employment Gap in EU-27, 2021.
Source: Based on Eurostat (2023a, 2023b, 2023c).

among nations with the most minor gender inequalities in absolute terms (below 7 pp).

The employment rate is a crucial social indicator that holds great analytical significance in the analysis of labor market dynamics. Here, the term "gender gap" refers to the variation in employment rates between men and women in the working-age population, which is defined as those between the ages of 20 and 64. The gender employment gap in the EU was estimated at 10.8 percentile points (pp) for Year 2021, meaning that males who are of working age were more likely than women to be employed, as illustrated in Fig. 6.2.

The gender-based employment gap varies significantly throughout EU Member States. Lithuania (1.4%) showed a very small gap in 2021, followed by Finland (2.0 pp), Estonia (3.7 pp), and Latvia (4.8 pp). Furthermore, the gender pay gap did not surpass 5 percentage points in any of these four EU nations. On the other hand, five Member States – namely, Czechia (15.4 pp), Malta (16.4 pp), Italy (19.2 pp), Greece (19.8 pp), and Romania (20.1 pp) – reported gaps that were equivalent to or higher than 15 pp. The considerably lower participation of women in the labor market in these countries can be blamed for the apparent difference in the gender employment gap.

The employment rate for the general demographic of people aged 20–64 varied from 62.6% in Greece to 81.7% in the Netherlands in Year 2020. The employment rate was higher than, or less than 5 percentage points, the EU average of 73.1% among the EU Member States with the smallest gender employment discrepancies. However, among the countries with the biggest gender employment inequalities, equal to or greater than 15%, the employment rate fell short of the EU norm in Greece (62.6%), Italy (62.7%), and Romania (67.1%), while it exceeded it in Malta (79.1%) and Czechia (80.0%).

The concept of an "unadjusted" gender pay gap provides a thorough analysis of the disparities in hourly salary rates between men and women. As a percentage of the average gross hourly wages of men, this indicator measures the difference between the median gross hourly wages of men and women (Eurostat, 2021). Because it does not take account of all the variables that affect the gender pay gap – such as differences in work experience, educational background, or occupational roles – it is known as "unadjusted."

Within the EU, according to Eurostat, women earn less per hour than men. In the overall economy for Year 2021, women's average gross hourly earnings were 14.4% lower than those of men across the EU. There is a significant difference in the gender wage gap between EU Member States. The gender wage gap in 2018 ranged from 2.2% in Romania and 1.4% in Luxembourg to 5.5% in Italy and 5.8% in Belgium. On the other hand, it reached its highest point to 20.1% in Germany and Czechia, 20.4% in Austria, and 21.8% in Estonia.

When expressed in purchasing power standards (PPS), the average gross hourly wages of workers in each Member State in 2021 varied greatly, ranging from 6.4 PPS in Bulgaria to 20.9 PPS in Denmark. Pay disparities between nations were found to be minimal, with 8.6 PPS in Portugal and 19.4 PPS in Luxembourg. These differences were below the 10% mark.

In contrast, the nations with the largest gender pay gaps (more than 20%) reported incomes ranging from 9.0 PPS in Estonia to 18.4 PPS in Germany.

The difference between the average yearly wages of men and women is affected by the larger incidence of part-time work among women, along with the gender pay gap, which relies on hourly earnings. The "gender hours gap," which measures the difference between the average monthly hours paid to men and women and is represented as a percentage of the average hours paid to men, serves as an example of this phenomenon.

In the EU, in 2021, women earned 12% fewer hours of labor per month on average than males did. Whereas part-time solutions for women vary significantly between EU nations, the number of hours for which males are paid stays rather stable. With a gender hour difference of 27%, the Netherlands sticks out in particular. This means that female employees there receive compensation for 27% fewer hours of labor per month than their male colleagues. In contrast, both Bulgaria and Romania reported a 1% gender hours gap, which is a negligible difference.

Examining gender differences in employment is essential, in addition to taking into account the gender pay gap and the gender hours gap, since these also significantly contribute to the difference in average earnings between men and women. To provide a comprehensive view of the gender pay gap, a new composite indicator has been created. This statistic calculates the total effect of three significant variables: the number of hours worked per month (before part-time work is taken into account), the average hourly salary, and the employment rate. In comparison to males, it evaluates the overall effects of these variables on the average wages of all adults and working-age women, regardless of their job situation (Eurostat, 2021).

In Year 2021, the gender disparity in total earnings within the EU was striking, with a significant gender overall earnings gap of 36.2%, as meticulously documented in Fig. 6.3. This gender earnings gap exhibited notable diversity across

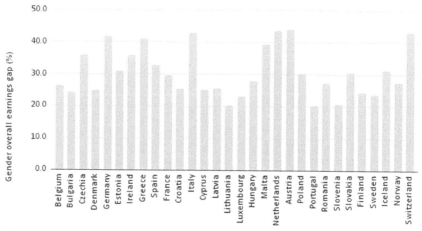

Fig. 6.3.   Gender Overall Earnings Gap in EU-27 (%, 2021). *Source*: Based on Eurostat (2023a, 2023b, 2023c).

the EU Member States, encompassing a spectrum from the comparatively modest disparities of 20.4% in Lithuania and Portugal to the substantial chasm of 44.2% witnessed in Austria.

The presented findings in Fig. 6.3 delineate distinct patterns among the EU Member States in terms of gender overall earnings gaps. There is a noticeable group of countries where the gender pay gap is less than 30%. Particularly, gender overall earnings gaps are comparatively smaller in Lithuania (20.4%), Portugal (20.4%), the Slovenian Republic (20.7%), Luxembourg (23.2%), Sweden (23.8%), Bulgaria (24.2%), the nation of Finland (24.5%), Denmark (25.1%), Cyprus (25.2%), the Republic of Croatia (25.5%), Latvia (25.7%), Belgium (26.4%), Romania (27.3%), Hungary (28.1%), as well as France (29.6%). On the other hand, a diverse group of nations have significant gender income disparities that surpass the 40% mark. Greece (41.2%), Germany (41.9%), Italy (43.1%), the Netherlands (43.7%), and Austria (44.2%) are noteworthy instances. These variations underscore the heterogeneous nature of gender-based economic inequalities within the EU, necessitating targeted policy measures and empirical investigations to comprehend and address the underlying determinants contributing to such divergent magnitudes across Member States.

The depicted graph (Fig. 6.4) affords a nuanced comprehension of the multifaceted dynamics inherent in the broader gender economic disparities, specifically encapsulating the gender earnings gap, gender employment gap, and gender hours gap. At the EU level, the composite analysis reveals distinct contributions to the overarching gender earnings gap, with discernible proportions delineated as follows: 36.7% attributed to the gender pay gap, 29.3% to the gender employment gap, and 34.0% to the gender hours gap. This elucidation underscores the imperative for targeted policy interventions addressing each facet comprehensively, thereby fostering a more equitable economic landscape conducive to gender parity within the EU. Further empirical investigations and policy implementations

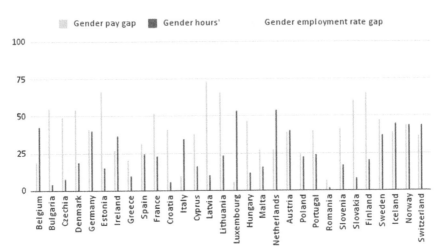

Fig. 6.4.   Contributions to the Gender Overall Earnings Gap in EU-27, 2021.
Source: Based on Eurostat (2023a, 2023b, 2023c).

are warranted to cultivate a more profound understanding and amelioration of the intricate interplay between these divergent elements influencing gender-based economic differentials.

Ways of Fostering Female Entrepreneurship

Governments have the capacity to foster female entrepreneurship within the realm of the green economy through the formulation and enactment of policies and initiatives that specifically target the distinctive challenges encountered by women entrepreneurs (Radović-Marković & Živanović, 2019). Several avenues for government support include facilitating financial access, facilitating educational and mentorship programs, gender-disaggregated data collection, the establishment of a women's entrepreneurship policy framework, and gender-sensitive climate investment.

First, the formidable challenge of obtaining financial resources, particularly during the inception and expansion phases of female entrepreneurship, can be addressed through government intervention. This support may manifest in the form of enhanced access to credit facilities, grants, and other financial instruments (Fallah & Soori, 2023). Second, women entrepreneurs often face difficulties in accessing educational and training opportunities, which, in turn, can limit their ability to acquire new skills and knowledge essential for business development. Government efforts to provide training and mentorship programs can be instrumental in cultivating new competencies and offering guidance in navigating the complexities of business growth (Agrawal et al., 2023). Third, the systematic collection, analysis, and evaluation of comprehensive, gender-disaggregated data can shed light on gender disparities across various economic sectors, with particular attention to women's entrepreneurship. Governments can harness these data to formulate tailored policies and initiatives that address the unique challenges experienced by women entrepreneurs (Halabisky et al., 2023). Fourth, the creation of a dedicated policy framework designed to confront the distinct hurdles faced by women entrepreneurs can serve as a catalyst for their growth and development. This framework should encompass policies aimed at improving financial access, fostering training opportunities, and facilitating access to other essential resources (Solano, 2023). Lastly, policies oriented toward amplifying climate investment while incorporating gender-sensitive considerations are paramount for extending support to women entrepreneurs and laborers operating within climate-vulnerable settings. Government endeavors to invest in green technologies and renewable energy can engender fresh opportunities for women entrepreneurs (Döhlen Wedin, 2023).

In summary, governments possess the potential to nurture female entrepreneurship in the green economy by implementing policies and initiatives that are tailored to mitigate the unique challenges faced by women entrepreneurs. These measures include enhancing financial access, instituting training and mentorship programs, collecting gender-disaggregated data, formulating a dedicated women's entrepreneurship policy framework, and advancing climate investments that are sensitive to gender-related factors.

The imperative to foster female entrepreneurship in the private sector within the EU has garnered scholarly attention, reflecting a burgeoning awareness of the need for gender-inclusive economic policies. Various strategies have been proposed in the extant literature to cultivate an environment conducive to female entrepreneurship, thereby addressing the prevailing gender disparities in business ownership and leadership roles. Primarily, scholars posit that enhancing women's access to financial resources constitutes a pivotal factor in fostering female entrepreneurship (Brush et al., 2019; Verheul & Thurik, 2001). Policies facilitating equitable access to funding mechanisms, such as venture capital and business loans, can ameliorate the financial barriers that often impede women from initiating and scaling entrepreneurial ventures.

Moreover, educational interventions are underscored as instrumental in empowering aspiring female entrepreneurs by equipping them with the requisite skills and knowledge (Kelley et al., 2015; Neneh, 2020). Targeted training programs, mentorship initiatives, and networking opportunities contribute to bridging the entrepreneurial gender gap by enhancing women's business acumen and self-efficacy. Additionally, scholars emphasize the significance of comprehensive policy frameworks and institutional support mechanisms (Welter et al., 2020). Enabling legislative environments that prioritize gender equality, coupled with the establishment of support structures such as women-focused business incubators and networks, fosters an ecosystem conducive to female entrepreneurship (Brush et al., 2008; OECD, 2019). Also, acknowledging the intersectionality of gender roles, policies promoting work–life balance are identified as crucial in facilitating women's entry and sustained engagement in entrepreneurship (Voronov & Vince, 2012). Provisions such as flexible working arrangements and childcare facilities contribute to mitigating the challenges that often deter women from pursuing entrepreneurial endeavors. Furthermore, the role of role models and networks is emphasized in academic discourse (Marlow et al., 2019). Establishing and promoting networks of successful female entrepreneurs, coupled with the visibility of women in leadership roles, serves as both inspirational and pragmatic guidance for prospective female entrepreneurs. In conclusion, fostering female entrepreneurship in the private sector within the EU necessitates a multifaceted approach encompassing financial inclusivity, educational empowerment, policy advocacy, work–life balance, and the cultivation of supportive networks. By amalgamating these strategies, policymakers can contribute to dismantling the persistent barriers inhibiting women's full participation and success in entrepreneurial ventures.

The Challenges Faced by Female Workers

Despite their potential contributions, female workers often encounter gender-specific challenges such as unequal pay, limited access to finance, and social norms that restrict their mobility (Duflo, 2012). Addressing these challenges is crucial for harnessing the full potential of female workers and building a resilient, green economy. The pivotal role of female workers in contributing to a green and resilient economy is undeniable. However, despite their considerable potential, female workers frequently encounter a range of gender-specific challenges that hinder their participation and full engagement in this transition (Unay-Gailhard & Bojnec, 2019). This section explores these challenges, encompassing issues of unequal pay, limited access to finance, and social norms that restrict their mobility and opportunities. Addressing these challenges is not only a matter of gender equality but also a vital component in harnessing the full potential of female workers in building a green, resilient economy (Anderson et al., 2021).

One of the most glaring challenges faced by female workers is the persistent issue of unequal pay. The gender pay gap remains a global concern, with women typically earning less than their male counterparts for equivalent work (Blau & Kahn, 2017). Unequal pay not only undermines the economic well-being of female workers but also perpetuates gender inequalities, making it more challenging for women to invest in sustainable entrepreneurship or pursue opportunities in green sectors. The inability to earn on par with male colleagues can serve as a deterrent for women in terms of career advancement and investment in sustainable business initiatives.

Female entrepreneurs and workers often confront limited access to financial resources, a critical impediment to their active participation in building a green economy. This gender-based financial constraint is attributed to a variety of factors, including the lack of collateral, discrimination in credit access, and the absence of networks and mentorship opportunities (Coleman, 2007). Without equitable access to financial resources, female workers face difficulties in securing capital for green entrepreneurship ventures or for further education and skills development in green industries.

Social norms and cultural expectations can further compound the challenges faced by female workers. In many societies, traditional gender roles and expectations limit the mobility and decision-making authority of women (Kabeer, 2005).

These norms can deter women from pursuing careers in male-dominated fields, such as science and technology, which are instrumental in the transition to a green economy. The lack of mobility and autonomy restricts women's ability to access green job opportunities, entrepreneurial ventures, or education in sustainable practices.

The challenges confronted by female workers in the context of transitioning to a green and resilient economy are multifaceted. Unequal pay, limited access to finance, and social norms restricting mobility are critical impediments to women's active participation in this process. Addressing these challenges is not only a matter of gender equality but also a necessity for fostering sustainable entrepreneurship and achieving environmental sustainability. Policymakers, businesses, and civil society must work together to eliminate these barriers and create an inclusive environment that allows female workers to maximize their contributions to a resilient, green economy.

The challenges encountered by female workers during maternity leave and childbirth within the EU constitute a multifaceted domain, subject to diverse socio-economic, legal, and organizational dynamics. The scholarly literature provides nuanced insights into the complexities surrounding this critical aspect of gender equality and workplace policies. The EU boasts a comprehensive legal framework addressing maternity rights; however, significant variations persist among Member States, leading to disparities in the extent and nature of protection afforded to female workers (European Parliament, 2019). Discrepancies in the duration and compensation of maternity leave across countries contribute to divergent experiences for female employees during this pivotal life stage. Research underscores the enduring challenges faced by women in maintaining career trajectories post-maternity leave, contributing to the perpetuation of the gender pay gap (Kunze & Troske, 2020). The interruption of professional continuity during maternity leave can result in diminished career prospects and earnings, underscoring the need for targeted policies to mitigate these repercussions. Maternity-related discrimination and stigmatization persist within workplaces despite legal safeguards (Plantenga & Remery, 2009). Negative attitudes toward pregnant employees or those on maternity leave contribute to a challenging professional environment for women, necessitating organizational efforts to foster inclusivity and combat discriminatory practices. The implementation of supportive organizational policies emerges as a crucial determinant in alleviating challenges faced by female workers during maternity leave (Heymann et al., 2017). Flexible work arrangements, on-site childcare facilities, and inclusive workplace cultures contribute to a more positive and conducive environment for women returning to work post-childbirth. The psychosocial well-being of female workers during maternity leave remains a pertinent concern. Balancing professional and caregiving responsibilities, coupled with societal expectations, can lead to stress and mental health challenges (Eurofound, 2018). Comprehensive policies addressing mental health support during this period are imperative for fostering overall well-being. In conclusion, the challenges encountered by female workers during maternity leave and childbirth in the EU necessitate a concerted effort to harmonize legal provisions, combat workplace discrimination, and implement

176 Bianca-Florentina Nistoroiu et al.

supportive organizational policies. A comprehensive approach addressing the intersectionality of legal, economic, and socio-cultural factors is imperative for fostering gender equity in the realm of maternity rights within the European workforce.

Conclusions

The pursuit of a green, resilient economy is inherently tied to the crucial role of entrepreneurship in fostering innovation and sustainable practices. However, achieving this transition in an equitable and effective manner necessitates the integration of gender inclusivity into the core of these efforts. Female workers and entrepreneurs, who are often underrepresented in entrepreneurship and green sectors, possess unique and indispensable capabilities for shaping a green and resilient future. Their contributions are pivotal not only in terms of economic growth but also for mitigating environmental degradation and fostering sustainable development.

The existing gender disparities, as elucidated earlier, including unequal pay, limited access to finance, and social norms constraining women's mobility and opportunities, represent significant barriers that must be overcome. Gender-sensitive policies and initiatives are essential to create an enabling environment for female workers and entrepreneurs. These measures should encompass efforts to close the gender pay gap, increase access to finance for women-led businesses, and challenge and transform societal norms that perpetuate gender-based discrimination.

In this context, studies have shown that gender-inclusive policies and measures not only empower women but also contribute to the broader goals of economic and environmental sustainability (Duflo, 2012; Kabeer, 2005). Gender equality in the workplace enhances productivity and fosters a diverse and inclusive work culture, which is instrumental for innovation and green entrepreneurship. It also enables female workers to more effectively participate in the green economy, supporting the development of renewable energy, sustainable agriculture, and clean technology, among others.

To sum up, a green, resilient economy is contingent on addressing the gender disparities within entrepreneurship and the workforce. By fostering gender inclusivity and implementing policies that empower female workers and entrepreneurs, society can better harness their potential in building a more sustainable and resilient future.

A green, resilient economy hinges on entrepreneurship as a driving force for innovation and the implementation of sustainable practices. However, the effectiveness and equity of this transition depend significantly on integrating gender inclusivity at its core. Female workers and entrepreneurs occupy a unique and indispensable role in shaping the trajectory of a green and resilient future. Their contributions extend far beyond mere gender equality and have profound implications for economic growth, environmental sustainability, and social well-being.

As emphasized in the preceding sections, female workers often face a multitude of gender-specific challenges, including unequal pay, limited access to financial resources, and the constraints imposed by deeply ingrained social norms. These barriers not only affect individual women but also have ripple effects on the broader economy and environmental outcomes. Addressing these challenges is not only a matter of social justice but an absolute necessity for harnessing the full potential of women in building a green economy.

Mitigating the gender pay gap is not only an essential step toward gender equality but also a strategy to ensure that female workers have the resources they need to engage actively in green sectors and sustainable business initiatives. Studies have demonstrated that closing the gender pay gap can lead to increased economic productivity, stimulate consumer demand, and improve the overall quality of the workforce. When women receive equal pay for equal work, they are better positioned to invest in sustainable practices, green entrepreneurship ventures, and professional development, thus catalyzing the transition to a more sustainable economy.

Furthermore, gender-inclusive policies to enhance women's access to financial resources and entrepreneurial support can catalyze their participation in green sectors, driving innovation and green technology adoption. Financial institutions, governments, and businesses must collaborate to ensure that women-led businesses have equitable access to credit, venture capital, and mentorship opportunities in the green economy. Additionally, addressing the deeply entrenched social norms that limit women's mobility and opportunities is imperative. Encouraging cultural shifts that support women's entry into traditionally male-dominated fields, such as science, technology, engineering, and mathematics (STEM), is essential for achieving a green, resilient economy. By challenging these norms, societies can open the door to more women contributing to fields integral to environmental sustainability, including renewable energy, sustainable agriculture, and clean technology.

In conclusion, building a green and resilient economy necessitates the simultaneous pursuit of gender equality and environmental sustainability. Female workers and entrepreneurs hold the potential to be transformative agents in this endeavor, and fostering their active participation is an investment in a brighter and more sustainable future for all. Gender-inclusive policies and measures must be integrated into the approach, ensuring that the full spectrum of talent and potential is utilized to create a greener, more equitable, and prosperous future.

References

Agrawal, R., Bakhshi, P., Chandani, A., Birau, R., & Mendon, S. (2023). Challenges faced by women entrepreneurs in South Asian countries using interpretive structural modeling. *Cogent Business & Management*, *10*(2), 2244755.

Anderson, C. L., Reynolds, T. W., Biscaye, P., Patwardhan, V., & Schmidt, C. (2021). Economic benefits of empowering women in agriculture: Assumptions and evidence. *The Journal of Development Studies*, *57*(2), 193–208.

Atahau, A. D. R., Sakti, I. M., Huruta, A. D., & Kim, M. S. (2021). Gender and renewable energy integration: The mediating role of green-microfinance. *Journal of Cleaner Production, 318*, 128536.

Blau, F. D., & Kahn, L. M. (2017). The gender wage gap: Extent, trends, and explanations. *Journal of Economic Literature, 55*(3), 789–865.

Brush, C. G., de Bruin, A., & Welter, F. (2019). A gender-aware framework for women's entrepreneurship. *International Journal of Gender and Entrepreneurship, 11*(2), 95–110.

Brush, C. G., Edelman, L. F., & Manolova, T. S. (2008). *Women entrepreneurs and the global environment for growth: A research agenda.* Edward Elgar Publishing.

Coleman, S. (2007). Access to capital and terms of credit: A comparison of men-and women-owned small businesses. *Journal of Small Business Management, 45*(3), 341–362.

Döhlen Wedin, A. (2023). Towards a gender-sensitive adaptation to climate change. Retrieved from HYPERLINK "https://linkprotect.cudasvc.com/url?a=https%3a%2f%2furn.kb.se%2fresolve%3furn%3durn%3anbn%3ase%3akth%3adiva-326701&c=E,1,PqwLriZq3PGetxHlADTb843tTc93-PDRHxn8JlIcW01XwYo_-zPpiYpXKASzsUAmFYH3GsQxVm5_ns2eay3JjTJoH1oi2yswN63JDuLfPNq5--Sb0tNbH_sIpw,,&typo=1"https://urn.kb.se/resolve?urn=urn:nbn:se:kth:diva-326701

Duflo, E. (2012). Women's empowerment and economic development. *Journal of Economic Literature, 50*(4), 1051–1079.

Eurofound. (2018). *Burnout in the workplace: A review of data and policy responses in the EU.* https://www.eurofound.europa.eu/publications/report/2018/burnout-in-the-workplace

European Parliament. (2019). *Maternity and paternity leave across EU Member States.* https://www.europarl.europa.eu/news/en/headlines/society/20190118STO25721/maternity-and-paternity-leave-across-eu-member-states

Eurostat. (2021). *Gender pay gap statistics.* Eurostat. Available at: https://ec.europa.eu/eurostat/statistics-explained/index.php?title=Gender_pay_gap_statistics#:~:text=For%20the%20economy%20as%20a,in%20Estonia%20(Figure%201).

Eurostat. (2023a). *Gender pay gap statistics.* Retrieved August 5, 2023, from https://ec.europa.eu/eurostat/statistics-explained/index.php?title=Gender_pay_gap_statistics#Gender_pay_gap_levels_vary_significantly_across_EU

Eurostat. (2023b). *Gender statistics.* Retrieved August 5, 2023, from https://ec.europa.eu/eurostat/statistics-explained/index.php?title=Gender_statistics#Earnings

Eurostat. (2023c). Labour market database. Retrieved August 5, 2023, from https://ec.europa.eu/eurostat/web/labour-market/database.

Fallah, M. R., & Soori, M. (2023). Presenting a framework for the successful entry of women entrepreneurs into green entrepreneurship. *Journal of Science and Technology Policy Management, 14*(3), 467–486.

Foss, L., Henry, C., Ahl, H., & Mikalsen, G. H. (2019). Women's entrepreneurship policy research: A 30-year review of the evidence. *Small Business Economics, 53*, 409–429.

Grown, C., Bahadur, C., Handbury, J., & Elson, D. (2006). The financial requirements of achieving gender equality and women's empowerment. SSRN Electronic Journal. 10.2139/ssrn.923851.

Halabisky, D., Jiménez, M.C., Koreen, M., Marchese, M., & Shymanski, H. (2023). Addressing gender disparities in access to finance for business creation. Joining Forces for Gender Equality : What is Holding us Back? | OECD iLibrary. Available at: https://www.oecd-ilibrary.org/sites/aa4719c3-en/index.html?itemId=%2Fcontent%2Fcomponent%2Faa4719c3-en (Accessed: 05 January 2024).

Heymann, J., Raub, A., & Earle, A. (2017). Breastfeeding policy: A globally comparative analysis. *Bulletin of the World Health Organization, 95*(9), 609.

Kabeer, N. (2005). Gender equality and women's empowerment: A critical analysis of the third Millennium Development Goal 1. *Gender & Development, 13*(1), 13–24.

Kelley, D., Singer, S. and Herrington, M. (2015). 2016 global report. *Global Entrepreneurship Monitor*.

Kunze, A., & Troske, K. (2020). Life-cycle patterns of women's labor force participation: A cohort view. *Journal of Labor Economics, 38*(3), 779–809.

Langowitz, N. and Minniti, M. (2007). The entrepreneurial propensity of women. *Entrepreneurship theory and practice, 31*(3), 341–364.

Lee, C. W., & Huruta, A. D. (2022). Green microfinance and women's empowerment: Why does financial literacy matter? *Sustainability, 14*(5), 3130.

Lopez, C., & Contreras, O. (2020). *Gender equality discussion within the G20.* Milken Institute W20.

Macías-Prada, J. F., Silva, Y., & Zapata, Á. M. (2023). The role of universities in Latin American social entrepreneurship ecosystems: A gender perspective. *International Journal of Gender and Entrepreneurship, 16*(1), 47–68. https://doi.org/10.1108/IJGE-03-2023-0081.

Marlow, S., Hicks, S. and Treanor, L. (2019). Gendering entrepreneurial behaviour. *Entrepreneurial behaviour: individual, contextual and microfoundational perspectives,* 39–60.

Neneh, B. N. (2020). Women entrepreneurs and access to finance: A review of empirical literature. *Journal of Innovation and Entrepreneurship, 9*(1), 1–26.

Njuki, J., Eissler, S., Malapit, H.J., Meinzen-Dick, R., Bryan, E. and Quisumbing, A.R. (2021). *A review of evidence on gender equality, women's empowerment, and food systems.* International Food Policy Research Institute.

OECD. (2019). *Bridging the digital gender divide.* OECD Publishing.

Okeke-Uzodike, O.U.E. (2019). Sustainable women's entrepreneurship: A view from two BRICS nations. *Journal of International Women's Studies, 20*(2), 340–358.

Plantenga, J., Remery, C., Figueiredo, H. and Smith, M., 2009. Towards a European Union gender equality index. *Journal of European Social Policy, 19*(1), 19–33.

Radović-Marković, M., & Živanović, B. (2019). Fostering green entrepreneurship and women's empowerment through education and banks' investments in tourism: Evidence from Serbia. *Sustainability, 11*(23), 6826.

Sanchez-Riofrio, A. M., Lupton, N. C., Camino-Mogro, S., & Acosta-Ávila, Á. (2023). Gender-based characteristics of micro, small and medium-sized enterprises in an emerging country: is this a man's world? *Journal of Entrepreneurship in Emerging Economies, 15*(3), 652–673.

Solano, G. (2023). A level playing field for migrant entrepreneurs? The legal and policy landscape across EU and OECD countries. *International Migration, 61*(2), 27–47.

Unay-Gailhard, İ., & Bojnec, Š. (2019). The impact of green economy measures on rural employment: Green jobs in farms. *Journal of Cleaner Production, 208,* 541–551.

Verheul, I., & Thurik, R. (2001). Start-up capital: Does gender matter? *Small Business Economics, 16*(4), 329–346.

Voronov, M., & Vince, R. (2012). Integrating emotions into the analysis of institutional work. *Academy of Management Review, 37*(1), 58–81.

Welter, F., Baker, T., & Wirsching, K. (2020). Three waves and counting: The rising tide of contextualization in entrepreneurship research. *Small Business Economics, 54*(1), 21–41.

Chapter 7

Analysis of Trends in Youth Unemployment in the European Union: The Role and Importance of Youth Entrepreneurship

Nataša Papić-Blagojević and Biljana Stankov

Novi Sad School of Business, RS Serbia

Abstract

Youth unemployment is one of the crucial problems facing modern society. Although the findings of the Organisation for Economic Co-operation and Development (OECD) and European Commission (EC) suggest that around 40% of young people are interested in starting their own business after finishing formal education, current studies indicate that the entrepreneurial potential of young people is still underutilized. The analysis of the trend of youth unemployment in the countries of the European Union (EU) in the period from 2009 to 2022 conducted in this chapter gave a clear insight into the decreasing tendency of youth unemployment from 15 to 29 years of age in the last 10 years. However, although there is a tendency for the youth unemployment rate to fall, it is still significantly higher than the unemployment of other age categories. Further analysis carried out in this chapter was related to testing three trend models on a selected data set on youth unemployment. The most precise measures, mean absolute deviation (MAD) and adjusted R^2, unequivocally indicated the selection of the quadratic trend model as the most appropriate for the observed data set, given that the MAD value was the lowest (444.55) and the adjusted R^2 coefficient was the highest (81.88%). Furthermore, through a comparative analysis of the linear and quadratic trend models, the authors predicted youth unemployment in the coming period and

Entrepreneurship and Development for a Green Resilient Economy, 181–204

Copyright © 2024 by Nataša Papić-Blagojević and Biljana Stankov

Published under exclusive licence by Emerald Publishing Limited

doi:10.1108/978-1-83797-088-920241007

concluded that by applying the estimated equations of both trend models, a further decline in youth unemployment in the EU could be expected.

Keywords: Youth unemployment; entrepreneurship; support programs; European Union; trend forecasting

Introduction

In the process of finding a job or developing their own business through self-employment, young people face numerous obstacles, including a lack of entrepreneurial role models, experience in the labor market, and entrepreneurial skills. To encourage young people to be self-employed, many countries are developing various support programs, including entrepreneurship education, training programs (as a form of non-formal education), teaching and mentoring in entrepreneurship, business incubators and funding of start-up programs.

The European Union Youth Strategy (2019–2027), through its objectives, strives to support young people in their personal development, encourage and provide them with the necessary resources to become active citizens involved in democracy and society while at the same time improving policies aimed at young people and making an effort to eradicate youth poverty. Concurrently, when designing and implementing active labor market and skills development policies to help workers move on to new occupations and jobs, it is important to ensure that young people are actively engaged and their needs are addressed (International Labour Organization, 2022).

The highly variable and turbulent social and business environment indicates the importance of creating and managing dynamic careers with a socially responsible approach. In such circumstances, young people should be given reliable and solid support in order to be encouraged to implement business ideas in accordance with their capabilities while at the same time effectively cooperating with others. Developing and maintaining the entrepreneurial way of thinking of individuals, but also teams and working groups, can significantly contribute to the achievement of the mentioned goals.

According to the OECD/EC (2021) Report, nearly half of young people indicate that they would prefer to be an entrepreneur rather than work as an employee, and more than 40% of university students report that they plan to become entrepreneurs within five years of their graduation. Despite this high interest in entrepreneurship, very few young people are working on start-ups. The EU identified the problem and recognized the need of young entrepreneurs at the beginning of their entrepreneurial venture for additional financial resources and timely information, expert advice, quality training and education, which it offers through numerous programs explained below in this chapter. Bearing in mind that small- and medium-sized enterprises (SMEs) are essential for the development of any economy, both in developed countries and in countries in transition (Jovičić Vuković, Jošanov-Vrgović, et al., 2020), the development of these programs to encourage young entrepreneurs is essential for the development of SMEs in general.

In order to create a complete picture of the importance and role of youth entrepreneurship, this chapter also analyzed the trend of youth unemployment concerning possible future trends in the countries of the EU.

EU Explanation of Entrepreneurial Mindset

Dealing with the problem of youth unemployment, as well as with the realization of their entrepreneurial ventures, as one of the ways to reduce the unemployment rate, the EU forms a reference framework that explains the entrepreneurial mindset. Naumann (2017) states that a vast and growing body of knowledge regarding entrepreneurial mindset addresses the challenges of coping with and adapting to complex, dynamic, and uncertain environments.

The European Entrepreneurship Competence Framework – EntreComp is based on a detailed explanation of entrepreneurial knowledge, skills, traits, and attitudes of individuals capable of simultaneously creating financial benefits and contributing to the increase of cultural and social values for the wider community. In the context of EntreComp, entrepreneurship is defined as the capacity to act upon opportunities and ideas and transform them into value for others. The value that is created can be financial, cultural, or social. The framework tends to answer the question: What are an entrepreneurial spirit and an entrepreneurial mindset, and what does it mean to be entrepreneurial? The aim of the EC during the creation of this framework was to provide support and encourage the implementation of activities to improve the entrepreneurial capacities of all citizens and organizations in the EU.

Considering that in the total employment in the EU, entrepreneurial ventures implemented in the form of micro-enterprises and SMEs participate with as much as 67% (Bergner et al., 2017), the importance of this framework is especially highlighted. It is known that youth entrepreneurship as a way to reduce unemployment and social exclusion of young people is almost at the top of the political agenda of the EU, with a particular emphasis on stimulating their innovation and creativity (*EU Youth Strategy – Employment and Entrepreneurship*, https://youth.europa.eu/strategy/employment-entrepreneurship_en).

Research conducted in 2022 by the EC (Directorate-General for Employment, Social Affairs and Inclusion, Ipsos European Public Affairs) shows that almost half of the young respondents in the EU would consider starting their own business but have not yet undertaken activities to realize that. Young people also declared that they mainly acquired entrepreneurial knowledge during their education in schools and universities. However, they certainly expect to be further educated on entrepreneurial skills, traits, and attitudes through various informal forms of education. Young people in France and Romania are the least interested in seeking entrepreneurial education in schools or universities when starting an entrepreneurial venture, unlike those in Luxembourg, who showed a significant interest in these types of education. Cyprus's youth would rather acquire the necessary knowledge using various online content; on the other side, members of the young population in Denmark and Sweden would rather use more informal forms of entrepreneurial education. The results of this study also indicate an interesting fact that young women prefer training in schools and universities, in contrast to young men who, for the same purpose, prefer to use online content (European Commission, 2023c).

EntreComp, in the context of both formal and informal entrepreneurial education, as well as in the establishment of an entrepreneurial mindset, can provide significant support to the young, entrepreneurially oriented population of the EU. EntreComp stands for equality in providing opportunities for the development of entrepreneurial competencies while simultaneously supporting entrepreneurial attitudes and developing entrepreneurial knowledge and skills.

The EntreComp framework factsheets state that being entrepreneurial means more than being prepared for self-employment or launching a start-up. The framework focuses on how people and organizations can address challenges, seize opportunities, and drive change in a rapidly changing world. This framework defines key entrepreneurial competencies, classified into three areas: Ideas and opportunities, Resources, and Actions (Fig. 7.1).

Within each area, five related competencies are combined, which makes a total of 15 entrepreneurial competencies included in the EntreComp framework (Fig. 7.2). The competencies are then expanded into individual outcomes that indicate the meaning and understanding of the competencies in a practical sense. The learning outcomes clearly indicate the learner's knowledge, understanding, and abilities, which are then graded within eight levels of achievement, from beginner to expert.

The key contribution of this framework is to define and explain the entrepreneurial mindset through the competencies mentioned above. The EntreComp offers an overview of interconnected and interrelated competencies that make someone entrepreneurial (McCallum et al., 2018).

The exceptional value of the framework is reflected in the fact that the entrepreneurial competencies are not directly related to the establishment of a new company and starting a business but to the entrepreneurial mindset in general. Creativity and innovation, manifested in the processes of finding new ways of performing certain business activities, are given particular importance both in the current progress of a business career and in creating new business ideas.

One of the key objectives of implementing the EntreComp Framework relates to realizing entrepreneurial education. Special attention should be paid to this type of education already within the primary education level (higher grades) and certainly at the secondary and higher education levels. A particular accent should be placed on the application of acquired knowledge in a specific business environment. Attention should be paid to raising the level of entrepreneurial knowledge and skills within various initiatives of local communities, as well as at workplaces. In this context, it is emphasized that entrepreneurial competence is recognized as "competence for life," which is relevant for personal development, advancement in business, and starting new entrepreneurial ventures.

By producing a common definition of entrepreneurship as a competence, the framework aims to establish a bridge between the worlds of education and work

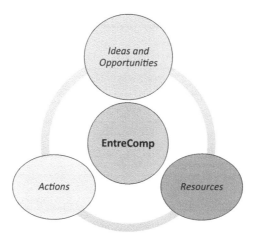

Fig. 7.1.   EntreComp Competence Areas. *Source*: European Commission (2018).

EntreComp		
IDEAS AND OPPORTUNITIES	**RESOURCES**	**ACTIONS**
1. Spotting oppurtunities 2. Creativity 3. Vision 4. Valuing ideas 5. Ettichal and sustainable thinking	1. Self-awareness and Self-efficacy 2. Motivation and perseverance 3. Mobilizing resources 4. Financial and economic literacy 5. Mobilizing others	1. Taking the initiative 2. Planning and management 3. Coping with uncertainty, ambiguity and risk 4. Working with others 5. Learning through experience

Fig. 7.2.   EntreComp Competences into Each Area. *Source*: European Commission (2018).

and to be taken as a reference de facto by any initiative that aims to foster entre-preneurial learning. The framework is a flexible source of inspiration to be used or adapted to support different contexts (Bacigalupo et al., 2016).

Following the EntreComp framework, depending on the dynamics of acquir-ing entrepreneurial competencies and achieving the desired learning outcomes, learner progress is manifested through eight stages, from essential to expert levels (Fig. 7.3).

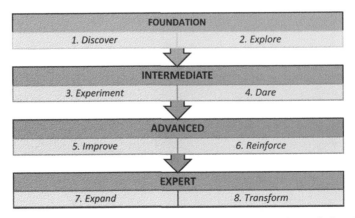

Fig. 7.3.   EntreComp Profession Levels. *Source*: European Commission (2018).

In the process of gaining entrepreneurial competencies at the first level, "foundation," the learner initially needs external support and help from teachers, mentors, colleagues, advisors, etc., which decreases toward the end of the level. On the other hand, the autonomy of the learner increases. The learner at the second level, "intermediate," gradually becomes independent, begins to do certain things following his ideas and capabilities, continues cooperation with participants at the same professional level, and by the end of this stage gradually begins to take responsibility for the activities undertaken. After that, the learner is ready to move to the next stage, "advanced," as with minimal and direct assistance, he begins to cooperate with other participants and take responsibility for his own decisions. At the beginning of the last "expert" stage, the learner can participate in complex events and take responsibility for his contribution. All previously developed competencies now encourage him to accept new challenges and to realize research development and innovative activities. By going through all the described levels, the final goal is achieved: The learner is able to provide excellence in business and transform the way work is done. The EU classifies entrepreneurial competencies among the key competencies of lifelong learning. Through their development, in addition to personal satisfaction, full employment and social inclusion is achieved (Figel, 2007).

The EntreComp application aims to implement activities to support and encourage the development of entrepreneurship in different countries, regions, and cities to exchange experiences and present positive business practices. Emphasis would be placed on those practices that have demonstrated a high degree of success in the process of creating a coherent methodology to support the development of an entrepreneurial mindset at all levels. The EntreComp framework is efficiently applied in the teaching process in educational institutions of the EU in order to adapt the outcomes of entrepreneurial learning to the specific context, that is, to specific users (e.g., students, entrepreneurs, policymakers, etc.). McCallum et al. (2018) emphasized at the beginning of the framework application for educational purposes that the increasing number of user experiences will bring positive effects and influence the better shaping of EntreComp in the future. In addition, its application is also very significant in an informal context, given that it helps individuals to recognize and correctly assess their entrepreneurial competencies.

Assistance and Support Programs for Young Entrepreneurs in the EU

EU Definition of Micro-Enterprises and SMEs

SMEs and entrepreneurs, especially those operating within the non-financial business sector, are given special importance in the EU. They contribute significantly to the growth and development of the European economy, added value, and annual turnover increase and encourage employment growth. The experience of developed countries shows that a successful SME sector is an important developmental factor for efficient economic development, as well as for solving many economic and social issues (Jovičić Vuković, Jošanov-Vrgović, et al., 2020). De Man et al. (2016) and later Dvoulety and Lukeš (2016) chronologically described the historical development of the entrepreneurial framework and policies for SMEs in the EU. Milestones were the declaration of an entrepreneurial, innovative, and open Europe in the Lisbon Agenda 2000 (Grimm, 2011), the publication of the Green Paper on Entrepreneurship by the European Commission (2003a, 2003b), the publication of the definition of SMEs and entrepreneurs in 2003, and the application of the Small Business Act as well as the principle "thinking small first."

Research by numerous authors indicates the importance of SMEs and entrepreneurs in the development and progress of the European economy. It is the fastest-growing sector of international trade which contributes to economic growth (Kushnir et al., 2010) with a share of around 50% in global gross domestic product (GDP) and 60% in global employment (Bamiatzi & Kirchmaier, 2014; Clark, 2021; Gerlach-Kristen et al., 2015). Dvoulety (2018, p. 411) points out that entrepreneurial activity in Europe represents 17% of all economic activities of residents aged 15–64. It is estimated that SMEs make up to 99% of companies that operate in the non-financial business sector of the EU, that they employ close to 100 million people and participate in the total employment of the EU with as much as 67%. By researching the economic activities of EU residents over the age of 15, the EC concluded that as much as 17% of this population are entrepreneurs.

From 2008 onward, the non-financial business sector of the EU is dominated by micro-enterprises employing up to 10 workers. One-employee and family businesses are a very attractive form of entrepreneurship in Europe (Stankov & Roganović, 2022). The same authors emphasize that after analyzing quantitative indicators on the number of employees in the EU non-financial business sector, it can be concluded that 65% of workers are employed in SMEs, that is, 29.2% of workers are employed in micro-enterprises. The EC points out that at the beginning of the second decade of the 21st century, as many as 21 million micro-enterprises and SMEs were active in the EU. Within the non-financial business sector, as many as 99.8% of companies belong to the SME sector, that is, 93% of them are micro-enterprises. Micro-enterprises are the most common type of organization and business chosen by youth in the EU.

Young entrepreneurs need appropriate assistance and support in order to start, develop, and maintain their businesses and thereby become part of the business environment of the EU. A potential threat to entrepreneurship development, especially micro-enterprises, can be foreign investors interested in investing in the EU. In that context, Stankov et al. (2015) emphasize that manufacturing is one of the most attractive economic sectors to foreign investors, and it is going to attract the most investors in Europe. The EC defines measures and implements various activities in order to provide support and encourage the development and survival of entrepreneurs. The ability to use incentives and financial resources, as well as access to various support programs, depends on the conditions of fulfillment which are contained in the definition of SMEs and entrepreneurs in the EU. In the scientific literature, some studies emphasize the importance of a precise and clear definition of SMEs as a prerequisite for the creation and application of adequate incentive measures and assistance (Dannreuther, 2007; Wapshott & Mallett, 2018).

The SMEs definition in the EU went through different phases that were marked by the activities of the EC in terms of the adoption of Recommendation 96/280/EC from 1996, then Recommendation 2003/361/EC from 2003, and the implementation of the Initial Impact Assessment program from 2017.

In the EC Recommendation 96/280/EC (https://eur-lex.europa.eu/legal-content/EN/TXT/?uri=CELEX%3A31996H0280), the following criteria for defining SMEs are stated: number of employees, value of annual turnover, annual value of the balance sheet, and independence criterion. At the beginning of the 21st century, the EC showed its intention to adapt the previous definition of SMEs to the changes that have occurred in the new business environment. The EC Recommendation 2003/361/EC (entered into force in 2005; https://eur-lex.europa.eu/legal-content/EN/TXT/?uri=celex%3A32003H0361) points out that the appropriate qualitative conditions must be fulfilled before determining to which group a given company belongs (micro-enterprise or SME).

According to Recommendation 2003/361/EC, certain novelties are introduced, and every entity that performs economic activity is considered an enterprise, regardless of the legal organizational form. It primarily refers to one-person and family businesses engaged in craft and similar businesses, which are particularly attractive to the young population. Once the described qualitative conditions are met, the company is further categorized into the appropriate group (micro-enterprise or SME) based on the remaining three quantitative criteria (number of employees, value of annual turnover, and value of the balance sheet). By comparing the previous EC recommendation from 1996 with the EC recommendation adopted in 2003, specific changes can be observed, the most significant of which is that in the structure of the SME sector, in addition to SMEs, micro-enterprises also appear. At that time, a key turning point was made, favoring young entrepreneurs because the classification of micro-enterprises in this sector and their definition created the preconditions for using the benefits of incentive measures and programs of the EU.

With the EC Initial Impact Assessment in 2017 (https://op.europa.eu/en/publication-detail/-/publication/c721f802-9ce7-11e7-b92d-01aa75ed71a1/language-en), another step forward was made, and a revision of the SMEs definition, which was applied based on the EC Recommendation 2003, was proposed. The aim of the revision was to create an efficient tool that would help to correctly identify precisely those enterprises that really need financial assistance and support. The new definition was based on two basic levers, financial and legal (El Madani, 2018).

By comparing the definition of a micro-enterprise by the EC, the World Bank (WB), and the OECD, it is noted that agreement has been reached regarding the quantitative criterion indicating the number of employees (<10). Furthermore, the EC and the WB also deal with financial determinants, unlike the OECD, which relies only on the number of employees. The EC definition states that micro-enterprises achieve an annual turnover and balance sheet total of up to 2 million euros, while the WB definition supports annual values of up to 3 million euros (El Madani, 2018).

Entrepreneurs who fulfill the criteria defined by the EC become qualified for participation in various EU business assistance and support programs.

Key Support to Young Entrepreneurs in the EU

Research on the factors that most motivate young people to become entrepreneurs in all EU member states highlights the desire to realize entrepreneurial ideas following their interests. This research conducted in 2022 by the EC (Directorate-General for Employment, Social Affairs and Inclusion, Ipsos European Public Affairs) indicates that 41% of young respondents in Hungary, Romania, and Slovakia opted for the mentioned answer, while in Sweden and Malta, it is as many as 60%. Starting their own business and getting more prosperous are important goals that young entrepreneurs would strive to achieve. Almost a third of respondents in Luxembourg would like to impact the environment with their entrepreneurial business positively. At the same time, the same number of young people in Malta and Cyprus want to realize their innovative ideas in entrepreneurial practice. The research has also led to interesting results indicating that young males are more driven by the desire to become richer than young females who primarily want to "follow their own dream or passion" as entrepreneurs and create their own businesses.

The EU has long recognized that young entrepreneurs need help and support at multiple levels. When starting a business, young people primarily need financial assistance. Financial programs of the EU related to granting loans, providing guarantees, and using other financial instruments that imply the return of approved funds are not based on direct financing by the EC. In this domain, the EU directs financial support to entrepreneurs through local, regional, and national institutions, as well as banks and investment funds. EU support in these circumstances implies the approval of a larger volume of financial resources than usual, a reduction in the interest rate or the number of requirements that the interested entrepreneur must first fulfill. In this context, the European Investment Bank (EIB) Group stands out as a key link in the implementation of the financing program for youth entrepreneurship.

EIB and European Bank for Reconstruction and Development (EBRD) programs are oriented toward providing financial support to entrepreneurs through loans, guarantees, donations, and other financial instruments and advisory support. The key goal to be achieved is to make financing access easier, encourage innovation development, improve competitiveness, and support the sustainable development of entrepreneurs. Through various programs, the EIB supports the entrepreneurial activities of young people and allocates significant funds for the development of start-ups and micro-enterprises. Also, it offers unique guarantees for financing innovative entrepreneurial ventures of young people to make it as simple as possible to obtain financial resources. The EBRD also supports the implementation of training programs for getting innovative skills and supports local financial institutions that give loans to women entrepreneurs and young entrepreneurs, as well as loans for the digitalization of entrepreneurial business.

Among other programs providing financial support to the SME sector and young entrepreneurs, the following stand out: COSME, EFSI, InnovFin, EaSI, and CCSGF.

COSME (Program for the Competitiveness of Enterprises and SMEs) is oriented toward improving the competitiveness of SMEs and entrepreneurs by providing easier access to funding sources, supporting internationalization and access to foreign markets, creating a competitive business environment, and encouraging the development of an entrepreneurial culture.

EFSI (European Fund for Strategic Investments) is an operational mechanism for implementing the investment plan, and it functions under the management of the EIB and the European Investment Fund (EIF). EFSI has a special section for SMEs and provides close to 5.5 billion euros for their financing. It directs funds to entrepreneurs with exceptional potential and supports approving loans to entrepreneurs actively involved in research and development activities, innovation, and social activities within the framework of other EU programs.

InnovFin (EU Finance for Innovators) is another program that supports research and innovation. It includes many financial instruments and advisory services provided by the EIB Group in cooperation with the EC.

EaSI (EU Program for Employment and Social Innovation) financially supports micro-enterprises, members of vulnerable groups, and social enterprises. The purpose of approved financial resources is determined and refers to investments in sustainable employment, improvement of working conditions, provision of adequate social protection, and reduction of social exclusion and poverty.

CCSGF (Cultural and Creative Sector Guarantee Facility) represents a program that provides guarantees to financial institutions that, among other things, deal with financing entrepreneurs doing business in the cultural and creative sector. Financial institutions receive free training to understand this sector's needs better and adapt financial instruments to specific uses for cultural and creative purposes. The Creative Europe program supports youth entrepreneurship development in various ways by encouraging transnational cooperation, mobility, innovation development, and access to the markets of cultural and creative organizations and young professionals.

In addition to the dominant need for financial resources in realizing an entre-preneurial venture, young people also strongly need timely and helpful informa-tion, appropriate expert advice, and quality education and training. Supporting the development of innovative and creative entrepreneurial ideas is also very important. Vapa-Tankosić and Stankov (2017) researched the application of tax incentives in Croatia and concluded that the system of tax incentives in this country is fully harmonized with European standards and that in addition to tax incentives for micro-entrepreneurs, there are also incentives for realization devel-opment and innovation activities in the process of introduction and moderniza-tion of products, production series, processes, and technologies.

The results of the Ipsos research on youth and entrepreneurship speak precisely about the expression of the mentioned needs among the young entrepreneurial population in the EU. Every third respondent in the Czech Republic points out the availability of education and training as the most helpful support for starting a business. Young, new entrepreneurs in Cyprus would need mentoring and coach-ing the most. Young people in the EU also said they need support in information and mutual networking to approach clients more efficiently. The younger the age of the respondents, the need for education and training is more pronounced.

In order to best meet the expectations of young entrepreneurs and satisfy their needs, the EC has created several instruments aimed primarily at networking entrepreneurs and timely and quality information; below are some of them.

The Enterprise Europe Network realizes various programs in order to help entrepreneurs who strive to innovate their businesses and enter international mar-kets. Belonging to the network provides the possibility of more accessible access to market information, faster removal of legal and administrative obstacles, and reaching a more significant number of business partners.

Erasmus for Young Entrepreneurs represents a cross-border exchange program that offers new, potential entrepreneurs or entrepreneurs who have started their businesses during the past three years, the opportunity to learn from experienced entrepreneurs who do business in another country. At the same time, a young entrepreneur will acquire valuable knowledge and skills, make contacts, and start cooperation with other entrepreneurs, organizations, and institutions.

SME Internationalization Support is a program for entrepreneurs based on pro-viding information about foreign markets and assistance to European entrepreneurs who want to internationalize their business and access markets outside Europe.

The European Cluster Collaboration Platform supports the networking of clus-ters operating in different economic sectors and assists in establishing interna-tional cooperation and connecting the most successful clusters.

The Your Europe Business Portal is a practical guide for doing business in Europe that provides helpful information to entrepreneurs who want to start a business outside the home country's market, that is, in other markets of EU member states.

The Single Portal on Access to Finance supports and assists SMEs and entre-preneurs in finding appropriate sources of financing provided by the EU.

The SME Assembly brings together representatives of the EC, representa-tives of the EU member states, scientific workers, and members of European and national entrepreneur associations. At the Assembly, they discuss key issues concerning the EU's SME policy. It is realized every year as part of the final moment of the European SME Week.

European SME Week is a significant event organized by the EC to promote entrepreneurship in Europe. Current entrepreneurs are provided with assistance in getting information about the various forms of support available, while potential entrepreneurs are encouraged to realize their entrepreneurial ideas and start a business.

Analyze of the Youth Unemployment in the EU

Unemployment is one of the critical problems facing young people around the world. The prolonged employment crisis forces young people to be less selective in choosing a job and, consequently, to establish more unstable working relationships that bring less satisfaction and earnings. As a rule, levels and rates of unemployment move cyclically, and apart from the influence of business cycles, unemployment is also influenced by trends in the labor market, as well as demographic changes.

In 2022, the unemployment rate in the EU for the age group of 15–74 reached a historical minimum of 6.2%, which is also the lowest rate since 2009. Over six consecutive years, from 2014 to 2019, the unemployment rate steadily declined (Eurostat, 2023b). When analyzing the available data for the member states of the EU for the category of young people up to 25 years of age, a downward trend in the youth unemployment rate can also be observed in the mentioned period: in 2015, it averaged 22.37%, in 2016 – 20.64%, 2017 – 18.51%, and 2018 – 16.70% (Eurostat, 2023a).

Fig. 7.4 shows the trend of the youth unemployment ratio (for the age group 15–29 years old) from 2009 to 2022 in the countries of the EU, which in the observed period is continuously above the overall unemployment presented with data for the age category 15–74.

This youth unemployment ratio indicates the share of youth unemployment in the total population of the same age. At the same time, the rates are higher if only young people participating in the labor force are taken into account. Apart from this trend, it can be observed that the unemployment rate of persons aged 25–74 in the entire period maintained a slightly lower level compared to the total level of unemployment represented by the data for the age category of 15–74. Fig. 7.4 also shows that during the period of the COVID-19 crisis (from the beginning of 2020 to the end of 2021), there was a significant increase in the youth unemployment ratio, unlike other age categories where the growth is less pronounced, that is, the line shows an almost even movement of unemployment in the crisis period, which indicates more stable employment of other age categories.

According to the OECD/EC Report (2021), the COVID-19 pandemic has had a negative impact on many young people since they have had difficulties getting the best out of their education and finding jobs in a labor market with increasing unemployment. Also, evaluation evidence suggests that youth entrepreneurship schemes can have a role as part of the government's policy response to growing youth unemployment during an economic crisis. From November

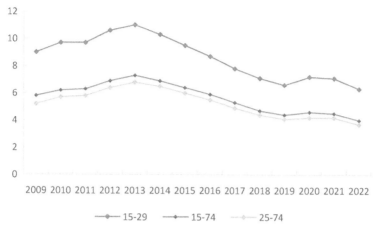

Fig. 7.4.   Trends in the Unemployment Ratio in the EU from 2009 to 2022.
Source: Adapted by the author based on data from Eurostat.

2020, unemployment among under-25s in the EU averaged 17.7%, an increase of 2.8% compared to the previous year. The highest youth unemployment rates were recorded in Spain (40.9% in November 2020), Italy (29.5%), Lithuania (28.4%), and Sweden (24.4%) (Youth Business International, 2021). It is also observed that the unemployment rate varies significantly at different levels of education, for example, as the level of education increases, the unemployment rate decreases. An exception to this rule is present only in Denmark, Luxembourg, and Malta, where people with a high level of education face higher unemployment than those with a medium level of education.

Regardless of some conflicting examples, it is essential to present to young people that "education is the foundation of development and survival of society together with economic, political, and cultural growth" (Jovičić Vuković, Damnjanović, et al., 2020), so the choice of a higher education institution is one of the most important decisions for future students, and it depends on many factors, for example, the perception of quality (Vukadinović et al., 2023), but also personal preferences and information obtained from the external environment.

The upward trend in youth unemployment forced the member states of the EU to respond to this crisis through numerous measures, including the Youth Guarantee, which enables young people up to the age of 30 to receive a quality job offer, continuation of the educational process, or apprenticeship within four months of finishing school or job loss. Addressing youth unemployment in Europe is imperative, not only for the well-being of young people but also to ensure sustainable, inclusive growth and global social cohesion (Youth Business International, 2021). For this reason, forecasting the future trend of youth unemployment in the countries of the EU is considered one of the most important in reducing unemployment to the lowest possible level by applying appropriate measures in the years to come.

Research Methodology

According to Filipović and Papić-Blagojević (2013), forecasting is the most important problem in time series analysis, for example, observing changes over time and projecting future trends. Time series forecasting assumes that the factors that have influenced activities in the past and present will continue to do so in approximately the same way in the future in order to identify and isolate these component factors to make predictions (Levine et al., 2011). Žižić et al. (2003) start from the assumption that certain factors have a permanent effect on the development of the phenomenon in a particular area, while others temporarily divert the course of the phenomenon from that direction, up or down. All these factors together represent a mechanism, a process that generates a specific time series.

Newbold et al. (2020) point out that a standard model for the behavior of time series identifies various components, and traditionally, four are represented in most time series: trend component, seasonality component, cyclical component, and irregular component. A trend in a time series is a persistent, long-term rise or fall; seasonality is a pattern in a time series that repeats itself at known regular intervals of time (Moore et al., 2011); cyclic fluctuations are repeated at intervals that are often unequal and longer than a year, while the irregular component consists of periodic oscillations. Sometimes, some simpler models could fit better to collected data, and on the other hand, more sophisticated ones are more convenient (Vujko et al., 2018).

In order to get a clearer picture of youth unemployment in the countries of the EU, the trend method was used in this chapter, and the authors tested the linear, exponential, and quadratic trend models on a selected set of data. The data were taken from the Eurostat database and adapted for research. The statistical trend model assumes that the overall development of the phenomenon in time is being studied, and the observation of the phenomenon in a specific successive series of finite periods represents the process of evaluating the trend model (Žižić et al., 2003). The estimated trend function is presented as follows:

$$\hat{Y}_i = b_0 + b_1 x + \cdots + b_k x^k$$

where $\hat{Y}_i$ is the estimated value of the dependent variable Y, x is the independent variable, and b_0, b_1, ..., b_k are the parameters of the set. The estimated trend functions for the linear, exponential, and quadratic models differ from the general model.

The linear trend method is very suitable for application in situations when we investigate long-term time series with one-year time periods (Stankov et al., 2023) and when the time series shows an approximately straight-line tendency. Suppose the long-term tendency of the phenomenon shows a stable relative change, for example, shows approximately the same pace of growth or decline of the phenomenon. In that case, using the exponential trend model for the selected data set is appropriate. If the time series data show some long-term quadratic downward or upward movement, a quadratic trend model can be used for the chosen data.

In the case of applying several different models to the same data set, it is necessary to compare the obtained results in order to select the most suitable forecasting model correctly. One way is to compare the adjusted R^2 coefficient for each model individually, where it is considered that the model with the higher coefficient is more suitable. The adjusted R^2 can be given as an adjusted coefficient of multiple determination (Bajpai, 2009):

$$\text{Adjusted } R^2 = 1 - \frac{\text{SSE}/n - k - 1}{\text{SST}/n - 1}$$

where SSE represents the sum of squares unexplained by the regression and SST total variation. The representativeness of the trend model is better when its value is closer to 1, as well as when there are small differences between the original values of the time series and the trend value (Stankov et al., 2023).

Also, a possible way of comparing results and making a proper conclusion is through residual analysis, wherein in the good-fitting model, the residuals represent the irregular component of the time series. According to Levine et al. (2011), the most accurate measure is the MAD, for example, the mean of the absolute differences between the actual and predicted values in a time series:

$$\text{MAD} = \frac{\sum_{i=1}^{n} \left| Y_i - \hat{Y}_i \right|}{n}$$

If the model fits the selected data set perfectly, then the MAD will be zero. When comparing two or more prediction models, the one with the lowest MAD should be chosen as the best.

Research Results and Discussion

In order to research the tendency of youth unemployment aged 15–29 in the EU, the data were selected from the available Eurostat database (Eurostat, 2023a). The data are presented in the form of a time series covering the period from 2009 to 2022; the number of observations is 14. The selected data are presented in Table 7.1, where the second column of data shows the number of unemployed youth in thousands, the third column represents the youth unemployment ratio, that is, the share of youth unemployment in the total population of the same age, while the fourth column shows unemployment rates of young people participating in the labor force.

Based on the data presented, it can be seen that the highest youth unemployment during the observed period was in 2012 (8,107,000) and 2013 (8,296,000). That period was followed by a gradual decline that led to the lowest youth unemployment in 2022 (4,483,000). When comparing the unemployment ratio and the unemployment rate, it is noticeable that the latter is significantly higher because the unemployment of only those young people who are economically active is taken into account, so school children and students are not included in this group. For example, the youth unemployment ratio in 2021 is 7.1%, while the unemployment rate in the same year is 13%.

Analysis of Descriptive Measures

To further process the data presented in Table 7.1, only data representing the total number of unemployed youth expressed in thousands were selected. Based on these data, descriptive statistics measures were calculated and presented in Table 7.2.

Based on Table 7.2, by interpreting the selected measures of descriptive statistics, the following can be concluded: the average number of unemployed youth in the observed period was approximately 6,462,571 persons; the average deviation of unemployed youth by years compared to the average number of unemployed youth amounts to 1,359,418 persons; the range between the highest and lowest number of unemployed persons is 3,813,000, while the lowest number of unemployed in the observed period is 4,483,000, and the highest is 8,296,000. The observed data set has a negative skewness ($\alpha_3 = -0.146$), which means that the values were left inclined relative to the mean (Živkov et al., 2023), and the kurtosis value ($\alpha_4 = -1.729$) is negative, too; that means a flatter distribution than the bell-shaped distribution.

Table 7.1.   Youth Unemployment in the EU Countries from 2009 to 2022.

Year	Number of Unemployed Youths (in Thousands)	Unemployment Ratio (%)	Unemployment Rate (%)
2009	7,337	9.0	16.3
2010	7,619	9.7	17.5
2011	7,518	9.7	17.6
2012	8,107	10.6	19.3
2013	8,296	11	20.1
2014	7,740	10.3	19.0
2015	7,054	9.5	17.5
2016	6,458	8.7	16.0
2017	5,754	7.8	14.3
2018	5,151	7.1	13.0
2019	4,763	6.6	12.1
2020	5,159	7.2	13.6
2021	5,037	7.1	13.0
2022	4,483	6.3	11.3

Source: Author's adaptation of data available on Eurostat (https://ec.europa.eu/eurostat).

Table 7.2. Descriptive Measures of Youth Unemployment in the EU from 2009 to 2022.

Type of Measure	Measures' Value
Mean	6,462.571429
Standard error	363.3196412
Median	6,756
Mode	N/A
Standard deviation	1,359.417619
Sample variance	1,848,016.264
Kurtosis	−1.728884953
Skewness	−0.146422983
Range	3,813
Minimum	4,483
Maximum	8,296

Source: Author's calculation of data available on Eurostat (https://ec.europa.eu/eurostat).

Trend Forecasting of Youth Unemployment in the EU

With the aim to assess the development tendency of youth unemployment (aged 15–29) in the countries of the EU, a linear, exponential, and quadratic trend model was applied to the selected data. The results shown in Table 7.3 compare selected measures of model accuracy to choose the trend model that best matches the selected data.

Based on the results, it can be seen that the quadratic trend model is the most appropriate because this model has the highest value of the adjusted R^2 coefficient; precisely, 81.88% of the variations in the number of unemployed youth in the period from 2009 until 2022 can be explained by applying a quadratic trend model. Considering the high value of this coefficient, it can be concluded that the representativeness of the quadratic trend model is very high for the observed data set.

Another measure favoring choosing the quadratic trend model is the MAD value, which is the lowest in this model and amounts to 444.55. In the case of

Table 7.3. Comparative Measures for Selection of Best-fitting Trend Model.

Regression Statistics	Linear Trend	Exponential Trend	Quadratic Trend
R^2	0.802102282	0.816241873	0.846682649
Adjusted R^2	0.785610806	0.800928696	0.818806766
MAD	477.2276295	525.1768113	444.5453689

Source: Author's calculation.

comparing two or more prediction models, as is the case in our example, the one with the lowest MAD value is chosen as the best one. According to the MAD criterion, the linear trend model is in second place in relevance, where the MAD is 477.23. A comparison of the models and the obtained results is made below to further analyze the quality of the selected trend models for a given data set.

Comparative Analysis of Linear and Quadratic Trend Models for Forecasting Youth Unemployment

The estimated trend function is used to evaluate the linear trend model for the given data set, the number of unemployed youth in the period from 2009 to 2022 in EU countries. The estimated linear trend function is:

$$\hat{Y}_i = 8,354.31 - 291.04x$$

where $\hat{Y}_i$ represents the estimate of the average values of the number of unemployed youth, x data indicating time, while the remaining numerical values are the estimated parameters b_0 and b_1. To calculate these coefficients, the abbreviated method of least squares (Žižić et al., 2003) based on the transformation of the series x was used. The value of the parameter b_0 = 8,345.31 shows the predicted number of unemployed youth in thousands in the countries of the EU in 2009. Coefficient b_1 is an indicator of average absolute growth, and since, in this case, it is negative, -291.04, we conclude that the number of unemployed young people decreased by 291,040 on average per year.

Based on the linear trend equation and the calculated coefficients, the estimated values for all observed data can be determined, which are presented in Table 7.4.

Following these calculations, the trend line is plotted in Fig. 7.5, together with the observed time series data.

Based on Fig. 7.5, it can be concluded that there is a pronounced negative trend. At the same time, the adjusted R^2 indicates that the linear trend model over the time series explains 80.21% of the variation in the number of unemployed youth.

Finally, based on the estimated coefficients and the linear trend equation, it is possible to predict the trend in youth unemployment in the coming period. Thus, it can be expected that the number of unemployed youth in 2023 will amount to 4,279,791, in 2024 to 3,988,754 persons, and in 2025 to 3,697,716, while in 2026, it can be expected that there will be 3,406,679 unemployed youth in the EU. Based on this prediction, it can be expected that in the years to come, the downward trend in the number of unemployed youth aged 15–29 will continue.

As we concluded earlier, the quadratic trend model is selected as the most appropriate for the observed data set, so the parameters b_0, b_1, and b_2 are evaluated using the least squares method. The estimated quadratic trend model is calculated as follows:

$$\hat{Y}_i = 7,855.7 - 41.725x - 19.178x^2$$

Table 7.4. Estimated Values of the Number of Unemployed Youth Using the Linear Trend Method.

Year	Number of Unemployed Youths (in Thousands)	Predicted Values
2009	7,337	8,354.314
2010	7,619	8,063.277
2011	7,518	7,772.24
2012	8,107	7,481.202
2013	8,296	7,190.165
2014	7,740	6,899.127
2015	7,054	6,608.09
2016	6,458	6,317.053
2017	5,754	6,026.015
2018	5,151	5,734.978
2019	4,763	5,443.941
2020	5,159	5,152.903
2021	5,037	4,861.866
2022	4,483	4,570.829

Source: Author's calculation.

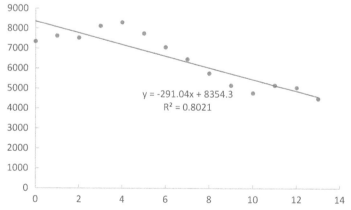

Fig. 7.5. The Linear Trendline of Youth Unemployment in the EU from 2009 to 2022. *Source*: Author's calculation. *Note*. The dots represent the values of the original data of the observed time series, while the linear trend is represented by the line..

Table 7.5. Estimated Values of the Number of Unemployed Youth Using the Quadratic Trend Method.

Year	Number of Unemployed Youths (in Thousands)	Predicted Values
2009	7,337	7,855,689
2010	7,619	7,794.787
2011	7,518	7,695.528
2012	8,107	7,557.914
2013	8,296	7,381.944
2014	7,740	7,167.618
2015	7,054	6,914.936
2016	6,458	6,623.899
2017	5,754	6,294.506
2018	5,151	5,926.757
2019	4,763	5,520.652
2020	5,159	5,076.192
2021	5,037	4,593.376
2022	4,483	4,072.204

Source: Author's calculation.

Based on the calculated coefficients, it is possible to determine the estimated values for all observed data (Table 7.5), and according to the value of the coefficient b_0, it can be concluded that the predicted number of unemployed persons in 2009 was 7,855,700.

Fig. 7.6 graphically shows a quadratic trend line interpolated between empirical time series data that successfully approximates the movement of unemployed youth from 2009 to 2022.

Fig. 7.6 shows a downward trend in youth unemployment, which exceeded the quadratic trend line from 2012 to 2015 and 2020 to 2021; in 2022, a new decline happened after the end of the COVID-19 pandemic.

Based on the estimated quadratic trend model, it is possible to predict the future trend of youth unemployment in the EU. For example, to forecast the movement in the following years by applying the quadratic trend equation, it can be expected that the number of unemployed youths in 2023 will amount to 3,512,676 persons, 2,914,792 in 2024, 2,278,553 in 2025, and 1,603,958 in 2026, so we could expect that the downward trend in youth unemployment would continue.

By comparing the obtained prediction results using the linear model and the quadratic trend model, it can be seen that the decline in the number of unemployed youth aged 15–29 has been confirmed through the application of both models, with the fact that it is significantly more pronounced when forecasting

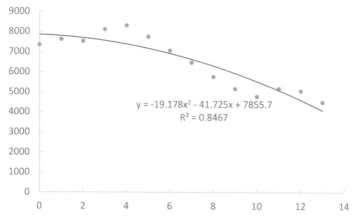

Fig. 7.6.   The Quadratic Trendline of Youth Unemployment in the EU from 2009 to 2022. *Source*: Author's calculation. *Note:* The dots represent the values of the original data of the observed time series, while the quadratic trend is represented by the line.

with the estimated quadratic trend equation has been done. Regardless of the optimistic assessment of both models, it is more realistic to expect that the downward trend in the number of unemployed youth in the EU will rather follow the dynamics of the linear trend prediction, taking into account the effect of other factors, which are not included in the research on this occasion.

Conclusion

Various assistance and support programs created by the EC contribute to the reduction of youth unemployment in the EU and the increase in the number of successful young entrepreneurs. Through this research, the authors concluded that the European Entrepreneurship Competence Framework – EntreComp significantly contributed to the development and improvement of entrepreneurial knowledge, skills, characteristics, and attitudes of young entrepreneurs. By incorporating this framework into formal and informal education programs, learners can simultaneously create financial benefits for their businesses and contribute to increasing cultural and social values for the wider community. Throughout the EntreComp application, the EU contributes to implementing activities to support and encourage the development of entrepreneurship in different countries, regions, and cities to exchange experiences and present positive business practices, as well as to support the development of an entrepreneurial mindset at all levels.

Based on the available data in the Eurostat database and prepared for further analysis, the authors compared the youth unemployment ratio and unemployment rate with total unemployment. The trend of the youth unemployment ratio (for the age group 15–29 years old) from 2009 to 2022 in the countries of the EU was continuously above the overall unemployment presented with data for the age category 15–74. This trend in youth unemployment forced the member states of the EU to respond to this crisis through numerous measures focused on raising entrepreneurial spirit among youth and encouraging them to become active citizens involved in democracy and society.

Further, the authors assessed the development tendency of youth unemployment (aged 15–29) in the EU by applying a linear, exponential, and quadratic trend model to the selected data. When choosing the best forecasting method for the data set, the most accurate measure, MAD, was used, which shows the absolute differences between the actual and predicted values in a time series. According to this criterion, the quadratic trend model was the most suitable for further analysis due to the lowest MAD value (444.55), while the linear trend model (MAD = 477.23) is in second place regarding relevance. With the high representativeness of both models, the authors evaluated the linear and quadratic trend models based on selected data on youth unemployment and predicted the future trend ending in 2026. The trend line in both cases was negative, for example, it had a decreasing tendency.

By analyzing the trend of youth unemployment and applying appropriate forecasting models, the authors concluded that the youth unemployment rate could be expected to decrease in the coming years. Still, further support from the EU through appropriate policies aimed at young people is necessary in order to ensure financial and other essential support in starting their entrepreneurial venture. Through the described support programs, the EU will continue to influence youth entrepreneurship development in the coming period, encouraging innovative and creative entrepreneurial ideas to reduce unemployment and social exclusion of young people.

References

Bacigalupo, M., Kampylis, P., Punie, Y., & Van den Brande, G. (2016). *EntreComp: The entrepreneurship competence framework*. Publication Office of the European Union in Luxembourg.

Bajpai, N. (2009). *Business statistics*. Pearson.

Bamiatzi, V. C., & Kirchmaier, T. (2014). Strategies for superior performance under adverse conditions: A focus on small and medium-sized high-growth firms. *International Small Business Journal, 32*(3), 259–284.

Bergner, S. R., Bräutigam, M. E., & Spengel, C. (2017). *The use of SME tax incentives in the European Union* [Discussion Paper 17-006, ZEW-Centre for European Economic Research]. (pp. 1–125).

Clark, D. (2021). *Number of SMEs in the European Union 2008–2021, by size*. https://www.statista.com/statistics/878412/number-of-smes-in-europe-by-size/

Dannreuther, C. (2007). A zeal for a zeal? SME policy and the political economy of the EU. *Comparative European Politics, 5*(4), 377–399.

De Man, P., Munters, A., & Marx, A. (2016). *Entrepreneurship policy: A multi-dimensional and multi-level assessment, publications*. Office of the European Union.

Dvouletý, O. (2018). Determinants of self-employment with and without employees: Empirical findings from Europe. *International Review of Entrepreneurship, 16*(3), 405–426.

Dvouletý, O., & Lukeš, M. (2016). Review of empirical studies on self-employment out of unemployment: Do self-employment policies make a positive impact? *International Review of Entrepreneurship, 14*(3), 361–376.

El Madani, A. (2018). SME policy: Comparative analysis of SME definitions. *International Journal of Academic Research in Business and Social Sciences, 8*(8), 100–111.

European Commission. (2018). *EntreCompe: The European entrepreneurship competence framework*. Publications Office of the European Union in Luxembourg.

European Commission. (2003a). *Commission recommendation of 6 May 2003 concerning the definition of micro, small and medium-sized enterprises*. http://eur-lex.europa.eu/legal-content/EN/TXT/?uri=CELEX:32003H0361

European Commission. (2003b). *Green paper on entrepreneurship in Europe*. http://ec.europa.eu/invest-in-research/pdf/download_en/entrepreneurship_europe.pdf

European Commission. (2023c). *Social entrepreneurship and youth – Flash eurobarometer 513*. https://europa.eu/eurobarometer/screen/home

Eurostat. (2023a). *Unemployment by sex and age – Annual data*. https://ec.europa.eu/eurostat/data/database

Eurostat. (2023b). *Unemployment statistics and beyond*. https://ec.europa.eu/eurostat/statistics-explained/index.php?title=Unemployment_statistics_and_beyond#Trends_in_the_unemployment_rate

Figel, J. (2007). *Key competences for lifelong learning – European reference framework*. Office for Official Publications of the European Communities in Luxembourg.

Filipović, L., & Papić-Blagojević, N. (2013). *Kvantitativne metode*. Alfa-graf NS.

Gerlach-Kristen, P., O'Connell, B., & O'Toole, C. (2015). Do credit constraints affect SME investment and employment? *The Economic and Social Review, 46*(1), 51–86.

Grimm, H. M. (2011). The Lisbon agenda and entrepreneurship policy: Governance implications from a German perspective. *Public Administration, 89*(4), 1526–1545.

International Labour Organization. (2022). *Global employment trends for youth 2022: Investing in transforming futures for young people*. ILO.

Jovičić Vuković, A., Damnjanović, J., & Papić-Blagojević, N. (2020). Service quality of the higher vocational education. *Management: Journal of Sustainable Business and Management Solutions in Emerging Economies, 27*(1), 21–30. https://doi.org/10.7595/management.fon.2020.0025

Jovičić Vuković, A., Jošanov-Vrgović, I., Jovin, S., & Papić-Blagojević, N. (2020). Socio-demographic characteristics and students' entrepreneurial intentions. *Stanovništvo, 58*(2), 57–75. https://doi.org/10.2298/STNV200423007J

Kushnir, K. M., Mirmulstein, L., & Ramalho, R. (2010). *Micro, small, and medium enterprises around the world: How many are there, and what affects the count*. [Analysis note, World Bank/IFC MSME Country Indicators].

Levine, D. M., Stephan, D. F., Krehbiel, T. C., & Berenson, M. L. (2011). *Statistics for managers using Microsoft excel*. Pearson Education, Inc.

McCallum, E., Weicht, R., McMullan, L., & Price, A. (2018). *EntreComp into action-Get inspired, make it happen: A user guide to the European entrepreneurship competence framework* (No. JRC109128). Publications Office of the European Union.

Moore, D. S., McCabe, G. P., Alwan, L. C., Craig, B. A., & Duckworth, W. M. (2011). *The practice of statistics for business and economics* (3rd ed.). Palgrave MacMillan.

Naumann, C. (2017). Entrepreneurial mindset: A synthetic literature review. *Entrepreneurial Business and Economics Review, 5*(3), 149–172.

Newbold, P., Carlson, W. L., & Thorne, B. M. (2020). *Statistics for business and economics* (9th ed.). Pearson Global Edition.

OECD/EC. (2021). *The missing entrepreneurs 2021: Policies for inclusive entrepreneurship and selfemployment*. OECD Publishing. https://doi.org/10.1787/71b7a9bb-en

Stankov, B., Markov, J., & Milošević, I. (2015). FDI by economic activities and investment incentives in Bulgaria and Serbia. *Management: Journal of Sustainable Business and Management Solutions in Emerging Economies, 20*(77), 61–69. https://doi.org/ 10.7595/management.fon.2015.0026

Stankov, B., & Roganović, M. (2022). Providing support and encouraging the development of small and medium enterprises in the European Union. *Akcionarstvo (Shareholding), 28*(1), 21–45.

Stankov, B., Roganović, M., & Mihajlović, M. (2023). Researching trends and forecasting future values of fruit exports and imports of the Republic of Serbia. *Economics of Agriculture, 70*(1), 29–46.

The European Union Youth Strategy. (2019–2027). Resolution of the Council of the European Union and the Representatives of the Governments of the Member States meeting within the Council on a framework for European cooperation in the youth field (OJ C 456, 18.12.2018, pp. 1–22). https://eur-lex.europa.eu/legal-content/EN/ TXT/?uri=celex%3A42018Y1218%2801%29

Vapa-Tankosić, J., & Stankov, B. (2017). Investment incentives effectiveness in attracting foreign investors in the Republic of Croatia and the Republic of Serbia – Research on tax incentives. In S. Đuričin, I. Ljumović, & S. Stevanović (Eds.), *Opportunities for inclusive and resilient growth* (pp. 141–159). Institute of Economic Sciences in Belgrade.

Vujko, A., Papić-Blagojević, N., & Gajić, T. (2018). Applying the exponential smoothing model for forecasting tourists' arrivals in Serbia – Example of Novi Sad, Belgrade and Niš. *Economics of Agriculture, 65*(2), 465–484. https://doi.org/10.5937/ ekoPolj1802757V

Vukadinović, M., Papić-Blagojević, N., & Jovičić Vuković, A. (2023). The effect of demographic variables on the assessment of cooperation and objectivity in the teaching process of higher education institutions. *CADMO, 2*(2022), 72–84. https://doi.org/ 10.3280/CAD2022-002005

Wapshott, R., & Mallett, O. (2018). Small and medium-sized enterprise policy: Designed to fail? *Environment and Planning C: Politics and Space, 36*(4), 750–772.

Youth Business International. (2021). *Youth business Europe programme – Impact report.* Citi Foundation. https://www.youthbusiness.org/file_uploads/Youth-Business-Europe-Programme--Impact-Report.pdf

Živkov, D., Stankov, B., Papić-Blagojević, N., Damnjanović, J., & Račić, Ž. (2023). How to reduce the extreme risk of losses in corn and soybean markets? Construction of a portfolio with European stock indices. *Agricultural Economics – Czech, 69*(3), 109–118. https://doi.org/10.17221/371/2022-AGRICECON

Žižić, M., Lovrić, M., & Pavličić, D. (2003). *Metodi statističke analize.* Ekonomski Fakultet Beograd.

Chapter 8

Competitiveness of SMEs in Relation to the Green, Resilient Economy

Catalin Popescu, Gabriela Oprea, Daniela Steluţa Uţă, Augustin Mitu and Alina Gabriela Brezoi

Petroleum-Gas University of Ploiesti, Romania

Abstract

The European Union (EU) is providing a wide range of instruments to its members in implementing a green, resilient economy. These instruments are not designed only for governments and state representatives but also for small businesses and entrepreneurs. The ability of those two-targeted audiences to understand and adopt these instruments, as well as their way to react and profit from the EU-stated drives, determines one's country capacity to absorb European funding and create economic growth. The present chapter proposes a presentation of the new European model for economic growth and of the advantages proposed with the European Green Deal, the European proposal to the world for a resilient, adaptable, and environmentally friendly economy.

Keywords: Competitiveness of SMEs; economic growth; green, resilient economy; transition mechanism; modeling economics

1. Introduction

The 2018 IPCC report states that all sectors of the economy, and actors at all scales from individuals to governments, must take urgent action to reduce greenhouse gas emissions. Small and medium enterprises (SMEs) are important actors whose use of energy and potential for energy and carbon savings were largely overlooked by efficient policy in the United Kingdom and European Union (EU)

Entrepreneurship and Development for a Green Resilient Economy, 205–227
Copyright © 2024 by Catalin Popescu, Gabriela Oprea, Daniela Steluţa Uţă, Augustin Mitu and Alina Gabriela Brezoi
Published under exclusive licence by Emerald Publishing Limited
doi:10.1108/978-1-83797-088-920241008

(Fawcett & Hampton, 2020). This aspect changed once with the 2019 Frans Timmermans Green Deal Agenda.

One question tackles SMEs: can they adapt to environmental regulation and still not only make a profit but also become more competitive?

Specialists Alam et al. (2022) conducted a vast research that examines the impact of climate change on SMEs innovation in developing countries. Their findings show that there is a strong correlation between the ability of the company to strive through innovation and adapt to climate change, regardless of its industry. Zilberman et al. (2018) previously showed that innovation is a key point for SMEs in agriculture, but their conclusion can be generalized to a wider range of activities. Other studies (Slominski, 2018) state that in times of crises, SMEs' competitiveness determines their resilience and ability to adapt. The same study states that in times of crises, the EU policymakers pay more attention to economic problems rather than climate change, as it happened during the COVID-19 pandemic (Belitski et al., 2022).

This chapter intends to summarize the EU mechanisms set out to enhance SMEs' competitiveness and reduce the pollution at the EU level and to set out indicators to assess an SME's competitiveness in order to evaluate its impact on economic growth and climate change.

2. Literature Review

According to Yadav et al. (2018), when quoting the World Bank report from 2015, formal SMEs contribute up to 60% of total employment and up to 40% of gross domestic product (GDP) in emerging economies. Globalization council study reveals that SMEs have more flexibility than multinational corporations (MNCs) to easily adapt and change to meet important environmental and social targets.

According to Schaefer et al. (2020), governments and business support organizations continue to promote SME environmental engagement mainly on the basis of a "win–win" rationale, where pro-environmental investments will simultaneously reduce costs or increase competitiveness (European Commission, 2011; Revell et al., 2010). However, securing SME engagement is difficult (Gadenne et al., 2009; Revell & Blackburn, 2007), as SMEs often struggle to comply with environmental regulation (Baden et al., 2009; Cassells & Lewis, 2011) or remain unconvinced by conventional "win–win" arguments (Vickers et al., 2009).

Kaesehage et al. (2019) identified three types of "climate entrepreneurs," those types being triggered by different motivation in order to adopt an environmentally friendly attitude:

- Climate opportunists – they are primarily driven by financial motivations linked to a short-term temporal understandings of climate change.
- Traditional entrepreneurs – demonstrate motivations that stem from their generational view of time and their community focus, coupled with a local understanding of place.
- Integrative entrepreneurs – exhibit both financial and socio-environmental motivations, which are linked to their fluid understanding of time and place and a blend of self-interest and an interest in society's well-being.

In order to increase the entrepreneurs' engagement in climate change mitigation, EU policies must address differently to each type of entrepreneurs. Same authors (Kaesehage et al., 2019) conclude that policymakers should advance and follow entrepreneurs' ways of addressing climate change by questioning people's understanding of themselves in time and place – and their accompanying lay knowledge, personal values, and practices.

Climate change, population growth, and current rate of consumption at a global scale have prompted academic and business communities to challenge the current models of production toward more circular approaches (Mura et al., 2020). According to Uvarova et al. (2020), the circular economy seeks for solutions of climate change and environmental challenges, encourages minimizing the waste and the consumption, engages customers to use products longer, and enables the efficiency of resources. In these conditions, the circular economy seeks for opportunities to balance the industrial and economic growth with the environment, health, and welfare of the society, and without the support of EU policies, it may not have the appropriate implementation due to the SMEs' resilience to change.

In order to attract SMEs in greening their activities, policymakers must appeal to policy tools that do not sacrifice their economic growth. If SMEs are not informed about the relevant greening measures and their costs and benefits, it could be difficult for them to deliver both green and inclusive growth (Koirala, 2019).

Some studies (e.g., Terzić, 2022) show that sustainable competitiveness promoted by EU policies can be achieved when appropriate micro- and macro-economic indicators are considered in correlation with the EU's Green Deal goals and the economic- and environmental-specific goals of each EU country.

3. The New European Model for Economic Growth

The EU and its Member States adopt various approaches and economic policies to promote economic growth. Economic policies in Europe vary by country and are influenced by several factors, such as the current state of the economy, the specific needs of each country, and economic development objectives.

However, the EU has developed different strategies and initiatives to promote sustainable economic growth and competitiveness in Europe. These include the Digital Agenda for Europe, the Investment Plan for Europe (also known as the Juncker Plan), the Digital Single Market, and many others. Additionally, in recent years, concepts such as the "Circular Economy" and the "Green New Deal" have been promoted to address environmental issues and support sustainable economic growth.

The economic growth model of the EU and its Member States evolves based on various factors, including the global economic context, political changes, and the strategic orientations of both the EU and national governments.

In general, the EU promotes an approach to economic development that combines economic growth with environmental and social objectives, including support for a greener economy, carbon emission reduction, and the stimulation of innovation and competitiveness. In the coming years, the EU may focus on implementing the goals set within the European Green Deal, aiming for a transition toward a more sustainable and climate-resilient economy.

4. European Green Deal

The European Green Deal is an ambitious plan of the EU announced in December 2019, representing a strategic framework for transforming Europe into a more environmentally friendly, low-carbon, and ecologically sustainable economy (the main targets of the European Green Deal in Fig. 8.1). The primary objective of the European Green Deal is to make the EU the world's first region to achieve climate neutrality by 2050 (Sikora, 2021). Climate neutrality means that greenhouse gas emissions will be significantly reduced or entirely offset, through carbon absorption measures, such as tree planting or carbon capture technologies.

The main elements and objectives of the European Green Deal include:

(1) Climate Neutrality by 2050: In order to achieve neutrality, the EU intends to reduce all greenhouse emissions from all economic sectors.
(2) "Farm to Fork" Strategy: The strategy intends building short distribution food chains that will ensure financial support for farmers that practice sustainable agriculture and fresh products for local and regional citizens. A secondary objective of this strategy is to reduce food waste. This strategy is a cornerstone of the European Green Deal and is instrumental in working toward the United Nations sustainable development goals (SDGs) (EU Communication From the Commission, 2020).
(3) Building Renovation: The European Green Deal proposes a revolution in the energy efficiency of buildings in the EU, with the objective of renovating 35 million homes by 2030. Another objective of the European Commission

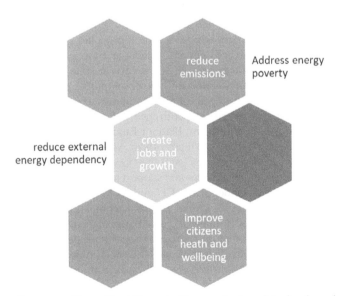

Fig. 8.1.   European Green Deal Targets. *Source*: Authors' design based on targets set out on the European Green Deal.

is the reduction of land consumption. The greatest potential for sustainable development comes from the recovery and rehabilitation of existing building stock, referred to as industrial brownfield land redevelopment (Sessa et al., 2022).

(4) Investments in Clean Energy: The EU promotes investments in renewable energy and support the transition to a low-carbon energy system.

(5) Sustainable Mobility: The European Green Deal promotes eco-friendly transportation, including the development of railway networks and the promotion of low-carbon vehicles.

(6) Biodiversity Protection: The plan includes measures to protect and restore natural ecosystems in Europe and address biodiversity loss.

(7) Social Justice and Just Transition: The European Green Deal commits to ensuring that the transition to a green economy takes into account social aspects, protecting jobs, and supporting communities affected by economic changes.

The EU had developed a various range of funding projects and a legislative framework in order to implement and sustain, on long-term basis, the Green Deal. It is a comprehensive and complex plan aimed at the profound transformation of the European economy to address the climate and environmental challenges of the 21st century.

Below are some of the key initiatives and programs of the EU for implementing the European Green Deal, detailed by Fleming and Mauger (2021):

(1) Just Transition Fund (JTF): JTF provides funding and technical assistance to help regions affected by transition to adapt and thrive in the new economy. The fund will be allocated with 7.5 billion euros, but for each € of investment from this fund, EU Member States have to add contributions via their share of the European Regional Development Fund (ERDF) or European Social Fund Plus (ESF+), or via co-financing.

(2) Just Transition Mechanism (JTM): The aim of this mechanism is to support regions most affected by the transition. The scheme is part of the InvestEU program and should attract private investments for up to 45 billion euros.

(3) ERDF: ERDF finances projects that contribute to sustainable regional development and job creation in EU regions. It supports investments in green infrastructure, innovation, and energy efficiency.

(4) Cohesion Fund (CF): This fund supports countries with lower incomes in reducing development disparities between regions. Funds can be used for environmental and green infrastructure projects.

(5) Next-Generation EU: This EU economic recovery program allocates resources to support economic recovery after the COVID-19 pandemic and to promote the green and digital transformation of the European economy.

(6) Fit for 55 Package: This comprehensive set of legislative initiatives is designed to contribute to reducing the EU's greenhouse gas emissions by at least 55%. It includes a revision of the carbon emissions trading system. A growing scholarship argues single instruments like carbon pricing alone cannot achieve that

decarbonization (Skjærseth, 2021). The program sets out ambitious targets for renewable energy as well as measures to promote clean transportation.

(7) European Circular Economy Package: This package aims to reduce waste production and promote recycling and sustainable resource use. It includes directives on plastic waste, sustainable packaging, and extended producer responsibility.

(8) Sustainable Finance Action Plan: This plan aims to channel private investments into sustainable and green projects and activities. It includes the EU taxonomy for sustainable activities and regulations on disclosing environmental, social, and governance (ESG) information.

These initiatives and programs represent the EU's commitment to combating climate change, protecting the environment, and promoting a greener and more sustainable economy. The European Commission proposed ambitious targets for reducing the CO_2 emissions of new cars and vans:

✓ 55% reduction of emissions from cars by 2030;
✓ 50% reduction of emissions from vans by 2030;
✓ 0 emissions from new cars by 2035.

As the European Green Deal sets its more ambitious target of reducing greenhouse gas emissions by 55% (up from 40%) by 2030 compared to 1990 levels, according to Etires (2022), the EU is currently considering the following new targets for 2030:

• Increasing the share of energy from renewable sources to 40% of total EU energy consumption (up from 32%).
• Increase in energy efficiency by 36% (for final energy consumption) and 39% (for primary energy consumption) – up from 32.5% – compared to 2007 projections of consumption levels without energy efficiency measures. This would represent a 9% overshoot of projections made in 2020. In addition, reducing energy consumption is essential to bring down both emissions and energy costs for consumers and industry. The Commission proposes to increase energy efficiency targets at the EU level and makes them binding, to achieve by 2030 an overall reduction of 36%–39% for final and primary energy consumption.

The European Commission is advocating for a more ambitious objective in the reduction of CO_2 emissions from new cars and vans. This initiative is part of a broader timeline of significant milestones:

(1) In December 2019, the Commission introduced the European Green Deal, which made a commitment to achieving climate neutrality by 2050. This signaled a fundamental shift toward environmental sustainability.

(2) In March 2020, the Commission proposed the European Climate Law, seeking to establish the 2050 climate neutrality target as legally binding legislation. This aimed to ensure a robust and enduring framework for climate action.

(3)   In September 2020, the Commission set forth a new EU target to achieve a minimum 55% reduction in net emissions by 2030 and incorporated it into the European Climate Law. This demonstrated a strong commitment to intermediate climate goals.

(4)   In December 2020, European leaders endorsed the Commission's proposed target of reducing net emissions by at least 55% by 2030. This marked a consensus among EU Member States on the urgency of climate action.

(5)   In April 2021, a political agreement was reached on the European Climate Law through the European Parliament and Member States. This highlighted the collaborative effort to turn climate ambitions into concrete legislation.

(6)   In June 2021, the European Climate Law officially came into effect, solidifying the EU's commitment to climate neutrality by 2050 as a legally binding obligation.

(7)   In July 2021, the Commission unveiled a package of proposals aimed at reshaping the European economy to align with the 2030 climate targets. The European Parliament and Member States initiated negotiations to adopt this legislative package, indicating active engagement in climate policy.

(8)   In September 2021, the New European Bauhaus initiative was launched, accompanied by new actions and funding. This initiative aimed to integrate sustainability and esthetics in architecture and design.

(9)   In October 2022, the Council and the European Parliament reached a provisional political agreement on more stringent CO_2 emission performance standards for new cars and vans. This represented a significant step toward reducing emissions from the transportation sector.

(10) By 2030, the EU is firmly committed to achieving a substantial reduction in emissions, aiming for at least a 55% decrease compared to 1990 levels. This reflects a tangible interim goal in the journey toward climate neutrality.

(11) The ultimate objective is for the EU to attain climate neutrality by 2050, marking a profound transformation toward a sustainable and green future.

These proposals not only focus on emission reduction but also present substantial opportunities for European industries by creating markets for clean technologies and products. They will have a pervasive impact on entire value chains across sectors such as energy, transport, construction, and renovation. This transformation will ultimately foster the creation of sustainable, local, and well-compensated job opportunities throughout Europe.

The Commission's strategy includes elevating the binding target for renewable energy sources in the EU's energy mix to 40% and promoting the adoption of renewable fuels like hydrogen in industries and transport through additional targets. Furthermore, a key component of emission reduction involves lowering energy consumption, which is essential for reducing both emissions and energy costs for consumers and industries alike. To achieve this, the Commission proposes increasing energy efficiency targets at the EU level and making them legally binding, aiming for an overall reduction of 36%–39% in final and primary energy consumption by 2030. This multifaceted approach underscores the EU's commitment to a sustainable and low-carbon future. The European Green Deal is not a single strategy that provides the solution for Europe's many environmental- and climate-related challenges. Rather, it presents a collection of targets, intentions, and objectives that will be implemented over the next years (Fetting, 2020).

5. Enhancing Resilience and Crisis Preparedness

Enhancing resilience and preparedness for crises are critical aspects for modern society, economies, and communities, particularly in the face of increasingly complex and varied threats. This topic can be approached from several perspectives:

1. Economic Resilience:
   o A resilient economy can absorb shocks and crises without suffering severe damage. This may involve diversifying the economy to reduce reliance on a single sector, creating financial safety nets such as emergency funds, and implementing flexible fiscal policies.
2. Community Resilience:
   o Resilient communities are those that are prepared for natural disasters or other types of crises. This entails developing evacuation plans, educating the public about safe behaviors during crises, and building resilient infrastructure.
3. Climate Resilience:
   o In the context of climate change, it is crucial to prepare for extreme weather events such as floods, hurricanes, wildfires, and droughts. This can mean investing in climate-resilient infrastructure and adapting to the new climate realities.
4. Cyber Resilience:
   o In the digital age, cyber crises can be as severe as natural ones. Developing the capacity to prevent, detect, and respond to cyberattacks is essential for modern society.
5. Health Resilience:
   o Pandemics, such as COVID-19, have highlighted the importance of preparedness in health-care systems. This involves developing strategic stockpiles of medical equipment, training health-care personnel, and creating pandemic response plans.
6. Personal Resilience:
   o Education and training in survival skills and stress management can play a significant role in developing individual resilience in the face of crises.
7. International Cooperation:
   o Resilience development is not limited to national borders. International cooperation and the exchange of knowledge and resources can strengthen the ability to address crises at a global level.

In conclusion, building resilience and preparedness for crises are complex efforts that encompass economic, social, and technological aspects. A holistic approach and collaboration across different sectors of society are essential to ensure that we are prepared to confront current and future challenges.

6. The JTM

The JTM is a crucial component of the European Green Deal and is an instrument created by the EU to ensure that the transition to a more sustainable, low-carbon economy is fair and leaves no one behind. This mechanism focuses on regions and economic sectors that may be more severely affected by the transition to a greener economy and aims to provide support for retraining and sustainable development.

Here are some key aspects related to the JTM and the need for promoting a resilient economy:

(1) Support for Affected Sectors and Regions: The JTM aims to assist regions and sectors heavily reliant on high-carbon industries in adapting to the new economic conditions. This may involve investments in vocational training, the creation of new jobs in green sectors, and the development of sustainable infrastructure.
(2) Social Justice: The JTM places a strong emphasis on ensuring that the transition to a greener economy is socially equitable. This means taking into account the impact on workers and affected communities and ensuring that they are not left behind in the transition process.
(3) Creation of Green Jobs: An important part of the JTM is promoting the creation of new jobs in green sectors and developing skills for the workforce in these areas. This can contribute to the revitalization of regional economies and support sustainable development.
(4) Promotion of Resilient Economy: Transitioning to a low-carbon, sustainability-oriented economy is essential for building resilience to climate change and other crises. A resilient economy involves investments in climate-resilient infrastructure, the promotion of energy efficiency, and diversification of energy sources.
(5) Cooperation and Financing: Implementing the JTM requires close cooperation between EU Member States, the private sector, and nongovernmental organizations. Adequate financial resources must also be allocated to support transition-related projects and initiatives.

In conclusion, the JTM plays a crucial role in ensuring that the transition to a more resilient and environmentally sustainable economy occurs in an equitable and inclusive manner. This is essential not only for addressing the challenges related to climate change but also for promoting sustainable development and the social well-being of European citizens.

7. Competitiveness of SMEs and European Statistics

The competitiveness of SMEs is a topic of significant importance for national economies and sustainable economic development. SMEs are often considered the backbone of economies, as they constitute a substantial portion of private businesses and have a significant impact on employment and innovation. Here are some key aspects related to the competitiveness of SMEs:

(1) Access to Financing: To be competitive, SMEs need access to adequate and reasonably priced financing. Governments and financial institutions need to develop policies and instruments that facilitate SMEs' access to credit, investments, and venture capital.
(2) Innovation and Technology: SMEs that invest in innovation and technology are often more competitive in the long run. Governments can support these efforts through research and development (R&D) programs and by facilitating technology transfer.
(3) Education and Workforce Development: Workforce training and development are essential to enhance the competitiveness of SMEs. Training and lifelong learning initiatives can help SMEs improve productivity and adapt to technological changes.
(4) Access to International Markets: Expanding to international markets can enhance the competitiveness of SMEs. Governments can support exports and SME internationalization through favorable trade agreements and export promotion services.
(5) Regulatory and Administrative Framework: Simplifying administrative procedures and reducing bureaucracy can help SMEs operate more efficiently and be more competitive.
(6) Inclusivity and Diversity: Governments can promote SME competitiveness by ensuring that all categories of entrepreneurs, including women and minorities, have equal access to resources and business opportunities.
(7) Public Funding: Public funding initiatives, such as grants or subsidies for SMEs, can significantly contribute to enhancing their competitiveness, especially in key sectors or during economic crises.
(8) Collaboration with Academic and Research Institutions: The link between SMEs, academia, and research institutions can stimulate innovation and the development of new products or services, thus increasing their competitiveness.

In conclusion, the competitiveness of SMEs is essential for economic development and employment. Governments, nongovernmental organizations, and the private sector play a crucial role in developing and implementing policies and programs to support and improve the competitiveness of these vital enterprises.

Quantifying the competitiveness of SMEs can be a complex process and involves the assessment of multiple factors. Here are several methods and indicators that researchers and analysts use to quantify the competitiveness of SMEs:

(1) Productivity: Labor and capital productivity is an important indicator of competitiveness. It can be measured by relating production or revenue to the number of employees or invested capital.
(2) Cost Efficiency: A competitive SME is capable of producing or offering services at lower costs or achieving higher profits than its competitors.

Cost efficiency can be assessed through an analysis of production costs, operational expenses, and profit margins.

(3) Innovation: The ability to innovate and develop new products or services and bring them to market can be a significant indicator of competitiveness. It can be evaluated through the number of patents obtained, R&D investments, or the introduction of innovative products/services.

(4) Product/Service Quality: The quality of the products or services offered by an SME can influence competitiveness. It can be assessed through customer reviews, quality tests, or quality certifications.

(5) Access to International Markets: Expanding into international markets can enhance an SME's competitiveness. The more successful an enterprise is in exporting or has a stronger presence in international markets, the more competitive it is.

(6) Reputation and Brand: A positive reputation and a strong brand can influence an SME's competitiveness. This can be evaluated through market research and brand awareness surveys.

(7) Flexibility and Adaptability: The ability to adapt to rapid changes in the business environment can be a significant indicator of competitiveness. It can be assessed by analyzing how the SME has managed past changes and its capacity to adapt to new requirements and opportunities.

(8) Financial Indicators: Financial indicators such as turnover, profitability, liquidity, and growth rate can be used to assess the financial competitiveness of an SME.

(9) Competitor Analysis: Comparing with direct competitors can provide insights into an SME's competitiveness regarding market share, pricing, profit shares, and other relevant indicators.

(10) Customer and Stakeholder Assessments: Customer, supplier, and other stakeholder opinions and feedback can offer valuable information regarding an SME's competitiveness.

It is important to note that there is no universal method for quantifying the competitiveness of SMEs, as it can vary depending on the industry, region, and other specific factors. Typically, analysts use a combination of indicators and methods to gain a more complete picture of an SME's competitiveness.

To analyze the competitiveness of an organization, the following indicators are presented:

(1) Labor Productivity: This indicator measures the efficiency of work within a company by evaluating the production or revenue generated by each employee. The higher the value or production each employee can generate, the more competitive the company is considered. An increase in labor productivity may indicate the adoption of more efficient work practices or investments in staff development.

(2) Market Share: This indicator determines the proportion of the market that the company holds in its industry or a specific region. A larger market share

may suggest a stronger position in the industry and a greater capacity to influence prices or attract new customers.

(3)   Profitability: This is a key indicator that quantifies the company's profitability. It may include measures such as net profit margin (profit in relation to revenue) and return on invested capital (profit in relation to the total investments of the company). Higher profitability indicates a more competitive and efficient use of resources.

(4)   Innovation: This indicator measures the level of creativity and development within the company. The number of new products or services can assess this indicator or services developed, the number of patents obtained, or the level of investment in R&D. Innovative firms are often considered more competitive in the long run.

(5)   Operational Costs: This indicator involves monitoring and comparing the company's operational costs with those of competitors or the industry as a whole. A company that can control or reduce operational costs over time can become more competitive.

(6)   Product/Service Quality: The quality of products or services provided by the company is a key factor in competitiveness. Measuring customer satisfaction levels or using other metrics to assess quality can provide insights into how well the company fits into the market.

(7)   Degree of Digitalization: This indicator evaluates the level of adoption of digital technology in the company's operations. The better prepared a company is for the digital age, the more competitive it becomes in an increasingly digitally connected world.

(8)   Access to Financing: Access to financing is crucial for the development and growth of a company. This indicator assesses the company's ability to obtain financing for investments in innovation, expansion, and other initiatives that improve competitiveness.

(9)   Workforce: Analyzing the skills level of employees and the company's ability to attract and retain talent is essential in determining competitiveness. A skilled and loyal workforce can provide a significant competitive advantage.

(10)   Sustainability: Sustainability refers to the company's efforts regarding social responsibility and the environment. A company that can integrate sustainable and responsible business practices into its operations can gain favor with customers and have a long-term competitive advantage.

(11)   Customer and Supplier Relationships: Evaluating the company's relationships with customers and suppliers is important to understand the level of loyalty and collaboration. A company with strong relationships can benefit from greater support in terms of access to resources and customers.

(12)   Operational Flexibility: The company's ability to adapt quickly to changes in the market or industry is crucial to remaining competitive. Operational flexibility allows the company to adjust and innovate in the face of new challenges and opportunities.

8. The Connection Between the Competitiveness of SMEs and the Concept of a "Green, Resilient Economy"

The evolution of competitiveness among SMEs in Europe is a complex subject and depends on a variety of factors, including the economic context, government policies, and changes in the business environment. In general, the competitiveness of European SMEs has evolved positively in certain areas but remains a subject of concern and development in others. Here are some trends and relevant factors in the evolution of competitiveness among European SMEs:

(1) Innovation and Technology: In recent years, there has been an increasing emphasis on innovation and technology in the European business environment. SMEs that invest in technology and innovation have tended to become more competitive and expand their businesses into international markets.
(2) Government Support: European governments have developed various programs and initiatives to support SMEs. These include access to financing, facilitating exports, promoting entrepreneurship, and investments in regional development.
(3) Access to International Markets: SMEs' participation in international trade has significantly increased. The EU has entered into trade agreements and developed export promotion programs to help SMEs expand their operations into international markets.
(4) Digitalization: Digitalization has become a priority, and SMEs that have adopted digital technologies have gained significant competitive advantages. The COVID-19 pandemic accelerated the adoption of digital technologies in the business environment.
(5) Access to Financing: Access to financing remains a concern for many European SMEs, especially those in less developed regions. However, funding initiatives, such as European structural and investment funds, have been created to address this issue.
(6) Regulation and Bureaucracy: Simplifying administrative procedures and reducing bureaucracy have been a significant focus to enhance SME's competitiveness.
(7) Key Sectors: Key sectors such as information technology, renewable energy, healthcare, and the environment have experienced significant growth in competitiveness, with many European SMEs in these fields making a global impact.
(8) Resilience in the Face of Crises: The recent experience of the COVID-19 pandemic highlighted the importance of SME resilience. The ability to adapt rapidly and survive during crises has become a key factor in competitiveness.

The evolution of competitiveness among European SMEs is influenced by multiple factors and can vary from one country to another and from one sector to another. Nevertheless, it is clear that SMEs play a vital role in the European economy and will continue to be drivers of growth and innovation in the region.

European governments and EU institutions continue to develop policies and programs to support and stimulate SME competitiveness in the future.

In fact, European structural and investment funds contain:

(1) ERDF that promotes balanced development in the different regions of the EU.
(2) ESF – supports employment-related projects throughout Europe and invests in Europe's human capital – its workers, its young people, and all those seeking a job.
(3) CF – funds transport and environment projects in countries where the gross national income (GNI) per inhabitant is less than 90% of the EU average.
(4) European agricultural fund for rural development (EAFRD) – focuses on resolving the particular challenges facing EU's rural areas.
(5) European maritime and fisheries fund (EMFF) – helps fishermen to adopt sustainable fishing practices and coastal communities to diversify their economies, improving quality of life along European coasts.

The ERDF represents, according to cohesiondata.ec.europa.eu, the only source of European funding for research and innovation, for competitiveness of SMEs and, as well as, for Information & Communication Technologies, between 2014 and 2020. In Fig. 8.2 (for 2014–2020 period) and in Fig. 8.3 (for 2021–2027 period) of this chapter, one can observe the ERDF planned funding for the two periods, for each country.

ERDF, CF, ESF, and Youth Employment Initiative are the main drivers for EU countries in supporting and developing SMEs.

Fig. 8.4 of this chapter presents the distribution of ERDF funding for SMEs by intervention code (in million euros). The main individual support to SMEs is directed toward generic productive investment SMEs, followed by SME business development, support to entrepreneurship, and incubation.

Fig. 8.5 of this chapter presents the distribution of ERDF funds by thematic objective, the competitiveness of SMEs being the second most financed objective.

SMEs are experiencing a decline in their competitive edge when compared to large corporations.

The ECA's special reports set out the results of its audits of EU policies and programs. According to the audit made by Audit Chamber II Investment for cohesion, growth, and inclusion spending areas, headed by ECA Member Iliana Ivanova, EU Member States aimed at funding a large number of SMEs rather than targeting the key factors that limit SME competitiveness. This approach led to a decrease of efficiency in using European funds and had no lasting influence on competitiveness.

The data cover more than 530 programs available (adopted) and include the EU and national co-financing covered by the adoption decision. Financial allocations in the program financial table may change over time (i.e., transfers between themes, between funds). The first wave of major changes took place at the end of 2017 as a result of the allocation of the "technical adjustment" and the increase in the allocation to the Youth Employment initiative.

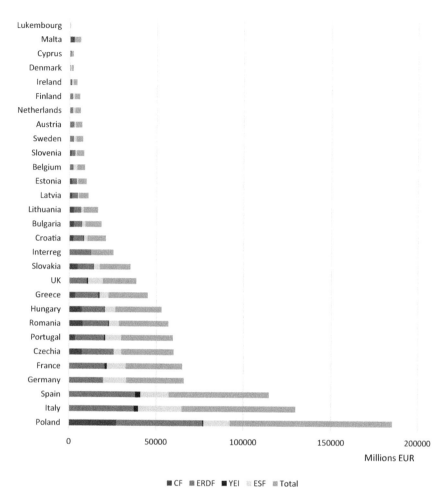

Fig. 8.2. Cohesion Policy Budget by Country, EUR Million, Funding Period 2014–2020. *Source*: Information processed by the authors based on the data retrieved from https://cohesiondata.ec.europa.eu/cohesion_overview/14-20.

For the 2021–2027 program period, the EU remains committed to providing financial support for initiatives aimed at enhancing the competitiveness of SMEs. This support encompasses several key areas:

(1) ERDF Funding: The ERDF for the period 2021–2027 will continue to promote SME's competitiveness as part of its broader policy objective. This objective includes a focus on R&D, information and communication technology (ICT), and skills enhancement. These areas are critical for SMEs to stay competitive in today's dynamic business landscape.

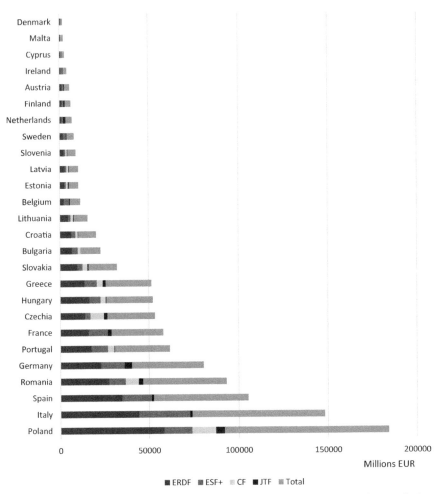

Fig. 8.3.   Cohesion Policy Budget by Country, EUR Million, Funding Period 2021–2027. *Source*: Information processed by the authors based on the data retrieved from https://cohesiondata.ec.europa.eu/cohesion_overview/21-27.

(2) REACT-EU: As of October 2021, REACT-EU has allocated an additional €6.6 billion to the 2014–2020 ERDF funding, adjusting for 2020 price levels. This infusion of funds is dedicated to supporting businesses, with a particular emphasis on addressing the economic challenges posed by the COVID-19 pandemic.

(3) Horizon Europe: Horizon Europe, the EU's flagship research and innovation program, has specifically earmarked €7.1 billion to foster innovation among SMEs. This allocation is designed to stimulate R&D activities within SMEs, driving innovation across various sectors.

(4) InvestEU: The InvestEU program will provide financing options tailored to the needs of SMEs and mid-cap companies looking to make strategic business

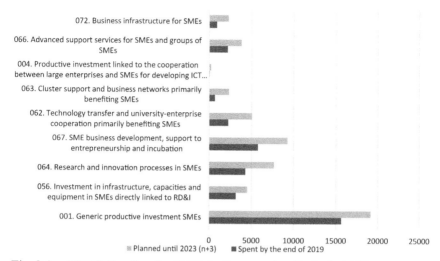

Fig. 8.4. ERDF Funding for SMEs by Intervention Code (in Million Euros). *Source*: Retrieved from European Court of Auditors, "ERDF support for SME competitiveness," Special report, Number 8/2022, https://www.eca.europa.eu/Lists/ECADocuments/SR22_08/SR_SME_Competitiveness_EN.pdf.

investments. This initiative aims to facilitate access to capital for smaller businesses, enabling them to expand and grow.

(5) Recovery and Resilience Facility (RRF): The RRF is another vital funding mechanism that will offer support to SMEs. It is important to note that this funding has to be allocated by 2023 and fully utilized by 2026. The RRF plays a significant role in helping SMEs recover from the economic impacts of crises and build resilience for the future.

In summary, the EU's commitment to strengthening SME's competitiveness for the 2021–2027 program period involves a multifaceted approach, encompassing financial support through various funds and programs. These initiatives aim to bolster the innovation capacity, economic resilience, and overall competitiveness of SMEs across Europe.

The connection between the competitiveness of SMEs and the concept of a "Green, Resilient Economy" is complex and significant in the current context of concerns related to climate change and sustainable development. Here are several ways in which these two concepts are interconnected:

(1) Green Innovation and Technology: To become competitive in a green, resilient economy, SMEs need to invest in green innovation and technologies. Developing innovative products and services, such as renewable energy sources, energy efficiency, or emission reduction technologies, can create new business opportunities and enhance competitiveness in the market.

(2) Access to Green Financing: A green, resilient economy often involves significant investments in sustainable technologies and practices. SMEs require access

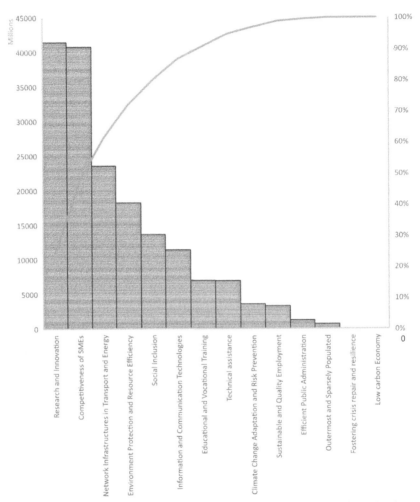

Fig. 8.5.   2014–2020 Period: ERDF Planned Funding by Thematic Objective (in Million Euros). *Source*: Information processed by the authors based on the data retrieved from https://op.europa.eu/webpub/eca/special-reports/competitiveness-08-2022/en/index.html#chapter10.

to specific funding to develop such projects. Governments and financial institutions can play a crucial role in providing green financing options for SMEs.

(3) Demand for Green Products and Services: Awareness and concern for the environment are growing among consumers and businesses. SMEs that produce or offer green products and services can attract increased demand and gain competitiveness in a changing business environment.

(4) Resource Efficiency and Resource Savings: A green economy involves the efficient use of natural resources and waste reduction. SMEs that adopt resource-efficient practices can save costs and remain competitive in the long term.

(5) Adaptation to Climate Risks: A green, resilient economy also focuses on adapting to climate change and managing associated risks. SMEs that are prepared to address climate change impacts can avoid major losses and remain competitive.
(6) Brand Image Benefits: Commitment to and implementation of green practices can improve the brand image of SMEs and enhance the trust of customers and business partners, which can have a positive impact on competitiveness.

9. Conclusion

In conclusion, the competitiveness of SMEs is closely linked to the development of a green, resilient economy. By adopting sustainability-oriented practices and strategies, SMEs can gain significant competitive advantages in a changing business environment and contribute to achieving SDGs and combating climate change.

For the 2014–2020 program period, the ERDF regulation did not mandate Member States to align the measures for enhancing SME's competitiveness within ERDF programs with national or regional strategies. Consequently, the Commission had limited means to ensure that ERDF funding was directed to areas with the greatest growth potential.

In 2019, just before the COVID-19 pandemic, the ERDF aimed to provide direct support to 0.8 million SMEs out of nearly 25 million in the EU (approximately 3.3% of all SMEs). Member States adopted various approaches, with some concentrating ERDF support on a few hundred companies, while others distributed it more widely. For instance, Ireland aimed to provide funding to over 67,000 SMEs (around 25% of all SMEs in the country), whereas Austria's ERDF program supported only 435 companies. Consequently, the funding per SME varied significantly among Member States. When ERDF programs spread funding across too many SMEs, there was a high risk that the support lacked the critical mass required to influence significantly SMEs' competitiveness.

In 2020, in response to the COVID-19 pandemic, many Member States reprogrammed their ERDF programs under the CRII/CRII+ and REACT-EU initiatives. This reprogramming led to additional funding for SMEs and a significant increase in the number of SMEs targeted, particularly in Italy.

In the four audited Member States, the 2014–2020 ERDF support for SME's competitiveness encouraged SMEs to invest, but its effectiveness in enhancing their competitiveness was hindered by various shortcomings in the funding approach adopted by Member States' managing authorities. These shortcomings included:

(1) Calls for project submissions often did not address all relevant obstacles to competitiveness faced by beneficiary SMEs, primarily co-financing specific productive investments without leading to demonstrable improvements in the SMEs' competitive situation in terms of operations, market position, internationalization, financial situation, or innovation capacity.
(2) Calls rarely financed investments in other value-adding processes that could enhance long-term SME competitiveness (e.g., boosting R&D capabilities or market penetration). Few projects provided tailored advisory services to overcome specific competitiveness hurdles.

(3) Projects primarily supported individual SMEs rather than groups of enterprises, limiting ERDF outreach to SMEs.

(4) Project funding primarily used non-competitive calls and selection procedures where every application meeting minimum criteria received financing.

(5) Financing took the form of grants rather than repayable forms of support (e.g., loans or guarantees). However, the use of repayable support could have assisted more businesses.

Moreover, some beneficiary SMEs would have made the same investments even without EU funding, and in some cases, ERDF support negatively affected the economic prospects of non-beneficiary SMEs competing in the same markets, reducing the overall net impact of EU support.

Recommendation 1 – Review the design of ERDF calls: The Commission should encourage and assist Member States in designing calls that promote the submission of proposals more likely to enhance effectively SMEs competitiveness. This involves organizing calls that address multiple factors limiting competitiveness within a project, strengthen cooperation between SMEs and other entities, and support SME participation in advisory services and networks.

Timeframe: By the end of 2023.

Recommendation 2 – Review ERDF selection procedures for grant awards: The Commission should encourage and support Member States in reviewing ERDF selection procedures, particularly for grant financing, aiming to select projects through non-competitive processes only when justified and based on ambitious selection criteria and thresholds to achieve optimal outcomes.

Timeframe: By the end of 2023.

Recommendation 3 – Prioritize the use of repayable aid for SME competitiveness: The Commission should encourage and support Member States in prioritizing financial instruments, such as loans, guarantees, or equity, for funding SME's competitiveness. Grants should only be used when necessary (e.g., addressing market failures) or to achieve specific policy objectives (e.g., promoting a circular, green, and equitable economy), and, whenever possible, grants should be combined with financial instruments.

9. Further Discussions

According to the ECA Special Report Number 8 from 2022, on evaluating the ERDF support for SME competitiveness, program design weaknesses decrease effectiveness of funding.

Based on the report, a number of recommendations can be made in order to increase the effectiveness of EU funding in all directions: ERDF, ESF+, and CF. The report states that even though the role of ERDF funding was to increase SME's competitiveness, the implemented and evaluated projects failed to do so, due to a number of unforeseen hurdles:

- Hurdles linked to human resources (e.g., insufficient availability of skills, qualified labor force, labor cost, etc.).
- Regulatory and administrative hurdles (e.g., high administrative costs due to public bureaucracy).

- External hurdles (e.g., unfair competition, access to information).
- Hurdles linked to production (e.g., high production costs, low productivity).
- Hurdles linked to R&D (e.g., intellectual property rights, access to relevant R&D networks).

As it is shown in the above list, the main hurdles encountered by the projects and unforeseen by the EU funding directions is linked to human resources, and this specific obstacle is relatively spread throughout the entire Europe not only in a specific area. This is why the authors of this chapter recommend a different approach in writing project proposals and establishing indicators for future proposals in accessing EU funds.

One of the main recommendations is that the projects proposals to be not only recommended but encouraged to set out objectives and actions that can be financed from different funds. This is the course of action that can be deduced from the 2021–2027 Cohesion Policy overview (Fig. 8.6).

Another point of discussion is if the EU efforts in sustaining the Green Deal have the desired impact on climate change. A major concern of specialists is that regardless of EU efforts in reducing energy consumption and investments in alternative green energy in order to reduce impact on climate change (EU is the fourth biggest greenhouse gas emitter after China, the United States, and India), the changes are too far gone to be controlled.

According to the publication of the European Parliament, the efforts are paying off, and with a coherent strategy, by 2050, Europe can achieve its goal of zero net emissions.

Authors Harriet Bulkeley and Peter Newell (2023) state in their book *Governing Climate Change* that climate change

> needs to be consider as a multi-level problem in which, different levels of decisions-making – local, regional, national and international – as well as new spheres and arenas of governance that cut across such boundaries are involved in both creating and addressing climate change.

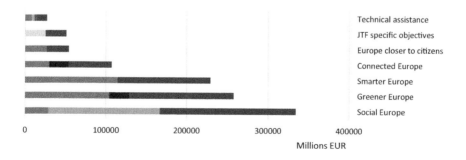

Fig. 8.6. Cohesion Policy, Budget by Theme, 2021–2027 (in Million Euros). *Source*: Information processed by the authors based on the data retrieved from https://cohesiondata.ec.europa.eu/cohesion_overview/21-27.

In this perspective, citizens, small and large companies, local, national, and international governance forms can be co-interested and engaged in shifting climate change.

Acknowledgments

This work was supported by a grant of the Petroleum-Gas University of Ploiesti, Project Number 11067, within Internal Grant for Scientific Research.

References

Alam, A., Du, A. M., Rahman, M., Yazdifar, H., & Abbasi, K. (2022). SMEs respond to climate change: Evidence from developing countries. *Technological Forecasting and Social Change, 185*, 122087. https://www.sciencedirect.com/science/article/pii/S0040162522006084#bb0055

Baden, D. A., Harwood, I. A., & Woodward, D. G. (2009). The effect of buyer pressure on suppliers in SMEs to demonstrate CSR practices: An added incentive or counter productive? *European Management Journal, 27*(6), 429–441. https://doi.org/10.1016/j.emj.2008.10.004

Belitski, M., Guenther, C., Kritikos, A. S., & Thurik, R. (2022). Economic effects of the COVID-19 pandemic on entrepreneurship and small businesses. *Small Business Economics, 58*, 593–609. https://doi.org/10.1007/s11187-021-00544-y

Bulkeley, H., & Newell, P. (2023). *Governing climate change*. Taylor & Francis.

Cassells, S., & Lewis, K. (2011). SMEs and environmental responsibility: Do actions reflect attitudes? *Corporate Social Responsibility and Environmental Management, 18*(3), 186–199. https://doi.org/10.1002/csr.269

Etires, E. (2022). *European energy: Complex issues and contemporary solutions*. Analytics, EU Law & Governance|Integrin Dk|EG in Europe: New Directions in the EU's political economy for skilled workforce. For those wanting to know more about modern EU. https://www.integrin.dk/2022/05/18/european-energy-complex-issues-and-contemporary-solutions

European Commission. (2020). Communication from the Commission to the European Parliament, the Council, the European Economic and Social Committee and the Committee of the Regions, Brussels. https://eur-lex.europa.eu/resource.html?uri=cellar:ea0f9f73-9ab2-11ea-9d2d-01aa75ed71a1.0001.02/DOC_1&format=PDF

European Commission. (2011). *A resource efficient Europe: Flagship initiative under the European 2020 strategy* (COM (2011) 21). https://www.eea.europa.eu/policy-documents/a-resource-efficient-europe-flagship

Fawcett, T., & Hampton, S. (2020). Why & how energy efficiency policy should address SMEs. *Energy Policy, 140*, 111337. https://doi.org/10.1016/j.enpol.2020.111337

Fetting, C. (2020, December). *The European Green Deal* [ESDN Report, ESDN Office]. https://www.esdn.eu/fileadmin/ESDN_Reports/ESDN_Report_2_2020.pdf

Fleming, R. C., & Mauger, R. (2021). Green and Just? An update on the 'European Green Deal'. *Journal for European Environmental & Planning Law, 18*(1–2), 164–180. https://doi.org/10.1163/18760104-18010010

Gadenne, D. L., Kennedy, J., & McKeiver, C. (2009). An empirical study of environmental awareness and practices in SMEs. *Journal of Business Ethics, 84*, 45–63. https://doi.org/10.1007/s10551-008-9672-9

Kaesehage, K., Leyshon, M., Ferns, G., & Leyshon, C. (2019). Seriously personal: The reasons that motivate entrepreneurs to address climate change. *Journal of Business Ethics, 157*, 1091–1109. https://doi.org/10.1007/s10551-017-3624-1

Koirala, S. (2019). *SMEs: Key drivers of green and inclusive growth* [OECD Green Growth Papers, No. 2019/03, OECD Publishing]. https://doi.org/10.1787/8a51fc0c-en

Mura, M., Longo, M., & Zanni, S. (2020). Circular economy in Italian SMEs: A multi-method study. *Journal of Cleaner Production, 245*, 118821. https://doi.org/10.1016/j.jclepro.2019.118821

Revell, A., & Blackburn, R. (2007). The business case for sustainability? An examination of small firms in the UK's construction and restaurant sectors. *Business Strategy & the Environment, 16*, 404–420. https://doi.org/10.1002/bse.499

Revell, A., Stokes, D., & Chen, H. (2010). Small businesses and the environment: Turning over a new leaf? *Business Strategy & the Environment, 19*, 273–288. https://doi.org/10.1002/bse.628

Schaefer, A., Williams, S., & Blundel, R. (2020). Individual values and SME environmental engagement. *Business & Society, 59*(4), 642–675. https://doi.org/10.1177/0007650317750134

Sessa, M. R., Russo, A., & Sica. F. (2022). Opinion paper on green deal for the urban regeneration of industrial brownfield land in Europe. *Land Use Policy, 119*, 106198. https://doi.org/10.1016/j.landusepol.2022.106198

Sikora, A. (2021). European Green Deal – Legal and financial challenges of the climate change. *ERA Forum, 21*, 681–697. https://doi.org/10.1007/s12027-020-00637-3

Skjærseth, J. B. (2021). Towards a European Green Deal: The evolution of EU climate and energy policy mixes. *International Environmental Agreements, 21*, 25–41. https://doi.org/10.1007/s10784-021-09529-4

Slominski, P. (2018). Energy and climate policy: Does the competitiveness narrative prevail in times of crisis? In G. Falkner (Ed.), *EU policies in times of crisis* (pp. 125–140). Routledge.

Terzić, L. (2022). Towards European Union's Green Deal: The importance of sustainable competitiveness and eco-innovation for achieving prosperity in EU-27 member states. *Uluslararası Ekonomi ve Yenilik Dergisi, 8*(2), 195–218. https://doi.org/10.20979/ueyd.1100207

Uvarova, I., Atstaja, D., & Korpa, V. (2020). Challenges of the introduction of circular business models within rural SMEs of EU. *International Journal of Economic Sciences, IX*(2), 128–149. https://doi.org/10.20472/ES.2020.9.2.008

Vickers, I., Vaze, P., Corr, L., Kasparova, E., & Lyon, F. (2009). *SMEs in a low carbon economy: Final report for BERR enterprise directorate.* Department of Business, Innovation & Skills. https://eprints.mdx.ac.uk/4163/1/SMEs_in_a_low_carbon_economy.pdf

Yadav, N., Gupta, K., Rani, L., & Rawat, D. (2018). Drivers of sustainability practices and SMEs: A systematic literature review. *European Journal of Sustainable Development, 7*(4), 531–531. https://doi.org/10.14207/ejsd.2018.v7n4p531

Zilberman, D., Lipper, L., McCarthy, N., & Gordon, B. (2018). Innovation in response to climate change. In L. Lipper, N. McCarthy, D. Zilberman, S. Asfaw, & G. Branca (Eds.), *Climate smart agriculture. Natural resource management and policy* (Vol. 52, pp. 49–74). Springer. https://doi.org/10.1007/978-3-319-61194-5_4

Chapter 9

Challenges in Protecting Green Energy Entrepreneurs in Wheat Industry Against Financial Risk: The Portfolio Optimization Approach

Boris Kuzman[a] and Dejan Živkov[b]

[a]*Institute of Agricultural Economics, Serbia*
[b]*Novi Sad business school, Serbia*

Abstract

This chapter tries to hedge extreme financial risk of entrepreneurs who work with wheat by combining wheat with four stock indices of developed and emerging European markets in a portfolio. Extreme risk of the portfolios is measured by the parametric and historical value-at-risk (VaR) metrics. Portfolios that target maximum return-to-VaR ratio are also constructed because different market participants prefer different goals. Preliminary equicorrelation results indicate that integration between wheat and emerging markets is lower (0.218) vis-à-vis the combination of wheat and developed markets (0.307), which gives preliminary advantage to emerging markets in diversification efforts. The results show that portfolios with emerging stock indices have significantly lower parametric (–0.816) and historical (–0.831) VaR than portfolios with developed indices, –1.080 and –1.295, respectively. As for optimal portfolios, the portfolios with developed indices have a slight upper hand. This chapter shows that parametric VaR is not a good measure of extreme risk, because it neglects the third and fourth moments.

Keywords: Parametric value-at-risk; historical value-at-risk; portfolio optimization; equicorrelation; GJR-GARCH model

Entrepreneurship and Development for a Green Resilient Economy, 229–250
Copyright © 2024 by Boris Kuzman and Dejan Živkov
Published under exclusive licence by Emerald Publishing Limited
doi:10.1108/978-1-83797-088-920241009

1. Introduction

Global warming is one of the most topical issues of today, which puts the use of biofuels in the foreground. On the other hand, biofuel production opens new opportunities for numerous market agents and entrepreneurs to develop businesses in this sphere. Ethanol is frequently used as an alternative to fossil fuels, and wheat is one of the most commonly used raw materials to produce ethanol. However, the close relationship between ethanol and wheat makes wheat susceptible to high price swings due to the volatile nature of ethanol prices. This creates a lot of uncertainty for farmers, traders and entrepreneurs who work with wheat on a daily basis.

This is the reason why risk hedging of wheat becomes an increasingly important topic in the international community (see, e.g., Czudaj, 2020; Tonin et al., 2020; Živkov et al., 2019). As a matter of fact, wheat price has suffered major price changes in the last six years, and several factors have contributed to this development. For instance, agricultural production varies year by year due to weather extremes (Petković et al., 2020), while competition for land between agricultural and industrial crops, that is, biofuels, intensifies (Baležentis, 2015; Petković et al., 2023). Wheat price is closely linked with the movements of other major commodities, particularly corn, which also experienced an excessive volatility in the previous period (Živkov et al., 2020). Prices of inputs, such as seeds, fuels and fertilizers, are very important for successful cultivation of wheat, and they all recorded significant price changes in the previous years, which is particularly true for oil (Gazdar et al., 2019; Kuzman et al., 2021). Economic growth and global demographic increase, especially in developing countries, influence growing demand for food (Hovhannisyan & Devadoss, 2020). On top of that, the corona virus outbreak created an unprecedented negative situation globally, impacting the agricultural sector as well (Szeles & Saman, 2020). On the other hand, the war in Ukraine significantly contributed to the global food insecurity, sending the price of wheat to over 1,200 USD cents per bushel in May 2022 (see Fig. 9.1).

Due to unfavorable global circumstances in recent years, entrepreneurs in the wheat industry face with extreme risk of wheat price that could create very serious problems for their normal functioning and business. Therefore, this study tries to answer whether a creation of a multivariate portfolio with wheat can mitigate very high financial risk that wheat entrepreneurs suffer. In this process, we make two multivariate portfolios of five assets, combining wheat with four stock indices of Western European countries (WEC) and Central and Eastern European countries (CEEC). In particular, we consider four stock indices of the largest WEC – Germany, France, Great Britain and Italy, and the largest CEEC – Poland, the Czech Republic, Hungary and Romania. We intentionally select four developed and four emerging European stock indices because developed stock markets are, by definition, more integrated than the emerging markets, which means that mutual correlation of developed stock indices is higher than the correlation of the emerging counterparts. In the procedure of portfolio designing, this is an important issue because low correlation between the assets in a portfolio is a crucial factor for the creation of an efficient portfolio.

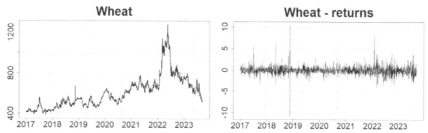

Fig. 9.1.   Empirical Dynamics of Wheat Price and Returns. *Source*: Authors' calculation. *Note*: Price of wheat is expressed in US cents per bushel.

In order to provide a clear result about the level of integration of stock indices, we first estimate multivariate dynamic equicorrelation, using the multivariate DECO-GJR-GARCH model, introduced by Engle and Kelly (2012). DECO calculates the temporal covariance matrix, where single average dynamic correlation between the selected assets is estimated. In this procedure, DECO eliminates the computational and presentation difficulties of high dimension data, which are the characteristic of a multi-asset portfolio. This model serves as a preliminary analysis, and it is useful for our purposes because it quantifies the time-varying correlation level between all the assets in the portfolios. This result may indicate which portfolio provides better hedging of wheat, since lower correlation between the assets in a portfolio gives better hedging results.

The main goal of this chapter is to find the optimal combination of assets in the portfolios that would have minimal extreme risk for wheat entrepreneurs. We observe extreme risk of portfolios from the aspect of downside risk, which is measured by parametric value-at-risk (VaR). Unlike common variance that takes into account equally positive and negative returns, downside risk observes only negative returns, and this is why investors rather prefer to know downside risk of a portfolio than its variance. Parametric VaR assumes that a portfolio follows normal distribution, which means that only the first two moments are considered for this calculation. VaR measures the maximum loss that a portfolio might endure, taking into account a specified time frame with a certain probability level (Živkov, Kuzman, et al., 2023). We want to target extreme risk of the portfolio, so we calculate the potential loss at a 99% probability level, which means that we observe only 1% of negative returns that are placed at the left tail of the distribution. Performing the minimum-VaR portfolio optimization in a multi-asset framework is a very complex and elaborate procedure, so relatively few papers used this methodology (see, e.g., Abuaf et al., 2018; Gatfaoui, 2019; Hammoudeh et al., 2013). According to our best knowledge, this is the first chapter that constructs a minimum-VaR portfolio with wheat and stocks, and this is where we find a motive to do this research.

Besides minimum-VaR portfolios (hereafter MVaRP), we also calculate two optimal portfolios that target maximum-modified Sharpe ratio. This ratio shows the relation between average realized excess returns and VaR, and the portfolio with the highest mSharpe ratio is called an optimal portfolio (hereafter OVaRP).

We calculate both types of portfolios because not all market participants want to pursue a minimum-risk portfolio, that is, some of them want to find the best return-to-risk relation, so this gives a wider perspective of our research.

As a complementary analysis, we additionally construct MVaRP and OVaRP portfolios with historical VaR. This additional approach is taken because parametric VaR lies on a very strict assumption that asset follows normal distribution. This is highly unlikely to be found in daily financial and commodity time series. Therefore, risk assessment with parametric VaR might be biased. In order to offer an alternative and also allow comparison, we construct all the portfolios with historical VaR as a target. Historical VaR does not require any prior distributional assumptions. In other words, it calculates the exact empirical VaR of any time series. On the other hand, the cons of using historical VaR are that it cannot be used for predicting unless there is a reasonable assumption that the past will be repeated in the future. This chapter does not deal with forecasting, but we only analyze realized returns. Constructing both parametric and historical VaR portfolios, we can check to what extent parametric VaR portfolios overestimate or underestimate realized downside risk. This can indicate whether parametric VaR is an appropriate risk measure in the process of wheat extreme risk hedging or not. Besides, it will show whether the structure of the portfolios has changed and how much.

Besides introduction, the rest of this chapter is structured as follows: Second section gives literature review. Third section explains used methodologies – DECO-GJR-GARCH model and VaR portfolio optimization. Fourth section is reserved for dataset and descriptive statistics. Fifth section presents empirical results in four subsections. Sixth section shows positive and negative implications of the results, while the last section concludes.

2. Literature Review

Papers that investigated risk hedging of agricultural commodities are relatively scarce, while even fewer have researched hedging of wheat in a portfolio. For instance, Hernandez et al. (2021) investigated the portfolio allocation and risk contribution characteristics of nine agricultural commodities (wheat, corn, soybeans, coffee, sugar cane, sugar beets, cocoa, cotton and lumber). They reported that sugarcane, followed by wheat and corn, is the largest risk contributor to total portfolio risk. On the other hand, cocoa, lumber and cotton bear the lowest risk in the portfolio. They claimed that cocoa and lumber are the most desirable for investment. Rehman et al. (2019) found important practical implications for portfolio managers in the commodity markets, analyzing four precious metals, oil, gas, copper, coal and wheat. They reported that crude oil offers more diversification benefits when combined with gold or silver, but minimal diversification benefits are found when crude oil is combined with wheat or platinum. Gas futures provide more diversification opportunities when combined with copper, wheat, platinum or palladium, while coal gives maximum diversification benefits when combined with gold, silver or wheat. The paper of Naeem et al. (2022) researched the safe-haven and hedging potential of oil and gold against industrial metals and agricultural commodities, using quantile-on-quantile regression. They covered the sample between January 2000 and December 2018, which further splits up into two sub-periods based on the global financial crisis (GFC). They found that oil (gold) has a lower correlation with metals and agriculture in the pre-GFC period than post-GFC. In addition, the quantile-to-quantile regression for two time periods (pre-GFC and post-GFC) was used to examine whether oil (gold) serves as a hedge (safe-haven) during the two periods. They reported that oil was a safe-haven for metals and agricultural commodities pre-GFC but lost that ability post-GFC. Besides, they examined the hedge ratio and hedge effectiveness pre- and post-GFC and concluded that oil had higher hedge effectiveness than gold during the pre-GFC period. Elliott et al. (2020) researched the risk reduction and price received when agricultural producers adopted new-generation grain contracts (NGGCs) to hedge corn and soybean production. They considered the Accumulator, Average Price, Price Plus, Minimum Price and Price Protection contracts and compared the performance measures of the average bushel price that would be received by corn and soybean producers, the change in daily value of the portfolio and the Sharpe ratio. They reported that the Price Plus contracts performed best overall during the 2008–2017 period, obtaining the highest bushel price and the highest average Sharpe ratio for both corn and soybeans.

The study of Chen et al. (2022) analyzed the dynamic correlation between global crude oil futures and seven agricultural commodity futures. In the research, they used the consistent dynamic conditional correlation (DCC) and dynamic equicorrelation models. They found that the dynamic correlation between the global crude oil futures market and China's agricultural futures market is weak compared to the global agricultural futures market. They asserted that soybean oil has the strongest correlation with crude oil, while Dalian Commodity Exchange (DCE) corn and Zhengzhou Commodity Exchange wheat have the weakest correlation with crude oil. They contended that the hedge ratio and optimal hedging weight change continuously over the sample period, which means that hedging strategies should be updated continuously. Important finding is that the combination of Brent oil and agricultural commodities portfolio is more effective compared to West Texas Intermediate (WTI) oil and agricultural commodities. Huang and Xiong (2023) investigated hedging properties and portfolio performance of the futures-spot combination in China. They examined 15 commodities in the selection of metals, agricultural goods and energy commodities. They used a quantile-based hedging analytic framework and found that almost all commodity futures are good hedges for the corresponding spot prices and can act as safe-havens under extreme market conditions. They claimed that hedge ratios should be appropriately increased when futures prices are in both bearish and bullish markets. Regarding different commodities, they asserted that metals perform the best, agricultural commodities are the second best, while energy commodities perform relatively poorly. Naeem et al. (2021) investigated whether cryptocurrencies are hedge and safe-haven for commodities. They focused on individual commodities from four groups, including metal, agriculture, precious metal and energy, and combined these with four major cryptocurrencies – Bitcoin, Ethereum, Litecoin and Ripple. They reported that cryptocurrencies are most effective for hedging commodities from metals and agricultural groups and least effective for energy commodities. Živkov, Stankov, et al. (2023) tried to reduce the extreme risk of corn and soybeans by constructing multivariate portfolios with developed and emerging European stock indices. They measured extreme risk with conditional VaR. The authors addressed two different goals that investors might prefer, constructing portfolios with the lowest risk and highest return-to-risk ratio. According to the results, corn and soybeans had relatively high portfolio shares because they have a very low pairwise correlation with the stock indices. They claimed that portfolios with emerging European indices had better risk-reducing results, considering both agricultural commodities because these indices are less risky than developed indices.

3. Used Methodologies

3.1. DECO-GJR-GARCH Model

Before portfolio construction, we calculate dynamic equicorrelation between the assets in the two portfolios. This gives a preliminary insight into which stock indices (WEC or CEEC) have lower dynamic correlation with wheat. In the DECO model, all pairwise correlations between the assets are equal, whereas their common equicorrelation is time varying, which makes the estimation process much easier and quicker. We assume the presence of an asymmetric effect in stock indices, so we use the GJR-GARCH model in the univariate specification. Equations (1) and (2) present how mean and variance equations of the GJR-GARCH model look like:

$$y_t = C + \phi y_{t-1} + \varepsilon_t; \ \varepsilon_t \sim z_t \sqrt{\sigma_t^2} \tag{1}$$

$$\sigma_t^2 = c + \alpha \varepsilon_{t-1}^2 + \beta \sigma_{t-1}^2 + \gamma \varepsilon_{t-1}^2 I_{t-1}; \ I_{t-1} = \begin{cases} 1 \ if \ \varepsilon_{t-1} < 0 \\ 0 \ if \ \varepsilon_{t-1} > 0 \end{cases}. \tag{2}$$

All mean equations are specified in an autoregressive form of order (1), which is enough to resolve a serial correlation problem of the selected time series. C and c are constants in the mean and variance equations. y_t is 5×1 vector of stock indices and wheat, whereas ε_t is the 5×1 vector of error terms. Symbol z_t describes an independently and identically distributed process. In conditional variance equation, parameter β describes the persistence of volatility, while α measures the ARCH effect. Parameter γ measures an asymmetric effect, that is, if $\gamma > 0$ than negative shocks impact volatility more than positive shocks, and vice versa. I_{t-1} is a dummy variable.

Positive definiteness of the variance–covariance matrix H_t is presented in Equation (3):

$$H_t = D_t^{1/2} R_t D_t^{1/2} \tag{3}$$

where $R_t = [\rho_{ij,t}]$ is the conditional correlation matrix, while the diagonal matrix of the conditional variances is given by $D_t = diag(h_{1,t}, \ldots, h_{n,t})$. Engle (2002) stated that the right-hand side of Equation (3) can be modeled directly by proposing the following dynamic correlation structure:

$$R_t = (Q_t^*)^{-1/2} Q_t (Q_t^*)^{-1/2} \tag{4}$$

$$Q_t^* = diag(Q_t) \tag{5}$$

$$Q_t = [q_{ij,t}] = (1 - a - b)S + au_{t-1}u'_{t-1} + bQ_{t-1}, \tag{6}$$

where $u_t = [u_{1,t}, \ldots, u_{n,t}]'$ is the standardized residuals, $u_{i,t} = \varepsilon_{i,t}/h_{i,t}$. $S = [s_{i,j}] = E[u_t u'_t]$ is $n \times n$ unconditional covariance matrix of u_t, while a and b are non-negative scalars satisfying $a + b < 1$. The resulting model is called the DCC model. However, Aielli (2013) proved that the estimation of the covariance matrix Q_t in this way is inconsistent because $E[R_t] \neq E[Q_t]$ and suggested the consistent DCC (cDCC) model for the correlation-driving process:

$$Q_t = (1 - a - b)S^* + a\left(Q_{t-1}^{*1/2} u_{t-1} u'_{t-1} Q_{t-1}^{*1/2}\right) + bQ_{t-1}, \tag{7}$$

where S^* is the unconditional covariance matrix of $Q_{t-1}^{*1/2} u_t$. Engle and Kelly (2012) suggested that ρ_t can be modeled by using the cDCC process to obtain the conditional correlation matrix Q_t and then taking the mean of its off-diagonal elements. This approach they called the dynamic equicorrelation (DECO) model, while the scalar equicorrelation is defined as in Equation (8):

$$\rho_t^{DECO} = \frac{1}{n(n-1)}\left(J'_n R_t^{cDCC} J_n - n\right) = \frac{2}{n(n-1)}\sum_{i=1}^{n-1}\sum_{j=i+1}^{n}\frac{q_{ij,t}}{\sqrt{q_{ii,t}q_{jj,t}}} \tag{8}$$

where $q_{ij,t} = \rho_t^{DECO} + a_{DECO}\left(u_{i,t-1}u_{j,t-1} - \rho_t^{DECO}\right) + b_{DECO}(q_{ij,t} - \rho_t^{DECO})$, which is the (i, j)th element of the matrix Q_t from the cDCC model. Scalar equicorrelation is then used to estimate the conditional correlation matrix:

$$R_t = (1 - \rho_t)I_n + \rho_t J_n, \tag{9}$$

where J_n is an $n \times n$ matrix of ones, and I_n is an n-dimensional identity matrix. This process allows representing the comovement degree of a group of assets in a portfolio with a single time-varying correlation coefficient.

3.2. Portfolio Optimization Procedure

We combine wheat with the four developed and emerging European stock indices in the two portfolios, where our goals are minimum-VaR and maximum-mSharpe ratio. In order to achieve a minimum-VaR portfolio, we first have to construct a minimum-variance portfolio, which can be done by solving Equation (10), according to Živkov, Kuzman, et al. (2022):

$$\min \sigma_p^2 = \min \sum_{i=1}^{n} w_i^2 \sigma_i^2 + \sum_{i=1}^{N} \sum_{j=1}^{N} w_i w_j \sigma_i \sigma_j \rho_{i,j}, \tag{10}$$

where σ_p^2 is a portfolio variance, σ_i^2 is the variance of a particular asset i, w_i denotes the calculated weight of an asset i in a portfolio, while $\rho_{i,j}$ is the correlation coefficient between the particular pair of assets (i and j). The first condition that needs to be fulfilled in every portfolio optimization process is that the sum of all weights of assets is equal to one, while all individual weights are somewhere in between zero and one:

$$\sum_{i=1}^{N} w_i = 1; \ 0 \leq w_i \leq 1 \tag{11}$$

Every portfolio with minimum variance has corresponding mean value, which is weighted average portfolio return (r_p), and it can be calculated as in Equation (12):

$$r_p = \sum_{i=1}^{n} w_i r_i. \tag{12}$$

First (r_p) and second (σ_p) moments from Equations (12) and (10), respectively, are used to construct a minimum parametric VaR of a portfolio (VaR$_p$), that is, VaR$_p = r_p + Z_\alpha \sigma_p$. Z_α is the left quantile of the normal standard distribution. Minimum-VaR$_p$ portfolio optimization can be achieved by solving expression (13):

$$\min \text{VaR}_p(w), \sum_{i=1}^{n} w_i r_i. \tag{13}$$

Besides the minimum-VaR portfolio, we also calculated a portfolio with a maximum-mSharpe ratio, which is OVaRP. The modified Sharpe ratio was proposed by Gregoriou and Gueyie (2003), and it has a form like in Equation (14), where R_p is an average daily return of a portfolio, and R_f is a risk-free rate. We take yields of 3M treasury bills for the risk-free rate:

$$\text{Modified Sharpe ratio} = \frac{R_i - R_f}{\text{VaR}}. \tag{14}$$

In the process of portfolio optimization, the optimal portfolio can be found by solving expression (15). w^T is the weights of individual assets in the portfolio with the number of returns T:

$$\max \left\{ \frac{w^T r - r_f}{\text{VaR}(w)} \right\}. \tag{15}$$

Fig. 9.2 graphically illustrates the VaR-efficient frontier line (VaR-EFL), where positions of all portfolios and MVaRP and OVaRP can be found. VaR-EFL contains all possible portfolios with different combinations of assets. In particular, portfolios that are placed on the gray line in Fig. 9.2 are called efficient portfolios because an increase in risk also implies an increase in return, which is acceptable (see Živkov, Balaban, et al., 2022). The choice of the portfolio in this line depends on risk preferences of every investor. On the other hand, portfolios that are placed on the black line are called inefficient portfolios because an increase in risk follows a decrease in return, which is an unacceptable choice for every investor. Portfolio on the curvature of the line is called the minimum-VaR portfolio, and it has the lowest extreme risk of all other portfolios. On the other hand, the portfolio that has the highest modified Sharpe ratio is called an optimal portfolio, and it is placed at a tangent point of line drawn from Y axis on VaR-EFL.

4. Dataset and Descriptive Statistics

This study uses daily data of wheat spot prices and four stock indices of WEC and CEEC. The selected WEC indices are as follows: FTSE250 (Great Britain), DAX (Germany), CAC (France) and FTSE-MIB (Italy), while CEEC indices are as follows: WIG (Poland), PX (the Czech Republic), BUX (Hungary) and BET (Romania). Data span ranges from January 2017 to August 2023, and all the selected time series are retrieved from the stooq.com website. All time series are transformed into log-returns ($r_{i,t}$) according to the expression: $r_{i,t} = 100 \times \log(P_{i,t} / P_{i,t-1})$, where P_i is the daily price of a particular asset. Wheat log-returns are synchronized separately with WEC and CEEC indices. Table 9.1 shows the first four moments, Ljung–Box tests for level and squared residuals, Dickey–Fuller generalized least squares (DF-GLS) test and calculated parametric and historical VaR values of every asset.

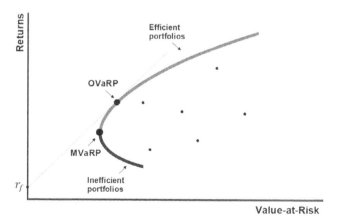

Fig. 9.2.   VaR-EFL. *Source*: Authors' illustration.

Table 9.1.   Descriptive Statistics of the Wheat and Stock Indices.

	Mean	Standard deviation	Skewness	Kurtosis	LB(Q)	LB(Q^2)	DF-GLS	Parametric VaR	Historical VaR
Wheat	0.041	0.972	0.641	28.938	0.000	0.000	−4.112	−2.220	−1.975
FTSE250	0.009	1.104	−0.766	16.573	0.000	0.000	−21.978	−2.559	−3.509
DAX	0.006	0.554	−0.749	18.602	0.153	0.000	−35.331	−1.282	−1.744
CAC	0.009	0.540	−1.129	19.217	0.014	0.000	−34.559	−1.246	−1.748
FTSE-MIB	0.004	0.603	−2.428	33.619	0.000	0.000	−17.591	−1.398	−1.783
WIG	0.001	0.546	−1.599	22.096	0.005	0.000	−15.665	−1.270	−1.535
PX	0.012	0.421	−1.304	18.660	0.000	0.000	−16.339	−0.968	−1.276
BUX	0.007	0.593	−1.719	17.682	0.000	0.000	−4.977	−1.372	−1.810
BET	0.012	0.479	−2.143	26.141	0.000	0.000	−4.923	−1.101	−1.722

Source: Authors' calculation.

Notes: LB(Q) and LB(Q^2) tests refer to p-values of Ljung–Box Q-statistics of level and squared returns of 10 lags. Assuming only constant, 1% and 5% critical values of the DF-GLS test with 10 lags are −3.435 and −2.864, respectively.

Table 9.1 indicates that all average returns are very close to zero, while wheat has the highest mean. This could mean that wheat potentially has the largest share in the optimal portfolio. Also, wheat is one of the riskiest assets, according to the standard deviation, which justifies combining wheat with the stock indices. FTSE250 is the riskiest one taking into account the observed sample. First two moments are used to calculate parametric VaR, and according to the results in Table 9.1, the level of the standard deviation is perfectly in line with the parametric VaR values. On the other hand, all four moments are considered in calculating historical VaR. This means that values of parametric and historical VaR differ, because all the assets have non-normal properties of the third and fourth moments. In particular, stock indices have negative skewness, which means that more negative returns are placed to the left of the mean. The opposite applies to wheat because wheat has positive skewness. According to Table 9.1, parametric VaR of all stock indices underestimates realized downside risk because all indices have negative skewness and very high kurtosis, which suggests the presence of outliers. On the other hand, parametric VaR of wheat is higher than the historical counterpart because wheat has a positive third moment, and this lowers historical VaR. These results indicate that parametric and historical VaR portfolios will probably differ in their structure as well as in the size of downside risk.

Autocorrelation is present in all assets except DAX, and all assets have a problem with heteroscedasticity. The DECO-GJR-GARCH model could resolve these issues. All assets have no unit root, according to the DF-GLS test, which is a necessary precondition for the GARCH modeling. Parametric and historical VaR values are also included in the descriptive statistics because the risk level of assets in a portfolio is a very important factor when portfolio optimization determines how much shares every asset will have. For instance, FTSE250 has the highest VaR, while wheat follows. This means that these two assets will probably have relatively low shares in the portfolio. How much low also depends on the level of pairwise correlations between the assets in the portfolio. It is interesting to notice that all VaR values perfectly coincide with standard deviation values. This is the case because the standard deviation is the most important ingredient in the calculation of parametric VaR.

5. Empirical Results

5.1. Equicorrelation Estimation

This subsection presents the results of the calculated equicorrelations between wheat and the stock indices. The level of estimated equicorrelations serves as a preliminary analysis, which can give us a clue which portfolio potentially have lower extreme risk. Table 9.2 contains the estimated DECO-GJR-GARCH parameters, while Fig. 9.2 shows the estimated equicorrelations of both portfolios.

α parameters in Table 9.2 indicate that the effect of shocks to the conditional variance is not present in all assets. On the other hand, volatility persistence is detected in all the markets because all β parameters are highly statistically significant. The asymmetric effect is found in almost all the markets, where the wheat

Table 9.2.   Estimated Parameters of the DECO-GJR-GARCH Model in Two Portfolios.

	Wheat	FTSE250	DAX	CAC	FTSE-MIB	Wheat	WIG	PX	BUX	BET
Panel A. GJR-GARCH parameter estimation with ASEAN stock indices										
α	0.411**	0.025*	0.001	-0.009	-0.014	0.124*	0.028	0.061***	0.056**	0.081
β	0.406***	0.830***	0.822***	0.798***	0.849***	0.840***	0.823***	0.841***	0.806***	0.711***
γ	-0.329*	0.232***	0.248	0.353***	0.234*	-0.101*	0.181*	0.116***	0.184**	0.342
Panel B. Diagnostic tests										
LB(Q)	0.420	0.602	0.451	0.262	0.672	0.651	0.394	0.445	0.853	0.625
LB(Q^2)	0.184	0.875	0.313	0.539	0.282	0.962	0.987	0.877	0.318	0.997
Panel C. Estimates of DECO model										
a_{DECO}	0.083**					0.099**				
b_{DECO}	0.742***					0.715***				

Source: Authors' calculation.

Notes: LB(Q) and LB(Q^2) numbers indicate *p*-values at 10 lags.

***, **, and * represent statistical significance at the 1%, 5% and 10% levels, respectively. Estimated parameters of wheat in two portfolios are different because sample size of wheat is different in two portfolios due to time series' synchronization.

market reports a negative γ parameter, while all stock markets have positive γ parameters. A positive γ parameter implies that negative shocks increase the volatility more than the positive shock, and this is a common finding for stock markets. On the other hand, the reverse applies for the wheat market. Panel B shows Ljung–Box test statistics of the standard and squared residuals, and it is clear that a serial correlation and heteroscedasticity is not present in the residuals, which suggest a good specification of the models. Estimated a_{DECO} and b_{DECO} parameters are positive and significant, which means that market shocks have an effect on equicorrelations, while both equicorrelations are dependent on past correlations. Statistically significant DECO parameters signal reliability of the estimated equicorrelations.

Fig. 9.3 reveals that assets in the WEC portfolio are more integrated vis-á-vis assets in the CEEC portfolio because average dynamic equicorrelation is higher in the portfolio with WEC (0.307) than in the portfolio with CEEC (0.218). This means that the CEEC portfolio potentially has better risk-minimizing results. Besides, the WEC indices are riskier than the CEEC indices (see Table 9.1), which is another argument that speaks in favor of the CEEC portfolio. In this regard, we hypothesize that the CEEC portfolio is better, while the next section discloses exactly how much better than the WEC counterpart. It should be noticed that both equicorrelations recorded a rise at the beginning of 2020, which can be related without a doubt to the pandemic outbreak.

5.2. Construction of the Parametric VaR Portfolios

This section tries to prove the hypothesis made in the previous section that the portfolio with the CEEC indices has better results in terms of extreme risk. Table 9.3 shows calculated shares of assets in the two portfolios with the minimum-parametric VaR and maximum-mSharpe goals. The previous section has calculated two equicorrelations, but these results cannot be used to explain the findings in Table 9.3 because they show average correlation between the assets. On the other hand, we need to know correlations between every pair of assets in order to offer a viable explanation regarding the shares of assets in the portfolios.

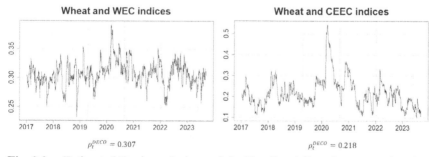

Fig. 9.3.   Estimated Equicorrelations of the Two Portfolios. *Source*: Authors' calculation.

To this end, Table 9.4 contains pairwise Pearson correlations between the assets in the two portfolios, and it is used, along with Table 9.1, to explain the findings in Table 9.3. Table 9.4 indicates that wheat has a very low correlation with all stock indices. As a matter of fact, in most cases, pairwise correlations between wheat and the indices are negative, which is very good for diversification, while pairwise correlations between the stock indices are relatively high. In particular, the pairwise correlations are higher among the WEC indices, than the CEEC indices, which gives a potential advantage to the CEEC indices.

Table 9.3.   Calculated Shares of Assets in the Created Parametric VaR Portfolios.

Portfolios with WEC Indices			Portfolios with CEEC Indices		
Assets	**MVaRP (%)**	**OVaRP (%)**	**Assets**	**MVaRP (%)**	**OVaRP (%)**
Wheat	24	97	Wheat	15	0
FTSE250	0	0	WIG	8	0
DAX	26	3	PX	44	100
CAC	50	0	BUX	4	0
FTSE-MIB	0	0	BET	29	0
Σ	100	100	Σ	100	100

Source: Authors' calculation.

Table 9.4.   Pairwise Correlations Between the Assets in the Two Portfolios.

Selected Assets	Wheat	FTSE250	DAX	CAC	FTSE-MIB
Wheat	1	0.009	−0.015	−0.002	−0.012
FTSE250	0.009	1	0.822	0.840	0.744
DAX	−0.015	0.822	1	0.940	0.878
CAC	−0.002	0.840	0.940	1	0.885
FTSE-MIB	−0.012	0.744	0.878	0.885	1
Average ρ	−0.004	0.483	0.525	0.533	0.499

Selected Assets	Wheat	WIG	PX	BUX	BET
Wheat	1	0.020	−0.014	−0.038	−0.050
WIG	0.020	1	0.552	0.595	0.435
PX	−0.014	0.552	1	0.566	0.517
BUX	−0.038	0.595	0.566	1	0.409
BET	−0.050	0.435	0.517	0.409	1
Average ρ	−0.016	0.320	0.324	0.306	0.262

Source: Authors' calculation.

In the parametric VaR portfolio with WEC indices, three out of five assets have a positive share in MVaRP, that is, wheat (24%), DAX (26%) and CAC (50%). On the other hand, only wheat and DAX have a share in OVaRP. CAC has the highest share of 50% in MVaRP because CAC has the lowest parametric VaR (–1.246). Although CAC has the highest average correlation with other indices (0.533), this does not prevent CAC to have the highest share in MVaRP. DAX has the second-best share of 26% because DAX has the second-lowest parametric VaR (–1.282). Wheat has the third-best share of 24%, although wheat has the second-highest parametric VaR (–2.220), and this is probably because wheat has a negative correlation with DAX and CAC. In OVaRP, wheat has the highest share of 97% because wheat has by far the highest mean (0.041), although wheat has the second-largest VaR. DAX has 3% in OVaRP, probably because DAX has the highest negative correlation with wheat (–0.015).

As for portfolio with CEEC, PX has the highest share of 44%, while BET is the second best with 29%, but the reasons are different why these indices take the two-best positions in the portfolio. In other words, PX has the highest share because PX has the lowest VaR (–0.968), while BET is the second best due to the lowest average correlation with other CEEC indices (0.262). In spite of very high VaR, wheat is the third one with 15% because wheat has a negative average correlation with all other CEEC indices (–0.016). WIG and BUX have the share of 8% and 4%, respectively, because these two have the highest VaR values, –1.270 and –1.372, respectively. In OVaRP, PX has the share of 100% because PX has the highest return-to-VaR ratio. Relatively low share of wheat in the two minimum-VaR portfolios is in line with the findings of Hernandez et al. (2021), who also reported that wheat is one of the riskiest agricultural commodities.

5.3. Construction of the Historical VaR Portfolios

This section presents the results of the constructed historical VaR portfolios, and Table 9.5 shows the structure of these portfolios. It is obvious that the structure of parametric and historical VaR portfolios is significantly different

Table 9.5.   Calculated Shares of Assets in the Created Historical VaR Portfolios.

Portfolios with WEC Indices			**Portfolios with CEEC Indices**		
Assets	**MVaRP (%)**	**OVaRP (%)**	**Assets**	**MVaRP (%)**	**OVaRP (%)**
Wheat	46	97	Wheat	22	67
FTSE250	11	0	WIG	19	6
DAX	11	0	PX	45	9
CAC	21	3	BUX	0	8
FTSE-MIB	11	0	BET	14	10
Σ	100	100	Σ	100	100

Source: Authors' calculation.

(see Tables 9.3 and 9.5), which means that third and fourth moments play an important role in the portfolio construction process. For instance, wheat has 24% in the parametric MVaRP with WEC, while in the historical MVaRP, the share is 46%. The reason lies in the fact that the historical VaR of wheat is lower than the parametric counterpart due to the positive skewness of wheat. In this regard, portfolio optimization gives higher share to wheat in the historical VaR portfolio, than in the parametric VaR portfolio. In addition, CAC dominates with 50% in the parametric VaR portfolio, while in the historical VaR portfolio, the share of CAC is significantly reduced to 21%. The reason is the relatively high historical VaR of CAC (–1.748), which is due to very high negative skewness (–1.129) and relatively high kurtosis (19.217). In OVaRP, the structure is not changed, that is, the major share goes to wheat with 97% because wheat has the highest average returns.

As for the portfolios with the CEEC indices, the structures of the two VaR portfolios are also different. In particular, the share of wheat increases from 15% to 22% in the historical MVaRP, the share of WIG also increases from 8% to 19%, while the share of PX slightly increases from 44% to 45%. On the other hand, BUX and BET recorded decrease in the historical MVaRP due to a significant increase of their historical VaR compared to parametric VaR. In other words, parametric VaR of the BUX and BET indices is –1.372 and –1.101, respectively, whereas their historical VaR amounts –1.810 and –1.722, respectively. In the historical OVaRP, the situation is completely different. The most significant change is recorded in the share of PX, which is reduced from 100% to 9%, while the share of wheat is increased from 0% to 67%. The rationale could be the fact that historical VaR of wheat is smaller, while of PX is higher compared to the parametric counterparts.

5.4. Comparative Analysis of the Parametric and Historical VaR Portfolios

This section compares performances of the created portfolios from the two aspects: WEC versus CEEC and parametric versus historical portfolios. As for the choice between WEC and CEEC indices, it can be seen that the WEC portfolios are riskier, regardless of whether one looks at parametric or historical portfolios. In other words, CEEC indices better hedge extreme risk of wheat. The reasons are threefold. First, the CEEC indices are less risky compared to the WEC counterparts. Second, the CEEC stock markets are less integrated, which is good for diversification. Third, the CEEC indices have higher negative average correlation with wheat (–0.016) compared to the WEC indices (–0.004).

On the other hand, higher risk implies higher reward, which means that the WEC portfolios are better from the modified Sharpe ratio. In other words, combining the WEC indices with wheat produces slightly better optimal portfolios than it is the case with CEEC indices. It is up to investors to decide whether they want slightly higher reward at the expense of significantly higher risk.

Results in Tables 9.1 and 9.6 are transferred to the graphical presentation in Fig. 9.4. In other words, Fig. 9.4 shows the two VaR-EFLs in the portfolios with

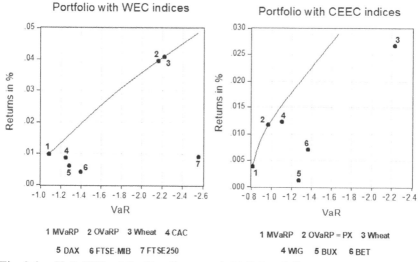

Fig. 9.4.   VaR-EFL of the Two Parametric VaR Portfolios. *Source*: Authors' calculation.

Table 9.6.   Performances of Parametric and Historical VaR Portfolios.

	Portfolios with WEC		Portfolios with CEEC	
	Parametric	**Historical**	**Parametric**	**Historical**
MVaRP	−1.080	−1.295	−0.816	−0.831
OVaRP	0.018	0.021	0.012	0.015

Source: Authors' calculation.

WEC and CEEC stock indices. MVaRP and OVaRP are on the EFL, whereas all other assets are also inserted in the plots. In order to preserve space, only parametric VaR portfolios are presented in this chapter.

It can be seen that Point 3 is significantly distanced from Point 1 in both plots, which means that both portfolios are very good in reducing extreme risk of wheat. In addition, it is interesting to notice the position of Point 2, which is an optimal portfolio. In the left plot, Point 2 is in the upper-right corner, while in the right plot, it is in the lower-left corner. It shows visually that the WEC portfolio offers higher reward but at the expense of higher extreme risk. In the right plot, the position of the optimal portfolio is equal to the PX index because PX takes 100% in the parametric OMVaRP (see Table 9.3).

Comparing the portfolios from the aspect in which VaR is used – parametric or historical, it can be seen that parametric portfolios have lower extreme risk vis-á-vis historical VaR portfolios. The difference is pretty significant in the case of the WEC portfolio, while in the case of the CEEC portfolio, the difference is smaller. This is a clear indication that parametric VaR underestimates extreme risk, which might lead to wrong investment decisions. In other words, parametric VaR is not a good measure of extreme risk because it neglects third and fourth moments. This means that investors should avoid using parametric VaR when time series are skewed to the left with high kurtosis values. In this regard, the better choice is historical VaR, but historical VaR cannot be used for forecasting, unless there is a strong assumption that past will be repeated. In this regard, the semiparametric VaR model can be regarded as a better solution because it considers all the four moments in calculating and predicting extreme risk (see Živkov, Manić, et al., 2022).

6. Implications of the Results for Wheat Entrepreneurs

The results show that significant extreme risk hedging of wheat can be achieved if wheat is combined with European stock indices in the portfolio. However, hedging financial risk can have numerous implications for wheat entrepreneurs, both positive and negative, depending on the specific circumstances and strategies employed.

6.1. Positive Implications

As for positive implications, probably the most important benefit is price stability of wheat. Hedging can help reduce the financial risk associated with fluctuations in wheat prices. This is particularly important for wheat entrepreneurs that rely on wheat as a key input or revenue source. Performing the hedging, they can lock in a price for their wheat, thus protecting themselves from adverse price movements.

In addition, hedging wheat can provide wheat entrepreneurs with predictability of cost and cash flows. For businesses that rely on wheat as a key input (e.g., bakeries or food manufacturers), hedging can provide predictability in input costs, helping with budgeting and financial planning. Hedging also provides predictability in cash flows, making it easier for businesses to plan and budget. Farmers can estimate their income more accurately, and food processors can budget for raw material costs.

Previous two benefits imply the third one, which is related to market competitiveness. In other words, hedging allows businesses to remain competitive in the market by offering stable prices to customers. This can help retain customers and maintain market share. Also, for businesses in the wheat supply chain, such as food manufacturers, hedging can help protect profit margins by mitigating the impact of price spikes in wheat.

The last positive implication of wheat hedging might be related to access to financing. In other words, lenders may be more willing to extend credit to farmers and businesses that have hedged their wheat price risk. This is because hedging reduces the uncertainty associated with repayment.

6.2. Negative Implications

Besides gains that hedging might bring, there are also several negative implications that should be mentioned. For instance, implementing hedging strategies can be costly, involving transaction fees, spreads and margin requirements, which can erode profits of entrepreneurs if not managed carefully.

Hedging financial risk might imply missed opportunities if wheat prices move in a favorable direction, for instance, prices rise in favor of wheat producers. In this scenario, producers that have hedged their positions may miss out on potential profits. Hedging locks in a specific price, which may be lower than the market price at a later date.

Hedging financial risk is not an easy job, which means that hedging strategies can be complex, requiring expertise and a good understanding of financial markets and risk management. Inexperienced participants may make costly mistakes or take on more risk than intended. An important factor in effective hedging also plays the market dynamics of wheat and auxiliary instruments in the portfolio. In other words, the effectiveness of a hedge depends on the correlation level between the hedge instrument (e.g., stock indices) and the underlying asset (wheat). If the correlation is high, the hedge may not provide the desired level of protection. Aforementioned factors can lead to over-hedging or under-hedging, implying that the appropriate level of hedging can be challenging. Over-hedging can limit potential gains, while under-hedging may expose a business to more risk than desired.

At the end, the existence of possible regulatory and compliance issues should be mentioned. In other words, engaging in hedging activities may subject businesses to regulatory requirements and reporting obligations. Failure to comply with these regulations can result in legal and financial consequences.

Generally speaking, hedging financial risk associated with wheat can be a valuable risk management tool when used appropriately. It can protect against adverse price movements and provide stability to cash flows, but it also comes with costs, complexity and the potential for missed opportunities. It is important for individuals and businesses to carefully assess their risk exposure and financial goals when implementing hedging strategies. Additionally, seeking advice from financial professionals or risk management experts can be beneficial in making informed hedging decisions.

7. Conclusion

The price of wheat has experienced huge oscillations in recent years, which happened as a consequence of the pandemic and the war in Ukraine, and also because wheat is used for ethanol production. In an effort to mitigate extreme financial risk of wheat, this chapter combines wheat with developed and emerging European stock indices in multivariate portfolios. Extreme risk of the portfolios is measured by the VaR metric. In particular, we use both parametric and historical VaR in the process of portfolio construction, which gives us an opportunity to compare performances of both portfolios. Also, in this way, it can be assessed whether parametric VaR is a good measure of extreme risk. Besides the minimum-VaR portfolio, we also construct a maximum-Sharpe portfolio because different market participants may prefer different goals. As a preliminary analysis, we estimate equicorrelation of both portfolios with the **DECO-GJR-GARCH** model.

These findings serve as an indication which portfolio might have better hedging performances.

According to the DECO results, the portfolio with CEEC indices is less integrated, which implies lower correlation between the assets, and this is a good characteristic for the diversification efforts. In particular, average equicorrelation with the WEC indices is 0.307, while for the CEEC indices, it amounts to 0.218. Also, the estimated DECO models show that a significant increase of equicorrelations happened at the beginning of 2020, which can be directly linked with the onset of the pandemic.

Regarding the results of the created portfolios, several findings are worth mentioning. In the parametric MVaRP with WEC indices, the highest share of 50% has CAC index, while DAX and wheat follow with 26% and 24%, respectively. On the other hand, in MVaRP with CEEC, the highest share has PX with 44%, while BET and wheat follow with 29% and 15%, respectively. Wheat has relatively high share in both portfolios, although wheat has relatively high risk, and the reason is negative correlation with stock indices. As for the optimal portfolios, only wheat and DAX constitute a portfolio of WEC indices, where wheat dominates with 97%. In OVaRP with CEEC, only PX has a place in the portfolio because it has the highest mSharpe ratio.

On the other hand, in the historical VaR portfolios, the share of wheat increases in both WEC and CEEC portfolios because the historical VaR of wheat is lower than its parametric VaR. Also, the structure of the historical VaR portfolios is significantly different compared to the parametric portfolios because the historical VaR values of the assets are significantly different vis-á-vis the parametric VaR values. In the historical OVaRPs with the WEC and CEEC indices, wheat dominates with 97% and 67%, respectively.

Comparing the performance of WEC and CEEC portfolios, the latter has significantly lower VaR than the former, which means that combination of wheat and the CEEC indices gives much better hedging of extreme risk. As for OVaRP, the results give a slight upper hand to the WEC portfolio. On the other hand, when parametric and historical VaR portfolios are compared, it is clear that parametric VaR is lower than historical VaR in both portfolios with the WEC and CEEC indices. This strongly indicates that parametric VaR underestimates extreme risk, which means that parametric VaR is not an appropriate measure of extreme risk and can lead to wrong investment decisions.

The results of this chapter can be very helpful for wheat producers, traders or investors because it can teach them how to hedge extreme financial risk of wheat in the multivariate portfolio. This chapter also sends an important message that parametric VaR is not a suitable measure of extreme risk because it ignores third and fourth moments. Future studies may try to optimize a portfolio with different risk-minimizing goals, for example, semiparametric VaR, which takes into account all four moments. In this way, it would be useful to compare the results of historical and semiparametric VaR in order to see the discrepancy between these two measures. This would show whether semiparametric VaR is a better risk measure than parametric VaR.

Acknowledgements

The paper is a part of research financed by the MSTDI RS, agreed in decision no. 451-03-66/2024-03/200009 from 5.2.2024.

References

Abuaf, N., Ayala, T., & Sinclair, D. (2018). Global equity investing: An efficient frontier approach. *International Finance, 22*, 1–16.

Aielli, G. P. (2013). Dynamic conditional correlation: On properties and estimation. *Journal of Business and Economic Statistics, 31*, 282–299.

Baležentis, T. (2015). The sources of the total factor productivity growth in Lithuanian family farms: A Färe-Primont Index approach. *Prague Economic Papers, 24*, 225–241.

Chen, Z., Yan, B., & Kang, H. (2022). Dynamic correlation between crude oil and agricultural futures markets. *Review of Development Economics, 26*(3), 1798–1849.

Czudaj, R. L. (2020). The role of uncertainty on agricultural futures markets momentum trading and volatility. *Studies in Nonlinear Dynamics and Econometrics, 24*, 20180054.

Elliott, L., Elliott, M., Slaa, C.T., & Wang, Z. (2020). New generation grain contracts in corn and soybean commodity markets. *Journal of Commodity Markets, 20*, 100113

Engle, R. F. (2002). Dynamic conditional correlation: A simple class of multivariate generalized autoregressive conditional heteroskedasticity models. *Journal of Business and Economic Statistics, 20*, 339–350.

Engle, R. F., & Kelly, B. (2012). Dynamic equicorrelation. *Journal of Business Economics and Statistics, 30*, 212–228.

Gatfaoui, H. (2019). Diversifying portfolios of U.S. stocks with crude oil and natural gas: A regime-dependent optimization with several risk measures. *Energy Economics, 80*, 132–152.

Gazdar, K., Hassan, M. K., Safa, M. F., & Grassa, R. (2019). Oil price volatility, Islamic financial development and economic growth in Gulf Cooperation Council (GCC) countries. *Borsa Istanbul Review, 19*, 197–206.

Gregoriou, G. N., & Gueyie, J-P. (2003). Risk-adjusted performance of funds of hedge funds using a modified Sharpe ratio. *Journal of Wealth Management, 6*, 77–83.

Hammoudeh, S., Santos, P. A., & Al-Hassan, A. (2013). Downside risk management and VaR-based optimal portfolios for precious metals, oil and stocks. *North American Journal of Economics and Finance, 25*, 318–334.

Hernandez, J. A., Kang, S. H., & Yoon, S.-M. (2021). Spillovers and portfolio optimization of agricultural commodity and global equity markets. *Applied Economics, 53*, 1326–1341.

Hovhannisyan, V., & Devadoss, S. (2020). Effects of urbanization on food demand in China. *Empirical Economics, 58*, 699–721.

Huang, H., & Xiong, T. (2023). A good hedge or safe haven? The hedging ability of China's commodity futures market under extreme market conditions. *Journal of Futures Markets, 43*(7), 968–1035.

Kuzman, B., Petković, B., Denić, N., Petković, D., Ćirković, B., Stojanović, J., & Momir Milić, M. (2021). Estimation of optimal fertilizers for optimal crop yield by adaptive neuro fuzzy logic. *Rhizosphere, 18*, 100358.

Naeem, M. A., Farid, S., Balli, F., & Shahzad, S. J. H. (2021). Hedging the downside risk of commodities through cryptocurrencies. *Applied Economics Letters, 28*(2), 153–160.

Naeem, M. A., Hasan, M., Arif, M., Suleman, M. T., & Kang, S. H. (2022). Oil and gold as a hedge and safe-haven for metals and agricultural commodities with portfolio implications. *Energy Economics, 105*, 105758.

Petković, D., Petković, B., & Kuzman, B. (2023). Appraisal of information system for evaluation of kinetic parameters of biomass oxidation. *Biomass Conversion and Biorefinery, 13*(2), 777–785.

Petković, B., Petković, D., Kuzman, B., Milovančević, M., Wakil, K., Ho, L. S., & Jermsittiparsert, L. (2020). Neuro-fuzzy estimation of reference crop evapotranspiration by neuro fuzzy logic based on weather conditions. *Computers and Electronics in Agriculture, 173*, 105358.

Rehman, M. U., Bouri, E., Eraslan, V., & Kumar, S. (2019). Energy and non-energy commodities: An asymmetric approach towards portfolio diversification in the commodity market. *Resources Policy, 63*, 101456.

Szeles, M. R., & Saman, C. (2020). Globalisation, economic growth and Covid-19. Insights from international finance. *Romanian Journal of Economic Forecasting, 23*, 78–92.

Tonin, J. M., Vieira, C. M. R., de Sousa Fragoso, R. M., & Filho, J. G. M. (2020). Conditional correlation and volatility between spot and futures markets for soybean and corn. *Agribusiness: An International Journal, 36*, 707–724.

Živkov, D., Balaban, S., & Joksimović, M. (2022). Making a Markowitz portfolio with agricultural futures. *Agricultural Economics – Zemedelska Ekonomika, 68*(6), 219–229.

Živkov, D., Manić, S., Đurašković, J., & Gajić-Glamočlija, M. (2022). Oil hedging with a multivariate semiparametric value-at-risk portfolio. *Borsa Istanbul Review, 22*(6), 1118–1131.

Živkov, D., Kuzman, B., & Subić, J. (2019). How do oil price changes impact the major agricultural commodities in different market conditions and in different time-horizons? *Economic Computation and Economic Cybernetics Studies and Research, 53*(4), 159–175.

Živkov, D., Kuzman, B., & Subić, J. (2020). What Bayesian quantiles can tell about volatility transmission between the major agricultural futures? *Agricultural Economics – Zemedelska Ekonomika, 66*(5), 215–225.

Živkov, D., Kuzman, B., & Subić J. (2022). Measuring risk-adjusted performance of the selected soft agricultural commodities. *Agricultural Economics – Zemedelska Ekonomika, 68*(3), 87–96.

Živkov, D., Kuzman, B., & Subić, J. (2023). Multifrequency downside risk interconnectedness between soft agricultural commodities. *Agricultural Economics – Zemedelska Ekonomika, 69*(8), 332–342.

Živkov, D., Stankov, B., Papić-Blagojević, N., Damnjanović, J., & Račić, Ž. (2023). How to reduce extreme risk of losses in corn and soybean markets? Construction of a portfolio with European stock indices? *Agricultural Economics – Zemedelska Ekonomika, 69*(3), 109–118.

Chapter 10

Assessing the Impact of Green Entrepreneurial Activities on Organizational Financial Performance: An Employee's Perceptual Approach

Claudiu George Bocean, Anca Antoaneta Vărzaru, Dorel Berceanu, Dalia Simion, Mădălina Giorgiana Mangra and Marian Cazacu

University of Craiova, Romania

Abstract

In recent decades, there has been a significant increase in global concern regarding the impact of economic activities on the environment and climate change. In this context, green entrepreneurship has become a growing trend in the business world. One of the most important benefits of green entrepreneurship is enhancing energy efficiency and resource utilization. By reducing the resources required to produce a product or deliver a service, green entrepreneurship can contribute to cost reduction and operational efficiency improvement. By implementing sustainable business practices, organizations can enhance their image in the eyes of consumers and attract new customers who are environmentally conscious. This chapter addresses the identified gap in the literature regarding the influence of green entrepreneurial activities on organizational financial performance from the perspective of employees in organizations engaged in such activities (waste reduction, waste recycling, energy conservation, air pollutant reduction, packaging reduction, sustainable transportation). Organizational financial performance is measured through perceived performance compared to the previous year and performance relative to expectations.

Entrepreneurship and Development for a Green Resilient Economy, 251–275
Copyright © 2024 by Claudiu George Bocean, Anca Antoaneta Vărzaru, Dorel Berceanu, Dalia Simion, Mădălina Giorgiana Mangra and Marian Cazacu
Published under exclusive licence by Emerald Publishing Limited
doi:10.1108/978-1-83797-088-920241010

Two visible financial indicators have been selected for analysis: turnover and net profit.

Keywords: Green entrepreneurship; green entrepreneurial activities; financial performance; organizational performance; perceptual approach

Introduction

In the current era, awareness of climate change, environmental degradation, and the depletion of natural resources has reached unprecedented levels in our society. With these significant challenges, sustainable development and environmental protection have become essential priorities for governments, organizations, and individuals. Green or ecological entrepreneurship has gained increasing importance in this context, representing an innovative approach to combining economic success with environmental responsibility.

Green enterprises no longer solely pursue profits but also consider their impact on the environment and the communities in which they operate. By implementing eco-friendly practices and technologies, these organizations commit to reducing their ecological footprint, minimizing the consumption of natural resources, and protecting biodiversity. More and more companies, from startups to multinational corporations, realize that sustainable development is not just a trend or legal requirement but an imperative necessity to ensure a prosperous and balanced future.

Green entrepreneurship not only contributes to environmental protection but can also bring significant economic benefits. Adopting sustainable practices can lead to long-term cost savings by reducing energy consumption, efficiently using resources, and responsibly managing waste. Environmentally conscious consumers are increasingly attracted to products and services offered by eco-friendly companies, which enhance customer demand and loyalty.

In addition to financial benefits, green entrepreneurial activities enhance competitive advantages. In an ever-changing market where consumers become more informed and demanding regarding companies' ethical and ecological practices, a sustainable approach can provide a distinct advantage over competitors. Therefore, organizations that adopt a long-term vision focused on sustainable development can achieve strategic advantage and ensure a strong market position.

As we face global challenges such as climate change, biodiversity degradation, and resource depletion, green entrepreneurial activities have evolved from alternative options to a vital necessity. Understanding that economic development cannot be separated from environmental responsibility has led to a fundamental shift in how we perceive businesses and their impact on the world. Thus, enterprises that adopt an innovative and sustainable approach can play a crucial role in building a fairer, healthier, and more prosperous future for future generations. Our research focuses on analyzing the effects that green entrepreneurial activities can have on the financial performance of organizations. While most previous research has focused on the ecological benefits of such activities, this study highlights the perceptual perspective to understand and evaluate how these ecological initiatives influence the financial performance of the involved organizations.

By adopting a perceptual approach, this study aims to provide a complex perspective on the interactions between employees, customers, and the organization concerning the commitment and implementation of green entrepreneurial activities. This way, potential synergies between social responsibility and financial performance will be highlighted, facilitating a better understanding of how environmental concerns become critical to organizations' success and sustainable growth.

This chapter begins with an introduction that presents the research problem, followed by a review of relevant literature. Then, the study's methodology is described, and the obtained results are presented. The "Discussion" section interprets and analyzes the results. Finally, this chapter concludes with the conclusions, summarizing the main findings and potential future research directions.

Literature Review

Social Responsibilities Toward the Environment

Globalization and digitization have continuously redefined the social context of business. In an increasingly complex world, organizations significantly impact individuals, the planet, and their capacity to sustain sustainable development. Globalization has created a borderless market, continuously fueling economic growth. However, this evolution has also led to imbalanced development, intensifying the division between the rich and the poor and generating social conflicts. Amid this reality, businesses are becoming increasingly aware that they cannot be separated from the rest of society. There is a strong interdependence between businesses and society, and the role of business organizations in building a better future is increasingly recognized and encouraged. It is no longer sufficient for organizations to pursue solely financial objectives, but they must consider their impact on society and the environment (Bustamante et al., 2021).

Thus, business organizations are called upon to assume new roles in this era of social responsibility. They must act as agents of change and contribute to addressing social and environmental issues, promoting equity, and supporting sustainable development. At the same time, these organizations can benefit from more robust relationships with the community, employees, and consumers by adopting a responsible and ethical approach (Çalıyurt, 2021). By adopting responsible business practices, organizations can build a better future, reduce social inequalities, protect the environment, and promote general well-being. This paradigm shift encourages collaboration between organizations, governments, and civil society to address global challenges and build a sustainable and equitable business environment (Dathe et al., 2022).

The awareness of the close link between business and society has grown, and business organizations have become aware of their responsibility to contribute to social progress and environmental protection. Striking a balance between financial objectives and social responsibility has become essential for creating a better and sustainable future (Mitra & Schmidpeter, 2021).

In today's world, survival and profit are no longer sufficient to consider a company socially acceptable. The new requirements impose high levels of transparency regarding information disclosure and corporate governance and address social issues that concern society, such as environmental pollution, child labor, and corruption. Organizations face increasing pressure to improve social and environmental aspects and to behave as responsible corporate citizens. Faced with these challenges, organizational leaders make complex decisions and must balance the demands and expectations related to corporate social responsibility (CSR).

Organizations must adopt innovative approaches to implement CSR and develop partnerships with other entities, including governments, nongovernmental organizations, and local communities (Opkara & Idowu, 2013). In this way, they contribute to solving social and environmental issues, promote sustainability, and support sustainable development within the communities in which they operate. Successfully implementing CSR is not just a matter of reputation but can also bring significant benefits to the organization, such as attracting and retaining talent, increasing customer loyalty, and strengthening relationships with investors (Dimitropoulos & Koronios, 2021).

Implementing CSR does not have a uniform approach but depends on the specificities of each organization and the environment in which it operates. However, organizations need to adopt an integrated and strategic approach to CSR, ensuring that its principles and values are incorporated into all aspects of the business. By responsibly managing their social and environmental impact, organizations play a crucial role in building a more sustainable future and achieving long-term success (Bustamante et al., 2021).

A recent theoretical perspective that has influenced the understanding of CSR is sustainable development. In 1987, the Brundtland Commission systematically emphasized the link between poverty, environmental degradation, and economic development. Sustainable development is defined as meeting the needs of the present without compromising the ability of future generations to meet their own needs, extending the responsibility of firms both intragenerational and intergenerational. As such, firms are expected to consider traditionally underrepresented stakeholders, such as the environment and future generations. However, significant tensions exist between CSR and the debate on sustainable development, although many CSR scholars have adopted the "triple bottom line" (Elkington, 1994).

In the current business context, there is an increasing public demand for business leaders to incorporate social issues into their strategies, given the current social and political climate. Managers consistently respond to the demands of various stakeholder groups to allocate resources for CSR. These pressures come from stakeholders such as employees, consumers, communities, and the environment (McWilliams & Siegel, 2001). Employee pressures include increased public recognition of certain employee rights in the workplace, such as non-discrimination in the recruitment, dismissal, and promotion processes. Similarly, consumer pressure involves the production of safe products and providing more extensive information to consumers. Community and environmental pressures involve investments in pollution reduction equipment, ensuring that business operations do not endanger the local community's safety, etc.

A study by Buhanita (2015) on European companies highlighted additional dimensions of CSR, such as the ecological, social, economic, and stakeholder dimensions. These dimensions reflect concerns regarding the environmental impact, social responsibility toward the community and employees, financial performance, and relationships with various stakeholders. CSR includes three fundamental principles of sustainable development: economic growth, social equity, and environmental protection (Lee & Jung, 2016). Operationally, CSR can be defined as a method through which a business achieves its economic, social, and environmental objectives, simultaneously addressing the needs of both shareholders and stakeholders. Active engagement in CSR is a crucial competence for organizational leaders, as by adopting positive social practices and developing sustainable policies and strategies, they can achieve measurable impact in the community and the environment (Çalıyurt, 2021).

Researchers have explored whether CSR is an indispensable component of organizational operations in addition to defining the concept of CSR. A dominant theory suggests that the socially solid performance of a company is achieved when there is a well-defined association between financial performance and social responsibility. Leaders in various industries increasingly know the need to balance financial objectives, social involvement, and environmental protection to ensure sustainable organizational sustainability (Boaventura et al., 2012).

It is essential to balance social responsibility, environmental management, and economic viability throughout the supply chain to achieve long-term economic performance and meet the needs and expectations of stakeholders. Companies must be responsible in their relationship with employees, customers, local communities, and the environment.

Engaging in CSR brings multiple benefits to a company. In addition to improving the image and reputation, responsible social and environmental practices increase customer loyalty and attract new consumers concerned about social and environmental aspects. Employees feel motivated and engaged in an organization that adopts responsible policies and engages in community actions, which leads to increased productivity and staff retention (Laasch, 2021).

It is essential to mention that CSR is not just a practice limited to individual companies but can be extended and integrated throughout the supply chain. Collaborating and communicating with suppliers, partners, and distributors lead to the implementation of high ethical and ecological standards in all stages of the production and distribution process. Engaging in CSR is a direct economic benefit (Hahn, 2022). Studies show that responsible management of social and environmental issues leads to long-term cost savings by reducing risks, optimizing resource usage, and improving operational efficiency. Integrating social responsibility into a company's operations and maintaining a balance between financial, social, and environmental aspects are crucial factors in achieving long-term economic performance and meeting the needs of all stakeholders. Through active engagement in CSR, companies can build strong relationships with stakeholders, gaining their trust and support while contributing to solving social and environmental issues (Dathe et al., 2022).

Green Entrepreneurship Activities

The evaluation of the impact of green entrepreneurial activities on organizational financial performance is a significant topic of interest in a world dominated by environmental concerns and sustainable development (Guo & Wang, 2022). Among the most common green entrepreneurial activities are waste reduction, recycling, energy conservation, air pollutant reduction, packaging reduction, and promoting sustainable transportation (Liu et al., 2022). These activities aim to protect the environment and bring significant financial benefits to organizations, providing a conducive framework for assessing their impact on financial performance (Dubey et al., 2015).

Waste reduction and recycling have become essential elements in addressing sustainability and environmental protection within organizations in various industries. As the world faces climate change and resource depletion challenges, adopting these practices becomes increasingly important for enterprises as they offer significant financial and social responsibility benefits (Leonidou et al., 2015).

One of the significant advantages of waste reduction and recycling is related to cost savings. Organizations significantly reduce waste management and disposal expenses by minimizing the generated waste and implementing efficient recycling processes. Instead of directing resources toward waste fees and disposal costs, funds can be redirected to other key organization activities, contributing to increased profitability and improved financial performance (Dubey et al., 2015).

In addition to cost savings, employee involvement in these environmental initiatives is crucial to their successful implementation. They drive an organizational culture that promotes environmental responsibility and employee engagement in more sustainable practices. Well-informed and aware employees of the importance of waste reduction and recycling are more likely to make significant contributions and actively engage in implementing these strategies (Guo et al., 2020). Thus, open communication and proper training can increase employee involvement and create a united team in achieving environmental objectives. Employee involvement in ecological practices extends the benefits beyond the organization's boundaries. Since employees are active community members, environmentally conscious and involved employees have a positive impact outside the organization. They are ambassadors of sustainable practices in the community where they live and work, influencing and motivating others to adopt responsible environmental behaviors (Qian & Burritt, 2009).

Waste reduction and recycling are essential pillars in organizations' environmental strategies. These initiatives generate significant cost savings and increase operational efficiency and financial performance. Employee involvement in these activities is crucial for their success and sustainability since their motivation and awareness strengthen the organizational culture and benefit the wider community (Dean & McMullen, 2007). Adopting a sustainable approach with active employee participation is essential to building a greener and more ecologically responsible future.

Implementing efficient waste reduction and recycling policies and techniques within organizations leads to significant cost savings. Organizations save financial and material resources by minimizing generated waste and optimizing production processes, which can be reinvested in innovation, research, and development. Thus, these investments in sustainable practices can lead to increased operational efficiency and improved long-term financial performance. Recycling is an essential component of a sustainable waste management approach. By recovering and reusing resources, organizations reduce their dependence on new materials and diminish their environmental impact. Recycling contributes to conserving natural resources and protecting biodiversity, which is crucial for maintaining ecological balance (Lin & Chen, 2018).

Employee involvement in these ecological initiatives is crucial to their success and sustainability. Informed and motivated employees can become active agents of change within organizations. By understanding the importance of waste reduction and recycling, they contribute innovative ideas and efficient solutions to implement these strategies. Moreover, employees involved in social and environmental responsibility activities may be more motivated, loyal, and proud of their contribution to a more sustainable future (Leonidou et al., 2015). Organizational culture also plays an essential role in strengthening the commitment to green practices. An open culture that encourages active employee involvement and recognizes their contributions to sustainability creates a united internal community focused on the organization's environmental goals (Kalyar et al., 2019).

In addition to internal benefits, adopting a sustainable approach enhances the organization's reputation in the eyes of the public and business partners. Environmentally conscious consumers increasingly support responsible companies, leading to increased market share and customer loyalty. Business partners and investors may also be attracted to the organization's commitment to sustainability as an indicator of long-term performance and responsible risk approach. Waste reduction and recycling are critical to organizations' efficient and responsible resource management. These practices bring significant financial and environmental benefits, increasing operational efficiency and environmental protection. By involving employees and adopting a sustainable approach, organizations can build a greener and more ecologically responsible future, enhancing long-term sustainability and success (Leonidou et al., 2015).

Energy conservation is undoubtedly a vital component in modern enterprises' environmental strategies. In a world where energy resources are limited, and climate change is an increasingly severe threat, adopting energy conservation practices is essential to minimize environmental impact and achieve significant cost savings. Active employee involvement in these initiatives is a critical factor in the success of sustainability efforts. Employees can adopt simple but effective measures to conserve energy in offices and organizational facilities. These may include shutting down computers and other equipment during breaks, using energy-efficient light bulbs, and adjusting lighting based on needs. Moreover, efficient building insulation and intelligent heating and cooling systems to optimize energy consumption are other measures that employees can implement (Dubey et al., 2015).

Regarding production processes, employees also play a crucial role in energy conservation. Identifying and eliminating energy inefficiencies in workflows and used equipment led to significant savings. Moreover, employees can be trained and involved in developing more efficient energy use practices, reducing consumption during production processes, and increasing the organization's operational efficiency (Aguilera-Caracuel & Ortiz-de-Mandojana, 2013). Employee involvement in energy conservation can be encouraged through awareness campaigns and training regarding the importance and benefits of these practices. Such initiatives educate employees about the impact of energy consumption on the environment and illustrate how each gesture makes a significant difference in global environmental protection efforts (Wahga et al., 2018).

Energy conservation benefits from a financial and environmental perspective and improves the organization's quality of life and comfort. Reducing energy consumption leads to a more pleasant and healthier atmosphere in offices and facilities, thus enhancing employee productivity and well-being. Energy conservation is a crucial pillar in organizational environmental strategies, and active employee involvement is essential for the success of these initiatives. Employees significantly reduce the environmental impact and achieve cost savings by adopting responsible behaviors and developing efficient energy utilization practices. Therefore, energy conservation is an ecological necessity and an opportunity for organizations to progress toward a more sustainable and energy-responsible future (Qian & Burritt, 2009).

Reducing air pollutants has become a significant priority for organizations worldwide as awareness of the negative impact of pollution on the environment and human health grows (Yang, 2018). Confronting the challenges of climate change and air pollution, organizations are taking an active role in environmental protection and sustainability promotion. Implementing cleaner technologies and sustainable practices in production processes and daily operations is crucial in reducing pollutant emissions (Leonidou et al., 2015). Adopting renewable energy sources, investing in more energy-efficient equipment, and optimizing production processes to minimize waste and harmful emissions are essential. Through such measures, organizations significantly improve air quality in their communities (Guo et al., 2020).

Employees are vital in reducing air pollutants as they are directly involved in organizations' day-to-day activities. By encouraging employee involvement in adopting responsible practices, such as using low-emission means of transportation or carpooling, organizing awareness activities regarding air quality importance, or appropriately recycling waste, organizations educate and motivate their staff to become more environmentally aware of their impact (Chaudhry & Amir, 2020).

Building a proactive organizational culture regarding environmental protection and human health can be achieved by promoting ethical values and social responsibilities. Encouraging open communication and employee involvement in environmental decisions leads to closer collaboration and innovative ideas to address air pollution challenges. Employees who feel actively engaged in environmental protection initiatives are more motivated and dedicated to supporting these objectives, strengthening the organization's commitment to fighting pollution. Local communities value responsible organizations that commit to protecting the environment and reducing their negative impact on health. Such efforts can bring mutual benefits, strengthen community relations, and lead to a positive image and enhanced reputation for the organization (Dubey et al., 2015).

Reducing packaging and promoting sustainable transportation are two essential components of green entrepreneurial activities, significantly impacting sustainable and ecologically responsible development (Guo & Wang, 2022).

Packaging represents a significant part of commercial activities; however, excessive or inadequate use of packaging leads to increased waste generation and negative environmental impacts (Dai et al., 2015). By adopting measures to reduce packaging or using recyclable and biodegradable packaging, organizations contribute to minimizing waste and protecting the environment. More efficient packaging strategies result in significant cost savings by reducing resources and costs associated with production, storage, and transportation. Environmentally aware consumers are more likely to support products and services offered by organizations that adopt eco-friendly practices. As such, a responsible approach to packaging management strengthens customer relationships and fosters loyalty to the brand (Leonidou et al., 2015).

Promoting sustainable transportation is another crucial initiative in environmental protection efforts. Replacing traditional means of transportation with less polluting alternatives, such as electric vehicles or those powered by renewable energy, reduces greenhouse gas emissions and improves air quality (Schaper, 2010). Implementing more efficient logistics strategies, such as optimizing transportation routes and using more ecologically friendly transportation means, leads to significant fuel and resource savings (Yang, 2018). Improving transportation efficiency reduces logistics and transportation-related costs, and more reliable and faster transportation enhances customer satisfaction and contributes to the organization's market competitiveness (Song et al., 2021).

Employee involvement in adopting these packaging reduction and sustainable transportation practices plays a vital role in ensuring the success of these efforts. Employees can be trained and motivated to adopt responsible behavior concerning packaging use and proper waste management. Moreover, they can be engaged in developing more efficient transportation strategies and offer feedback and innovative ideas to optimize logistics activities (Guo & Wang, 2022).

Reducing packaging and promoting sustainable transportation are critical aspects of green entrepreneurial activities, bringing significant ecological and financial benefits. Organizations protect the environment and achieve cost savings by adopting measures to reduce packaging and utilizing more efficient and eco-friendly transportation. Employee involvement in these efforts is essential to strengthen the organization's sustainability-oriented culture and create an engaged and motivated internal community focused on achieving the organization's environmental goals. Through eco-friendly practices, organizations progress toward a greener, more responsible, and sustainable future (Sun et al., 2016).

The evaluation of the impact of green entrepreneurial activities on organizational financial performance from the employees' perspective represents a highly relevant and valuable research domain in sustainable development (Liu et al., 2022). These activities contribute to environmental protection and offer significant advantages in financial performance and organizational competitiveness (Liu et al., 2022). Through active involvement and employee awareness of the importance of these initiatives, organizations build a sustainable and environmentally responsible culture, bringing benefits both to businesses and society as a whole.

Based on these considerations, we have formulated two research hypotheses:

H1. Waste reduction activities are the most frequently associated activities with organizational CSR in the employees' perception.

H2. Green entrepreneurial activities positively influence organizational financial performance in the employees' perception.

Research Methodology

To examine the relationships between variables and investigate the activities that influence organizational performance, we employed structural equation modeling (SEM). SEM allows for testing hypotheses regarding the relationships between observed and latent variables. Hair et al. (2017) highlighted that SEM is a "multivariate technique that combines aspects of multiple regression and factor analysis to estimate a series of inter-correlated dependent relationships simultaneously." The variables defining entrepreneurial activities are waste reduction, recycling, energy conservation, air pollutant reduction, packaging reduction, and promoting sustainable transportation. The variables defining organizational financial performance concerning the previous year and expectations are profit and turnover. The studied variables, including sociodemographic variables, are presented in Table 10.1.

The empirical study involved conducting a survey based on a questionnaire, which took place from September 2022 to November 2022 among 431 employees of organizations in Romania. We used the stratified random sampling method based on three sociodemographic variables: gender, age, and education. The sample was established with a confidence level of 95% and a margin of error of 4.723%.

Results

The first category of activities commonly associated with CSR focuses on environmental protection. Variable $v1$ assesses respondents' perceptions regarding their organizations' engagement in waste reduction activities. The frequency analysis of the values recorded for this variable reveals that only 19.7% of the respondents declare that their organization is highly engaged in waste reduction activities (Fig. 10.1).

The analysis of responses for Variable $v2$ reveals the level of waste recycling perceived by the respondents within their organizations. Only 20% highly appreciate the waste recycling activities within their organizations, while 29.7% consider these activities sufficient. About 30.3% of the respondents state that their organization

Table 10.1.   Multivariate Tests on the Relationships Between CSR and Environmental Protection Activities.

Latent Variables	Items	Scales
Demographic variables	Gender	Male (1), female (2)
	Age	18–30 years (1), 31–40 years (2), 41–50 years (3), over 50 years (4)
	Education	High school (1), bachelor (2), master, or PhD (3)
Green entrepreneurial activities	Reducing waste ($v1$)	To a great extent
	Recycling ($v2$)	Sufficient
	Conserving energy ($v3$)	An average level
		To a lesser extent
	Reducing air pollutants ($v4$)	Not at all
	Reducing packaging ($v5$)	
	Sustainable transport ($v6$)	
CSR	CSR level ($v7$)	Strongly agree (5)
		Partially agree (4)
		Moderate (3)
		Partially disagree (2)
		Strongly disagree (1)
Perceived performance	Net profit compared to last year ($v8$)	A substantial increase over the previous year (5)
	Turnover compared to last year ($v9$)	An increase compared to the previous year (4)
		Same as last year (3)
		The decrease compared to the previous year (2)
		The substantial decrease compared to the previous year (1)
Expected performance	Net profit compared to expectations ($v10$)	Much higher than expected (5)
	Turnover compared to expectations ($v11$)	Greater than expectations (4)
		Up to expectations (3)
		Less than expected (2)
		Much lower than expected (1)

Source: Developed by the authors based on the literature review.

is engaging in waste recycling activities to a small extent, while 20% believe their organization has a moderate level of waste recycling activities (Fig. 10.2).

The investigation of Variable $v3$ led to the idea that in the perception of only about a quarter of the respondents, the organizations they belong to undertake sufficient actions for energy conservation. A significant percentage of respondents (over a third) consider energy conservation a minor concern for their organization (Fig. 10.3).

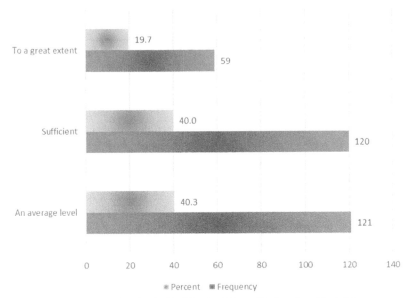

Fig. 10.1. Frequency Analysis Within the Waste Reduction Variable.
Source: Developed by the authors based on collected data.

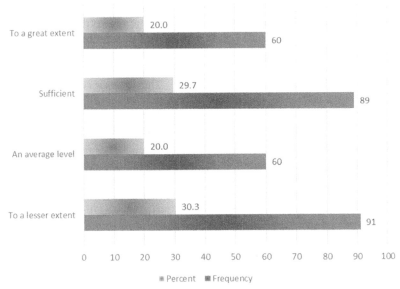

Fig. 10.2. Frequency Analysis Within the Waste Recycling Variable.
Source: Developed by the authors based on collected data.

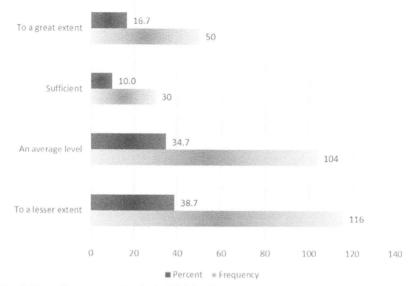

Fig. 10.3.   Frequency Analysis Within the Energy Conservation Variable.
Source: Developed by the authors based on collected data.

Variable $v4$ examines employees' perception of reducing air pollutants within their organization. It can be observed from the investigation of the frequency values recorded for this variable that most respondents appreciate that their organization shows a high and very high level of action for reducing air pollutants. Only 29% of the respondents rated the actions of reducing air pollutants in their organization as moderate (Fig. 10.4).

The analysis of responses for Variable $v5$ reveals a predominantly positive perception of employees regarding the actions of organizations in reducing packaging. Most respondents (77%) consider that their organization regularly undertakes activities to reduce packaging quantities, with 23% stating that their organization is at a moderate level regarding packaging reduction actions (Fig. 10.5).

The investigation of Variable $v6$ led to the finding that in the perception of the majority of respondents, organizations undertake actions toward ensuring sustainable transportation (Fig. 10.6).

To investigate *H1* regarding green entrepreneurship activities, we conducted a multivariate analysis of variance for the applied variables, considering one set for CSR (CSR level – $v7$) and another set for environmental activities – $v1$–$v6$ (waste reduction, waste recycling, energy conservation, air pollution reduction, packaging reduction, sustainable transportation). Table 10.2 presents the multivariate tests performed using SPSS in the analysis of variance (ANOVA).

The Wilks' lambda test showed that the model is statistically significant. For all six variables characterizing environmental protection activities, the p-values were <0.001. The observed power was 1.000 for most variables, with only $v3$ and $v6$

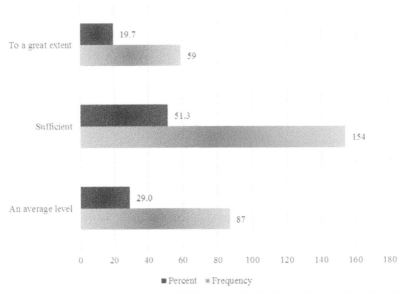

Fig. 10.4.   Frequency Analysis Within the Air Pollution Reduction Variable.
Source: Developed by the authors based on collected data.

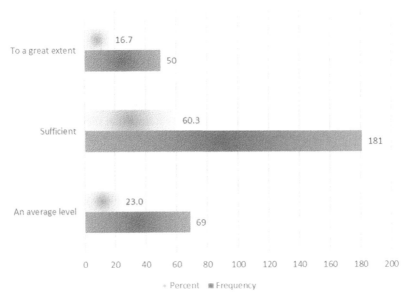

Fig. 10.5.   Frequency Analysis Within the Packaging Reduction Variable.
Source: Developed by the authors based on collected data.

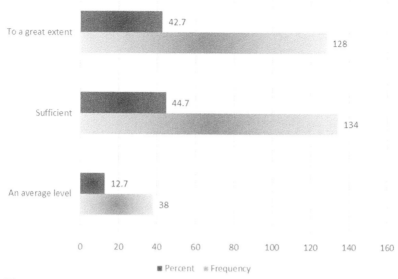

Fig. 10.6.   Frequency Analysis Within the Sustainable Transportation Variable.
Source: Developed by the authors based on collected data.

having a slightly lower power than 1.000 but very close to this value, indicating over 99% chance of a significant result. The effect size (partial eta squared) indicated that waste recycling activities ($v2$), air pollution reduction ($v4$), and packaging reduction ($v5$) are the activities most associated with respondents' perceptions of CSR.

To identify the influence of each environmental protection activity on the CSR level, we calculated the estimated parameters for each dependent variable (Table 10.3).

The analysis of significance levels of independent variables concerning the dependent Variable $v7$ shows that organizations' actions toward increasing sustainable transportation are not strongly associated with the variable describing the level of CSR activities. The effect size (partial eta squared) is illustrated in Fig. 10.7. From the analysis of Fig. 10.7, we found that the most important environmental protection activity associated with the CSR level is the reduction of air pollutants, followed by waste reduction and recycling.

The conclusion drawn from the ANOVA is that CSR is described by entrepreneurial activities related to waste reduction, followed by packaging reduction and air pollution reduction, according to the respondents' perceptions in the research (which validates *H1*).

The investigation of *H2* involved studying the influence of green entrepreneurial activities on organizational financial performance in the perception of employees engaged in such activities (waste reduction, waste recycling, energy conservation, air pollution reduction, packaging reduction, and ensuring sustainable transportation). Organizational financial performance is measured through

Table 10.2.   Multivariate Tests on the Relationships Between CSR and Green Entrepreneurship Activities.

Effects		Value	F	Hypothesis df	Error df	Significance	Partial Eta Squared	Observed Power
Intercept	Pillai's trace	0.390	61.978	3.000	291.000	0.000	0.390	1.000
	Wilks' lambda	0.610	61.978	3.000	291.000	0.000	0.390	1.000
	Hotelling's trace	0.639	61.978	3.000	291.000	0.000	0.390	1.000
	Roy's largest root	0.639	61.978	3.000	291.000	0.000	0.390	1.000
$v1$	Pillai's trace	0.142	16.059	3.000	291.000	0.000	0.142	1.000
	Wilks' lambda	0.858	16.059	3.000	291.000	0.000	0.142	1.000
	Hotelling's trace	0.166	16.059	3.000	291.000	0.000	0.142	1.000
	Roy's largest root	0.166	16.059	3.000	291.000	0.000	0.142	1.000
$v2$	Pillai's trace	0.389	61.674	3.000	291.000	0.000	0.389	1.000
	Wilks' lambda	0.611	61.674	3.000	291.000	0.000	0.389	1.000
	Hotelling's trace	0.636	61.674	3.000	291.000	0.000	0.389	1.000
	Roy's largest root	0.636	61.674	3.000	291.000	0.000	0.389	1.000
$v3$	Pillai's trace	0.089	9.476	3.000	291.000	0.000	0.089	0.997
	Wilks' lambda	0.911	9.476	3.000	291.000	0.000	0.089	0.997
	Hotelling's trace	0.098	9.476	3.000	291.000	0.000	0.089	0.997
	Roy's largest root	0.098	9.476	3.000	291.000	0.000	0.089	0.997

		Value	F					
v4	Pillai's trace	0.536	112.260	3.000	291.000	0.000	0.536	1.000
	Wilks' lambda	0.464	112.260	3.000	291.000	0.000	0.536	1.000
	Hotelling's trace	1.157	112.260	3.000	291.000	0.000	0.536	1.000
	Roy's largest root	1.157	112.260	3.000	291.000	0.000	0.536	1.000
v5	Pillai's trace	0.247	31.760	3.000	291.000	0.000	0.247	1.000
	Wilks' lambda	0.753	31.760	3.000	291.000	0.000	0.247	1.000
	Hotelling's trace	0.327	31.760	3.000	291.000	0.000	0.247	1.000
	Roy's largest root	0.327	31.760	3.000	291.000	0.000	0.247	1.000
v6	Pillai's trace	0.104	11.243	3.000	291.000	0.000	0.104	0.999
	Wilks' lambda	0.896	11.243	3.000	291.000	0.000	0.104	0.999
	Hotelling's trace	0.116	11.243	3.000	291.000	0.000	0.104	0.999
	Roy's largest root	0.116	11.243	3.000	291.000	0.000	0.104	0.999

Source: Developed by the authors based on collected data.

Table 10.3.   Estimated Model Parameters on the Relationships Between CSR and Green Entrepreneurship Activities.

Dependent Variable	Independent Variables	*B*	Standard Error	*t*	Significance	Partial Eta Squared	Observed Power
*v*7	Intercept	3.013	0.259	11.632	0.000	0.316	1.000
	*v*1	−0.211	0.035	−5.981	0.000	0.109	1.000
	*v*2	−0.127	0.026	−4.824	0.000	0.074	0.998
	*v*3	0.092	0.021	4.458	0.000	0.064	0.993
	*v*4	0.663	0.046	14.366	0.000	0.413	1.000
	*v*5	−0.116	0.046	−2.541	0.012	0.022	0.716
	*v*6	0.047	0.034	1.392	0.165	0.007	0.284

Source: Developed by the authors based on collected data.

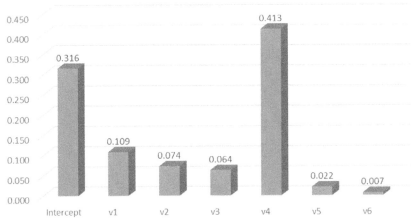

Fig. 10.7.   Effect Size Within the Level of CSR Activities. *Source*: Developed by the authors based on collected data.

perceptions of performance compared to the previous year and performance compared to expectations regarding profit and turnover.

We used SEM to test the direct relationships between green entrepreneurial activities and organizational financial performance. The tested model assumes the existence of direct relationships between variables defining green entrepreneurial activities and variables defining financial performance concerning the previous year and expectations. The model, obtained using SMARTPLS v3.0, is illustrated in Fig. 10.8.

The constructed model is formative, with CSR variables comprising the concept of CSR. The latent variables are CSR, the level of profit and turnover of the

Fig. 10.8. PLS Model Applied to Direct Relationships Between Green Entrepreneurial Activities and Financial Performance Compared to the Previous Year
and Expectations.
Source: Developed by the authors based on collected data.

Table 10.4. Multicollinearity of Variables in the PLS Model.

	VIF
*v*1	1.545
*v*2	1.915
*v*3	1.113
*v*4	2.308
*v*5	1.876
*v*6	1.193
*v*8	1.067
*v*9	1.492
*v*10	2.080
*v*11	1.570

Source: Developed by the authors based on collected data.

company in 2022 compared to the previous year, and the profit and turnover of
the company in 2022 compared to expectations.

It is necessary to avoid the multicollinearity of variables, meaning that the
variance inflation factor (VIF) should be less than 3 to be valid. Table 10.4 presents the VIF values for the previous model.

The model is relevant, presenting significant indicators for its validity Standardized
Root Mean Square Residual (SRMR) = 0.078 < 0.08; Normed Fit Index (NFI)
= 0.951 > 0.9). The path coefficients obtained using bootstrapping within the
Partial least squares (PLS) model are presented in Table 10.5.

All relationships established between green entrepreneurial activities and
indicators of organizational financial performance are significant ($p < 0.001$).
However, differentiation in the intensity of relationships is evident. This could
be explained by the fact that green entrepreneurial activities create high expectations. More environmentally responsible behavior by the organization will lead

Table 10.5.   Path Coefficients in the PLS Model.

	Path Coefficient	Standard Deviation	*t* Statistics	*p*-Values
CSR – turnover compared to the previous year	0.861	0.079	9.1	0.005

Source: Developed by the authors based on collected data.

to long-term growth in indicators of organizational financial performance (net profit and turnover). Based on the results obtained through structural equation modeling, we confirm the validation of *H2* regarding the existence of a significant positive direct relationship between green entrepreneurial activities and organizational financial performance.

Discussions

Developing partnerships and collaborations between the private sector, nongovernmental organizations, and governmental institutions significantly promotes environmental and social responsibility and sustainable development. These partnerships facilitate the exchange of resources, expertise, and knowledge, leading to more efficient solutions and maximizing the positive impact on society and the environment. In a rapidly changing world facing significant challenges, companies have an essential role in promoting social responsibility and sustainable development. Adopting strong CSR practices and strategies contributes to building a more equitable society, protecting the environment, and ensuring a sustainable future for all (Bustamante et al., 2021).

Given the importance of significant investments in CSR and the increasing availability of reporting systems, researchers have focused on developing efficient approaches to assess the effectiveness of these investments in the corporate community. In this regard, several independent third-party companies have emerged to evaluate individual companies' CSR activities, allowing stakeholders to assess their social and environmental commitment. However, regarding the SME sector, CSR evaluation has limited representation in the specialized literature (Ward, 2017).

The environmental CSR dimension focuses on organizations' environmental impact and involves adopting eco-friendly practices, responsible management of natural resources, and reducing polluting emissions. It is becoming increasingly crucial in climate change and environmental degradation. On the other hand, the social CSR dimension refers to organizations' responsibility toward the community they operate and their stakeholders. It involves supporting the local community through social development projects, promoting human rights, ensuring an ethical work environment, and fostering diversity within the organization. These two dimensions, environmental CSR and social CSR, along with the economic dimension, form a solid framework for evaluating CSR risk in three aspects: social, environmental, and governance (Szczanowicz & Saniuk, 2016). Thus, the multidimensional approach to CSR and classification into social, environmental, and governance dimensions provide organizations with a solid foundation to develop and implement effective CSR strategies, ensuring that their impact is positive and sustainable economically, socially, and environmentally (Bachnik et al., 2022).

It is essential to underline that investments in CSR should not be seen merely as additional expenses but as an opportunity to create sustainable value and contribute to overall societal development. Therefore, the comparative analysis of financial results in the context of social and environmental CSR provides organizations with a valuable framework for strategic decision-making and alignment with the needs and expectations of society (Mitra & Schmidpeter, 2021).

Theoretical Implications

The findings of our study open new perspectives and emphasize the importance of perceptual analysis in understanding the impact of green initiatives on organizational financial performance. First, the theoretical implications of this study reaffirm that employee involvement in green entrepreneurial activities plays an essential role in the success and sustainability of these initiatives. The perceptual approach reveals that employees are motivated and more engaged in an organization that adopts an environmentally responsible culture and promotes eco-friendly practices. Thus, employee involvement is critical to successfully incorporating green practices into the organizational culture and operations.

Our findings support the idea that the perceptual approach provides a more comprehensive and in-depth perspective in evaluating the impact of green entrepreneurial activities on organizational financial performance. Understanding employees' experiences, values, and perceptions regarding ecological initiatives adds a human and sensitive dimension to the study of this field, thus offering a more holistic view of the relationship between environmental responsibility and financial success. Besides these aspects, the perceptual approach can offer valuable clues in identifying the motivational and behavioral factors underlying employees' commitment and active participation in green practices. Understanding these aspects help develop more effective strategies to involve employees in environmental initiatives, directly impacting organizational financial performance.

This study also highlights the relevance and importance of management strategies that promote an organizational culture focused on sustainability and environmental responsibility. Thus, the research results can be helpful to managers and leaders, providing them with guidance and relevant information for developing sustainable policies and practices that support financial performance and employee engagement.

The perceptual approach reveals the crucial role of employees in successfully implementing green practices and brings a human and holistic perspective to the relationship between environmental responsibility and organizational financial success. The results of this study can be used as a foundation for developing efficient and sustainable strategies that encourage employees' involvement and commitment to environmental initiatives, benefiting both organizations and the environment.

Practical and Managerial Implications

The research results guide leaders and managers in developing sustainable policies and practices that support ecological objectives and maximize organizational financial performance. One of the main practical implications of this study is related to the importance of promoting an organizational culture focused on sustainability and environmental responsibility. Organizational leaders should develop and support a culture that encourages and motivates employees to engage in green practices and contribute to the company's environmental goals. In this sense, awareness and training sessions can be organized to inform and inspire employees to adopt more sustainable behaviors in their daily activities. Another practical implication is involving employees in the organizational decision-making process regarding green practices. Employees can be consulted and engaged in identifying and implementing ecological initiatives, making them feel more involved and responsible for the results. This involvement increases commitment and better integrates green practices into the organizational culture. Managers should be aware of the importance of stimulating and recognizing employees who contribute significantly to green entrepreneurial activities. Rewarding employees for their eco-friendly initiatives and environmental protection increases their motivation and commitment to these activities. Collaboration and involvement in joint projects to protect the environment enhance the organization's reputation and strengthen ties with the community. These partnerships provide opportunities for exchanging experiences and best practices, contributing to the organization's sustainable development. Promoting an organizational culture focused on sustainability, involving employees in the decision-making process, stimulating and recognizing their contributions, and developing partnerships with local communities are essential for successfully integrating green practices and achieving superior financial performance. The active involvement of employees in environmental initiatives can become a determining factor in the success and sustainability of organizations in a world increasingly concerned with environmental protection and sustainable development.

Conclusions

Our study investigated how ecological initiatives and an environmentally oriented organizational culture influenced employees' involvement, commitment, and satisfaction and, consequently, the financial performance of organizations. In this endeavor, we identified that employees' involvement in green entrepreneurial activities and efforts to protect the environment is not merely an obligation or requirement from the company but can be a significant motivational factor for employees. Commitment to the organization's environmental objectives can create a sense of pride and belonging, giving employees a broader perspective on contributing to a more significant cause. Consequently, this approach can lead to increased morale and team spirit, with beneficial effects on productivity and efficiency. Another important aspect highlighted by this study is that employees are more likely to feel motivated and engaged when the organization adopts a culture of environmental responsibility, integrating concern for sustainability and environmental impact at all decision-making and operational levels. Through such a culture, employees perceive their daily efforts as having a greater purpose and long-term relevance, which increases their commitment and loyalty to the organization.

Employees' satisfaction with the ecological organizational culture creates a positive dynamic and contagious effect on pro-environment attitudes and behaviors. Satisfied and motivated employees adopting more sustainable practices become internal ambassadors for ecological initiatives, inspiring and involving other colleagues in environmental protection efforts. This study emphasized the importance of the perceptual approach in evaluating the impact of green entrepreneurial activities on organizational financial performance from employees' perspectives. When organizations understand and adequately integrate employees' perspectives into their ecological strategies, they benefit from increased involvement and commitment, positively impacting their financial success and long-term sustainability. Thus, promoting an organizational culture that is environmentally responsible represents not only a moral initiative but also a source of competitive advantages and sustainable growth in a changing world where social and environmental responsibilities become increasingly crucial for business success.

Limitations and Future Research

Although our study brought a valuable and relevant perspective on evaluating the impact of green entrepreneurial activities on organizational financial performance from employees' perspective, it is essential to acknowledge and address some limitations that may influence the interpretation of our results and highlight possible directions for future research. One of the main limitations of this study concerns the use of a perceptual approach. Although employees' perspective provides a valuable understanding of how ecological initiatives influence their behavior and commitment, some subjects may report their opinions subjectively, thus influencing the results. In future research, mixed approaches can be adopted, including objective measurements of financial performance, to obtain a more complete and balanced picture. The temporal dimension of our research represents another limitation. Evaluating the impact of green entrepreneurial activities on financial performance may require a more extended period to identify and measure these initiatives' long-term effects adequately. In the future, longitudinal studies can be conducted, tracking organizations over a more extended period to observe the evolution of their financial performance after adopting ecological practices. Future research can also address different industries or economic sectors to obtain a more comprehensive and comparative understanding of the impact of green entrepreneurial activities on financial performance. Different sectors may have specific needs and challenges regarding social and environmental responsibility, and further research can guide sector-specific strategies and policies. A more detailed exploration of the work environment and organizational culture within organizations adopting green practices can be essential research directions. Understanding how organizational culture and management styles influence the implementation and impact of these initiatives can provide valuable insights for developing effective and sustainable strategies.

References

Aguilera-Caracuel, J., & Ortiz-de-Mandojana, N. (2013). Green innovation and financial performance. *Organization and Environment, 26*, 365–385. http://doi.org/10.1177/1086026613507931

Bachnik, K., Kazmierczak, M., Rojek-Nowosielska, M., Stefanska, M., & Szumniak-Samolej, J. (2022). *Corporate social responsibility and sustainability: From values to impact*. Taylor & Francis Ltd.

Boaventura, J. M. G., Silva, R. S. D., & Bandeira-de-Mello, R. (2012). Corporate financial and social performance: Methodological Development and the theoretical contribution of empirical studies. *Revista Contabilidade and Finanças, 23*(60), 232–245.

Buhanita, I. (2015). Dimensions in CSR: An evaluation of current definitions. *Romanian Journal of Journalism and Communication, 10*(4), 64–72.

Bustamante, S., Pizzutilo, F., Martinovic, M., & Olarte, S. H. (Eds.). (2021). *Corporate social responsibility and employer attractiveness: An international perspective*. Springer.

Çalıyurt, K. T. (Ed.). (2021). *New approaches to CSR, sustainability and accountability* (Vol. II). Springer.

Chaudhry, N. I., & Amir, M. (2020). From institutional pressure to the sustainable development of the firm: The role of environmental management accounting implementation and environmental proactivity. *Business Strategy and the Environment, 29*, 3542–3554. http://doi.org/10.1002/bse.2595

Dai, J., Cantor, D. E., & Montabon, F. L. (2015). How environmental management competitive pressure affects a focal firm's environmental innovation activities: A green supply chain perspective. *Journal of Business Logistics, 36*, 242–259. http://doi.org/10.1111/jbl.12094

Dathe, T., Dathe, R., Dathe, I., & Helmold, M. (2022). *Corporate social responsibility (CSR), sustainability and environmental social governance (ESG): Approaches to ethical management (management for professionals)*. Springer.

Dean, T. J., & McMullen, J. S. (2007). Toward a theory of sustainable entrepreneurship: Reducing environmental degradation through entrepreneurial action. *Journal of Business Venturing, 22*, 50–76. http://doi.org/10.1016/j.jbusvent.2005.09.003

Dimitropoulos, P., & Koronios, K. (2021). *Corporate environmental responsibility, accounting, and corporate finance in the E.U.: A quantitative analysis approach*. Springer.

Dubey, R., Gunasekaran, A., & Ali, S. S. (2015). Exploring the relationship between leadership, operational practices, institutional pressures, and environmental performance: A framework for green supply chain. *International Journal of Production Economics, 160*, 120–132. http://doi.org/10.1016/j.ijpe.2014.10.001

Elkington, J. (1994). Towards the sustainable corporation – Win–win–win business strategies for sustainable development. *California Management Review, 36*, 90–100.

Guo, Y., & Wang, L. (2022). Environmental entrepreneurial orientation and firm performance: The role of environmental innovation and stakeholder pressure. *SAGE Open, 12*, 21582440211. http://doi.org/10.1177/21582440211061354

Guo, Y., Wang, L., & Chen, Y. (2020). Green entrepreneurial orientation and green innovation: The mediating effect of supply chain learning. *SAGE Open, 10*, 215824401989879. http://doi.org/10.1177/2158244019898798

Hahn, R. (2022). *Sustainability management: Global perspectives on concepts, instruments, and stakeholders*. Rüdiger Hahn.

Hair, J. F., Hult, G. T. M., Ringle, C. M., & Sarstedt, M. A. (2017). *Primer on partial least squares structural equation modeling (PLS-SEM)* (2nd ed.). SAGE Publications Ltd.

Kalyar, M. N., Shoukat, A., & Shafique, I. (2019). Enhancing firms' environmental performance and financial performance through green supply chain management practices and institutional pressures. *Sustainability Accounting, Management and Policy Journal, 11*, 451–476. http://doi.org/10.1108/SAMPJ-02-2019-0047

Laasch, O. (2021). *Principles of management: Practicing ethics, responsibility, sustainability.* SAGE Publications Ltd.

Lee, S., & Jung, H. (2016). The effects of corporate social responsibility on profitability: The moderating roles of differentiation and outside investment. *Management Decision, 54*(6), 1383–1406.

Leonidou, L. C., Christodoulides, P., Kyrgidou, L. P., & Palihawadana, D. (2015). Internal drivers and performance consequences of small firm green business strategy: The moderating role of external forces. *Journal of Business Ethics, 140,* 585–606. http://doi.org/10.1007/s10551-015-2670-9

Lin, Y. H., & Chen, H. C. (2018). Critical factors for enhancing green service innovation: Linking green relationship quality and green entrepreneurial orientation. *Journal of Hospitality and Tourism Technology, 9,* 188–203. http://doi.org/10.1108/JHTT-02-2017-0014

Liu, N., Hu, H., & Wang, Z. (2022). The relationship between institutional pressure, green entrepreneurial orientation, and entrepreneurial performance – The moderating effect of network centrality. *Sustainability, 14,* 12055. https://doi.org/10.3390/su141912055

McWilliams, A., & Siegel, D. (2001). Corporate social responsibility: A theory of the firm perspective. *Academy of Management Review, 26*(1), 117–128.

Mitra, N., & Schmidpeter, R. (Eds.). (2021). *Corporate social responsibility in rising economies: Fundamentals, approaches, and case studies.* Springer.

Opkara, J. O., & Idowu, S. O. (Eds.). (2013). *Corporate social responsibility: Challenges, opportunities, and strategies for 21st century leaders.* Springer.

Qian, W., & Burritt, R. (2009). The development of environment management accounting: An institutional view. *Ecological Economics and Industrial Ecology, 24,* 233–248. http://doi.org/10.1007/978-1-4020-8913-8_12

Schaper, M. T. (Ed.). (2010). Understanding the green entrepreneur. In *Making ecopreneurs: Developing sustainable entrepreneurship* (pp. 7–20). MPG Book Group.

Song, S., Hossin, M. A., Yin, X., & Hosain, M. S. (2021). Accelerating green innovation performance from the relations of network potential, absorptive capacity, and environmental turbulence. *Sustainability, 13,* 7765. http://doi.org/10.3390/su13147765

Sun, J., Yao, M., Zhang, W., Chen, Y., & Liu, Y. (2016). Entrepreneurial environment, market-oriented strategy, and entrepreneurial performance: A study of Chinese automobile firms. *Internet Research, 26,* 546–562. http://doi.org/10.1108/IntR-05-2015-0138

Szczanowicz, J., & Saniuk, S. (2016). Evaluation and reporting of CSR in SME sector. *Management, 20*(1), 96–110.

Wahga, A. I., Blundel, R., & Schaefer, A. (2018). Understanding the drivers of sustainable entrepreneurial practices in Pakistan's leather industry. *International Journal of Entrepreneurial Behavior & Research, 24,* 382–407. http://doi.org/10.1108/IJEBR-11-2015-0263

Ward, S. (2017). *SME definition. The balance.* Retrieved July 27, 2023, from https://www.thebalancemoney.com/sme-small-to-medium-enterprise-definition-2947962

Yang, C. S. (2018). An analysis of institutional pressures, green supply chain management, and green performance in the container shipping context. *Transportation Research Part D: Transport and Environment, 61,* 246–260. http://doi.org/10.1016/j.trd.2017.07.005

Chapter 11

The Impact of the COVID-19 Pandemic on Dividend Policy Relevance to Firm Value: The Case of the Indonesian Banking Industry

Cliff Oliver Winoto and Felizia Arni Rudiawarni

Universitas Surabaya, Indonesia

Abstract

Banking industry is synonymous to larger dividend payment compared to other sectors. The complexity of dividend policy is further exacerbated by the occurrence of COVID-19 pandemic. This research is aimed to test the impact of COVID-19 pandemic on dividend policy relevance to firm value (FV). FV is measured by firm market value (MV) and TOBINSQ. Meanwhile, dividend policy is measured by dividend payout ratio and dividend yield ratio. This research used Indonesian Banking Companies listed in Indonesia Stock Exchange Period 2018–2022. This research does not find a significant impact of dividend policy on FV and supports Irrelevance Theory, both for pre-COVID-19 pandemic and during COVID-19 pandemic. However, this research finds differing significant impact on each bank's common equity tier that reflects the dynamic expectation imposed by the market for each common equity tier. This research also finds a more profound negative and significant impact of dividend policy on FV for state-owned banks compared to private banks. Furthermore, banking-specific performance measurement like a non-performing loan (NPL) and capital adequacy ratio (CAR) consistently impacts the banks' FV.

Keywords: Dividend policy; firm value; COVID-19; Irrelevance theory; signaling theory

Entrepreneurship and Development for a Green Resilient Economy, 277–296
Copyright © 2024 by Cliff Oliver Winoto and Felizia Arni Rudiawarni
Published under exclusive licence by Emerald Publishing Limited
doi:10.1108/978-1-83797-088-920241011

Introduction

Financial service firms, including banks, are associated with large, stable, and regular dividend payments (Gambacorta et al., 2020; Hutagalung et al., 2013). Banks tend to retain dividend payments instead of shifting to share repurchase as displayed by firms in other industries (Floyd et al., 2015); 49.5% of the Indonesia Stock Exchange (IDX) High Dividend 20 Index (IDXHIDIV20), based on the August 2022 release, is composed of banks. Three banks topped the Top 10 dividend payments in IDXHIDIV20, sequentially, as follows: PT Bank Mandiri (Persero) Tbk., PT Bank Central Asia Tbk., and PT Bank Rakyat Indonesia (Persero) Tbk. Meanwhile, PT Bank Negara Indonesia (Persero) Tbk. also manages to occupy the ninth position on the list.

Indonesian banks are under strict supervision from investors, Bank Indonesia, Otoritas Jasa Keuangan, and other interested stakeholders. Banks are required to maintain 6% Tier 1 capital and 4.5% common equity Tier 1 as mandated by Basel III. Capital adequacy requirement is stipulated under Financial Services Authority Regulations No. 11/POJK.03/2016 about Minimum Capital Adequacy Requirement for Commercial Banks (POJK 11). However, dividend disbursement is only alluded in Article 46 of POJK 11, which barely touches upon the subject. Banks are prohibited from paying dividends when there is a tendency to decrease capital or increase risk.

Dividend policy complexity increases as COVID-19 pandemic strikes. The COVID-19 pandemic's adverse effect has beaten down gross domestic product (GDP), goods and services trades, foreign direct investment, and money circulation (Rathnayaka et al., 2023). As a mitigation act against the pervasive spread of COVID-19 virus, the Indonesian government enacted large-scale social restriction in 2020 under Government Regulation No. 21 Year 2020 regarding large-scale social restriction in the effort to handle COVID-19.

During the 2008 financial crisis, dividend cuts were more prevalent in the financial service sector than in other sectors (Krieger et al., 2021). At the same time, as Signaling Theory suggests, dividend has been utilized as a signaling tool by managers (Al-Yahyaee et al., 2011; Black, 1976; de Wet & Mpinda, 2013; Floyd et al., 2015; Goddard et al., 2006; Ham et al., 2020; Karpavičius, 2014; Sarwar, 2013; Suwanna, 2012; Tekin & Polat, 2021). Dividend cuts or omissions might negatively affect the firm (Lie, 2005). Dividend gains importance for lower core capital banks during a crisis (Tripathy et al., 2021).

Despite the empirical evidences that many researchers have provided, the seminal paper by Miller and Modigliani (1961) lays an opposing foundation called Irrelevance Theory. This theory advocates the absence of information borne by dividends, hence the irrelevance in terms of FV. The FV should be measured by its ability to generate cash for investors. Share repurchase and institutional investors are of the many factors that reduce the importance of dividends (Amihud & Li, 2006; Fama & French, 2001; Grullon & Michaely, 2004; Lo et al., 2017). Budagaga (2020) found empirical evidence that supports the Irrelevance Theory in Middle Eastern and North African countries.

Therefore, to enrich the previous researches, this chapter will examine the impact of dividend policy relevance to FV in listed Indonesian banks. Additionally, this research will moderate the independent variable to accommodate the COVID-19 pandemic period. It is imperative to understand the difference in effect toward FV during the COVID-19 pandemic.

Theoretical Framework

Miller and Modigliani (1961), with their Irrelevance Theory, have sparked interest and debates on the dividend puzzle. Irrelevance Theory believes that dividend announcements and payment do not impact FV (Al-Malkawi et al., 2010). Budagaga (2020) explains that without dividend disbursement, retained earnings can be managed to produce future earnings and realized as capital gain in the future. This theory assumed effective market, market rational behavior, and perfect certainty. Miller–Modigliani Theorem also provides mathematical argumentation that dividend policy does not impact shareholders' value. Firms that pay dividends are consequently obliged to seek external funds to finance their investments. Gain from dividend payments is balanced by the increasing cost of external funds. This theory argues that the present value of dividend payments would equal the stock's terminal value.

Relevance Theory believes that dividend payments would contribute to increasing FV. Dividend has been empirically proven to be a value-relevant information for firm valuation (Al-Malkawi et al., 2010; Hussainey et al., 2011; Litzenberger & Ramaswamy, 1979; Miller & Scholes, 1982; Okafor et al., 2011). Siegel (2014) analyzes S&P 500 companies from 1957 to 2012 and classifies them into five classes based on dividend yield to the following: (1) highest, (2) high, (3) middle, (4) low, and (5) lowest. The highest and high dividend yield firms beat other classes in terms of rate of return.

A sub-theory of the Relevance Theory, called Dividend Signaling Theory, explains that dividend is useful to accommodate information asymmetry. Dividend communicates earning information from the firm internal team to external parties (Chen & Dhiensiri, 2009). Price movement is not derived from the dividend itself but is caused by the information content of the dividend. Dividend cut and omission negatively impacts FV (Baker et al., 2012; Lie, 2005; Miller & Rock, 1985). Lintner (1956) and Gordon (1959) explain that investors prefer a bird in the hand (dividend) compared to two birds in the bushes (capital gain).

Agency Theory is also used to justify dividend relevance. As the most liquid asset, cash presents management with unwanted agency problems (Dittmar et al., 2003; Labhane & Mahakud, 2016; Shi, 2019; Yeo, 2018; Zhang et al., 2016). Excess cash is perceived as a cause of agency problems, and dividend is viewed as a control tool (Hussain & Akbar, 2022; Kadioglu & Yilmaz, 2017; Trong & Nguyen, 2021).

Hypothesis Development

Al-Malkawi et al. (2010) summarize dividend (ir)relevance research that has been conducted and classify the findings as follows: (1) dividend payment increases FV (Suwanna, 2012; Thomsen, 2004); (2) dividend payment reduces FV (Habib et al., 2012); and (3) dividend payment does not affect FV (Al-Saedi, 2010; Budagaga, 2020). However, more research has been conducted on developed countries and less on emerging countries. Pinto et al. (2020) plotted dividend policy research and found that the top contributing countries have been the United States and the United Kingdom. Emerging countries have different characteristics than developed ones (Adaoglu, 2000). Developed countries are characterized by more efficient markets, extensive competition, sufficient liquidity, experiences, information availability, and higher taxes (Budagaga, 2020). Thus, this research proposed the following hypothesis:

H1. Ceteris paribus, dividend policy positively affects the value of banking industry companies listed on the IDX.

The financial services sector is more vulnerable to domestic and global shocks (Wang et al., 2018). The banking business model is prone to the contagion effect, as displayed during the 2008 financial crisis and 2015 eurozone crisis (Cecchetti & Schoenholtz, 2020). Customer's confidence crisis in banks' solvability level can spread quickly and create a first-mover advantage. Customers who cash out first will receive full returns, while those who are slow to withdraw potentially lose their savings. Several researchers provide evidence that firms are more inclined to cut, omit, or delay dividend payments during COVID-19 pandemic (Krieger et al., 2021; Pettenuzzo et al., 2023). Pandey and Kumari (2022) find that COVID-19 fails to generate significant abnormal returns as compared to previous years. However, some still find dividends as a potential signaling tool during the COVID-19 pandemic (Ali, 2022; Eugster et al., 2022). Thus, the different views on previous studies result in the following hypothesis:

H2. Ceteris paribus, COVID-19 pandemic moderates the effect of dividend policy on FV in Indonesian listed banks.

Research Method

This study uses a data panel. The observation consists of all banks listed in the IDX Period 2018–2022. The data are taken from www.idx.co.id, www.finance. yahoo.com and the corresponding company's website. This research uses data that fulfill the sample criteria, which are (1) the financial statement for the year should be published, (2) the financial statement uses Rupiah as the reporting currency, and (3) the reporting period ended every December 31 every year.

FV Calculation

The dependent variable in this research is FV. It is measured using two proxies: MV and Tobin's Q (TOBINSQ). MV is calculated using the following formula:

$$MV_{i,t} = \ln(P_{i,t} \quad SO_{i,t}) \qquad (1)$$

where $MV_{i,t}$ is the MV; $P_{i,t}$, the adjusted closing price; $SO_{i,t}$, number of shares outstanding; i, firm i; and t, period t (end of year).

Meanwhile, TOBINSQ is calculated using the following formula:

$$TOBINSQ_{i,t} = (MV_{i,t} + DEBT_{i,t}) / TA_{i,t} \qquad (2)$$

where $TOBINSQ_{i,t}$ is the value of firm; $MV_{i,t}$, the MV of firm; $DEBT_{i,t}$, the total liabilities book value; $TA_{i,t}$, the total assets book value; i, firm i; and t, the period t (end of year).

Dividend Policy Calculation

The independent variable is dividend policy (DIV). It is measured using two proxies: dividend payouts (DPOR) and dividend yield (DYR). DPOR is calculated using the following formula:

$$DPOR_{i,t} = DPS_{i,t} / EPS_{i,t} \qquad (3)$$

where $DPOR_{i,t}$ is the dividend payout ratio; $DPS_{i,t}$, the dividend per share; $EPS_{i,t}$, the earnings per share; i, the firm i and t, the period t (end of year).

Meanwhile, DYR is calculated using the following formula:

$$DYR_{i,t} = DPS_{i,t} / P_{i,t} \qquad (4)$$

Hypothesis Testing Design

$$FV_{i,t} = \alpha + \beta_1 DIV_{i,t} + \beta_2 COVID_{i,t} + \beta_3 DIV_{i,t} * COVID_{i,t} + \beta_4 RI_{i,t}$$
$$+ \beta_5 SIZE_{i,t} + \beta_6 NPL_{i,t} + \beta_7 CAR_{i,t} + \varepsilon_{i,t} \qquad (5)$$

where FV represents firm value, proxied by MV and TOBINSQ; DIV is dividend policy, proxied by DPOR and DYR. While COVID is a dummy variable, 1 for COVID-19 pandemic period (2020, 2021, and 2022) and 0 otherwise (2018 and 2019). RI refers to residual income (RI) following Budagaga (2020). SIZE is calculated as the natural logarithm of total assets. The two variables are the specific measurements of a bank's performance: NPLs and CAR. NPLs are the quality of assets a bank owns. NPL is the ratio of NPLs to total loans of Bank i in Year t, while CAR is used as an indicator of bank capital resilience. Banks with higher CAR levels are considered safer and have better resilience. CAR is calculated as the ratio of total equity to total assets (Saif-Alyousfi, 2020).

Data Analysis and Discussion

Table 11.1 shows sample selection criteria for the research object. The observation of the study consisted of 229 data, and samples that met the criteria were 218 data.

Table 11.1.   Sample Selection Criteria for Research Object.

Description	2018	2019	2020	2021	2022	Total
All banks listed in Indonesian Stock Exchange during 2018–2022	45	45	45	47	47	229
Criteria for eliminating the sample						
1. Firms that do not publish financial statement	−2	−2	0	0	−1	−5
2. Firms that do not use Indonesian Rupiah as reporting currency	0	0	0	0	0	0
3. Firms that do not end the reporting period on December 31 every year	0	0	0	0	0	0
4. Firms suspended from Indonesian Stock Exchange trading	−3	−2	−1	0	0	−6
Companies that fulfilled the criteria	**40**	**41**	**44**	**47**	**46**	**218**

Source: Authors' data processing.

Multiple Regression Result

Result Discussions and Theoretical Implications for the First Hypothesis

Table 11.2 depicts the results of the empirical test for our hypothesis. We use four models representing different measurements for FV (MV and Tobin's Q) and dividend policy (dividend payout ratio and dividend yield).

The first hypothesis is not supported, meaning dividend policy has an insignificant impact on FV. This result is consistent in all models (Models 1–4) used in this research. Our finding supports the Irrelevance Theory proposed by Miller and Modigliani (1961). This result does not support Relevance Theory, including Dividend Signaling Theory and Agency Theory. Dividend irrelevance shown in our findings can be viewed as the absence of information content and impact on cash inflows from investors' perspective. Dividend is not considered an effective tool to mitigate agency problems within banks (Budagaga, 2020). Stringent regulation and overseeing authorities in the banking industry might contribute to the insignificance of dividends in this sector, as those might be able to reduce agency problems.

The banking industry has been proven to adhere to a residual dividend policy (Al-Saedi, 2010). This policy prioritizes investment policies compared to dividend policies. As much as 75% of company directors in Indonesia also believe that

Table 11.2.   Multiple Regression Test Result.

	Dependent Variable: MV	**Dependent Variable: MV**	**Dependent Variable: TOBINSQ**	**Dependent Variable: TOBINSQ**
	Model 1	**Model 2**	**Model 3**	**Model 4**
Constant	4.040	2.500	−6.741	−6.877
(*t*-statistic)	(2.150)	(1.246)	(−0.608)	(−0.624)
DPOR	0.177	− (−)	0.195	− (−)
	(0.777)		(0.357)	
DYR	− (−)	−5.603	− (−)	0.016
		(−1.165)		(0.001)
COVID	0.243 ***	0.227 **	0.039	0.054
	(2.386)	(2.100)	(0.149)	(0.194)
DPORCOVID	−0.181	− (−)	−0.112	− (−)
	(−0.692)		(−0.178)	
DYRCOVID	− (−)	−2.539	− (−)	−2.451
		(−0.644)		(−0.258)
RI	−0.000	−0.000	−0.000 **	−0.000 **
	(−0.862)	(−0.934)	(−1.691)	(−1.685)
SIZE	0.814 ***	0.866 ***	0.230	0.235
	(13.761)	(13.562)	(0.650)	(0.668)
NPL	−6.582 ***	−6.435 ***	−9.946 **	−9.568 **
	(−3.172)	(−3.129)	(−1.759)	(−1.698)
CAR	1.140 ***	1.134 ***	3.713 ***	3.700 ***
	(6.279)	(6.238)	(5.851)	(5.831)
Adjusted R^2	0.575	0.577	0.523	0.523
F statistic	42.894 ***	43.249 ***	5.484 ***	5.481 ***
Testing	REM	REM	FEM	FEM

Source: Authors' data processing.

*, **, *** significant at 10%, 5% and 1% level, respectively. One-tailed test.

CEM = Common Effect Model; FEM = Fixed Effect Model; REM = Random Effect Model

cash dividends should be distributed as residuals after all investment options have been used up (Baker & Powell, 2012). Banks tend to prioritize fund allocation to investments that can provide a beneficial rate of return. The remaining uninvested funds are distributed to investors in the form of dividends (Smith, 2011). Therefore, banks' decision to distribute dividends can be interpreted as a lack of investment options. Conversely, a bank that does not pay dividends cannot be directly interpreted as a company with poor performance. Thus, dividends can only provide an overview of residual profits, not banks' earnings performance.

Result Discussions and Theoretical Implications for the Second Hypothesis

The second hypothesis is not supported, which means COVID-19 pandemic has an insignificant impact on the effect of dividend policy on FV. This result is consistent for all models used in this research. Our finding further supports the Irrelevant Theory in the banking industry, which means that even during crises like the COVID-19 pandemic, the dividend is irrelevant information that can be used as a signal from managers to investors.

This result means that dividend policy is not an important factor in determining company value during the COVID-19 pandemic. The scale and distribution of the impact of the COVID-19 pandemic may override individual company policies. Szczygielski et al. (2023) find that during the COVID-19 pandemic, Google search trends, stringent government responses, and mass media coverage described the systemic impact of the COVID-19 pandemic on stock returns. Among the 35 countries tested, the performance of shares in the Indonesian Stock Exchange is the most negatively affected by the government's strict policies. Restrictive measures taken by the government might have a positive impact on reducing the spread of the COVID-19 virus but have a negative impact on the economy in the long term (Bajra et al., 2023; Cross et al., 2020; König & Winkler, 2021).

Additional Testing

Sample Split Based on Banks' Core Capital

The size of a bank is determined by its core capital (KBMI). As the core capital increases, the bank's assets also increase proportionally. According to the laws set by the Indonesian Financial Services Authority, banks are classified into four groups based on their core capital. The ranking of Group 1 (KBMI 1) is based on its smallest core capital, whereas Group 4 (KBMI 4) is ranked largest due to its highest core capital. The diverse range of bank sizes listed on the IDX can impact the results. Fu et al. (2014) and Saif-Alyousfi (2020) propose that a positive correlation exists between a bank's size and its performance. Large banks can benefit from economies of scale. This research categorizes (Tables 11.3–11.6) the sample according to bank size, specifically based on core capital.

The results from the sample split based on core capital (KBMI) show differences in the impact of dividend policy on FV at each level of the core capital group. Dividend distribution by banks with low core capital grouped under KBMI 1 has a significant negative impact on FV. This negative impact gradually diminished as core capital increased to the KBMI 2 group, as evidenced by the reduced impact of dividend policy on FV to moderate impact at the 10% significant level. Meanwhile, banks with core capital classified in KBMI 3 show a positive impact of dividend distribution on FV. Large banks classified in KBMI 4 experience no impact of dividend policy on FV.

This result can be interpreted as the response of investors to the bank's dividend policy changes along with the increase in the bank's core capital. Dividend payment in lower-capital banks has the potential to erode bank capital and increase the risk of bank failure. In addition, the distribution of dividends indicates the

Table 11.3.   Multiple Regression Test Result for KBMI 1 Banks.

	Dependent Variable: MV	Dependent Variable: MV	Dependent Variable: TOBINSQ	Dependent Variable: TOBINSQ
	Model 1	**Model 2**	**Model 3**	**Model 4**
Constant	5.958	6.904	−7.115	6.525
(*t*-statistic)	(1.380)	(1.628)	(−0.373)	(−0.345)
DPOR	−1.205 **	− (−)	0.023	− (−)
	(−1.931)		(0.013)	
DYR	− (−)	−28.765 **	− (−)	6.932
		(−2.206)		(0.177)
COVID	0.258 **	0.295 **	0.263	0.329
	(1.718)	(1.959)	(0.593)	(0.735)
DPORCOVID	1.224 **	− (−)	0.067	− (−)
	(1.882)		(0.036)	
DYRCOVID	− (−)	−2.018	− (−)	−20.656
		(−0.092)		(−0.333)
RI	−0.000	−0.000	−0.000	−0.000
	(−0.470)	(−0.347)	(−0.610)	(−0.593)
SIZE	0.755 ***	0.726 ***	0.264	0.243
	(5.290)	(5.182)	(0.415)	0.386
NPL	−6.930 ***	−7.448 ***	−10.228 *	−10.038 *
	(−2.941)	(−3.171)	(−1.359)	(−1.330)
CAR	0.959 ***	0.908 ***	2.460 ***	2.441 ***
	(4.668)	(4.460)	(2.987)	(2.962)
Adjusted R^2	0.437	0.445	0.404	0.405
F statistic	14.279 ***	14.772 ***	3.259 ***	3.266 ***
Testing	REM	REM	FEM	FEM

Source: Authors' data processing.

*, **, *** significant at 10%, 5% and 1% level, respectively. One-tailed test.

CEM = Common Effect Model; FEM = Fixed Effect Model; REM = Random Effect Model

exhaustion of investment opportunities that drive future performance and can be interpreted as an obstacle to bank growth. Dividend distribution is also considered to have the potential to disrupt bank liquidity and increase operational risk. Farag et al. (2013) and Elbadry (2018) find that the bank's core capital serves to absorb risks. Banks with low core capital are expected to accumulate capital buffers during economic booms to avoid capital shortages during economic downturns (Repullo & Suarez, 2013; Valencia & Bolaños, 2018). Thus, the market punishes banks with high dividend payout rates by decreasing the FV since the

Table 11.4. Multiple Regression Test Result for KBMI 2 Banks.

	Dependent Variable: MV	Dependent Variable: MV	Dependent Variable: TOBINSQ	Dependent Variable: TOBINSQ
	Model 1	**Model 2**	**Model 3**	**Model 4**
Constant	38.914	8.281	−38.243	−39.249
(*t*-statistic)	(2.358)	(0.630)	(−1.904)	(−1.875)
DPOR	1.026	− (−)	−0.605	− (−)
	(0.949)		(−0.962)	
DYR	− (−)	−11.054 *	− (−)	−0.335
		(−1.492)		(−0.040)
COVID	−0.001	−0.001	−0.733 **	−0.655 **
	(−0.001)	(−0.003)	(−2.246)	(−1.821)
DPORCOVID	0.111	− (−)	1.272	− (−)
	(0.068)		(1.158)	
DYRCOVID	− (−)	−6.869	− (−)	7.199
		(−0.745)		(0.867)
RI	0.003	0.006 **	−0.001	0.001
	(0.704)	(2.010)	(−0.196)	(−0.189)
SIZE	−0.314	0.667 *	1.114 *	1.143 *
	(−0.610)	(1.633)	(1.773)	(1.745)
NPL	13.927 *	2.327	−0.157	−1.749
	(1.713)	(0.384)	(−0.029)	(−0.332)
CAR	1.994 **	2.895 ***	17.275 ***	17.261 ***
	(2.300)	(4.367)	(29.716)	(27.687)
Adjusted R^2	0.268	0.294	0.994	0.993
F statistic	2.311 *	2.489 *	275.678 ***	253.492 ***
Testing	REM	REM	FEM	FEM

Source: Authors' data processing.
*, **, *** significant at 10%, 5% and 1% level, respectively. One-tailed test.
CEM = Common Effect Model; FEM = Fixed Effect Model; REM = Random Effect Model

market considers that these kinds of banks do not prepare their core capital for economic buffers. Conversely, banks that have higher levels of retained earnings (meaning lower dividend payout) are valued higher by the market.

As core capital increases, the market tends to favor dividend payment. Banks with a higher level of capital adequacy allow banks to run operations with lower funding costs (Gambacorta et al., 2020). Thus, the distribution of dividends is no longer perceived as eroding bank capital. However, banks can use dividends as a positive signal for their performance and prospects in the future. This result aligns

Table 11.5.   Multiple Regression Test Result for KBMI 3 Banks.

	Dependent Variable: MV	**Dependent Variable: MV**	**Dependent Variable: TOBINSQ**	**Dependent Variable: TOBINSQ**
	Model 1	**Model 2**	**Model 3**	**Model 4**
Constant	11.892	13.784	2.144	1.316
(*t*-statistic)	(1.648)	(1.688)	(1.399)	(0.871)
DPOR	0.515 ***	4.655	0.050 *	− (−)
	(2.622)	(0.639)	(1.547)	
DYR	− (−)	0.172	− (−)	0.476
		(0.747)		(0.408)
COVID	0.115	0.172	0.012	0.001
	(0.646)	(0.747)	(0.415)	(−0.034)
DPORCOVID	−0.448 *	− (−)	−0.066 *	− (−)
	(−1.454)		(−1.437)	
DYRCOVID	− (−)	−6.823	− (−)	−0.453
		(−0.918)		(−0.442)
RI	0.001	0.000	−0.000	−0.000
	(1.181)	(0.550)	(−0.199)	(−0.535)
SIZE	0.559 ***	0.504 **	−0.033	−0.009
	(2.648)	(2.107)	(−0.726)	(−0.193)
NPL	−14.670 ***	−11.090 ***	−3.164 ***	−2.223 **
	(−3.460)	(−2.500)	(−2.501)	(−1.880)
CAR	3.156 **	2.566	0.139	0.188
	(1.819)	(1.287)	(0.383)	(0.497)
Adjusted R^2	0.263	0.181	0.816	0.801
F statistic	3.543 ***	2.578 **	13.333 ***	12.211 ***
Testing	REM	REM	FEM	FEM

Source: Authors' data processing.
*, **, *** significant at 10%, 5% and 1% level, respectively. One-tailed test.
CEM = Common Effect Model; FEM = Fixed Effect Model; REM = Random Effect Model

with the Dividend Signaling Theory and the Bird-in-Hand Theory. At this level, dividends are used to show the superiority of a bank compared to other banks.

The ability of dividends to signal is ultimately limited to a certain level of core capital. Banks in the KBMI 4 category (highest core capital) do not require dividends as a signal for the market. At the highest level of capital, investors pay more attention to RI, NPLs, and CAR.

During the COVID-19 pandemic period, our finding shows the opposite results. In the KBMI 1 sample group (lowest core capital), dividends have a

Table 11.6.   Multiple Regression Test Result for KBMI 4 Banks.

	Dependent Variable: MV	Dependent Variable: MV	Dependent Variable: TOBINSQ	Dependent Variable: TOBINSQ
	Model 1	**Model 2**	**Model 3**	**Model 4**
Constant	−53.766	−40.436	−17.510	−15.043
(*t*-statistic)	(−1.995)	(−1.642)	(−1.941)	(−1.628)
DPOR	0.146	− (−)	0.164	− (−)
	(0.135)		0.454	
DYR	− (−)	−2.380	− (−)	−2.615
		(−0.394)		(−1.152)
COVID	−0.030	0.036	0.066	−0.075
	(−0.057)	(0.102)	0.381	(−0.559)
DPORCOVID	−0.411	− (−)	−0.276	− (−)
	(−0.391)		(−0.784)	
DYRCOVID	− (−)	−2.201	− (−)	0.969
		(−0.448)		(0.526)
RI	−0.002 ***	−0.002 ***	−0.001 ***	−0.001 ***
	(−6.883)	(−7.094)	(−7.769)	(−6.842)
SIZE	2.510 ***	2.122 ***	0.544 **	0.471 *
	(3.236)	(2.998)	(2.095)	(1.771)
NPL	−45.079 **	−50.772 ***	−14.693 **	−13.506 **
	(−2.674)	(−3.236)	(−2.603)	(−2.293)
CAR	6.971 *	8.323 **	1.342	2.188 **
	(1.682)	2.752	(0.967)	(1.928)
Adjusted R^2	0.952	0.964	0.916	0.920
F statistic	38.604 ***	51.310 ***	21.624 ***	22.790 ***
Testing	FEM	FEM	FEM	FEM

Source: Authors' data processing.
*, **, *** significant at 10%, 5% and 1% level, respectively. One-tailed test.
CEM = Common Effect Model; FEM = Fixed Effect Model; REM = Random Effect Model

significant positive effect. On the contrary, in the KBMI 3 sample group, dividends have a significant negative effect. Dividend payments are shown to be influenced by the macroeconomic context that occurs (Abreu & Gulamhussen, 2013). This result means that banks with larger sizes tend to diversify business lines, while banks with lower core capital tend to serve the local market, thereby reducing the impact of the perceived economic shock (Castrén et al., 2006). During the COVID-19 pandemic, banks with low core capital could use dividends to send a signal that the bank's prospects were better than other banks. This result is in

Table 11.7.   Multiple Regression Test Result for Government-owned Banks.

	Dependent Variable: MV	Dependent Variable: MV	Dependent Variable: |TOBINSQ	Dependent Variable: TOBINSQ
	Model 1	Model 2	Model 3	Model 4
Constant	−9.584	−16.673	−3.781	−4.749
(*t*-statistic)	(−0.602)	(−1.199)	(−1.296)	(−1.774)
DPOR	0.157 *	− (−)	0.017	− (−)
	(1.325)		(0.778)	
DYR	− (−)	−8.559 **	− (−)	−1.255 *
		(−1.953)		(−1.487)
COVID	−0.201	−0.531 ***	−0.002	−0.063 **
	(−1.031)	(−2.890)	(−0.057)	(−1.787)
DPORCOVID	−0.047	− (−)	−0.085 **	− (−)
	(−0.185)		(−1.837)	
DYRCOVID	− (−)	4.634 *	− (−)	0.272
		(1.534)		(0.467)
RI	0.000	−0.000	−0.000 *	−0.000 *
	(0.622)	(−0.727)	(−1.405)	(−1.457)
SIZE	1.247 ***	1.472 ***	0.161 **	0.191 **
	(2.602)	(3.520)	(1.834)	(2.373)
NPL	−5.109 **	−3.696 **	−2.348 ***	−2.095 ***
	(−2.176)	(−1.886)	(−5.455)	(−5.554)
CAR	−1.319 *	−0.712	−1.689 ***	−1.553 ***
	(−1.492)	(−0.796)	(−10.419)	(−9.021)
Adjusted R^2	0.986	0.987	0.949	0.948
F statistic	182.632 ***	199.039 ***	48.302 ***	47.704 ***
Testing	FEM	FEM	FEM	FEM

Source: Authors' data processing.
*, **, *** significant at 10%, 5% and 1% level, respectively. One-tailed test.
CEM = Common Effect Model; FEM = Fixed Effect Model; REM = Random Effect Model

line with Tripathy et al. (2021), who found that dividends from lower core capital banks during a crisis have a better ability to send signals of financial health.

Sample Split Based on State-owned and Private Banks

Lin et al. (2010) found that state-owned companies prefer cash dividend distributions compared to private companies. So, this research will separate the sample between private banks and state-owned banks. The empirical results can be seen in Tables 11.7 and 11.8.

Table 11.8.   Multiple Regression Test Result for Private Banks.

	Dependent Variable: MV	Dependent Variable: MV	Dependent Variable: TOBINSQ	Dependent Variable: TOBINSQ
	Model 1	Model 2	Model 3	Model 4
Constant	4.468	3.182	−6.349	−6.252
(t-statistic)	(1.952)	(1.326)	(−0.526)	(−0.521)
DPOR	−0.144	− (−)	0.207	− (−)
	(−0.285)		(0.163)	
DYR	− (−)	−10.149 *	− (−)	0.314
		(−1.424)		(0.016)
COVID	0.288 **	0.286 **	0.058	0.090
	(2.333)	(2.319)	(0.179)	(0.276)
DPORCOVID	0.150	− (−)	−0.132	− (−)
	(0.293)		(−0.103)	
DYRCOVID	− (−)	0.294	− (−)	−4.660
		(0.045)		(−0.286)
RI	−0.000	−0.000	−0.000 *	−0.000 *
	(−0.795)	(−0.841)	(−1.565)	(−1.555)
SIZE	0.797 ***	0.842	0.219	0.216
	(10.941)	(10.950)	(0.561)	(0.557)
NPL	−5.745 **	−5.800 **	−10.516*	10.234 *
	(−2.161)	(−2.184)	(−1.440)	(−1.391)
CAR	1.151 ***	1.140 ***	3.750 ***	3.735 ***
	(6.030)	(5.947)	(5.351)	(5.336)
Adjusted R^2	0.528	0.533	0.517	0.518
F statistic	30.188 ***	30.825 ***	5.264 ***	5.270 ***
Testing	REM	REM	FEM	FEM

Source: Authors' data processing.
*, **, *** significant at 10%, 5% and 1% level, respectively. One-tailed test.
CEM = Common Effect Model; FEM = Fixed Effect Model; REM = Random Effect Model

State ownership in the banking industry in various countries has been empirically proven to worsen corporate performance and governance, which is shown in terms of inefficiency, high NPLs, inexpedient lending, lower main core capital, and slow growth (Cornett et al., 2010; Hau & Thum, 2010; Jia, 2009; La Porta et al., 2002). High concentration of state ownership coupled with weak corporate governance and negative market response can be indicators of tunneling (Chen et al., 2009). Tunneling is the practice of withdrawing cash from a company for the benefit of the majority shareholder to the detriment of the minority shareholder. Investors see cash issued for dividend payments as an opportunity cost that should be reinvested in the business to spur future growth and profits. Thus, the value of state-owned banks decreases along with an increase in the dividend distribution.

According to the Indonesia Minister of Finance Regulation, state-owned enterprises are classified as business entities that are obliged to distribute payments. State-owned enterprises – including state-owned banks – in their capacity as payers, are required to distribute dividends to shareholders, including the government. Hence, the distribution of dividends by state-owned banks is a procedural and obligatory matter, which cannot depict the company's performance accurately.

Univariate Analysis on Dividend Policy Variables

Univariate test results for the dividend policy variable in Tables 11.9 and 11.10 show that there is no significant difference between the DPOR and DYR variables during the COVID-19 pandemic and the non-COVID-19 pandemic. Therefore, this result supports our main findings that there is no significant impact of dividend policy on FV.

Table 11.9.   Mean of Dividend Policy Variables.

Variable	Mean	
	COVID	**NON-COVID**
DPOR	0.165	0.173
DYR	0.012	0.014

Source: Authors' data processing.

Table 11.10.   Univariate Analysis Result for Dividend Policy Variables.

		F	**Significance**	*t*
DPOR	Equal variances assumed	0.056	0.814	−0.154
	Equal variances not assumed			−0.160
DYR	Equal variances assumed	0.281	0.597	−0.631
	Equal variances not assumed			−0.646

Source: Authors' data processing.

Conclusion, Implication, Suggestion, and Limitations

This study examines the impact of dividend policy on FV in the banking industry. The results of this study show, in general, dividend policy does not affect the bank's FV. This result remains consistent during the COVID-19 pandemic. Our findings support the Irrelevant Theory, which believes that dividend policy does not impact FV.

This research finds that the impact of dividend policy on FV varies at each level of a bank's core capital. Dividend distribution by banks with low core capital tends to receive negative responses. However, this impact continues to diminish as the bank's core capital increases, where a dividend increase can be a positive signal for the market. During the COVID-19 pandemic, banks with low core capital were expected to pay large dividends to show superiority. Meanwhile, banks with larger core capital are expected to be more conservative and reduce dividend distribution. For banks with the highest core capital, the dividend policy does not affect company value, both under normal conditions and during the COVID-19 pandemic.

This study also finds that the impact of dividend policy is stronger on state-owned banks than private banks. This result can be interpreted as an indicator of tunneling in state-owned banks due to the concentration of government ownership in their capital structure. This negative impact persists for state-owned banks during the COVID-19 pandemic.

Empirical results show that specific indicators in the banking industry such as NPLs and capital adequacy are important indicators of bank value. This finding occurs consistently across all tests and samples, where an inverse relationship is found in NPLs with FV, and a positive relationship is found in capital adequacy with bank value.

This study has limitations that can serve as opportunities for future research. In the future, researchers may employ other methods, such as the price-to-earnings ratio (PER) or the price-to-book value ratio (PBV), to assess a bank's value, serving as proxies for determining the overall worth of the organization. Furthermore, future research can extend the research period to encompass additional crisis times, such as the financial crisis in 2008, in order to analyze and contrast the varying effects of dividend policy on bank value during each crisis.

References

Abreu, J. F., & Gulamhussen, M. A. (2013). Dividend payouts: Evidence from U.S. bank holding companies in the context of the financial crisis. *Journal of Corporate Finance, 22*(1), 54–65. https://doi.org/10.1016/j.jcorpfin.2013.04.001

Adaoglu, C. (2000). Instability in the Dividend Policy of the Istanbul Stock Exchange (ISE) Corporations: Evidence from an Emerging Market. *Emerging Market Review, 1*(3), 252–270. doi:10.1016/S1566-0141(00)00011-X.

Ali, H. (2022). Corporate dividend policy in the time of COVID-19: Evidence from the G-12 countries. *Finance Research Letters, 46*, 102493. https://doi.org/10.1016/j.frl.2021.102493

Al-Malkawi, H.-A. N., Rafferty, M., & Pillai, R. (2010). Dividend policy : A review of literatures and empirical evidence. *International Bulletin of Business Administration, 9*, 171–200. https://doi.org/10.12816/0037572

Al-Saedi, A. A. S. (2010). *The effect of dividend policy on market value* [Durham E-Theses]. http://etheses.dur.ac.uk/556/

Al-Yahyaee, K. H., Pham, T. M., & Walter, T. S. (2011). The information content of cash dividend announcements in a unique environment. *Journal of Banking and Finance, 35*(3), 606–612. https://doi.org/10.1016/j.jbankfin.2010.03.004

Amihud, Y., & Li, K. (2006). The declining information content of dividend announcements and the effects of institutional holdings. *Journal of Financial and Quantitative Analysis, 41*(3), 637–660. https://doi.org/10.1017/S0022109000002568

Bajra, U. Q., Aliu, F., Aver, B., & Čadež, S. (2023). COVID-19 pandemic–related policy stringency and economic decline: Was it really inevitable? *Economic Research-Ekonomska Istrazivanja, 36*(1), 499–515. https://doi.org/10.1080/1331677X.2022.2077792

Baker, H. K., & Powell, G. E. (2012). Dividend policy in Indonesia: Survey evidence from executives. *Journal of Asia Business Studies, 6*(1), 79–92. https://doi.org/10.1108/15587891211191399

Baker, M., Mendel, B., & Wurgler, J. (2012). *Dividends as reference points: A behavioral signaling approach.* The Review of Financial Studies, 29(3), 697–738. https://doi.org/10.1093/rfs/hhv058

Black, F. (1976). The dividend puzzle. *Journal of Portfolio Management, 2*, 5–8. https://doi.org/10.3905/jpm.1996.008

Budagaga, A. R. (2020). Determinants of banks' dividend payment decisions: Evidence from MENA countries. *International Journal of Islamic and Middle Eastern Finance and Management, 13*(5), 847–871. https://doi.org/10.1108/IMEFM-09-2019-0404

Castrén, O., Fitzpatrick, T., & Sydow, M. (2006). *What drives EU banks' stock returns? Bank-level evidence using the dynamic dividend-discount model* [Working Paper Series 677]. European Central Bank. http://www.ecb.int

Cecchetti, S. G., & Schoenholtz, K. L. (2020). Contagion: Bank runs and COVID-19. In R. Baldwin & B. W. di Mauro (Eds.), *Economics in the time of COVID-19* (pp. 77–80). CEPR Press.

Chen, D., Jian, M., & Xu, M. (2009). Dividends for tunneling in a regulated economy: The case of China. *Pacific Basin Finance Journal, 17*(2), 209–223. https://doi.org/10.1016/j.pacfin.2008.05.002

Chen, J., & Dhiensiri, N. (2009). Determinants of dividend policy: The evidence from New Zealand. *International Research Journal of Finance Economics, 34*, 18–28.

Cornett, M. M., Guo, L., Khaksari, S., & Tehranian, H. (2010). The impact of state ownership on performance differences in privately-owned versus state-owned banks: An international comparison. *Journal of Financial Intermediation, 19*(1), 74–94. https://doi.org/10.1016/j.jfi.2008.09.005

Cross, M., Ng, S. K., & Scuffham, P. (2020). Trading health for wealth: The effect of COVID-19 response stringency. *International Journal of Environmental Research and Public Health, 17*(23), 1–15. https://doi.org/10.3390/ijerph17238725

de Wet, J., & Mpinda, M. (2013). The impact of dividend payments on shareholders wealth: Evidence from the vector error correction model. *International Business & Economics Research Journal (IBER), 12*(11), 1451. https://doi.org/10.19030/iber.v12i11.8182

Dittmar, A., Mahrt-Smith, J., & Servaes, H. (2003). International corporate governance and corporate cash holdings. *The Journal of Financial and Quantitative Analysis, 38*(1), 111–133.

Elbadry, A. (2018). Bank's financial stability and risk management. *Journal of Islamic Accounting and Business Research, 9*(2), 119–137. https://doi.org/10.1108/JIABR-03-2016-0038

Eugster, N., Ducret, R., Isakov, D., & Weisskopf, J. P. (2022). Chasing dividends during the COVID-19 pandemic. *International Review of Finance, 22*(2), 335–345. https://doi.org/10.1111/irfi.12360

Fama, E. F., & French, K. R. (2001). Disappearing dividends: Changing firm characteristics or lower propensity to pay? *Journal of Financial Economics, 60*(1), 3–43. https://doi.org/10.1016/S0304-405X(01)00038-1

Farag, M., Harland, D., & Nixon, D. (2013). Bank Capital and Liquidity. *Bank of England Quarterly Bulletin, 2013 Q3*, 201–215. Available at SSRN: https://ssrn.com/abstract=2327437.

Floyd, E., Li, N., & Skinner, D. J. (2015). Payout policy through the financial crisis: The growth of repurchases and the resilience of dividends. *Journal of Financial Economics*, *118*(2), 299–316. https://doi.org/10.1016/j.jfineco.2015.08.002

Fu, X. M., Linb, Y. R., & Molyneux, P. (2014). Bank efficiency and shareholder value in Asia Pacific. *Journal of International Financial Markets, Institutions and Money*, *33*, 200–222. https://doi.org/10.1016/j.intfin.2014.08.004

Gambacorta, L., Oliviero, T., & Shin, H. S. (2020). *Low price-to-book ratios and bank dividend payout policies* [Working Paper No. 907, Monetary and Economic Department]. www.bis.org

Goddard, J., McMillan, D. G., & Wilson, J. O. S. (2006). Dividend smoothing vs dividend signalling: Evidence from UK firms. *Managerial Finance*, *32*(6), 493–504. https://doi.org/10.1108/03074350610666229

Gordon, M. J. (1959). Dividends, earnings, and stock prices. *The Review of Economics and Statistics*, *41*(2), 99–105.

Grullon, G., & Michaely, R. (2004). The information content of share repurchase programs. *Journal of Finance*, *59*(2), 651–680. https://doi.org/10.1111/j.1540-6261.2004.00645.x

Habib, Y., Kiani, Z. I., & Khan, M. A. (2012). Dividend policy and share price volatility: Evidence from Pakistan. *Global Journal of Management and Business Research*, *12*(5), 79–84. https://doi.org/10.1109/CHUSER.2012.6504314

Ham, C. G., Kaplan, Z. R., & Leary, M. T. (2020). Do dividends convey information about future earnings? *Journal of Financial Economics*, *136*(2), 547–570. https://doi.org/10.1016/j.jfineco.2019.10.006

Hau, H., & Thum, M. (2010). *Subprime crisis and board (in-)competence: Private vs. public banks in Germany* [Working Paper No. 45/FIN, Centre for Economic Studies and IFO Institute (CESifo)].

Hussain, A., & Akbar, M. (2022). Dividend policy and earnings management: Do agency problem and financing constraints matter? *Borsa Istanbul Review*, *22*(5), 839–853. https://doi.org/10.1016/j.bir.2022.05.003

Hussainey, K., Oscar Mgbame, C., & Chijoke-Mgbame, A. M. (2011). Dividend policy and share price volatility: UK evidence. *Journal of Risk Finance*, *12*(1), 57–68. https://doi.org/10.1108/15265941111100076

Hutagalung, S., Yahya, M. H., Kamarudin, F., & Osman, Z. (2013). The dividend payout policy – A study on Malaysian financial institutions. *Social Sciences & Humanities*, *21*, 127–148.

Jia, C. (2009). The effect of ownership on the prudential behavior of banks – The case of China. *Journal of Banking and Finance*, *33*(1), 77–87. https://doi.org/10.1016/j.jbankfin.2007.03.017

Kadioglu, E., & Yilmaz, E. A. (2017). Is the free cash flow hypothesis valid in Turkey? *Borsa Istanbul Review*, *17*(2), 111–116. https://doi.org/10.1016/j.bir.2016.12.001

Karpavičius, S. (2014). Dividends: Relevance, rigidity, and signaling. *Journal of Corporate Finance*, *25*(2014), 289–312. https://doi.org/10.1016/j.jcorpfin.2013.12.014

König, M., & Winkler, A. (2021). COVID-19: Lockdowns, fatality rates and GDP growth: Evidence for the first three quarters of 2020. *Intereconomics*, *56*(1), 32–39. https://doi.org/10.1007/s10272-021-0948-y

Krieger, K., Mauck, N., & Pruitt, S. W. (2021). The impact of the COVID-19 pandemic on dividends. *Finance Research Letters*, *42*(September), 101910. https://doi.org/10.1016/j.frl.2020.101910

La Porta, R., Lopez-De-Silanes, F., & Shleifer, A. (2002). Government ownership of banks. *The Journal of Finance*, *LVII*(1), 265–301.

Labhane, N. B., & Mahakud, J. (2016). Determinants of dividend policy of Indian companies. *Paradigm*, *20*(1), 36–55. https://doi.org/10.1177/0971890716637698

Lie, E. (2005). Operating performance following dividend decreases and omissions. *Journal of Corporate Finance*, *12*(1), 27–53. https://doi.org/10.1016/j.jcorpfin.2004.04.004

Lin, Y. H., Chiou, J. R., & Chen, Y. R. (2010). Ownership structure and dividend prefer-
    ence: Evidence from Chinas privatized state-owned enterprises. *Emerging Markets
    Finance and Trade, 46*(1), 56–74. doi:10.2753/REE1540-496X460106.
Lintner, J. (1956). Distribution of incomes of corporations among dividends, retained
    earnings, and taxes. *The American Economic Review, 46*(2), 97–113.
Litzenberger, R. H., & Ramaswamy, K. (1979). The effect of personal taxes and divi-
    dends on capital asset prices theory and empirical evidence. *Journal of Financial
    Economics, 7*, 163–195.
Lo, H. C., Wu, R. S., & Kweh, Q. L. (2017). Do institutional investors reinforce or
    reduce agency problems? Earnings management and the post-IPO performance.
    International Review of Financial Analysis, 52, 62–76. https://doi.org/10.1016/j.irfa.
    2017.04.004
Miller, M. H., & Modigliani, F. (1961). Dividend policy, growth, and the valuation of
    shares. *The Journal of Business, 34*(4), 411–433.
Miller, M. H., & Rock, K. (1985). Dividend policy under asymmetric information. *The
    Journal of Finance, 40*(4), 1031–1051. https://doi.org/10.1111/j.1540-6261.1985.
    tb02362.x
Miller, M. H., & Scholes, M. S. (1982). Dividends and taxes: Some empirical evidence. *Journal
    of Political Economy, 90*(6), 1118–1141. http://www.journals.uchicago.edu/t-and-c
Okafor, C. A., Mgbame, C. O., & Chijoke-Mgbame, A. M. (2011). Dividend policy and
    share price volatility in Nigeria. *Journal of Research in National Development, 9*(1),
    202–210.
Pandey, D. K., & Kumari, V. (2022). Do dividend announcements override the pandemic
    impacts? Evidence from the BSE 500 constituent firms. *Asia Pacific Management
    Review, 27*(3), 210–219. https://doi.org/10.1016/j.apmrv.2021.09.002
Pettenuzzo, D., Sabbatucci, R., & Timmermann, A. (2023). Payout suspensions during the
    Covid-19 pandemic. *Economics Letters, 224*, 111024. https://doi.org/10.1016/j.econ-
    let.2023.111024
Pinto, G., Rastogi, S., Kadam, S., & Sharma, A. (2020). Bibliometric study on dividend
    policy. *Qualitative Research in Financial Markets, 12*(1), 72–95. https://doi.org/
    10.1108/QRFM-11-2018-0118
Rathnayaka, I. W., Khanam, R., & Rahman, M. M. (2023). The economics of COVID-19:
    A systematic literature review. *Journal of Economic Studies, 50*(1), 49–72. https://doi.
    org/10.1108/JES-05-2022-0257
Repullo, R., & Suarez, J. (2013). The procyclical effects of bank capital regulation. *Review
    of Financial Studies, 26*(2), 452–490. https://doi.org/10.1093/rfs/hhs118
Saif-Alyousfi, A. Y. H. (2020). Determinants of bank shareholder value: Evidence from
    GCC countries. *International Journal of Managerial Finance, 16*(2), 224–252. https://
    doi.org/10.1108/IJMF-05-2019-0170
Sarwar, M. S. (2013). Effect of dividend policy on share holder's wealth: "A study of
    sugar industry in Pakistan." *Global Journal of Management and Business Research
    Finance, 13*(7), 1–9.
Shi, M. (2019). Overinvestment and corporate governance in energy listed companies:
    Evidence from China. *Finance Research Letters, 30*, 436–445. https://doi.org/
    10.1016/j.frl.2019.05.017
Siegel, J. J. (2014). *Stocks for the long run* (5th ed.). McGraw-Hill Education.
Smith, D. M. (2011). Residual dividend policy. In H. K. Baker (Ed.), *Dividends and dividend
    policy* (pp. 115–126). John Wiley and Sons. https://doi.org/10.1002/9781118258408.
    ch7
Suwanna, T. (2012). Impacts of dividend announcement on stock return. *Procedia – Social
    and Behavioral Sciences, 40*, 721–725. https://doi.org/10.1016/j.sbspro.2012.03.255
Szczygielski, J. J., Charteris, A., Rutendo Bwanya, P., & Brzeszczyński, J. (2023). Which
    COVID-19 information really impacts stock markets? *Journal of International*

Financial Markets, Institutions and Money, 84, 101592. https://doi.org/10.1016/j.intfin.2022.101592

Tekin, H., & Polat, A. Y. (2021). Do market differences matter on dividend policy? *Borsa Istanbul Review, 21*(2), 197–208. https://doi.org/10.1016/j.bir.2020.10.009

Thomsen, S. (2004). *Blockholder ownership, dividends and firm value in continental Europe* (pp. 1–37). Department of International Economics and Management. http://citeseerx.ist.psu.edu/viewdoc/summary?doi=10.1.1.175.7017%5Cnhttp://scholar.google.com/scholar?hl=en&btnG=Search&q=intitle:Blockholder+ownership,+dividends+and+firm+value+in+continental+Europe#1

Tripathy, N., Wu, D., & Zheng, Y. (2021). Dividends and financial health: Evidence from U.S. bank holding companies. *Journal of Corporate Finance, 66*, 101808. https://doi.org/10.1016/j.jcorpfin.2020.101808

Trong, N. N., & Nguyen, C. T. (2021). Firm performance: The moderation impact of debt and dividend policies on overinvestment. *Journal of Asian Business and Economic Studies, 28*(1), 47–63. https://doi.org/10.1108/JABES-12-2019-0128

Valencia, O. C., & Bolaños, A. O. (2018). Bank capital buffers around the world: Cyclical patterns and the effect of market power. *Journal of Financial Stability, 38*, 119–131. https://doi.org/10.1016/j.jfs.2018.02.004

Wang, G. J., Xie, C., Zhao, L., & Jiang, Z. Q. (2018). Volatility connectedness in the Chinese banking system: Do state-owned commercial banks contribute more? *Journal of International Financial Markets, Institutions and Money, 57*, 205–230. https://doi.org/10.1016/j.intfin.2018.07.008

Yeo, H. J. (2018). Role of free cash flows in making investment and dividend decisions: The case of the shipping industry. *Asian Journal of Shipping and Logistics, 34*(2), 113–118. https://doi.org/10.1016/j.ajsl.2018.06.007

Zhang, D., Cao, H., Dickinson, D. G., & Kutan, A. M. (2016). Free cash flows and overinvestment: Further evidence from Chinese energy firms. *Energy Economics, 58*, 116–124. https://doi.org/10.1016/j.eneco.2016.06.018

Chapter 12

Meat Consumption Patterns and Changes in Consumer Attitudes

Karoly Bodnar

Hungarian University of Agriculture and Life Sciences (MATE), Hungary

Abstract

The author presents the meat of the most common species consumed in Europe and their role in nutrition. The work focuses on the meat of mammals and birds; it does not deal with the importance of protein sources from other taxonomic categories. European meat consumption habits and consumer preferences are presented, taking into account religious, cultural and geographical differences. It examines the possibility of influencing and changing consumer behavior based on consumer opinions. It separately examines the reasons for the less preference of meat or the complete rejection of meat consumption among consumers. This chapter also points out the demographic effects, lifestyle changes and the economic effects of income conditions. It presents examples of the role of government propaganda and the marketing activities of producers or processors in encouraging consumption.

Keywords: Meat consumption; consumer behavior; cultural differences; animal species; rejection of meat

1. Introduction

One of the most ancient and natural sources for meeting the protein needs of the human body is protein from animal organisms. Animal meat not only satisfies the human need for nutrients with the necessary amino acids and protein but is also a source of many other useful substances (saturated and unsaturated fatty acids, vitamins, minerals, etc.). The type (species) and amount of meat consumed are influenced

Entrepreneurship and Development for a Green Resilient Economy, 297–318
Copyright © 2024 by Karoly Bodnar
Published under exclusive licence by Emerald Publishing Limited
doi:10.1108/978-1-83797-088-920241013

by many factors: geographical location, climate, access, cultural background, religious regulations, social trends, family customs, individual taste, ethical, animal protection and animal welfare aspects, health and animal health issues, solvent demand, etc. Knowing all this, it is not surprising that the source of animal protein intake can be animals belonging to many taxonomic categories. This work only intends to deal with the consumption of the meat of mammals and birds, and for reasons of scope, the consumption of milk and eggs was not included in the work either.

The purpose of this chapter is to provide a brief overview of the key factors in the consumption or rejection of certain types of meat. Monitoring changes in consumer behavior is of great importance in terms of promoting sustainable development. This can be attributed to the fact that producers, processors and trade must prepare for these changes in time.

This chapter is partly based on literary data and partly on the author's decades of own research results. The presentation of the data is supported by tables, figures and the author's own photos.

2. Meat Consumption in Europe

Meat consumption in developed countries, including among the European population, has undergone a significant transformation, both in terms of quantity and quality. The increase in quantity is clearly indicated by the fact that 50 years ago, the daily meat consumption was 17 g/person, while today, it is an average of 28 g/person/day. The development of the availability of individual types of meat is clearly shown by the fact that throughout history, the most important were beef and pork. The consumption of both types of meat increased continuously between the 1960s and 1990s, after which the amount of pork stabilized, while the consumption of beef began to decrease suddenly, and its place was gradually taken by poultry (Bonnet et al., 2020). This change can be traced back to a number of factors: the evolution of the price of various meats had a significant impact. Meat products have been replaced by dairy products for many consumers. This change can be traced back to many factors: the evolution of the price of various meats had a significant impact, but the change of the Common Agricultural Policy (CAP) (Santini et al., 2017), the social perception of the connection between ruminant animals and greenhouse gases (GHGs) also contributed.

There are several regulatory tools to influence consumption. Fiscal policy instruments can be such, although no special tax is levied on meat in the European Union, but from a tax point of view, there is already a difference between the various sectors with GHG emissions, and in Denmark, a high saturated fatty acid content is subject to a special tax (Jensen & Smed, 2013), while in Hungary, a high salt content of processed products is subject to a special tax.

Consumer behavior related to meat is shaped by a number of determining and mutually influencing factors (Fig. 12.1). Consumers' expectations, attitudes and quality judgments related to meat and meat products are heterogeneous, influenced not only by the sensory properties of meat but also by psychological, technological and marketing factors. Strengthening a more favorable attitude (e.g., through more effective communication) and ensuring that the meat meets

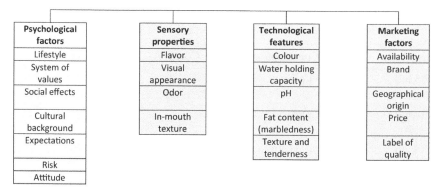

Fig. 12.1.   Components of the Main Factors Affecting Consumer Behavior.
Source: Author.

consumer expectations can increase the competitiveness of the products and their potential market share (Font-i-Furnols & Guerrero, 2014).

Effective means of influencing consumption are information campaigns that draw attention to the risk of consuming certain types of meat, as well as the preference for certain types of meat. This includes advertising, gastronomic programs, tastings, and labeling with special labels. These labels may indicate traceability, the fat content of the meat or meat product, the conditions of animal husbandry or the geographical origin.

In Spain, meat consumption is high, with a total of approximately 50 kg/person. They are planning to reduce it due to health, ethical and sustainability considerations. Farmers and meat processors are tasked with making efforts to ensure their survival, in addition to guaranteeing the well-being of the animals, to provide consumers with meat and information in order to offset the uncertainties of the external market, so that the consumer chooses a domestic product (Font-i-Furnols & Guerrero, 2014, 2022).

Influence of consumption based on environmentally conscious behavior and way of thinking is spreading rapidly in Western countries. These include the alleviation of climate change, the reduction of the area and water required for production, and the prioritization of animal rights or rejecting cage systems (Coker & van der Linden, 2022).

Meat consumption habits differ significantly from country to country, including in the Czech Republic and the United Kingdom. The British prefer ruminants, beef, veal and sheep, while pork is much more popular in the Czech Republic and in general in Central European countries (Table 12.1). This can presumably be traced back to the fact that the available fodder in the grain-producing areas favored the keeping of animals consuming cereals. In addition, meat consumption in the United Kingdom is characterized by higher-income consumer groups looking for high-quality meat much more than the same groups in the Czech Republic (Špička et al., 2021). Demand for higher quality increased across all income groups in the Czech Republic and in lower income groups in the United Kingdom, an important signal for meat producers and processors.

Table 12.1.   Meat Consumption Data in European Countries by the Results of Different Authors.

Meat Type	Consumption	Country	Source
All kind (total)	81.5 kg/year/capita	UK	Coker and van der Linden (2022)
All kind (total)	53 kg/year/capita	Spain	Chamorro et al. (2012)
All kind (total)	98 g/day/capita	The Netherlands	Dagevos and Verbeke (2022)
Beef	13.3 g/day/capita	UK	Stewart et al. (2021)
Beef	5.2 kg/year/capita	Romania	Pânzaru and Medelete (2021)
Beef	14.21 kg/year/capita	EU	Pânzaru and Medelete (2021)
Beef and veal	4.6 g/day/capita	Germany	De Boer et al. (2006)
Beef and veal	10.4 g/day/capita	Italy	De Boer et al. (2006)
Beef and veal	9.1 kg/year/capita	Czech Republic	Špička et al. (2021)
Game birds	0.4 g/day/capita	UK	Stewart et al. (2021)
Lamb	3.3 g/day/capita	UK	Stewart et al. (2021)
Mutton and goat	0.1 g/day/capita	Finland	De Boer et al. (2006)
Mutton and goat	5.4 g/day/capita	Greece	De Boer et al. (2006)
Pork	25 kg/year/capita	UK	Coker and van der Linden (2022)
Pork	6.7 g/day/capita	UK	De Boer et al. (2006)
Pork	22.7 g/day/capita	Austria	De Boer et al. (2006)
Pork	5.8 g/day/capita	UK	Stewart et al. (2021)
Pork	38.3 kg/year/capita	Romania	Pânzaru and Medelete (2021)
Pork	38.69 kg/year/capita	EU	Pânzaru and Medelete (2021)
Pork	43 kg/year/capita	Czech Republic	Špička et al. (2021)
Poultry	4.6 g/day/capita	Sweden	De Boer et al. (2006)
Poultry	11.7 g/day/capita	Ireland	De Boer et al. (2006)
Poultry	35.3 g/day/capita	UK	Stewart et al. (2021)
Poultry	26.9 kg/year/capita	Romania	Pânzaru and Medelete (2021)

Table 12.1.   (*Continued*)

Meat Type	Consumption	Country	Source
Poultry	23.06 kg/year/capita	EU	Pânzaru and Medelete (2021)
Sheep	0.4 kg/year/capita	Czech Republic	Špička et al. (2021)
Sheep and goat	1.3 kg/year/capita	Switzerland	Aepli and Finger (2013)
Sheep and goat	2.2 kg/year/capita	Romania	Pânzaru and Medelete (2021)
Sheep and goat	1.99 kg/year/capita	EU	Pânzaru and Medelete (2021)
Sheep and goat	2.5 kg/year/capita	Serbia	Faostat (2013)
Turkey	1.1 kg/year/capita	Spain	Chamorro et al. (2012)

Source: Author.

Meat consumption in the United Kingdom fell between 2008 and 2019, in line with meat purchase data from the Department for Environment, Food and Rural Affairs (Stewart et al., 2021). These data show that during the same period, weekly meat purchases at home decreased (−37 g), but the number and amount of meat purchases outside the household increased slightly (8 g) during the same period. The figures show that meat available for consumption in the United Kingdom has increased by 2.9 g/capita/day (taking into account changes in population).

The majority of poultry meat consumption per capita is chicken (but also includes turkey, duck, goose and guinea fowl) over a 50-year period and in eight European countries, but in the last 10 years, there have been sharp falls in Hungary, Spain and France and a long-term decline in Italy which is a trend. In the case of the Netherlands, a 10-year sharp decline starting in the mid-1990s was followed by strong growth in the early 2000s (Kanerva, 2013). The data for eight European countries show that urbanization is in many cases related to the increase in meat consumption. This relationship is particularly strong in Spain and Italy. Interestingly, the latter is the only country among the eight where beef consumption is significantly and positively related to urbanization. On the other hand, chicken consumption is positively and significantly correlated with urbanization in all but one of the examined countries (Finland). Furthermore, the only significant negative relationship is found in beef and sheep meat in Hungary and mutton in the United Kingdom.

Considering the social, cultural, economic, political, environmental and geographical similarities between the Netherlands and Belgium (especially in the Flemish part of the country) – as well as general health status and nutritional and food-related habits and eating culture – it is reasonable to assume that both Belgium and the Netherlands can reduce the average level of meat consumption.

Especially, if the two countries, that is, the Netherlands, were to improve to the 2019 Belgian food supply data, and Belgium to the 2020 Dutch household consumer basket data, then a further 10%–15% reduction in meat consumption could be achieved in both countries in the following years (Dagevos & Verbeke, 2022).

In the near future, it can be predicted that beef and veal will be replaced by chicken as the most sought-after meat, as well as an increase in the consumption of meat-based convenience foods in Spain (Chamorro et al., 2012).

The results of Aepli and Finger (2013) suggest that the factors determining the demand for Swiss sheep and goat meat are the prices of different meat categories, expenditures and different household characteristics and regional considerations. Their results confirm previous research that sheep and goat meat are substitutes for chicken and pork but complement beef. Their results provide insight into how to cope with the future challenges of Swiss sheep and goat farming. For example, the positive signs for the French-speaking area of Switzerland suggest that marketing efforts should be particularly focused on this area, where the consumption of sheep and goat meat has a significant tradition and is welcomed by consumers. One of the upcoming challenges for Swiss sheep and goat farmers will be, on the one hand, the liberalization of trade relations between Switzerland and the European Union and, on the other hand, price reductions as a result of the World Trade Organization (WTO) negotiations, as well as the intensifying competitive situation.

Proorocu et al. (2021) highlights that pork consumption varies greatly among pork-consuming countries and that consumers consider many quality characteristics in their purchasing decisions, and their expectations are heterogeneous. Based on the results, it can be concluded that the labeling of quality certificates (e.g., organic, geographical origin, method of keeping the animal or veterinary meat inspection) can be a competitive advantage. Therefore, marketers need to examine the quality of pork from several points of view based on consumer aspects.

The majority of respondents prefer to consume poultry meat because it is considered healthy, easily available, and last but not least, for example, chicken is a relatively cheap type of meat. According to 53.6% of Hungarian consumers, pork is the most consumed meat; 35% of men and 65% of women chose pork as the most consumed type of meat. Among pork lovers, the youngest age group accounted for 20%, 25- to 54-year-olds 65%, and 56- to 64-year-olds 15%. The popularity of pork appeared in proportion to the educational level of the respondents. More than 52% of the respondents said that they eat pork several times a week, while 33% of the respondents said that they eat pork once a week. However, the consumption of special types of pork (e.g., mangalitza) was hardly preferred by the respondents, partly due to the higher price and partly due to the significant fat content. Consumers were asked which part of the pig they liked best. Among the respondents, sirloin, blade sirloin and ham took the first three places. This was followed by shoulder with a price category similar to the first three types of meat, bacon and then the more expensive tenderloin (Bodnar & Privoczki, 2022). In recent times, inflation and the official price products introduced as a result have distorted this picture. The majority of consumers are looking for the cheapest type of meat and part of meat at the given moment.

Visiting restaurants and eating meat can often be a sign of status. To this day, eating in restaurants, especially expensive restaurants, often serves to emphasize a high social position. A similar statement also applies to meat consumption. The social importance of meat and restaurants in the diet and in a person's life can therefore go well with each other. At the same time, a certain polarization of meat consumption can be observed recently, where, on the one hand, the proportion of vegetarians is increasing, while the proportion of meat in the diet is increasing in other social groups (Ritzel & Mann, 2023). A correlation can be shown between individual meal occasions and the quantity and frequency of meat consumption. Age and gender of the consumer were seen as influencing factors. On Sundays and with family members, the amount consumed increased significantly. The probability of eating meat in a restaurant alone or among strangers increased, but the amount consumed decreased (Horgan et al., 2019).

According to observations, global meat consumption is constantly increasing as a result of population and income growth. However, price changes and other factors not only affect changes in the amount consumed but also the decisions of customers, who react by giving up red meat in favor of environmentally friendly (and consequently more expensive but considered healthier) white meat taking into account animal welfare. This factor was less decisive among the population with a higher income. The members of this group were much more sensitive to the quality, sensory properties and beneficial effects of meat dishes on health. Unfortunately, there are Polish respondents for whom meat and meat products are rarely part of their diet due to the high prices compared to their income, in this group they can almost be a luxury item. This phenomenon can therefore also be a measure of poverty in a part of society (Bereźnicka & Pawlonka, 2018).

Despite the fact that meat production has been linked to environmental degradation, consumption is increasing in many countries. Whitton et al. (2021) found evidence that meat consumption has peaked in several countries, but there is also evidence that consumption is still increasing in many countries. In many countries with emerging economies, there was a direct relationship between gross domestic product (GDP) per capita and meat consumption per capita during the years under review, but there was no relationship in higher-income countries. Their study shows that the substitution of poultry for beef has continued over the past two decades. Population growth and rising incomes in developing countries are behind the increased poultry consumption.

Based on estimates of income and demographic data, global meat consumption will continue to increase until 2050, mainly in low- and medium-developed countries (Parlasca & Qaim, 2022). In the second half of this century, global meat demand may begin to decline, although long-term trends are difficult to predict. According to researchers, only about 15% of the nutrients used to feed animals are in direct competition with human food. Thus, for many poor people living in developing countries, meat and livestock farming is still an important source of livelihood, and it also fulfills many other social functions, such as an asset, a status symbol, etc.

The consumer survey conducted in Ireland in 2021 among adult consumers for whom beef is a regular part of the evening meal, a decrease in beef consumption is expected. The increase in the number of weekly buyers of pork, turkey and meat substitute products indicates that these are probably substitute products. In Henchion et al. (2022) survey, chicken is probably not substitutable. The need for protein intake changes significantly with age, as well as the choice of the appropriate protein source. An aging person must decide to eat less meat or perhaps look for alternative sources of protein instead of meat. Alternative protein sources are available in different ways and to a different extent in European Union countries, which also has a strategic, cultural and social background (Grasso et al., 2021).

In Western European countries, researchers compared the spending on meat in predominantly Catholic countries (Italy, France, Spain, etc.) with predominantly Protestant countries (Netherlands, United Kingdom, Finland, Germany, etc.). Observing that the higher spending levels in the first group suggests that the difference can be partly explained by the attitude of Catholics toward meat consumption (it causes pleasure and is a sign of social status) (De Boer et al., 2006; Sans & Combris, 2015). In several European countries, a small transformation of consumption toward poultry meat and ruminant animals can be observed, the reason for which is the continuous increase in the number of Mohammedan immigrants.

During questionnaire surveys, it was found that when women are asked about their eating habits and diet, they usually indicate a lower consumption of meat than they actually are, especially if they had the opportunity to look into the statistics on meat production and consumption before. In general, male respondents are not influenced in their assessment of the quantity and quality of their own meat consumption by knowledge of the consumption registered in the given social environment (Ioannidou et al., 2023).

Italian studies consistently show that a large majority of consumers do not consider the environmental footprint of food when purchasing meat (Bimbo, 2023). The sensory properties of the product, price, brand, convenience and popularity are the factors that determine their decision. The results revealed that food production is not considered dangerous for the environment, but the transportation and packaging of food is considered responsible for the largest part of food-related GHG emissions and environmental pollution.

The meat industry must be prepared for how consumers relate to their meat purchase decisions, since the currently considered important criteria or characteristics that determine these decisions, for example, mainly the price and the appearance; in the near future, they may be replaced by some of the external features of the product, such as the labeling of the quality certificate, as well as the design and functionality of the packaging. The transformation of the dominance of the factors influencing the decision presumably also extends to the purchase of fresh meat, as well as to the store's own brands of processed meat products. It is a basic requirement that the meat on the market should not pose a health risk to consumers. To this end, a general procedure at slaughterhouses is the ante-mortem and post-mortem examination of the animals, the completion of which is certified by the seal of the examining veterinarian (Fig. 12.2).

The development of a consumer-centered approach and its application at a high level in practice through the supply chain enables the selection of meats that

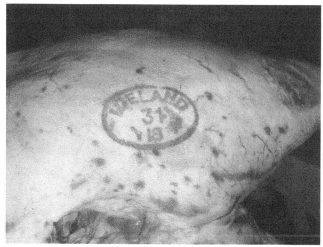

Fig. 12.2.   Veterinary Meat Inspection Seal on a Sheep Carcass (Iceland).
Source: Author.

offer combinations of the factors underlying the customer's decision to corre-
spond to the current purchasing attitudes (Henchion et al., 2014). In this context,
it is important to note that attributes are not equally important for all consumers,
and the set of attributes expected when purchasing meat differs among different
segments of the population.

3. Consumers' Choice of Other Meats

Eating meat in developed countries often means buying meat without bones
(Fig. 12.3), although traditionally most peoples' diets included all parts of animals,
and the food produced was not wasted. Differences in the cultural background and
traditions are shown up well in consumption statistics: 0.5 kg/capita in Denmark
versus 9.6 kg/capita in Ireland (De Boer et al., 2006; Sans & Combris, 2015).

The animal's head, tail, edible offal, etc. usually require more labor-intensive
kitchen preparation and special preparation techniques and recipes. Today, the
consumption of certain body parts or viscera is distasteful to many people, and
even meat eaters are often averse to it. Eating liver is still relatively common,
but preparing the kidneys, stomach, testicles, womb or udder, etc. of animals
is already highly divisive (Fig. 12.4). It is common that these inhibitions have a
psychological background rather than a matter of taste. This kind of aversion to
unusual meat parts must be respected; it is not fair to deceive the consumer even
with well-prepared and tasty food. At the same time, if someone likes these parts
or would like to try them, take the opportunity, because especially the edible viscera contain many valuable nutrients for the body. The situation is similar with
animal fats. Many people also avoid the use of lard when preparing meat dishes,
preferring to use vegetable oils. It is still a matter of debate as to which one is
healthier considering the advantages and disadvantages.

Fig. 12.3.   Ready-to-Cook, Deboned Meats at a Butcher's Counter (France).
Source: Author.

Fig. 12.4.   Bovine Offal and Lower-value Meat Parts (Italy). *Source*: Author.

The same duality can be observed in the case of some domestic and wild animals that are less often on the table, such as the domestic rabbit, horse, pigeon, huntable and exotic animals. The complete rejection of their consumption and its reasons will be discussed later.

In most countries, rabbit meat is available as live rabbit, fresh, pre-chilled meat, frozen, semi-finished products and ready meals.

In Mediterranean countries, domestic rabbit is served relatively often and in several forms (Table 12.2). Hungary's situation can be said to be special, because in addition to significant rabbit production, the sector is export oriented, and domestic consumption is negligible.

Table 12.2.   Rabbit Meat Consumption in Some European Countries.

Consumption (kg/year/capita)	Country	Source
0.50	Italy	Petracci et al. (2018)
0.52	Spain	Petracci et al. (2018)
0.37	France	Petracci et al. (2018)
0.27	Germany	Petracci et al. (2018)
0.15–0.2	Hungary	Kristóf (2022)
3	Malta	Debono (2018)
0.7–0.8	Hungary	Juráskó (2022)

Source: Author.

Consumption statistics are often misleading. In Hungary, the statistics do not include producers' own consumption; only store sales are taken into account. In Italy, the situation is reversed; in reality, only 52% of the officially reported amount is consumed (0.50 vs 0.92 kg); this is often due to the use of carcass-to-edible conversion factors (Petracci et al., 2018). In Hungary, the annual consumption of rabbit meat per person was recently 200 g, the goal was to increase this to at least 0.5–1 kg. There is a minimal increase, because you can get rabbits in more and more stores. With the support of the Rabbit Production Council, the Agricultural Marketing Centre and the Ministry of Agriculture, they launched a consumption-encouraging and informative campaign to promote rabbit meat with store tastings, demonstration kitchens and cooking shows. As a result of the store tastings, the turnover of pre-packaged rabbit meat increased significantly during the promotions (Bodnar, 2018).

In no country do consumers want to buy live rabbits and slaughter them at home, skin them, etc. (Rabbit farmers are an exception in this respect.) The freshness of the meat is the most important aspect in Spain and France, but not in Italy; however, frozen meat is not favored in any Mediterranean country. In France, they prefer whole carcasses and thighs much more than in Spain or Italy. Roast meat is popular in Spain and France, while the semi-finished product is popular in Italy and France (Szendrő et al., 2020). It can be concluded that it is not possible to show a general trend covering all countries. There is also a significant difference in whether the head remains on the carcass or whether it contains the edible offal. An increasingly common consumer demand is the origin and quality verified by labeling (Fig. 12.5). Stakeholders wishing to produce and export their products online must be aware of the expectations of customers in each country.

The consumption of rabbit meat among the younger generation is low; all countries are taking steps to make the young people more familiar with the favorable properties of rabbit meat (Szendrő et al., 2021). The phenomenon is also interesting because young children (unknowingly) have most likely already eaten rabbit, as this type of meat is a common ingredient in baby food. It seems like a good opportunity to expand the proportion and selection of semi-finished

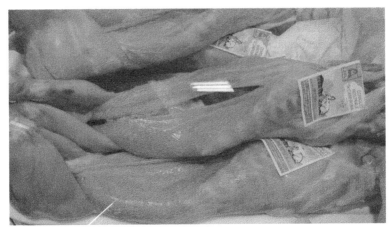

Fig. 12.5.   Rabbit Carcasses with Label of Origin (Italy). *Source*: Author.

products and ready-to-eat meals, which will at least attract those who have less time to cook or do not know proper preparation methods.

Another target group could be attracting elderly or sick people. When composing their diets, the high and easily digestible protein content and low fat content of rabbit meat speak in favor of more frequent consumption; however, due to its price, rabbit meat cannot compete with broiler chicken, which has similar properties. This is the main reason why it was not widely used in public catering or in the menus of the school canteens (González-Redondo & Rodrígez-Serrano, 2012). In addition to the popularity of the rabbit, it varies from nation to nation but also from family to family. Many recipes are used in Malta, while housewives in Hungary could list only 2–3 types of rabbit dishes.

European rabbit meat production is certainly facing a challenging period, characterized by a gradual decrease in consumption as a result of the ethical requirements arising during the purchasing decision of consumers, supplemented by structural weaknesses of the actors in the value chain. Effective renewal, survival and transmission of the rabbit meat industry to the next generations is possible only after analyzing the national market of each country. This can only be followed by communicating the already well-known excellent properties of rabbit meat to arouse the interest of a conscious customer group and generate demand (Cullere & Dalle Zotte, 2018).

The meat of hunted animals, perhaps the oldest consumed in human history, has now become a relatively divisive product. The consumer perception of game meat reflects strong extremes. There are those who consider it a premium product of special quality, there are those who consume it as a healthy, functional food and there are those who refuse to consume it for a variety of reasons. Game meat is constantly appearing on the European meat market, but a limited number of consumers are interested in it. Consumers' purchase decisions are more influenced by rational motives than emotional reasons. This suggests that the measurable quality characteristics of game meat should be presented in more detail by

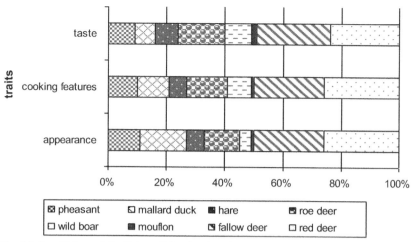

Fig. 12.6.   Value of Delight – Distribution by Game Species. *Source*: Bodnar et al. (2010).

producers and sellers on the market. The possibility of increasing the frequency of game eating is possible for those who pay attention to the special taste, high protein content, nutritional value and origin of the meat. Verified origin can also guarantee consumer safety (Niewiadomska et al., 2020).

A Swedish study shows that a combination of personal experiences with hunters and hunting, including the consumption of game meat, has a large effect on the perception of hunting, especially when hunting is aimed at obtaining meat. The level and frequency of game meat consumption seems to be similar in both urban and rural areas, but access to it is easier in the countryside. From the point of view of natural resource management, game meat supply is easier to influence than socialization processes. Simply providing people with game meat is unlikely to change attitudes. Social interactions related to meat are suitable for that. For example, a hunting story told during dinner is likely to have a greater positive effect than simply buying meat at the store (Ljung et al., 2015).

The value of delight of meats (Fig. 12.6) is measured by three different characteristics: appearance, cooking characteristics and taste. Different types of deer received the highest rating among all the characteristics and proved to be more special than the others (Bodnar et al., 2010). The most popular, desired and well-known specialties are red deer and fallow deer meat (24% and 26%).

Game meat is generally described as a healthy and natural food; the consumption of which has a beneficial effect on human nutrition and physiology. To support this, the daily requirement of the various elements was compared with the content of game meat. One portion of wild boar meat (200 g) seems to satisfy the daily intake of several important elements, above all phosphorus, iron, selenium and zinc (Bodnarne Skobrak et al., 2010).

The most readily available game species are usually those that can be hunted locally. The three most commonly eaten wild games in the Hungarian lowlands

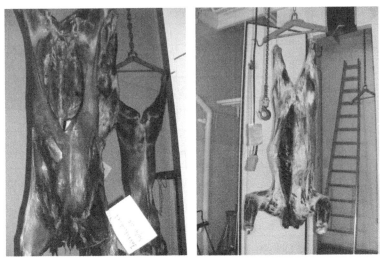

Fig. 12.7.   Moose (Left) and Brown Bear (Right) Carcasses in Cold Storage (Norway). *Source*: Author.

are wild boar, roe deer and pheasant. The non-hunters usually indicated the domestic huntable species as additional animals consumed, while the hunters also tasted the meat of other, often considered exotic, species (presumably abroad), for example, badger, antelope species, chamois, beaver, bear, moose (Fig. 12.7), grouse, marmot and crocodile (Bodnar & Kun, 2023). The selection is presumably constantly expanding, on the one hand, with the widening of the range of stores and, on the other hand, through hunting tourism.

By stimulating consumption, hunting provides funding for wildlife management and contributes to the conservation of natural values and hunting traditions.

4. Reduction and Rejection of Meat Consumption

The fact that meat has become a controversial topic of public debate has a negative impact on consumers and consumption, as it affects many sustainability topics. These include the relationship between global meat consumption trends and economic, social, environmental, health and animal welfare issues of sustainability (Parlasca & Qaim, 2022). Meat has a much larger environmental footprint than plant-based foods. The technological development of production can help increase the sustainability of meat production, but it is also necessary to change the level and structure of consumption, especially in countries with higher incomes, where people consume more meat on average, and a significant reduction is expected. However, this does not mean that a vegetarian lifestyle is mandatory for everyone. In addition, animal husbandry is an important source of income for many farms and households.

In recent decades, the amount of annual meat consumption per capita has gradually decreased in almost all of Europe. Several factors can play a role in

Fig. 12.8.   Vacuum-packed Horse Steak in Tray (France). *Source*: Author.

this, for example, the exaggerated negative role of meat consumption in obesity or the development of cardiovascular system and other diseases, as well as various epidemic animal diseases that occur from time to time in individual countries.

It is very common to hear those environmental considerations are behind the reduction or complete rejection of meat consumption. Ecological footprint and meat consumption – the two terms are often heard together. Also, in order to reduce our ecological footprint, we must reduce the amount of meat in our diet, or we must completely switch to a meat-free lifestyle.

Ethical and moral issues are often behind the total rejection of meat. This is especially true among young people, mainly women, who live in urban environments and only have pets or companion animals. Many people identify hunting and the operation of slaughterhouses with murder. Is it morally okay to eat meat? It is important to consider the nutritional benefits of eating meat! Are we anthropomorphizing animals when it comes to their welfare? What are the dangers of giving animals human characteristics? This phenomenon can be observed among pet owners (especially rabbits). People who engage in equestrian hobbies or sports find it unthinkable to consume horse and foal meat and its consumption used to be common in Europe, but today, a relatively narrow group is interested in it (Fig. 12.8).

At the same time, we often forget about the beneficial physiological effects of meat and its contents, and our decisions are often influenced by business interests and marketing tricks.

The study by Mathijs (2015) examined the question of whether human nutrition is, on the one hand, approaching a Western diet rich in animal protein and fat or a behavioral change toward consuming less meat. A clear relationship was found between the consumption of meat and meat products and income; the composition of meat consumption is less obvious. There was also no convincing answer to the question of whether, in addition to the weak but increasing signs of a reduction in meat consumption, which can be observed in a limited group of countries with high GDP; there are effects related to human health, animal welfare and the environment. Compared to more developed economies, meat consumption in Poland is influenced to a greater extent by the income situation of households. In Polish families, the main reason for the reduction of meat consumption is the low income (Bereżnicka & Pawlonka, 2018).

Cultural and religious traditions, social norms, the formation of identities and lifestyles influence and shape people's attitudes toward meat (Stoll-Kleemann & Schmidt, 2017). Meat has cultural significance for many people as an essential part of the diet. Such motivation is driven by powerful forms of symbolism associated with meat in many cultures, such as for Catholics, the lamb is eaten at Easter, but the meat-free period before Easter, fasting, is equally important. In Western thought and practice, there is a historical tradition that the consumption of red meat is driven by the desire to express human power, for example, the names of the guards of the Tower of London also indicate their status. On the other hand, in many cultures and religions, the consumption of certain types of meat, blood and offal is governed by complex rules and prohibitions, which may dictate the preference or avoidance of certain foods.

The effect of religion on meat consumption depends on the religion itself and on the extent to which individuals observe the laws of their religion. Most religions prohibit certain foods (such as pork in Judaism and Islam, or pork and beef in Hinduism and Buddhism), except for Christianity, which does not taboo meat (Bonne et al., 2007). One of the religions subject to food prohibition is Islam. Muslims must adhere to dietary regulations designed to promote their well-being. The halal dietary laws found in the Qur'an define which foods are "lawful" or permitted, thus prohibiting the consumption of pork, blood, dead meat and meat from animals not ritually slaughtered according to Islamic law. Following the rules of Islam is a personal decision of the individual whether to eat halal or not. According to a Belgian study, next to quality and taste, the method of cutting is responsible for the freshness of the meat, which explains why most consumers buy (halal) meat from an Islamic butcher (Bonne & Verbeke, 2006).

Significant differences can be observed according to how gender roles influence meat consumption. Gender has been identified as a key variable in many studies. Maleness has been consistently associated with increased meat consumption and a reluctance to eat more plant-based diets because it is not masculine enough, while females are generally identified with lower meat consumption and being more open to following a plant-based diet (Graca et al., 2019). The perception that eating meat is a masculine practice has distracted attention from the differences within a seemingly homogeneous group of men. The more men identify with non-traditional forms of masculinity, the weaker their attachment to meat, the more positive their tolerance toward vegetarians, and the stronger their inclination to reduce meat consumption. This challenges the stereotype that "real men eat meat" (De Backer et al., 2020; Rosenfeld & Tomiyama, 2021).

Reducing meat consumption can often be traced back to medical advice and health reasons. Many studies deal with the effect of meat on health, its advantages and disadvantages. Unfortunately, quite a lot of conflicting information appears in this area, so it is difficult for the consumer to adjust between the information, and it is even more difficult to find the balance between a diet rich in meat and a vegetarian lifestyle.

According to the results of several authors, meat in itself cannot be classified as healthy or unhealthy foods, on the one hand, meat provides essential amino acids and microelements such as iron, zinc and vitamin B12 (Schütz & Franzese, 2018), and on the other hand, the consumption of red (especially processed) meat can be associated with an increased risk of obesity, Type 2 diabetes, colon cancer and cardiovascular disease (Bonnet et al., 2020).

The development of global deadly diseases is attributed to a diet based on red meat. Nevertheless, a differential health effect between red meat subtypes appears in the literature. In a World Health Organization (WHO) report, processed meat products were classified in Group 1, that is, carcinogenic to humans, while fresh red meat was classified in Group 2, that is, potentially carcinogenic. Unfortunately, these effects have not been studied in the elderly, even though the increase in the elderly population would justify this in an extraordinary way (Kouvari et al., 2016). In patients over 45 years of age, a significant association was found between causes of death and high meat consumption in those consuming red meat and red processed meat compared to those with low consumption. Interestingly, the degree of saturated fatty acid intake did not show such a correlation (Dominguez et al., 2018).

Thanks to good communication from the health sector, households have really started to eat a wider variety of meats, and broiler is on more and more plates in Finland. Although meat consumption is widespread, it has become a lifestyle characteristic of the middle class. At the same time, the number of non-meat eaters spread, which has stabilized at around 6% at present (Vinnari et al., 2010).

In the case of game meat consumption, as a result of popular beliefs and misconceptions, several restraining forces often have to be fought in parallel, all of which work against consumption:

- Strong ethical and moral inhibitions can develop with hunting itself (even if it is aimed at obtaining meat), and the game regarding his shooting, taking his life.
- Game meat differs from domestic animal meat in many respects (color, texture, stronger smell, taste, etc.).
- The processing of shot game and the preparation of food require special skills and more effort (e.g., skinning and cutting) and time.
- There are those who abstain from consumption for health reasons, due to the occurrence of diseases (zoonosis) transmitted from animals to humans, which has been observed especially since the Bovine spongiform

Fig. 12.9.   Specially Aged Wild Boar Salami and Ham (Italy). *Source*: Author.

encephalopathy (BSE) epidemics in Western Europe. This can be observed even if it is known that the health status of the animals is determined both before and after being shot, and the body is subjected to a post-mortem meat examination. In Europe, for example, testing wild boar meat for *Trichinella* is common practice, so even non-heat-treated products (salami, ham) can be safely consumed (Fig. 12.9).

- A restraining force can be the shrapnel or bullet present in the shot body, which can cause metal and, in some cases, heavy metal contamination (Morales et al., 2018). During evisceration, hunters try to remove these by cutting out the location of the bullet, and they even scan animals transported to game processing plants with metal detectors.

German consumers are in a difficult decision situation. They gladly replace beef and mutton with chicken because they consider it healthier. At the same time, for reasons of animal welfare, they criticize the poultry and pig husbandry technology, compared to which, in their opinion, beef cattle husbandry is more natural and sustainable (Cordts et al., 2014).

The communication of those who oppose meat consumption is generally well-developed and effective. There are many promising results in strategies to promote "meat-free days." The topic of choosing one or more meat-free meals per week received rather positive feedback from certain consumer segments, especially those who already had a relatively low number of "meat" days and a relatively high use of alternative protein sources (De Boer et al., 2014). The decrease in meat consumption is also due to the better availability of alternative proteins (Whitton et al., 2021). It helps to win over consumers who want to change if non-traditional, plant-based meat-free dishes are prepared by imitating meat dishes (sight, texture, seasoning). An ever-expanding selection of meat-free shops and restaurants attracts a steadily growing population of vegetarians, semi-vegetarians, meat eaters and "vegans" alike.

5. Conclusion

Knowledge of different consumer groups can be important in managing the attitude toward meat in terms of a healthy lifestyle, in establishing the appropriate frequency of meat consumption and in making consumers realize the importance of the right meat. This determines the fate and future of not only consumers but also many producers (and other members of the value chain). On the demand side, education is probably the most effective way to spread healthier and more sustainable eating habits. Food education should be prioritized in primary schools, from school gardens to nutrition and environmental knowledge and farm visits (Pais et al., 2020). With this, we can begin to create a more livable future, since the role of children in this is twofold, as consumers and parents of the present and the future.

References

Aepli, M., & Finger, R. (2013). Determinants of sheep and goat meat consumption in Switzerland. *Agricultural and Food Economics, 1*(1), 1–11.

Bereżnicka, J., & Pawlonka, T. (2018). Meat consumption as an indicator of economic well-being – Case study of a developed and developing economy. *Acta Scientiarum Polonorum. Oeconomia, 17*(2), 17–26. https://doi.org/10.22630/ASPE.2018.17.2.17

Bimbo, F. (2023). Climate change-aware individuals and their meat consumption: Evidence from Italy. *Sustainable Production and Consumption, 36,* 246–256. https://doi.org/10.1016/j.spc.2023.01.009

Bodnar, K. (2018). A nyúlhús termékpálya hazai kihívásai (Challenges in the supply chain of Hungarian rabbit meat production). In Z. Egri & K. Bodnar (Eds.), *Logisztika a Dél-Alföldön, Logisztika Napja* (pp. 79–85). SZIE.

Bodnar, K., Benak, A., & Bodnarne Skobrak, E. (2010). Analyses of consumer preferences and attitudes on Hungarian game meat market (preliminary report). *Lucrari Stiintifice seria Agronomie, 53*(1), 9–12.

Bodnar, K. & Kun, L. L. (2023). Study of game meat consumption among Hungarian consumers. *Lucrari Stiintifice Management Agricol, 25,* 26–32.

Bodnar, K. & Privoczki, Z. I. (2022). Consumption patterns of pork in South-East Hungary. *Lucrari Stiintifice Seria I, 24*(1), 21–26.

Bodnarne Skobrak, E., Javor, A., Gundel, J., & Bodnar, K. (2010). Analyses of macro- and microelements of wild boar meat in three different regions of Hungary. *Lucrari Stiintifice Seria Agronomie 53*(1), 22–25.

Bonne, K., & Verbeke, W. (2006). Muslim consumer's motivations towards meat consumption in Belgium: Qualitative exploratory insights from means-end chain analysis. *Anthropology of Food, 5,* 2–24. https://doi.org/10.4000/aof.90

Bonne, K., Vermeir, I., Bergeaud-Blackler, F., & Verbeke, W. (2007). Determinants of halal meat consumption in France. *British Food Journal, 109*(5), 367–386. https://doi.org/10.1108/00070700710746786

Bonnet, C., Bouamra-Mechemache, Z., Réquillart, V., & Treich, N. (2020). Regulating meat consumption to improve health, the environment and animal welfare. *Food Policy, 97,* 101847. https://doi.org/10.1016/j.foodpol.2020.101847

Chamorro, A., Miranda, F. J., Rubio, S., & Valero, V. (2012). Innovations and trends in meat consumption: An application of the Delphi method in Spain. *Meat Science, 92*(4), 816–822.

Coker, E. N., & van der Linden, S. (2022). Fleshing out the theory of planned of behavior: Meat consumption as an environmentally significant behavior. *Current Psychology*, *41*(2), 681–690. https://doi.org/10.1007/s12144-019-00593-3

Cordts, A., Nitzko, S., & Spiller, A. (2014). Consumer response to negative information on meat consumption in Germany. *International Food and Agribusiness Management Review*, *17*(Special issue A), 83–106.

Cullere, M., & Dalle Zotte, A. (2018). Rabbit meat production and consumption: State of knowledge and future perspectives. *Meat Science*, *143*, 137–146. https://doi.org/10.1016/j.meatsci.2018.04.029

Dagevos, H., & Verbeke, W. (2022). Meat consumption and flexitarianism in the low countries. *Meat Science*, *192*, 108894. https://doi.org/10.1016/j.meatsci.2022.108894

De Backer, C., Erreygers, S., De Cort, C., Vandermoere, F., Dhoest, A., Vrinten, J., & Van Bauwel, S. (2020). Meat and masculinities. Can differences in masculinity predict meat consumption, intentions to reduce meat and attitudes towards vegetarians? *Appetite*, *147*, 104559. https://doi.org/10.1016/j.appet.2019.104559

De Boer, J., Helms, M., & Aiking, H. (2006). Protein consumption and sustainability: Diet diversity in EU-15. *Ecological Economics*, *59*(3), 267–274. https://doi.org/10.1016/j.ecolecon.2005. 10.011

De Boer, J., Schösler, H., & Aiking, H. (2014). "Meatless days" or "less but better"? Exploring strategies to adapt Western meat consumption to health and sustainability challenges. *Appetite*, *76*, 120–128. https://doi.org/10.1016/j.appet.2014.02.002

Debono, J. (2018, May 19). It's official: Maltese are highest consumers of rabbit in Europe. *MaltaToday*. https://www.maltatoday.com.mt/news/national/86827/its_official_maltese_are_highest_consumers_of_rabbit_in_europe

Dominguez, L. J., Bes-Rastrollo, M., Basterra-Gortari, F. J., Gea, A., Barbagallo, M., & Martínez-González, M. A. (2018). Should we recommend reductions in saturated fat intake or in red/processed meat consumption? The SUN prospective cohort study. *Clinical Nutrition*, *37*(4), 1389–1398. http://dx.doi.org/10.1016/j.clnu.2017.06.013

Faostat. (2013). Sheep and goat meat consumption per capita in Serbia. HelgiLibrary. https://www.helgilibrary.com/indicators/sheep-and-goat-meat-consumption-per-capita/serbia/

Font-i-Furnols, M., & Guerrero, L. (2014). Consumer preference, behavior and perception about meat and meat products: An overview. *Meat Science*, *98*(3), 361–371. http://dx.doi.org/10.1016/j.meatsci.2014.06.025

Font-i-Furnols, M., & Guerrero, L. (2022). Spanish perspective on meat consumption and consumer attitudes. *Meat Science*, *191*, 108874. https://doi.org/10.1016/j.meatsci.2022.108874

González-Redondo, P., & Rodríguez-Serrano, T. M. (2012, September 3–6). *Promotion of rabbit meat consumption in Spain* [Conference paper]. In Proceedings of the 10th world rabbit congress, Sharm El-Sheikh (pp. 955–959).

Graca, J., Godinho, C. A., & Truninger, M. (2019). Reducing meat consumption and following plant-based diets: Current evidence and future directions to inform integrated transitions. *Trends in Food Science & Technology*, *91*, 380–390. https://doi.org/10.1016/j.tifs.2019.07.046

Grasso, A. C., Hung, Y., Olthof, M. R., Brouwer, I. A., & Verbeke, W. (2021). Understanding meat consumption in later life: A segmentation of older consumers in the EU. *Food Quality and Preference*, *93*, 104242. https://doi.org/10.1016/j.foodqual.2021.104242

Henchion, M., McCarthy, M., Resconi, V. C., & Troy, D. (2014). Meat consumption: Trends and quality matters. *Meat Science*, *98*(3), 561–568. http://dx.doi.org/10.1016/j.meatsci.2014.06.007

Henchion, M., McCarthy, M., Zimmermann, J., & Troy, D. J. (2022). International comparisons, domestic influences and where to next? The case of Irish meat consumption. *Meat Science* , *193*, 108921. https://doi.org/10.1016/j.meatsci.2022.108921

Horgan, G. W., Scalco, A., Craig, T., Whybrow, S., & Macdiarmid, J. I. (2019). Social, temporal and situational influences on meat consumption in the UK population. *Appetite, 138*, 1–9.

Ioannidou, M., Lesk, V., Stewart-Knox, B., & Francis, K. B. (2023). Moral emotions and justifying beliefs about meat, fish, dairy and egg consumption: A comparative study of dietary groups. *Appetite, 186*, 106544.

Jensen, J. D., & Smed, S. (2013). The Danish tax on saturated fat–short run effects on consumption, substitution patterns and consumer prices of fats. *Food Policy, 42*, 18–31. https://doi.org/10.1016/j.foodpol.2013.06.004

Juráskó, R. (2022, September 29). *Situation of Hungarian rabbit production in 2021* [Conference paper]. In Proceedings of the 33 Hungarian conference on rabbit production, MATE, Kaposvár (pp. 7–11).

Kanerva, M. (2013). Meat consumption in Europe: Issues, trends and debates. [Artec-Paper No. 187, Universität Bremen].https://nbn-resolving.org/urn:nbn:de:0168-ssoar-58710-6

Kouvari, M., Tyrovolas, S., & Panagiotakos, D. B. (2016). Red meat consumption and healthy ageing: A review. *Maturitas, 84*, 17–24. http://dx.doi.org/10.1016/j.maturitas.2015.11.006

Kristóf, I. (2022, April 29). Fogyasszunk nyúlhúst: Egészséges és finom! [Let's eat rabbit meat: Healthy and delicious!] *Agrárágazat.*https://agraragazat.hu/hir/agrar-nyul-hus-termektanacs-agrarminiszterium-sirha-mezogazdasag/

Ljung, P. E., Riley, S. J., & Ericsson, G. (2015). Game meat consumption feeds urban support of traditional use of natural resources. *Society & Natural Resources, 28*(6), 657–669. https://doi.org/10.1080/08941920.2014.933929

Mathijs, E. (2015). Exploring future patterns of meat consumption. *Meat Science, 109*, 112–116. http://dx.doi.org/10.1016/j.meatsci.2015.05.007

Morales, J. S., Moreno-Ortega, A., Manual Angel, A.L., Casas, A. A., Cámara-Martos, F., & Moreno-Rojas, R. (2018). Game meat consumption by hunters and their relatives: A probabilistic approach. *Food Additives & Contaminants: Part A*, 35(9), 1739–1748. https://doi.org/10.1080/19440049.2018.1488183

Niewiadomska, K., Kosicka-Gębska, M., Gębski, J., Gutkowska, K., Jeżewska-Zychowicz, M., & Sułek, M. (2020). Game meat consumption – Conscious choice or just a game? *Foods, 9*(10), 1357. https://doi.org/10.3390/foods9101357

Pais, D. F., Marques, A. C., & Fuinhas, J. A. (2020). Reducing meat consumption to mitigate climate change and promote health: But is it good for the economy? *Environmental Modeling & Assessment, 25*, 793–807. https://doi.org/10.1007/s10666-020-09710-0

Pânzaru, R. L., & Medelete, D. M. (2021). Some considerations regarding meat consumption in Romania (2014–2018). *Scientific Papers Series Management, Economic Engineering in Agriculture and Rural Development, 21*(4), 403–408.

Parlasca, M. C., & Qaim, M. (2022). Meat consumption and sustainability. *Annual Review of Resource Economics, 14*, 17–41.https://doi.org/10.1146/annurev-resource-111820-032340

Petracci, M., Soglia, F., Baldi, G., Balzani, L., Mudalal, S., & Cavani, C. (2018). Technical note: Estimation of real rabbit meat consumption in Italy. *World Rabbit Science, 26*, 91–96. https://doi.org/10.4995/wrs.2018.7802

Proorocu, M., Petrescu, D. C., Burny, P., & Petrescu-Mag, R. M. (2021). Pork meat consumption, from statistics to consumer behavior: A review. *Porcine Research, 11*(1), 2–8.

Ritzel, C., & Mann, S. (2023). Exploring heterogeneity in meat consumption and eating out by using a latent class model. *British Food Journal, 125*(1), 132–144. https://doi.org/10.1108/BFJ-11-2021-1183

Rosenfeld, D. L., & Tomiyama, A. J. (2021). Gender differences in meat consumption and openness to vegetarianism. *Appetite, 166*, 105475. https://doi.org/10.1016/j.appet.2021.105475

Sans, P., & Combris, P. (2015). World meat consumption patterns: An overview of the last fifty years (1961–2011). *Meat Science, 109*, 106–111. http://dx.doi.org/10.1016/j.meatsci.2015.05.012

Santini, F., Ronzon, T., Perez Dominguez, I., Araujo Enciso, S. R., & Proietti, I. (2017). What if meat consumption would decrease more than expected in the high-income countries? *Bio-Based and Applied Economics Journal, 6*(1050-2018-3684), 37–56.

Schütz, J., & Franzese, F. (2018). *Meat consumption in old age: An exploration of country-specific and socio-economic patterns of eating habits of the European population.* [SHARE Working Paper Series 32-2018, Munich Center for the Economics of Aging (MEA)].

Špička, J., Eastham, J., & Arltová, M. (2021). How the income elasticity of meat consumption differs between social groups? A case of the UK and the Czech Republic. *AGRIS on-line Papers in Economics and Informatics, 13*(665-2022-499), 101–117. https://doi.org/10.7160/aol.2021.130409

Stewart, C., Piernas, C., Cook, B., & Jebb, S. A. (2021). Trends in UK meat consumption: Analysis of data from years 1–11 (2008–09 to 2018–19) of the national diet and nutrition survey rolling programme. *The Lancet Planetary Health, 5*(10), e699–e708.

Stoll-Kleemann, S., & Schmidt, U. J. (2017). Reducing meat consumption in developed and transition countries to counter climate change and biodiversity loss: A review of influence factors. *Regional Environmental Change, 17,* 1261–1277. https://doi.org/10.1007/s10113-016-1057-5

Szendrő, K., Szabó-Szentgróti, E., & Szigeti, O. (2020). Consumers' attitude to consumption of rabbit meat in eight countries depending on the production method and its purchase form. *Foods, 9,* 654. https://doi.org/10.3390/foods9050654

Szendrő, K., Szabó-Szentgróti, E., & Szigeti, O. (2021, November 3–5). *Consumers' motivation for (not) choosing rabbit meat – A global view* [Conference paper]. In Proceedings of the 12th world rabbit congress, Nantes (pp. 3–5).

Vinnari, M., Mustonen, P., & Räsänen, P. (2010). Tracking down trends in non-meat consumption in Finnish households, 1966–2006. *British Food Journal, 112*(8), 836–852.

Whitton, C., Bogueva, D., Marinova, D., & Phillips, C. J. (2021). Are we approaching peak meat consumption? Analysis of meat consumption from 2000 to 2019 in 35 countries and its relationship to gross domestic product. *Animals, 11*(12), 3466. https://doi.org/10.3390/ani11123466

Printed and bound by CPI Group (UK) Ltd, Croydon, CR0 4YY

21/11/2024

14596803-0003